ROUTING IN COMMUNICATIONS NETWORKS

ROUTING IN COMMUNICATIONS NETWORKS ❖ ❖ ❖ ❖

EDITOR

Martha E. Steenstrup

PRENTICE HALL, *Englewood Cliffs, New Jersey 07362*

Library of Congress Cataloging-in-Publication Data
Routing in communications networks /editor, Martha Steenstrup.
   p.   cm.
   Includes bibliographical references and index.
   ISBN 0-13-010752-2
   1. Telecommunication—Switching systems.   I. Steenstrup, Martha.
   TK5103.8.R68   1995
   621.382—dc2094-38723
   CIP

 This book was acquired, developed, and produced by
Manning Publications Co., 3 Lewis Street, Greenwich, CT 06830

   Managing Editor: Lee E. Fitzpatrick
   Copyeditor: David Lynch
   Typesetter: Aaron Lyon

© 1995 by Prentice-Hall, Inc.
A Simon & Schuster Company
Englewood Cliffs, New Jersey 07632

The author and publisher of this book have used their best effort in producing this book. These efforts include the development, research, and testing of the theories and programs to determine their effectiveness. The author and publisher make no warranty of any kind, expressed or implied, with regard to these programs and the documentation contained in this book. The author and publisher shall not be liable in any event for incidental or consequential damages in connection with, or arising out of, the furnishing, performance, or use of these programs.

Printed in the United States of America.
1 2 3 4 5 6 7 8 9 10 - VB - 98 97 96 95

ISBN 0-13-010752-2

Prentice-Hall International (UK) Limited, *London*
Prentice-Hall of Australia Pty. Limited, *Sydney*
Prentice-Hall Canada Inc., *Toronto*
Prentice-Hall Hispanoamericana, S.A., *Mexico*
Prentice-Hall of India Private Limited, *New Delhi*
Prentice-Hall of Japan, Inc., *Tokyo*
Simon & Schuster Asia Pte. Ltd., *Singapore*
Editora Prentice-Hall do Brasil, Ltda., *Rio de Janeiro*

Contents

Preface

Routing is a key component of every communications network. Over the past twenty-five years, the telecommunications field has evolved rapidly. Telephone and computer networks, now nearly ubiquitous, provide access to voice, data, and video services throughout the world. As networking technologies evolve and proliferate, researchers develop new traffic routing strategies. A fundamental understanding of the basic routing techniques and the factors that influence their behavior is critical in designing and selecting an appropriate routing strategy for a network. The main purpose of this book is to convey such an understanding to the reader.

The book comprises an edited collection of twelve chapters written by experts who have contributed to the theoretical and practical development of routing in communications networks. It is unique in covering the full range of routing techniques, including those for circuit-switched, packet-switched, high-speed, and mobile networks. The routing techniques presented are a cross section of those currently employed in large operational networks or slated for introduction into such networks. Through comparative study of these routing techniques, the reader will gain an understanding of their similarities and differences across a variety of networking technologies.

This book is designed to be used both as a textbook and as a reference work. As a textbook, the material is suitable for courses on routing, ranging in level from advanced undergraduate to advanced graduate. As a reference work, it is intended primarily for network researchers, designers, and managers. The reader is assumed to have some elementary knowledge of communications networks and how they function.

This book includes an introductory chapter offering a general perspective on routing in communications networks, followed by four major sections covering, respectively, routing in circuit-switched, packet-switched, high-speed, and mobile networks. Each section begins with an overview that relates the chapters contained within that section. This organization was chosen to aid the reader in understanding the similarities and differences among the various routing techniques and the reasons for them. In particular, it highlights the important factors influencing the design of the routing strategies discussed in each section.

All chapters in each of the four sections are self-contained and may be read independently. In each chapter, the authors describe a class of related routing techniques, motivate the theory behind those techniques, illustrate the performance of the techniques through results of analysis, simulation, or experience in actual networks, and include a bibliography for further reading. The authors also define terminology and acronyms specific to the class of techniques they describe and the type of networks in which those techniques are applied.

Together, the routing strategies presented in the book are representative of the principal traffic routing techniques currently employed in communications networks. Of course, it is not possible to include every routing technique here. Routing topics not treated in this book include bridging, intraswitch routing, and routing in satellite networks. Deciding which material to omit was very difficult, and I apologize to the researchers whose work is not presented here.

I am indebted to the authors who contributed to the book. Without their commitment, cooperation, and responsiveness in producing excellent chapters, this book would not exist. My deepest thanks go to all of them. I am also indebted to the reviewers for helpful suggestions in organizing the book and for detailed critiques of the chapters. In particular, Dave Piscitello, Bala Rajagopalan, Rich Sutton, and Ole Jacobsen provided invaluable advice. I am very grateful to Lee Fitzpatrick and Marjan Bace of Manning Publications for coordinating this entire effort. Finally, I thank Aaron Lyon for his deft computer typesetting and David Lynch for his careful copyediting of this book.

Martha Steenstrup

Contributors

Joseph Bannister
The Aerospace Corporation, M1-102
P. O. Box 92957
Los Angeles, CA 90009

Routing in Optical Networks

Flaminio Borgonovo
Dipartimento di Elettronica
    e Informazione
Politecnico di Milano
Piazza L. Da Vinci 32
20133 Milano, Italy

Deflection Routing

Israel Cidon
UMTV29-221
Sun Microsystems Labs, Inc.
2550 Garcia Avenue
Mountain View, CA 94043

Routing in the plaNET Network

Magda El Zarki
Department of Electrical Engineering
University of Pennsylvania
200 South 33rd Street
Philadelphia, PA 19104

On Routing in ATM Networks

Mario Gerla
Computer Science Department
UCLA
Los Angeles, CA 90024

Routing in Optical Networks

Richard J. Gibbens
Statistical Laboratory
University of Cambridge
16 Mill Lane
Cambridge, CB2 1SB
United Kingdom

Dynamic Alternative Routing

Roch Guérin
IBM Research Division
T. J. Watson Research Center
P. O. Box 704
Yorktown Heights, NY 10598

Routing in the plaNET Network

Sanjay Gupta
Department of Electrical and
        Computer Engineering
Illinois Institute of Technology
3301 South Dearbron Street
Chicago, IL 60616

On Routing in ATM Networks

Frank P. Kelly
Statistical Laboratory
University of Cambridge
16 Mill Lane
Cambridge, CB2 1SB
United Kingdom

Dynamic Alternative Routing

John W. Ketchum
GTE Laboratories, Inc.
40 Sylvan Road
Waltham, MA 02254

*Routing in Cellular Mobile Radio
Communications Networks*

Peter B. Key
Transport Design and Performance
BT Laboratories
Martlesham Heath
Ipswich, IP5 7RE
United Kingdom

Dynamic Alternative Routing

Milan Kovacevic
Center for Telecommunications
    Research and Department of
    Electrical Engineering
Columbia University
801 Schapiro Research Building
530 West 120th Street
New York, NY 10027

Routing in Optical Networks

Fidelia Kuang
Apple Computer, Inc.
1 Infinite Loop
Cupertino, CA 95015

AppleTalk Routing

Gregory S. Lauer
GTE Laboratories
40 Sylvan Road
Waltham, MA 02254

Packet-Radio Routing

Gary Scott Malkin
Xylogics, Inc.
53 Third Avenue
Burlington, MA 01803

Distance-Vector Routing

John Moy
Cascade Communications Corp.
5 Carlisle Road
Westford, MA 01886

Link-State Routing

Alan B. Oppenheimer
110 South Laurel Street
Ashland, OR 97520

AppleTalk Routing

Yakov Rekhter
IBM Research Division
T. J. Watson Research Center
P. O. Box 704, H3-D40
Yorktown Heights, NY 10598

Inter-Domain Routing: EGP, BGP, and IDRP

Keith W. Ross
Department of Systems
University of Pennsylvania
Philadelphia, PA 19104

On Routing in ATM Networks

Martha E. Steenstrup
Bolt Beranek and Newman, Inc.
10 Moulton Street
Cambridge, MA 02138

Introduction
Distance-Vector Routing

Introduction

The goal of routing in a communications network is to direct user traffic from source to destination in accordance with the traffic's service requirements and the network's service restrictions. This simple characterization belies the fact that routing is often realized as a complex system of distinct yet interdependent procedures shaped by potentially conflicting objectives and constraints. Objectives include maximizing network performance (e.g., delay and throughput) while minimizing the cost (e.g., equipment and facilities) of the network itself. Constraints are imposed by the underlying network switching technology, the dynamics of the switching network and user traffic, and the network services provided and user services requested.

As a multiobjective, multiconstraint optimization problem, routing is a rich area for research. The evolution of networking technologies constantly reveals new opportunities for routing research and development. Although routing techniques designed for older technologies have sometimes proven adequate for newer technologies, novel routing approaches are often required.

The eleven chapters in this book illustrate the wide variety of routing algorithms designed for various networking technologies, highlighting the relationships between algorithms and technologies. Historical as well as state-of-the-art routing strategies are presented, providing insight into evolutionary as well as revolutionary developments in communications network routing. To become better acquainted with the general routing

1

problem, the reader is encouraged to complete the remaining introductory material before delving into the chapters on specific routing techniques.

ROUTING FUNCTIONS

Although different networks employ different routing algorithms, all communications networks share a core of basic routing functionality. The first of the core routing functions is assembling and distributing network and user traffic state information which is used in generating and selecting routes. This state information includes service requirements and current locations of users, services provided by and resources available within the network, and restrictions on use of these services and resources. Moreover, state information may comprise both measured and predicted values obtained from the network and from external sources.

The second core routing function is generating and selecting feasible and even optimal routes based on user and network state information. Feasible routes are those which satisfy all the user- and network-imposed service constraints. Optimal routes are feasible routes that are "best" with respect to a specific performance objective. Depending upon the network performance objectives and service constraints, route generation and selection is often computationally intensive and may require heuristic approaches to produce acceptable results within a reasonable amount of time.

Forwarding user traffic along the routes selected is the last of the three core routing functions. Two distinct traffic forwarding paradigms are employed in communications networks: connection-oriented and connectionless approaches. Connection-oriented forwarding requires forwarding directives to be installed in the switches along a route prior to using the route for transporting user traffic. With connectionless forwarding, user traffic carries its own forwarding information in the form of either explicit directives for each individual switch along the route or implicit hints that may be independently interpreted by any switch in the network.

ROUTING AS A DYNAMIC SYSTEM

Routing, flow control, user traffic, and the network itself are distinct dynamic systems, each of which affects and is affected by the others. Specifically, routing and flow control are network control processes operating in a dynamic environment defined by the user traffic and the network. User traffic patterns, volumes, and service requirements, together with network service offerings, resource availability, and usage restrictions, determine the feasibility and optimality of routes within a network. By selecting routes that meet the objectives and constraints set by the user traffic and the network, routing determines which network resources are traversed by which user traffic. Flow control, in turn, determines how the traffic uses these network resources.

Flow control is distinct from routing and therefore is not covered in detail in this book. Nevertheless, the reader should be aware that routing and flow control are tightly coupled. Routing selects routes according to their performance characteristics, and flow control seeks to keep those characteristics within an acceptable range. More precisely, the objective of flow control is to decide whether to accept and when to transmit user traffic so as to reduce or prevent network congestion without unduly restricting network throughput. Flow control may be applied at multiple levels within a network, including user sessions, routes, and links. In general, flow control operates at a finer time scale than routing.

Almost all routing systems respond in some way to changes in network and user traffic state. However, routing systems vary widely in the types of state changes to which they respond and the speed of their responses.

At one extreme are static routing systems whose routing remains fixed independent of the current state of the users and the network. Static routing is based on expected rather than actual user and network behavior. In most static routing systems, routing is an integral part of network design, and hence rerouting occurs infrequently.

The objective of network design is to produce a network topology at minimal equipment cost that can, in conjunction with routing, accommodate the expected user traffic under specified network conditions. Network design is a combinatorial optimization problem whose input includes user traffic forecasts, network performance requirements, and network cost constraints. It often relies on long-term measurements of user traffic (for use in traffic forecasting) and network loading (for use in assessing performance of the network design). Network design usually requires intensive off-line computation for processing these measurements and producing acceptable designs, and hence is performed infrequently in response to long-range trends in user service demands.

Static routing involves virtually no real-time activities other than traffic forwarding and thus requires almost no computational resources within the network itself. Quasi-static routing systems are static routing systems that also modify traffic routing in response to exceptional events (e.g., link or switch failures) or at relatively long time intervals. Manual updating of network traffic routing is often sufficient in static and quasi-static routing systems as routing changes are infrequent.

At the opposite extreme are dynamic routing systems that autonomously update traffic routing by adapting in real time to perceived changes in user and network state. These state changes include not only link and switch outages but also fluctuations in user traffic and availability of network resources. Dynamic routing systems rely on active participation by entities within the network to measure user traffic and network peformance and to compute routes on demand, accounting for current user traffic and network state. Thus, dynamic routing requires memory and computational resources resident within the network for real-time information gathering and control decisions.

Most of the routing systems described in this book lie within the dynamic portion of the spectrum. The appropriate degree of dynamism for a given routing system depends on several factors, including the processing, memory, and transmission resources available to support the routing functions; the type and frequency of changes in network and user traffic state; the expected performance degradation resulting from a mismatch between selected routes and actual state; and the limitations or response delay imposed in assembling, propagating, and acting upon state information.

Routing in a highly dynamic network environment presents interesting challenges. A dynamic routing system that is able to keep up with rapid state changes may not always be practical because of the quantity of network resources required. When state changes are small, the routing system need not react to them. Instead, it may be able to maintain acceptable routes by basing its routing decisions on statistically derived rather than current state changes. When state changes are drastic enough to render current routes unacceptable, the routing system should strive to adapt to these changes in most cases. If, however, the period between successive state changes is shorter than the minimum possible response delay of the routing system, better performance may actually be achieved with a less dynamic routing system. Complicated cost and performance tradeoffs may therefore be necessary when designing a routing system for a specific networking environment.

DECENTRALIZING THE ROUTING SYSTEM

Each of the three basic routing functions may be implemented in either centralized or decentralized form. The degree of decentralization depends upon the desired dynamism, robustness, and manageability of the routing system.

With a centralized implementation, a single entity performs the given routing function. Centralized procedures are easy to manage because the functionality resides at a single entity, simplifying management functions such as modifying or isolating faults within the implementation. Moreover, if specialized resources are required to perform the routing function (e.g., computational engines capable of solving combinatorial optimization problems), these resources can be concentrated in one place, thus reducing costs.

There are, however, disadvantages to centralized implementations. When the central entity performing the routing function fails or is otherwise separated from the network, that routing functionality is unavailable for the duration of the separation. Also, a routing function's responsiveness to state changes depends upon the load on the entity providing that functionality and the distance between that entity and the portion of the network requiring that functionality. Thus, concentrating a routing function at a single entity limits the responsiveness of that function.

With a decentralized implementation, multiple peer entities perform the given routing function. If the functionality is replicated, each entity independently provides the functionality without exchanging results with its peers. If the functionality is distributed, peer entities independently provide portions of the functionality but must cooperate to provide the complete functionality by exchanging results. Such cooperation among peer entities may be either synchronous or asynchronous.

Although decentralization complicates management of the routing system, it has numerous advantages. Replicating functionality at multiple entities increases the fault tolerance of the routing system. It also reduces response delay by spreading the load among multiple entities and by enabling functionality to be placed close to the portions of the network that require it. Distributing functionality over multiple entities reduces the amount of routing system resources required at any single entity and also enables the routing system to grow incrementally with the size of the network. Most of the routing systems described in this book have been implemented as distributed procedures.

CIRCUIT SWITCHING AND PACKET SWITCHING

Traditionally, communications networks have been divided along the circuit-switching or packet-switching boundary. This classification distinguishes not only the underlying network switching technology but also the purposes for which the networks were developed.

Circuit-switched networks were originally designed to carry voice traffic, which is sensitive to ordering and to delay fluctuations. Historically, circuit switches were analog devices based on space-division multiplexing. Digital switching, however, has given rise to time-division multiplexing as a popular switching method. With circuit switching, transmission and switching resources are dedicated to a call along its path from source to destination, thus preventing queuing delays during a call. These resources remain dedicated to the call for its duration, regardless of whether the call uses all its resources. Dedicated but idle switching and transmission resources are not available for other calls.

The majority of circuit-switched networks are public networks developed by telephone companies for commercial purposes. Telephone companies seek to maximize their revenues by supplying dependable telephone service to large customer bases. Hence, they have expended considerable resources on designing their networks and managing their traffic routing so that they can accommodate their customers, with minimal design and management costs, even under adverse network loading and outage conditions.

Packet-switched networks were originally designed to carry delay-insensitive data traffic. Most packet-switched networks use statistical multiplexing to allocate switching and transmission resources to traffic on demand. Thus, packet switching ensures that if there is demand for currently unused resources, then traffic contending for those resources will be allowed access to them. Contention for resources may, however, force queuing, or even discarding of packets, when the traffic load offered to the resource exceeds its capacity.

Until recently, the majority of packet-switched networks were either private networks developed for specific purposes (e.g., airline reservation systems, banks) or public networks developed as government-subsidized research or infrastructure projects (ARPANET, NSFNET). Private networks have prompted development of routing strategies optimized for specific environments or uses. Research networks have encouraged development of experimental adaptive routing strategies, often behaving in ways that are difficult to predict a priori.

A PERSPECTIVE ON THE FUTURE OF ROUTING

Although circuit switching and packet switching began on parallel independent evolutionary tracks, they are beginning to merge. This convergent evolution is the result of two principal forces: user service demands and high-speed transmission and switching technologies.

The growth in number of powerful, easy-to-use, portable, and affordable personal computers, combined with globally accessible communications networks, has resulted in a large and growing user community with demands for sophisticated communications services. These user service requirements may be summed up as low-cost, high-quality, distributed multimedia services (e.g., voice, data, and video) available independent of user location. The principal global communications networks, namely the telephone networks and the Internet, have attempted to address these requirements in the following ways.

Telephone service providers have responded to user demands by developing new technologies. These include Broadband Integrated Services Digital Networks (B-ISDN) to support multimedia services and mobile cellular radio systems to provide location-independent services. Moreover, telephone networks, which historically have employed centralized, quasi-static traffic routing strategies, are now beginning to adopt dynamic routing strategies to increase call carrying capacity and network robustness, in a cost-effective manner.

The emergence of the Internet as a global data networking substrate has triggered many changes in its operation. Historically, the Internet has employed distributed, dynamic routing strategies that provide "best-effort" traffic handling with no service guarantees. Internet engineers are now developing protocol standards for providing service guarantees, efficient point-to-multipoint communication, and support for mobile users and networks. Internet service providers, as nascent commercial enterprises with paying customers, are beginning to grapple with the complicated network cost and performance issues that have confronted the telephone companies for many years. Moreover, the Internet's dramatic growth has created a need for reliable, manageable, and secure routing strategies that can accommodate very large networks.

Networking technologies most likely to meet the diverse service demands of tomorrow's sophisticated users are those which provide both circuit-switching and packet-switching capabilities. In fact, many of the high-speed networking technologies currently under development, such as fast packet switching and photonic networks, are actually hybrids of circuit switching and packet switching. Such technologies provide the perfect environment for cross-fertilization of circuit-switching and packet-switching routing techniques.

Ultimately, global user interconnectivity will not be provided by a single homogeneous networking substrate. Instead, it will almost certainly be provided by multiple independently managed, interconnected service providers offering different services and using different switching technologies. The principal problem for a routing system operating in such an environment will be efficient distribution, management, and synthesis of the large volume of diverse information used in routing traffic across the internetwork. In fact, this is likely to be one of the most challenging communications problems posed by the large, heterogeneous, and dynamic internetworks of the future.

PART I ❖ ❖ ❖ ❖

CIRCUIT-SWITCHED NETWORKS

Circuit switching is the oldest and most prevalent of the switching technologies for communications networks. Originally designed for voice communication, circuit-switched networks establish physical circuits from sources to destinations in response to users' demands for call connection. Each of these circuits and its switching and transmission resources is dedicated to the users at both ends, for the duration of the call.

The most familiar circuit-switched networks are the global telephone systems that carry primarily voice traffic. Within the telephone networks, however, gradual conversion from analog to digital transmission and switching technologies has enabled them to handle various types of traffic, including voice, data, and video.

Routing in circuit-switched networks has been driven primarily by the economic objectives of the telephone companies and by the switching technologies available. To ensure that their networks meet the expected peak traffic demands and recover quickly from failures and other unlikely events, the telephone companies devote many of their resources to traffic control and to network design. Network design is a combinatorial optimization problem that includes topological layout of switches and trunks as well as provisioning of these assets to handle projected traffic loads with the minimum-cost network. For a given design, the load on individual switches and trunks depends upon how the traffic is routed through the network. Thus, routing according to expected traffic is an integral part of the network design process.

Historically, the telephone networks have relied on static, preconfigured routes computed off-line at a central facility and subsequently loaded into the switches. The computed routes depend upon network topology and provisioning as well as forecasts of traffic demand but not upon current state of the network. To maximize the likelihood of continuing to provide the requested services amid changing network states, the central facility may provide each switch with multiple routes to each destination. These routes are of two types: (1) alternative routes for use when calls are blocked on the primary route and (2) time-dependent routes for use at different hours of the day. When unforeseen network problems arise, manual intervention may be necessary to reconfigure the set of routes at particular switches.

The advantages of off-line route computation include complete control over the routes selected (ensuring compliance with network design assumptions and thus predictable routing performance) and minimal processing requirements for switches. Disadvantages include slow adaptation to unpredicted events (often requiring human intervention), inability to optimize routes within the network, and the large amount of switch memory required to store the configured multiple routes per destination.

There were two reasons for applying relatively static routing to the telephone networks in the past. First, the switches did not have the processing capacity to determine network state and compute routes accordingly. Second, the telephone companies were reluctant to relinquish a large portion of network control to the network itself, because of the economic consequences if the network were to make incorrect routing decisions.

With the introduction of stored-program-control switches with high-speed processing capabilities, dynamic routing has become a feasible alternative for telephone network routing. The telephone companies have come to recognize that dynamic routing is profitable because it reduces both network trunking and operating costs along with call blocking under all conditions. Several major telephone companies have installed dynamic routing capabilities in their networks.

A dynamic call-routing strategy uses network state inforamtion in selecting a route for a call. With dynamic routing, the rate at which routes adapt to changes in network state depends in part upon whether route selection is based on global or local network state information. Distributing and collecting global state and computing and distributing routes based on this information usually limits the adaptation rate to the order of minutes. Using local state, however, switches may modify routes on a real-time (call-by-call) basis.

An important class of dynamic routing strategies are the *state-dependent routing* algorithms. State-dependent routing attempts to route each call so as to minimize the blocking probability of future calls. Hence, state-dependent routing relies upon knowledge of predicted traffic demands and requires switches to measure and collect network state information such as offered load and call-blocking rate.

Telephone networks that employ dynamic call-routing methods, such as state-dependent routing, gain increased reliability and throughput, simplification of design and management, and the ability to accommodate new features such as integrated services and dynamic trunking. The two chapters in this section, "Dynamic Alternative Routing" by R. J. Gibbens, F. P. Kelly, and P. B. Key, and "On Routing in ATM Networks" by S. Gupta, K. W. Ross, and M. El Zarki describe some of the most dynamic routing strategies deployed within the major telephone networks. Other important dynamic routing strategies, however, are not covered in this section but are briefly described below.

Kelly has developed an approach based on "implied costs,"[9] which seeks to apportion calls on routes according to the net expected revenue of the routes. The cost of carrying a call on a given route is the difference between the call's "worth" (which may be an arbitrary function) and the implied costs of the component links of the route. A link's implied cost captures the cost to the entire network of carrying an additional call on that link. These implied costs may be calculated in real time in a decentralized manner, thus yielding a local proportional routing scheme for adaptively maximizing expected revenue.

Learning automata have also been applied to the problems of route selection and next-node selection in telephone networks.[10,11] A learning automaton is a stochastic finite-state automaton that operates in a random environment, updating its action probabilities in response to inputs received from the environment in order to improve its performance according to a specified measure. In the context of routing in telephone networks, learning automata seek to minimize the expected number of blocked calls by distributing calls over routes according to a probability distribution that is continually updated using information about actual call blocking.

SELECTED SUGGESTIONS FOR FURTHER READING

1   M. Schwartz, *Telecommunication Networks: Protocols, Modeling and Analysis,* Reading: Addison-Wesley, 1987.

2   A. Girard, *Routing and Dimensioning in Circuit-Switched Networks,* Reading: Addison-Wesley, 1990.

3   B. R. Hurley, C. J. R. Seidl, and W. F. Sewell, "A Survey of Routing Methods for Circuit-Switched Traffic," *IEEE Communications Magazine,* Vol. 25, No. 9, September 1987, pp. 13–20.

4   *IEEE Communications Magazine,* Vol. 28, No. 10, October 1990.

5   T-K. G. Yum and M. Schwartz, "Comparison of Routing Procedures for Circuit-Switched Traffic in Nonhierarchical Networks," *IEEE Transactions on Communications,* Vol. COM-35, No. 5, May 1987, pp. 535–544.

6   D. Mitra and J. B. Seery, "Comparative Evaluations of Randomized and Dynamic Routing Strategies for Circuit-Switched Networks," *IEEE Transactions on Communications,* Vol. 39, No. 1, January 1991, pp. 102–116.

7   T. J. Ott and K. R. Krishnan, "State-Dependent Routing of Telephone Traffic and the Use of Separable Routing Schemes," *Proceedings of the Eleventh Teletraffic Congress,* Kyoto, September 1985.

8   K. R. Krishnan and T. J. Ott, "State-Dependent Routing for Telephone Traffic: Theory and Results," *Proceedings of the Twenty-Fifth IEEE Control and Decision Conference,* Athens, December 1986.

9   F. P. Kelly, "Routing in Circuit-Switched Networks: Optimization, Shadow Prices, and Decentralization," *Advances in Applied Probability,* Vol. 20, March 1988, pp. 112–144.

10 K. S. Narendra and M. A. L. Thathachar, "On the Behavior of a Learning Automaton in a Changing Environment with Application to Telephone Traffic Routing," *IEEE Transactions on Systems, Man, and Cybernetics,* Vol. SMC-10, No. 5, May 1980, pp. 262–269.

11 K. S. Narendra and P. Mars, "The Use of Learning Algorithms in Telephone Traffic Routing—A Methodology," *Automatica,* Vol. 19, No. 5, 1983, pp. 495–502.

CHAPTER 1   ❖ ❖ ❖ ❖

Dynamic Alternative Routing*

RICHARD J. GIBBENS, FRANK P. KELLY,
AND PETER B. KEY

CONTENTS

* Work supported by SERC Grant GR/F 94194 and a Royal Society University Research Fellowship.

Dynamic call-routing strategies, which route calls according to current network state, have been widely deployed in telephone networks over the past decade because of their ability to yield improved network performance at reduced network cost. This chapter describes an ingenious example of this type of routing strategy, Dynamic Alternative Routing (DAR), currently employed by British Telecom. DAR is an adaptive call-routing strategy that stochastically selects an alternative route when a direct route is not available and uses local information about the loading of outgoing trunks to determine the feasibility of selected routes. Dynamic routing strategies, such as DAR, which operate in a decentralized fashion and rely only on local information to make call-routing decisions, are particularly attractive because they are robust in the presence of failures, they consume a minimum of network resources, and they are simple to implement.

1.1 INTRODUCTION

Dynamic routing in a circuit-switched network is a way of providing flexibility at the switched level. Flexibility is required to adapt to changing and volatile traffic demands; to cope with forecasting uncertainties, shifts in traffic patterns, and the introduction of new services; and to provide resilience against individual network failures. In other words, dynamic routing, by allowing the path a call takes through the network to vary with time or the state of the network, enables the network to be used more efficiently, and also provides robustness. With performance measured by "grade-of-service"—the probability that a call will encounter network congestion— efficiency can translate into a cheaper network for given performance criteria, or into increased performance at a given cost.

When a demand is made upon the network, there are essentially two questions to answer. First, should the demand be accepted? Second, where should the demand be routed? In any dynamic routing scheme, these two concepts can be inextricably interwoven; however, for convenience we shall say that the first addresses the control issue, whereas the second affects routing. The first question is, in a sense, more fundamental and harder; it is important because, without control, the performance of a circuit-switched network can seriously degrade under a flexible routing scheme.

Dynamic routing is meant to find the "best" path through the network, that is, a short path that causes least damage to future calls. In its simplest form, dynamic routing attempts to find spare capacity in the network. This seeking can be done in a centralized or decentralized way, the former making use of a central processor to monitor the state of the network and recommend decisions. A centralized processor requires a separate control network, and the system is vulnerable to failures. In a decentralized or distributed scheme the intelligence is spread throughout the network.

In this chapter we concentrate on Dynamic Alternative Routing (DAR), which has been implemented in the British Telecom (BT) public switched-trunk network. DAR is a simple but effective dynamic routing strategy, which is decentralized and uses only local information. In particular, the only information required is whether trunk-reservation thresholds have been exceeded on a route, and the current recommended alternative route. The information can be localized even further by limiting knowledge to outgoing links from an exchange, and thus the scheme uses only as much information as Automatic Alternative Routing (AAR),[12] with the additional stored memory of the current best alternative.

Thus DAR contrasts markedly to the scheme of Bell-Northern,[8,9] and AT&T's Dynamic Nonhierarchical Routing (DNHR).[3,4,5] The former is centralized, time-delayed, and requires detailed information about circuit occupancies and traffic arrivals, whereas the latter uses a large off-line calculation to advise on choices of alternative routes, which can change hourly, coupled with a dynamic part similar in spirit to the scheme of Bell-Northern.

The organization of this chapter is as follows. In Section 1.2 we define DAR for a fully connected network, discuss the importance of trunk reservation, and see how the simplicity of the DAR scheme allows it to be readily modeled and easily modified to cope with circumstances. In Section 1.3 we describe a dual-parented implementation of DAR in the BT network, and in Section 1.4 we discuss the application of DAR to the BT international-access network. In Section 1.5 we describe a more general application of the sticky principle underlying DAR to a multiparented network, and provide a framework for comparing the performance of different routing schemes. An interesting topic touched on in Section 1.5 is joint control of large networks: if parts of a network belong to different operating companies[13] then it may be especially important that dynamic routing schemes be simple and decentralized.

In writing this chapter we have relied heavily on work carried out with a number of colleagues, particularly Roger Ackerley, Graham Cope, David Songhurst, Stephen Turner, and Phil Williams. The development and implementation of DAR would never have been possible without active support and involvement by a number of people, especially Henny Azmoodeh, Roger Stacey, and Martin Whitehead.

1.2 DAR FOR FULLY CONNECTED NETWORKS

We begin by describing the DAR scheme for a fully connected network.[12,14,27] A major aspect of the scheme is trunk reservation, which we discuss more fully in Section 1.2. Mathematical models of DAR have been important in illuminating the behavior of the scheme under a wide range of overload and failure conditions: these models are introduced in Section 1.3.

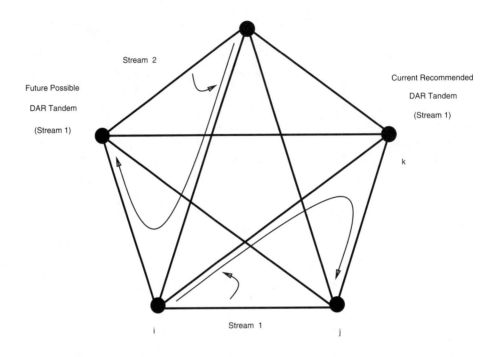

Figure 1.1   Fully connected network

1.2.1   The DAR Scheme

The DAR scheme operates as follows (see Figure 1.1). Suppose the network has N nodes, with link (i, j) having a capacity C_{ij}. Each link is assigned a trunk-reservation parameter and each source–destination pair stores the identity of its current tandem k for use in two-link alternative routes. Fresh-offered traffic between nodes i and j is first offered to the direct link and is always routed along that link if a circuit is free. Otherwise, the call attempts the two-link alternative route via tandem node k with trunk reservation applied to both links. If the call fails to be routed via k, this call is lost and, further, the identity of the tandem node is reselected (at random, perhaps) from the set $\{1, \ldots, N\} / \{i, j\}$. Notice especially that the tandem node k is not reselected if the call is successfully routed on either the direct link or the two-link alternative path.

Thus the DAR scheme has two main components: trunk reservation, to control overload behavior; and reset of the tandem node after loss of an overflowing call. Trunk reservation, an established mechanism,[37] is discussed further in Section 1.2.2. The reset mechanism, operating in a parallel distributed manner over the entire network, encourages DAR to seek out good routing patterns and is discussed further in Section 1.3.

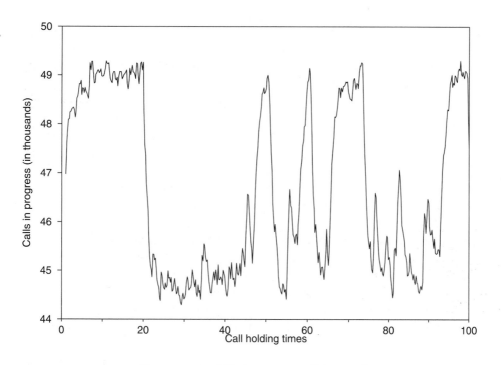

Figure 1.2 Instability in an uncontrolled network

The simplicity of the DAR scheme allows it to be readily modeled and easily modified to cope with circumstances. We illustrate these points in the rest of the chapter.

1.2.2 Trunk Reservation

A flexible or dynamic routing scheme gives an individual call a better chance of success, perhaps by increasing the number of ways it can traverse the network. The success of this call, however, could prevent the success of more than one other call, creating a less than satisfactory solution overall.[37] This is a symptom of the classic dichotomy between individual and social optimization. From the individual call's point of view, it wants as much freedom as possible so that it has the best chance of finding a path through the network; whereas to achieve a system optimum, we might have to limit an individual's freedom.

For example, consider a fully connected symmetric network such as that in Figure 1.1, where calls are offered between each node pair and the first-choice route is the direct link joining the two nodes. Now consider any dynamic routing scheme that seeks a two-link alternative path if the direct route is busy, and suppose that over a long period all such two-link alternatives are chosen an equal number of times. For instance, we could choose a two-link alternative at random, or by using one of the dynamic schemes such as DAR. Then under-overload calls are set up on two-link paths, which then cause other calls to overflow, bootstrapping the network into a state of high congestion. The network as a whole would be better off restricting calls to one-link paths.

At certain critical traffic levels the network with no controls can exhibit unstable behavior in which it flips between two quasi-stable states. This behavior was first predicted by simple fixed-point analytic models,[34] and has since been found in simulations.[1,2] Figure 1.2 shows an example of this behavior, where the total number of calls in progress is plotted for a 5-node symmetric fully connected network (10 links) with 5000 circuits on each link and 4900 Erlangs (a measure of traffic intensity expressed as the product of calls per unit time and average call-holding time) of traffic offered between each node pair, where DAR is used to search out a two-link alternative, and where no control is applied. In the low congestion state, almost 4900 Erlangs are carried on each route; however, for much of the time the network is in a highly congested state in which each link carries almost 5000 Erlangs with a significant proportion of two-link paths, and only about 4500 Erlangs are carried on each route. This total is much worse than if calls were restricted to one-link paths.

Trunk reservation against two-link overflow calls is an effective way of controlling this condition, where a trunk-reservation parameter of r on a link means that a two-link overflow call is accepted on that link only if more than r circuits are free, whereas the single-link calls are accepted onto the link whenever a circuit is free (a trunk-reservation parameter of 0). This tactic ensures, first, that under overload conditions the use of two-link alternatives is suppressed, and second, that performance under any load is always better than if we just used direct routing. Even for links of thousands of circuits, only a small trunk-reservation parameter is required (fewer than ten, say). For instance, in the example above, a trunk-reservation parameter of 4 is sufficient to ensure that the network stays in the low congestion state.

In practice it is sometimes difficult to implement trunk reservation on the second link of a two-link path; for example, the second link may not have the information necessary to differentiate between direct and overflow traffic. Fortunately, the undesirable overload behavior described above can be prevented by using trunk reservation on just the first link of two-link paths, with slightly higher levels of trunk-reservation parameter.

If a call is allowed to try more than one two-link alternative before it is lost (as in the schemes described in Section 1.5.3.1), then the unstable behavior described above becomes more pronounced and higher levels of trunk reservation parameter are necessary to control the network.[2,12,34] This is an example of a general principle: schemes that try harder to pack in alternatively routed calls are required to be more severely restrained by more vigorous use of trunk reservation.

Trunk reservation has more general uses, as a way of giving priorities to different streams of traffic, and we shall see such an example in Section 1.5.3.3.

1.2.3 Behavior and Modeling of DAR

One of the desirable properties of DAR is its speed of response. DAR locks on to a good path, and once a path or route ceases to become attractive, another is sought. This can be thought of as a learning scheme wherein the probabilities of choosing a particular overflow path are 1, 0, or $1 / (N - 2)$, depending on whether the last overflowing call was successful (thus retaining the designated current choice) or not. Although we can gain some idea of DAR's behavior by looking at how it operates for a single source-destination pair, we really need to step back and look at the whole network. On this canvas DAR is attempting, in a distributed manner, to pack calls onto the network subject to the control of trunk reservation, choosing two-link alternatives so that they do not interfere with each other.

The simplicity of the DAR scheme enables us to construct mathematical models of its long-run stationary behavior. This planning is important, for it then enables networks to be analyzed and dimensioned. Over a long period, each DAR choice will be changed an equal number of times, hence an equal number of calls will be lost on each choice. Thus, if p_t denotes the proportion of calls offered to tandem t and if b_t denotes the probability that they are blocked, then the blocking rate $p_t b_t$ is equal for all t. Hence

$$p_t \propto \frac{1}{b_t}$$

Thus the proportion of overflowing calls routed through any given tandem is *inversely* related to the blocking on that route: this is the essential means by which DAR adapts its routing to deal with overloads and failures. An approximation is to calculate b_t using a simple fixed-point model,[12,14,22,24] with each DAR stream assumed to behave as if it arises from a proportional routing scheme, with proportions p_t. Simulation results have validated the accuracy of this model for many or small DAR streams, but it can break down with a large DAR stream overflowing to a number of small routes, in which case a more delicate analysis is required.[11] Because DAR streams will be kept small in practice, the simple model above is very useful.

1.2.4 Implementation Issues

A simple way to implement DAR is to use routing tables with separate pointers for different DAR streams, thus adapting typical AAR implementations. For instance, in a fully connected network of N nodes, each exchange can have one routing table or DAR list consisting of all the nodes except itself ($N - 1$ elements), thus giving N tables in total for the network. In this case there is a small chance that the destination node will be chosen ($1 / (N - 1)$); however, if the network is large, this probably outweighs the disadvantage of having $N - 2$ separate tables in each exchange. For

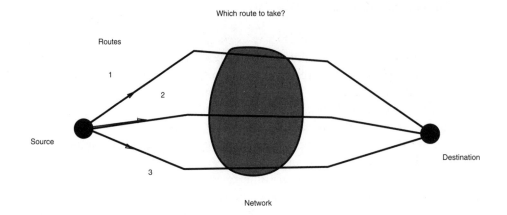

Figure 1.3   A routing problem

example, the latter requires more memory, and also is more complex to update as the network evolves.

Strictly speaking, the pointers should cycle through the table in a (pseudo-)random manner, but we could choose to step through the table. If the different streams step through the table using coprime steps, then we avoid "bunching" effects, where large (aggregated) streams of traffic follow each other in switching to recommended tandems.

Observe that the actions of routing schemes considered here occur on the fast time scale of call arrivals to the network. In contrast, network management and planning actions, such as decisions to modify the parameter settings of the routing scheme or upgrade link capacities, occur on a much slower time scale and usually are only partially automated. We must always keep in mind the importance of creating a sympathetic blend between the actions taken on these differing time scales.[12,26,29]

1.2.5   Variations

Although described above for a fully connected network, the principle behind DAR can be applied to different network structures. This principle can be described as a "sticky-random" or "back-the-winner" policy—use what worked last time; otherwise, choose a new alternative at random. Thus, for example, applying the principle to the three-route example in Figure 1.3, we continue to use route i while calls are not being lost on it, and as soon as we lose a call we choose another route from those possible at random. This is an example where we can use DAR without a fixed first choice. There are certain other straightforward extensions that can be made.

- If the DAR stream is large, it may be preferable to split it. This can be achieved by having a number of choices that are cycled through in turn, with each choice in this "cycle set" independently reset.

- The message to reset the current tandem can be sent before a call is lost. The "DAR reset message" can be returned if, for example, a call routed using DAR takes the last circuit on one of the links of the current choice route. Such anticipation tries to prevent the next call from being lost.

- Certain tandem nodes may be known to be better or worse than others. This can be reflected by increasing or decreasing their probability of selection. For example, some tandems might be barred as a network management action.

The variations have different implementation overheads. The simplest to implement is the last—we can increase the selection probability of tandems by repeating them in the routing table. Conversely, we might choose to delete some permanently, perhaps for transmission reasons, such as avoiding very long routes that introduce transmission delay, potentially degrading the speech quality or requiring additional echo cancellation equipment. However, although this is the simplest generalization to implement, we have to be careful—extra tables eat into the memory of exchanges, which is potentially a problem.

The "cycle set" could be implemented in a number of ways: if the large stream represents traffic to a number of destinations, then the numbering of the destinations themselves can be used to generate separate DAR streams (using later digits in the digit-decode). Or we could use a proportional-routing facility, (PTDP—proportional traffic-distribution facility) to distribute the traffic along a number of routes, and *then* use DAR.

The DAR reset is potentially more complex to implement, because it requires integration with the signaling messages. It is, however, a powerful method because it includes a state-dependent element. Indeed, if we also allow a number of DAR attempts then we can mimic a least-busy alternative-routing scheme (in Section 1.5.4, we formally compare the performance of least-loaded routing with DAR).

1.2.6 Simulated Grades of Service

Many simulation experiments have been performed to assess the accuracy of the model and to confirm the adaptiveness of routing patterns under DAR. Here we describe some experiments on 5-node and 14-node networks where grades of service were studied in detail.

- *5-node network* The network was simulated under normal load conditions and with one stream and two streams at 10 percent overload. For this case the stream grade of service of every stream from the analytical model lay within the 95

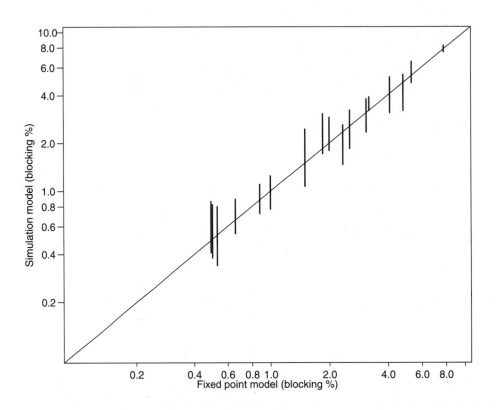

Figure 1.4   Comparison of fixed point and simulations in 5-node network

percent confidence limits of the simulation (illustrated in Figure 1.4). In addition, the calculated proportions of calls which are blocked on the direct link and which are offered to tandem nodes were plotted in 2-space with 95 percent confidence regions from the simulation, and again the agreement was good. Figure 1.4 shows the excellent agreement found between the grades of service given by the approximate fixed-point model and a network-simulation model.

- *14-node network*   The network was a subset of the BT main network, and was dimensioned in an analogous way, with target grades of service for the design-date traffic, 10 percent and 20 percent overload. The network was then simulated at general overloads of –5 percent, 0 percent, 5 percent, and 10 percent. Again the agreement between the analytic model and the simulation was very good. It is worth realizing that fixed-point models are generally least accurate at low blockings; however, in these examples the analytic results and simulation agreed well even at low blockings, when the overall grade of service was 0.03 percent. Figures 1.5 and 1.6 show in further detail the close correspondence

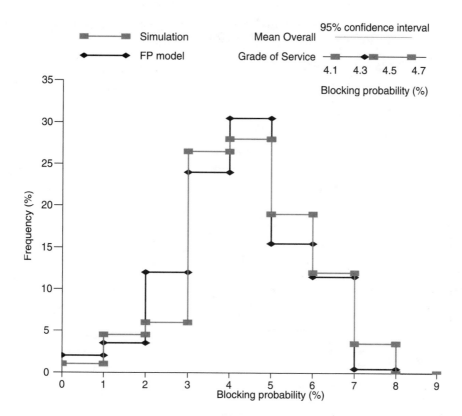

Figure 1.5   14-node network under 5 percent overload

between analytical and simulation models for 5 percent and 10 percent general overloads.

The approximation procedure can break down, for example, if the overflow is large and needs to be spread over a number of alternatives. In the most extreme example, there is no direct traffic on a link. DAR may still perform well in such circumstances, as simulation results show for the international-access example of Section 1.4.

1.3   DAR DUAL-PARENTED IMPLEMENTATION IN BT NETWORK

Work on dynamic routing in circuit-switched networks has concentrated mainly on fully connected networks for good reason, because economic pressures have generally led to core networks that are effectively fully connected. Increasingly, reliability

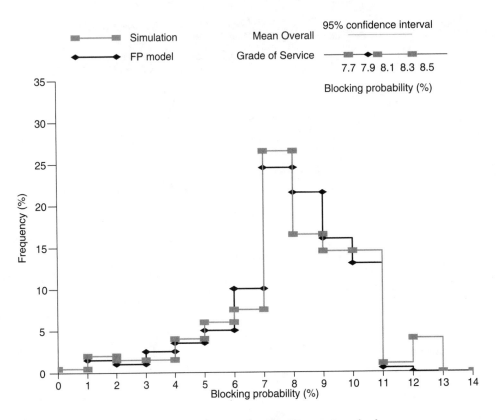

Figure 1.6   14-node network under 10 percent overload

considerations are leading to dual- and multiparented architectures, in which a call can enter (or leave) the core network at two or more access points (Figure 1.7). In this section we describe the implementation of DAR proposed by Stacey and Songhurst[36] for the dual-parented BT public switched network.

1.3.1   The Implementation

The network structure we consider is illustrated in Figure 1.7. The two levels are the *core* network and the *access* network. The nodes of the core network are fully connected, but nodes in the access network are connected to two or more nodes (*parents*) in the core network. In the BT network, nodes in the core network are known as *digital main switching units* (DMSUs), and nodes in the access network are called *local exchanges*.

A call from a local exchange in the access network is routed to a parent in the core network. Effectively, two "direct" routes are possible between origin and destination DMSUs because the destination local exchange is connected to both a "home" and a

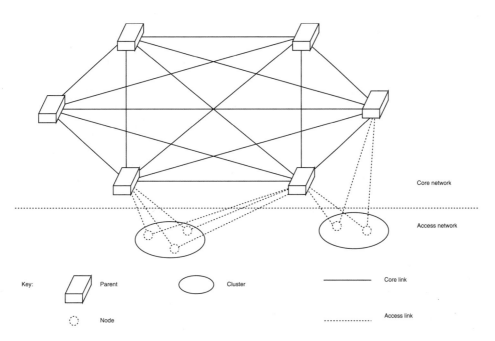

Figure 1.7 The network structure

"security" DMSU. These direct routes are the first two choices, following which the call may overflow to the current dynamic alternative, from where again it can be routed to either the "home" or "security" DMSU of the destination local exchange (see Figure 1.8). Loss of a call overflowing to the dynamic alternative triggers the selection of a new dynamic alternative path. Trunk reservation is used to give priority to direct traffic over alternatively routed traffic.

1.3.2 Discussion

In a fully connected network operating under DAR, a call has the opportunity to be carried on the direct route or on just one two-link path. Notice that in the implementation of DAR above a call has rather more opportunities to traverse the core network: a call that reaches a parent in the core network attempts two single-link paths across the core network before it tries to reach the dynamic alternative, from where it has two further potential paths.

If a call is blocked on the link from the local exchange to its first-choice parent, then it next attempts its other parent: whichever parent it reaches is the origin DMSU in Figure 1.8. Traffic may be balanced in several ways: outgoing traffic may try first the security DMSU, then the home DMSU, to balance incoming traffic, which tries first the home DMSU, then the security DMSU; or the choice of which

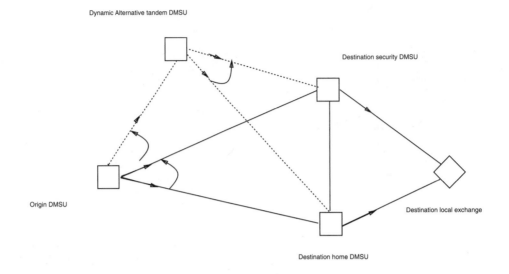

Figure 1.8   Dynamic alternative routing in a dual-parented network

parent to try first may be made randomly for both outgoing and incoming traffic. The simplicity of DAR allows its ready extension to multiparented networks, and in Section 1.5 we describe how further improvement in performance is possible if local exchanges, as well as core exchanges, adopt a sticky strategy.

1.3.3   Further Implementation Issues

What else needs to be done to implement such a scheme in a real network? Essentially some form of data-build for each exchange, which characterizes the DAR lists to be used together with a trunk-reservation policy. Some of the data-build issues have been discussed earlier. Using routing tables, the first two entries will be the destination parents, and the third choice a DAR choice. If we have N nodes, say, in the network, then for a dual-parented network, each DMSU can potentially use one of $N-4$ nodes as a DAR tandem (the 4 representing the home security of the origin and destination local). In fact, selection of the *other* source parent need not be prohibited. Thus DAR choice can be a pointer to a list with $N-3$ or $N-4$ entries accordingly. A single list of $N-1$ entries can be used, provided a mechanism is supplied for detecting if a DAR choice corresponds to a destination parent.

As the network evolves to a triple or multiparented architecture, DAR becomes the fourth or later choice in the routing tables, the previous choice being single-link hops across the network. This arrangement can be different for each exchange, and thus mixed parenting strategies are easy to accommodate within one framework.

1.3.4 Trunk-Reservation Policy

We have discussed in Section 1.2.2 the principles that motivate trunk reservation: traffic that uses a DAR choice uses more network resources than a directly routed call—two "core links" or four links in total as opposed to one core link (three links in total); therefore, trunk reservation should be applied against the DAR traffic. Ideally, trunk reservation should be set on both links of the DAR path; practically, however, this setup can be difficult to arrange, because an exchange doesn't normally use source information when deciding where to route. Hence trunk reservation can be applied just on the first link of the DAR path—a call attempts to complete to the destination parents, and if it cannot it overflows to the link connected to the recommended DAR tandem *provided* the number of free circuits is above its trunk-reservation threshold. Numerical results suggest little is lost by having trunk reservation applied to only the first link—all we have to do is set the trunk-reservation parameter a little higher than we would otherwise.

Simple ways of choosing trunk-reservation parameters have been suggested in reference 14 (more accurate models can use implied-cost methodology[21,23,26,29] or simulations over differing periods). Moreover the robustness of trunk reservation works to our advantage—the precise value is not critical, which helps because traffic values fluctuate over time, and are rarely known accurately. Trunk-reservation values related to circuit size and some notion of expected traffic, or *first-offered* traffic, will produce a simple policy that evolves as the network grows.

One may also use the last-chance trunk reservation: traffic that has percolated through the network to a destination parent has only one chance to complete, whereas outgoing traffic can overflow onto the other parent. Therefore, it makes sense to apply a small trunk-reservation parameter *against* outgoing traffic from the original local to its parent (see also Sections 1.5.3.3 and 1.5.5).

1.4 THE INTERNATIONAL-ACCESS NETWORK

We now discuss the use of dynamic routing schemes in non–fully connected networks, looking in particular at the BT international-access network.

1.4.1 The Problem

BT has a number of international gateways, or International Switching Centres (ISCs). These connect the trunk network of DMSUs to foreign administrations. For reliability, countries with large traffic volumes (for example, the U.S., France, and Germany) are connected to three of four ISCs, as shown in Figure 1.9. The network

- *Crankback*   A call is offered in turn to each ISC to which the destination country's ISCs are connected. If a country has circuits on, say, four ISCs, then the switching overhead can be large if a call tries each one. Furthermore, localized areas of congestion can occur, with calls being sent relentlessly to ISCs whose outgoing links are blocked. This inability to balance loads can have significant knock-on effects, as discussed below.

- *DAR with fixed-first choice*   The call is offered to a fixed first-choice ISC; but if this is unsuccessful, then a second choice is used, the selection made by DAR. The second choice is invoked if the call fails on the link to the ISC; if crankback is used, then the second choice can be tried if the call also fails on the international link beyond the ISC. A problem here is to allocate the first choices evenly.

- *DAR*   The call is offered to just one current-choice ISC. If the call is successful, then the current choice is retained; otherwise, the call is rejected and the current choice is reset. A disadvantage is that each call has only one choice, albeit a good one; but it does balance loads at ISCs very well.

1.4.3 Advantages of DAR

The last option, DAR, satisfies the requirements well, and its ability to choose its own ISCs makes everyday management easy. A particularly desirable feature of DAR is that in all studies to date, adding capacity to the network has always improved performance. But crankback does not do so—the localized congestion problem means that adding more circuits to a national link can increase congestion out of an ISC, causing the performance of some streams (that is, those which can use only that ISC) to deteriorate. Because the performance measure adopted by BT is the congestion seen by the worst streams, adding this extra capacity could well adversely affect BT's overall performance objective.

Similar effects have been observed when capacity is uniformly added into the access network,[38] or for countries whose busy hour does not coincide with the access network's. Indeed, the two effects are complementary, for adding capacity is equivalent to reducing traffic. The cost and performance curves in Figures 1.11 and 1.12 compare crankback and DAR in the afternoon (U.S. and total network) and morning (European) busy hours, where the performance criterion is the end-to-end congestion seen by the worst 20 percent of traffic.

These graphs highlight the counterintuitive behavior of crankback, where adding in capacity can make performance worse. Notice that here DAR is allowed only one attempt to connect through the network, whereas crankback has many. The processing overhead of crankback has to be added in as a real *cost* of the solution, whereas with DAR we could incur implementation cost through routing-table requirements: if DAR is implemented using routing tables then separate routing tables are required for each collection of 2, 3, 4, …, ISCs at each DMSU.

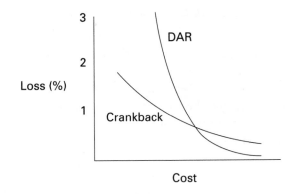

Figure 1.11   Afternoon performance during national-network and U.S. busy hour

This example also illustrates where the variations of DAR mentioned in Section 1.2.5 come into their own: using, say, proportionate routing to split the streams followed by DAR (an implementable alternative), or using DAR with two choices, gives better performance characteristics, which can be particularly beneficial for *small networks*. Repeating tandem nodes in a DAR list can also be used to improve performance.

The phenomenon mentioned above, that under certain routing schemes adding capacity to a network may degrade the network's performance, is an example of Braess's paradox. It has been observed in several models of network flow; a discussion is given in reference 25.

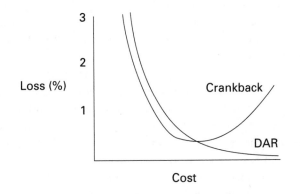

Figure 1.12   Morning performance during European busy hour

1.5 MULTIPARENTED NETWORKS

In this section we present a more formal analysis, from reference 15, of dynamic routing schemes for dual- and multiparented networks.

An important issue is the access network's role (see Figure 1.7) in dynamic routing. Because the access network and the core network may belong to different operating companies, it is especially important that dynamic routing schemes that involve both layers be simple and decentralized.[16]

1.5.1 Overview

To provide a framework for our discussion we now outline three families of dynamic routing schemes. The first family assumes that a call must enter the core network through a single defined parent, and must leave the core network through a single defined parent. The core network may, however, route the call between these two nodes as it pleases: either on the direct single link joining the parents, or on any of the two-link or longer paths through the core network between the two parents. A theoretical bound on the performance of any such scheme is available and simulations indicate that the bound can be approached by a scheme described as follows: each link calculates a trunk-reservation parameter as a function of its capacity and the traffic offered to the core network between the two parents it joins; a call offered to the core network between two parents is routed directly if possible, and if not is offered to a randomly ordered sequence of two-link paths joining the two parents until a path is found where both links are occupied below their respective trunk-reservation parameters; if no such two-link path exists the call is lost. This scheme is the special case ALBA(2) of the Aggregated Least-Busy Alternative family of schemes;[30,31,32] a major impetus for work on such schemes is AT&T's recent deployment of Real Time Network Routing.[6]

The second family of schemes we describe assumes that the network is able to route a call by any route through the core network connecting any parent of the originating node with any parent of the destination node. A bound on the performance of any such scheme is clearly given by Erlang's formula, with arguments the sum of the traffics offered to the core network and the sum of the link capacities of the core network. This bound is approached by a least-loaded routing scheme: route each call by one of the single-link routes through the core network able to carry it, and choose the one with most circuits free. The performance of this scheme considerably improves on the bound provided for schemes from the first family.

Dynamic routing schemes from the first family essentially ignore the multiparented structure; schemes from the second family are able to exploit the additional routes made available by multiple parents, which explains their improved performance. To implement a scheme from the second family, however, may be difficult: for example, the least-loaded routing scheme would require the originating node for a call to route the call to a parent whose identity depended on the instantaneous state of various links in the core network. We describe more easily implemented schemes able to achieve much of the improvement in performance possible by exploiting multiparenting. These schemes are based on two elementary principles: the *last-chance* principle, whereby a link gives priority to calls that will be lost if they are blocked; and the *sticky* principle, whereby a route that successfully carries a call is left as a preferred route, but a route that is unable to carry a call is replaced. For earlier work on the last-chance principle, see references 18, 19, and 23. For earlier work on sticky routing, see references 12, 17, 33, and 36.

In Section 1.5.3 we describe the various schemes more fully. In Section 1.5.4 we consider the performance of the three families of routing schemes for approximately symmetric networks, under various conditions of variable traffic and failure of links or nodes. To compare the schemes it is necessary to make some modeling assumptions about the form of the network and the traffic offered. We now describe these assumptions.

1.5.2 Modeling Assumptions

We consider a fully connected network of N "parents," numbered 1 to N. The undirected link from parent i to parent j has a capacity of $C_{i,j}$ circuits. Many of the schemes we consider will involve a trunk reservation parameter $r_{i,j}$. We set $C_{i,j}^2 = C_{i,j} - r_{i,j}$. A high-priority call offered to a link is accepted if any circuits are free, whereas a low-priority call is accepted only if fewer than $C_{i,j}^2$ circuits are being used.

Calls are generated between nodes, numbered 1 to n. In the dual-parented model, each node i is connected directly to two of the parents, which we call i_0 and i_1. We assume that these access links are nonblocking, or equivalently that they have infinite capacity, to concentrate on the issue of routing through the core network. Nodes that have the same two parents are said to be in the same cluster. Clusters that share a parent are said to be adjacent. Figure 1.7 is a schematic diagram of the network structure.

Calls from cluster i to cluster j arise as a Poisson process of rate $\lambda_{i,j}$; independent of other traffic streams each call has a holding time exponentially distributed with mean 1, independent of other calls and of the arrival processes; and a successfully routed call requires one circuit at each link on its route. We assume for simplicity that a call between two clusters is equally likely to be due to any node–node pair within those clusters. Calls between two nodes in the same cluster or in adjacent clusters can be successfully routed via access links only, not via the core network; because we are primarily considering effects in the core network, we omit such traffic.

To complete the description of a network, we must define which clusters are connected to which parents. The numerical results described in this section were obtained for a 24-node core network, with 36 clusters in the access network, each cluster including six nodes.[15]

1.5.3   The Schemes

1.5.3.1   Single-Parented Routing

The first family of schemes we consider we call *single-parented routing* (SPR). A call chooses a parent of its source node i and a parent of its destination node j without referring to the state of the network. It must enter the core network through the first parent and leave through the second. Thus the routing in the core network makes no use of multiparenting, and for each call the network is effectively single-parented. Subject to these conditions, however, a call may be carried on *any* route through the core network.

In reference 15 we find a lower bound on the network-loss probability of *any* SPR scheme. The bound is approached by a simple scheme. Each link calculates a trunk-reservation parameter as a function of its capacity and the traffic offered to the core network between the two parents it joins. A call offered to the core network between two points is routed directly if possible; if not, it is offered to a randomly ordered sequence of two-link paths joining the two parents until a path is found where both links are occupied below their respective trunk-reservation parameters; if no such two-link path exists the call is lost.

Figure 1.15 illustrates the lower bound on the performance of any SPR scheme, and simulation results for the SPR scheme just described, for a dual-parented network where the capacity of a typical link in the core network is 600 circuits. The load parameter ν measures the direct traffic offered to a typical link of the core network. For simulation results, the size of the plotting character is comparable to the standard error. We discuss these results further in Section 1.5.4.

1.5.3.2   Least-Loaded Routing

The second family of schemes we consider assumes that the network is able to route a call by *any* route. Observe that for a dual-parented network a call from node i to node j has then the choice of four possible direct routes through the core network, for it can choose to go via parent i_0 or i_1 of node i, and via parent j_0 or j_1 of node j.

Because each call passing through the core network must use at least one circuit from that network, a lower bound on the network-loss probability is given by Erlang's formula

$$E\left(\sum \lambda_{ij} , \sum C_{ij} \right)$$

where the summations run over all links ij of the core network.

An example of a scheme from our second family is Least-Loaded Routing (LLR), defined as follows. The scheme simply looks at the four possible direct routes through the core network that a call could take, and chooses the one with the greatest number of free circuits; if all four routes are full, the call is lost. Figure 1.15 illustrates the Erlang bound and the simulated performance of LLR, for the dual-parented network. For further discussion and examples of this class of bounds, see reference 12. We see that under a wide range of offered traffic the performance of LLR considerably exceeds that of the SPR schemes, and comes close to the Erlang bound. Notice especially that there is very little incentive to consider schemes other than LLR from within the second family of schemes—for example, schemes that allow a call to use two or more links within the core network. The Erlang bound in Figure 1.15 indicates how little remains to be won over LLR by *any* such scheme.

The LLR scheme may be hard to implement, however, relying as it does on having instantaneous information about the occupancy of links in the core network. Therefore we seek schemes which are able to gain most of the benefit of dual parenting, but which are simple and easy to implement. The schemes we consider are based on the two aforementioned simple principles, the last-chance principle and the sticky principle.

1.5.3.3 Last-Chance Principle

The use of a trunk-reservation parameter against calls that would absorb an excessive amount of network resource if they were carried is a familiar one, as discussed in Section 1.2.2. The last-chance principle, however, uses trunk reservation in a different way, namely to favor calls that are attempting their last possible route through the network and would therefore be lost if they were blocked. Theoretical analysis[23] indicates the considerable merit of this principle provided alternative routes use no more network resources than first choice routes.

Motivated by the principle, we define this simple last-chance scheme. A call chooses at random equiprobably from among its four direct routes across the core network; suppose it chooses the route via link $i_t j_s$. It is attempted on this link at low priority. If it fails there—that is, if there are no more than $r_{i_t j_s}$ free circuits on that link—it attempts the route via link $i_t j_{(1-s)}$ at high priority. If it cannot be carried there, because there are no free circuits on that link, the call is lost (see Figure 1.13). Observe that the call may be lost even though free circuits are available on the link $i_t j_s$: we discuss this point further in Section 1.5.4.

1.5.3.4 Sticky Principle

The sticky principle is that routes on which a call is carried are retained as preferred routes, routes on which a call is blocked are replaced. Thus nodes and parents are allowed to remember very limited information about the success or otherwise of previous calls. We further illustrate this principle in the following sticky scheme.

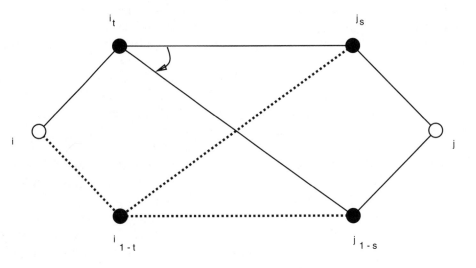

Figure 1.13 Routing a call from *i* to *j*

Node i has a current first-choice parent for calls to node j, i_t say, and parent i_t has a current first-choice route for calls to node j via either j_0 or j_1. We say that parent i_t is in state 0 for calls to node j if its first-choice route is via parent j_0 and state 1 if the first-choice route goes via j_1.

Now a call from i to j will be attempted via parent i_t. If i_t is in state s then it will attempt to route the call via j_s. If the call is successfully carried on $i_t j_s$ then the current first choices are unchanged. If the call is not successful there, it is attempted on the link from i_t to $j_{(1-s)}$. If it is carried there, i_t switches to state $(1-s)$. If it fails there also the call is lost and node i switches its first-choice parent for calls to node j to $i_{(1-t)}$. The last-chance and sticky principles are combined in the general sticky scheme flowcharted in Figure 1.14; a pure sticky scheme is obtained by setting the trunk-reservation parameter r_{ij} to zero.

Notice that the general sticky scheme uses very simple rules, which can be easily implemented. A further consequence of simplicity is that we can derive a fixed-point analytical model for the scheme,[15] as described in Section 1.2.3. The results of the analytical model are shown in Figure 1.15, for the sticky scheme with trunk-reservation parameter $r = 2$. Also shown are simulation results for the same scheme. The analytical model was used to choose the value $r = 2$ for the trunk-reservation parameter. This choice is optimal or nearly optimal for all the varied examples considered in this section.

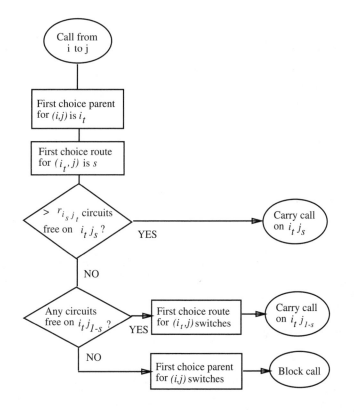

Figure 1.14   The general sticky scheme

1.5.4   Discussion

1.5.4.1   Relative Performance

Figure 1.15 collects results on the three families of schemes described in Section 1.5.3. It is interesting to view Figure 1.15 as part of a larger figure. At low offered traffics any reasonable scheme has (effectively) zero blocking, and we see in Figure 1.16 that for sufficiently high offered traffic all schemes again perform similarly. But as the traffic offered increases from a low level, blocking for the SPR bound rises before that for the sticky scheme, and thus there is a region where the sticky scheme has near-zero blocking, but the SPR scheme may have blocking of up to 2 percent.

Notice in Figure 1.15 how close the performances of the SPR and the LLR schemes are to their respective bounds. Although we do not have formal proof that the analytical model of the sticky scheme is a bound, the model's independence assumption would seem too favorable, and so we'd expect that simulations of the sticky scheme would also lie above their respective curve.

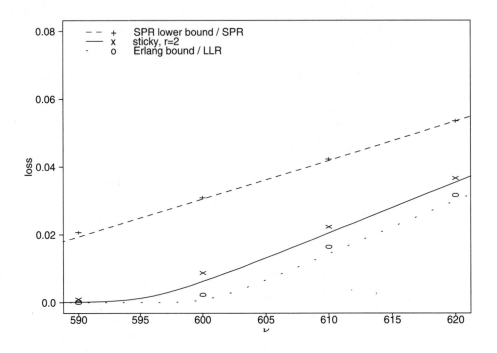

Figure 1.15   Comparison of three families

The active exploitation of multiparenting by the LLR scheme considerably improves performance over the best possible SPR schemes. Further, most of this improvement can be achieved by schemes as simple as the sticky scheme.

Although our illustrations concentrate on networks with link capacities on the order of 600 circuits, similar results hold for other capacities. For example, if link capacities are of order 120 circuits, then with load $v = 115$, the network-loss probability is around 0 percent, 0.7 percent, and 4 percent under the LLR, sticky, and SPR schemes.

1.5.4.2 Link Failures

Any scheme must be judged both by its level of blocking and by its ability to cope with mismatches of traffic and capacity in the network. The first sort of mismatch we consider is provided by considering the effect of link failures. As we fail links, we expect the blocking to increase as the capacity decreases, and indeed in Figure 1.17 (which takes the load $v = 610$ and fails random "general" links one after another) we see that the relative performance of the schemes is very similar to that of Figure 1.15.

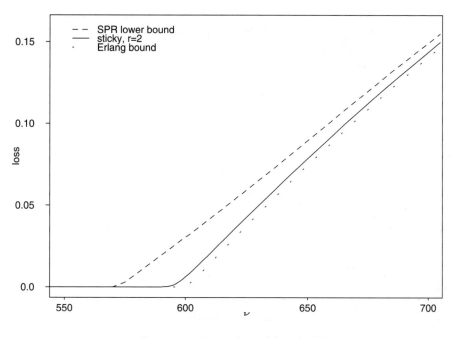

Figure 1.16   Comparison of three families

1.5.4.3   Traffic Mismatches

The general sticky scheme described in Figure 1.14 is based on both the sticky principle and, if trunk-reservation parameters are positive, the last-chance principle. In this section we show that these principles are essentially complementary.

The sticky scheme cannot gain any significant advantage over the simpler last-chance scheme when blocking probabilities on different routes are approximately the same, but the sticky scheme can show its superiority over the last-chance scheme when traffics and capacities are mismatched. In this case the sticky scheme can learn to direct more traffic toward less-loaded links, thus more effectively utilizing the capacity available in the network. As an example we consider an adjustment in the traffics offered between clusters, derived from an initially balanced traffic matrix. Two cluster–cluster pairs are chosen at random from among the set, S, of all cluster–cluster pairs providing traffic to the core network and an amount of offered traffic uniformly distributed on $[0, \alpha\lambda]$ is taken from one and put on the other. The two cluster–cluster pairs are removed from the set S, two more pairs are selected, and the same procedure applied, and so on until all pairs have been used. The effect is that traffic and capacity are mismatched, but the amount of traffic and capacity remains constant. Figure 1.18 shows results for networks that have been generated by this method for

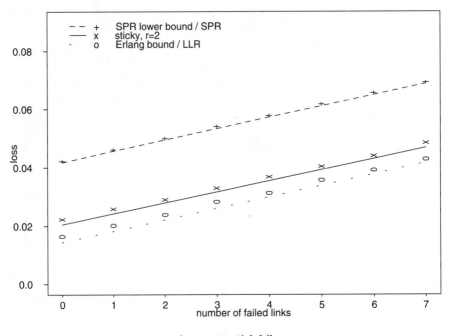

Figure 1.17   Link failures

load $v = 610$ and a range of α. Observe that as α increases, producing more highly asymmetric traffic patterns, the last-chance scheme degrades by nearly 50 percent, but there is no significant degradation in the performance of the sticky scheme. Indeed at the right-hand end of the graph the pure sticky scheme, with $r = 0$, is better than the last-chance scheme with $r = 2$. The sticky scheme is better able to divert traffic toward less-loaded parts of the network, thus providing far greater robustness against mismatches of traffics and capacities.

It may seem surprising that the sticky schemes are oblivious to the degree of traffic mismatch, and counterintuitive that the cases $r = 2$ outperform the cases $r = 0$. Because all routing in the core network is direct, surely it is perverse to deny access (by the choice $r = 2$) to free circuits? It is however our intuition that requires development. Recall that the link $i_t j_s$ in Figure 1.13 will carry traffic between several cluster–cluster pairs, because nodes i_t and j_s are each parents to more than a single cluster (see Figure 1.7). Some of these traffic streams will view the link $i_t j_s$ as first choice, some as second choice. A positive trunk-reservation parameter r favors those streams which will be lost if blocked, allowing traffic to be shared more evenly over the various links of the core network. Similarly the sticky scheme allows the proportions of traffic from node i to nodes i_0 or i_1 (in Figure 1.13) to adapt and load the core network more evenly, even in the presence of traffic mismatches. Several other schemes can of

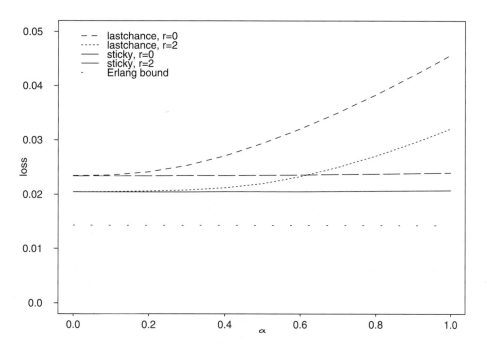

Figure 1.18 Traffic mismatches

course achieve a similar even loading: we have described LLR, and various schemes of intermediate complexity, involving crankback, for example, could be devised. In a multiparented network the routing strategy should encourage the capacity available throughout the core network to act as a single pooled resource.

1.5.4.4 Parent Failures

We now turn to the question of how fast the sticky scheme responds when a failure occurs. A scheme must be able to adapt as quickly as possible to a failure, with as few calls lost as possible. In our simulation at a certain time, a whole parent fails. If we consider just the traffic streams out of the clusters that are parented on the failed parent, then the effect of failing the parent is shown in gray in Figure 1.19. We see that at first the blocking from these clusters becomes very high, but that as calls attempt to go via the failed parent and are blocked, the states automatically flip and future calls are sent to the other parent, so that the blocking drops quite quickly. We can also derive an analytical model for this effect: before the parent fails, the blocking is the same on all the links in the network, and so the states are set equiprobably, and the sticky scheme is effectively the same as the last-chance scheme. Therefore just after the parent fails, the blocking out of the relevant clusters is the same as it would be

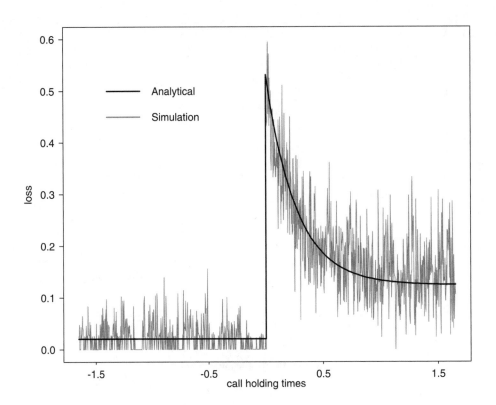

Figure 1.19   Node failure at time 0, local blocking

under the last-chance scheme, which, according to the analytical model, is 53 percent. When it has settled down, the blocking out of these clusters reaches the blocking for the sticky scheme, which is 12 percent. For our numerical example traffic from one cluster to another is generated at rate

$$\frac{4}{18}\nu$$

so traffic from one node to another is generated at rate

$$\frac{4}{18}\nu \cdot \frac{1}{n_c^2}$$

where n_c is the number of nodes in a cluster. If $\nu = 610$ and $n_c = 6$ then the rate at which traffic is generated between two given nodes is 3.765 Erlangs. Because each node–node pair has a state that, if it is set to the failed parent, flips as soon as it tries to send a call, the decay from the higher to the lower value is exponential of rate 3.765. This analytical result is portrayed as the solid curve in Figure 1.19 and we see that it agrees very closely with the observed results. Notice that the sticky scheme adapts as quickly as possible using only information gleaned from blocked calls. (LLR, of course, uses more information and adapts more quickly.)

Further discussion of reliability and robustness issues can be found in references 7, 12, 28, and 35; results on the speed of response of sticky and other schemes are reported in references 10, 20, and 33.

1.5.5 Multiparenting

All this analysis extends naturally from dual- to multiparented networks. The main reason for constructing networks with greater numbers of parents is to increase reliability in accessing the core network; for example, if one link from a node to a parent fails in the dual-parented case half the capacity is lost, whereas in the triple-parented case only one-third of the capacity is lost. This limitation does not trouble our analysis because we gave the access links infinite capacity. Nevertheless, greater numbers of parents can also reduce blocking by increasing the number of routes (and indeed the number of schemes) available, and in any case because many networks are moving to triple-parenting our scheme must generalize simply to such cases. Therefore we briefly discuss this generalization, using the triple-parented case as an example.

The last-chance and sticky routing rules work analogously, except that each call may attempt three routes, the first being chosen as in the dual-parented case, the other two being the other two routes from the first-choice parent in random order. The call is at high priority only on its last attempt. In the sticky scheme the first choices change in a way analogous to the dual-parented case. Changing to the multiparented case reduces the blocking still further (although we cannot expect a dramatic improvement, because in the dual-parented case we are already performing close to the Erlang bound) and provides even greater robustness in certain types of failure conditions (such as failure of a whole parent).

Throughout we have treated access links as nonblocking, but it is straightforward to generalize our simple schemes to the case where access links have finite capacity. If calls can overflow between the various access links connecting a node to its several parents, then trunk reservation in favor of a call on its last attempted access link will encourage efficient use of the access links.[18]

1.6 CONCLUSION

In this chapter we discuss how dynamic routing strategies can be used in circuit-switched telecommunication networks to improve the network's performance and robustness against failures and uncertain conditions. We present in detail the Dynamic Alternative Routing strategy, which uses a principle of sticky routing and trunk-reservation mechanisms in a simple and decentralized fashion to find and then efficiently utilize spare capacity in the network. We consider how this approach applies in a number of network architectures, including fully connected networks, dual- and multiparented networks, and international-access networks.

REFERENCES

1   R. G. Ackerley, "Hysteresis-Type Behaviour in Networks with Extensive Overflow," *British Telecom Technical Journal,* Vol. 5, No. 4, 1987.

2   J. M. Akinpelu, "The Overload Performance of Engineered Networks with Nonhierarchical Routing," *Proceedings Tenth International Teletraffic Congress,* Montreal, 1983.

3   G. R. Ash, R. H. Cardwell, and R. P. Murray, "Design and Optimization of Networks with Dynamic Routing," *Bell Systems Technical Journal,* Vol. 60, 1981, pp. 1787–1820.

4   G. R. Ash, A. H. Kafker, and K. R. Krishnan, "Servicing and Real-Time Control of Networks with Dynamic Routing," *Bell Systems Technical Journal,* Vol. 60, 1981, pp. 1821–1845.

5   G. R. Ash, "Use of a Trunk Status Map for Real-Time DNHR," *Proceedings of the Eleventh International Teletraffic Congress,* 1985.

6   G. R. Ash, J.-S. Chen, A. E. Frey, and B. D. Huang, "Real-Time Network Routing in a Dynamic Class-of-Service Network," *Proceedings of the Thirteenth International Teletraffic Congress,* Copenhagen, Amsterdam, North-Holland, 1991.

7   G. R. Ash, F. Chang, and D. Medhi, "Robust Traffic Design for Dynamic Routing Networks," *Proceedings of IEEE INFOCOM,* 1991.

8   W. H. Cameron, J. Regnier, P. Galloy, and A. M. Savoie, "Dynamic Routing for Intercity Telephone Networks," *Proceedings of the Tenth International Teletraffic Congress,* 1983.

9   F. Caron, "Results of the Telecom Canada High-Performance Routing Trial," *Proceedings of the Twelfth International Teletraffic Congress,* Amsterdam, North-Holland, 1988.

10 P. Chemouil, J. Filipiak, and P. Gauthier, "Performance Issues in the Design of Dynamically Controlled Circuit-Switched Networks," *IEEE Communications Magazine,* "Advanced Traffic Control Methods for Circuit-Switched Telecommunications Networks," Vol. 28, No. 10, October 1990.

11 G. A. Cope, "A Fixed Point Model of Dynamic Alternative Routing," *BT Internal Memo,* 1988.

12 R. J. Gibbens and F. P. Kelly, "Dynamic Routing in Fully Connected Networks," *IMA Journal of Mathematical Control and Information,* Vol. 7, 1990, pp. 77–111.

13 R. J. Gibbens, F. P. Kelly, G. A. Cope, and M. J. Whitehead, "Coalitions in the International Network," *Proceedings of the Thirteenth International Teletraffic Congress,* Copenhagen, Amsterdam, North-Holland, 1991.

14 R. J. Gibbens, F. P. Kelly, and P. B. Key, "Dynamic Alternative Routing—Modelling and Behaviour," *Proceedings of the Twelfth International Teletraffic Congress,* Amsterdam, North-Holland, 1988.

15 R. J. Gibbens, F. P. Kelly, and S. R. E. Turner, "Dynamic Routing in Multiparented Networks," *IEEE/ACM Transaction Networking,* Vol. 1, No. 2, 1993, pp. 261–270.

16 I. Hawker, "Future Trends in Digital Telecommunication Transmission Networks," *Electronics and Communication Engineering Journal,* December 1990.

17 B. Hennion, "Feedback Methods for Calls Allocation on the Crossed Traffic Routing," *Proceedings of the Ninth International Teletraffic Congress,* Torremolinos, October 1979.

18 P. J. Hunt and F. P. Kelly, "Strategic Issues in the Design of Circuit-Switched Networks," *Report for BT by the Stochastic Networks Group,* Cambridge, 1987.

19 A. R. Ingham and A. M. Elvidge, "Trunk Reservation with Automatic Alternative Routing," *Sixth UK Teletraffic Symposium,* London: IEEE, 1989.

20 A. Inoue, H. Yamamoto, and Y. Harada, "An Advanced Large-Scale Simulation System for Telecommunication Networks with Dynamic Routing," *Networks 89,* September 1989, pp. 77–82.

21 F. P. Kelly, "Routing in Circuit-Switched Networks: Optimization, Shadow Prices and Decentralization," *Advances in Applied Probability,* Vol. 20, 1988, pp. 112–144.

22 F. P. Kelly, "Fixed Point Models of Loss Networks," *Journal of the Australian Mathematical Society,* Series B, Vol. 31, 1989, pp. 204–218.

23 F. P. Kelly, "Routing and Capacity Allocation in Networks with Trunk Reservation," *Mathematics of Operations Reserved,* Vol. 15, 1990, pp. 771–793.

24 F. P. Kelly, "Loss Networks," *Annals of Applied Probability,* Vol. 1, 1991, pp. 317–378.

25 F. P. Kelly, "Network Routing," *Philosophical Transactions of the Royal Society,* Vol. 337, 1991, pp. 343–367.

26 P. B. Key, "Implied Cost Methodology and Software Tools for a Fully Connected Network with DAR and Trunk Reservation," *British Telecom Technology Journal,* Vol. 6, 1988, pp. 52–65.

27 P. B. Key and G. A. Cope, "Distributed Dynamic Routing Schemes," *IEEE Communications Magazine,* "Advanced Traffic Control Methods for Circuit-Switched Telecommunications Networks," Vol. 28, No. 10, October 1990.

28 P. B. Key and A. Elvidge, "Design and Analysis of a Highly Reliable Transmission Network," *Proceedings of the Thirteenth International Teletraffic Congress,* Copenhagen, Amsterdam, North-Holland, 1991.

29 P. B. Key and M. J. Whitehead, "Cost-Effective Use of Networks Employing Dynamic Alternative Routing," *Proceedings of the Twelfth International Teletraffic Congress,* Turin, Amsterdam, North-Holland, 1988.

30 D. Mitra, R. J. Gibbens, and B. D. Huang, "Analysis and Optimal Design of Aggregated-Least-Busy-Alternative rRouting on Symmetric Loss Networks with Trunk Reservations," *Proceedings of the Thirteenth International Teletraffic Congress,* Copenhagen, Amsterdam, North-Holland, 1991.

31 D. Mitra, R. J. Gibbens, and B. D. Huang, "State-Dependent Routing on Symmetric Loss Networks with Trunk Reservations, I," *IEEE Transactions on Communications,* Vol. 41, No. 2, 1993, pp. 400–411.

32 D. Mitra and R. J. Gibbens, "State-Dependent Routing on Symmetric Loss Networks with Trunk Reservations, II: Asymptotics, Optimal Design," *Annals of Operations Research,* Vol. 35, 1991, pp. 3–30.

33 D. Mitra and J. B. Seery, "Comparative Evaluations of Randomized and Dynamic Routing Strategies for Circuit-Switched Networks," *IEEE Transactions on Communications,* Vol. 39, 1991, pp. 102–116.

34 Y. Nakagome and H. Mori, "Flexible Routing in the Global Communication Network," *Proceedings of the Seventh International Teletraffic Congress,* Stockholm, 1973.

35 M. Pioro, M. de Miguel, and I. Pita, "Telecom Networks Evolution towards Secure Dynamic Structures," *International Teletraffic Congress Specialists' Seminar,* Cracow, 1991.

36 R. R. Stacey and D. J. Songhurst, "Dynamic Alternative Routing in the British Telecom Trunk Network," *International Switching Symposium,* Phoenix, 1987.

37 R. Weber, "A Simulation Study of Routing and Control in Communication Networks," *Bell Systems Technical Journal,* Vol. 43, 1964, pp. 2639–2676.

38 G. A. Wroe, G. A. Cope, and M. J. Whitehead, "Flexible Routing in the BT International Access Network," *Proceedings of the Seventh UK Teletraffic Symposium,* Durham, England: IEEE, 1990.

CHAPTER 2   ❖   ❖   ❖   ❖

On Routing in ATM Networks*

SANJAY GUPTA, KEITH W. ROSS, AND MAGDA EL ZARKI

CONTENTS

---

*   Supported in part by NSF Grant NCR-891447 and in part by AT Grant 5-23690.

Asynchronous transfer mode (ATM) was originally developed as a switching standard for support of broadband integrated services in public, switched telephone networks. More recently, it has also gained popularity as a networking substrate for private high-speed networks. A virtual-circuit, packet-switching technology as opposed to a circuit-switching technology, ATM nevertheless can provide a wide range of guaranteed qualities of service, when combined with appropriate techniques for route selection and traffic control. This chapter describes an innovative approach to ATM virtual-circuit route selection in accordance with users' service requirements. The basic route selection algorithm and its variants are derived from the Least Loaded Routing algorithm, which forms the basis of AT&T's Real-Time Networking Routing algorithm. To apply this telephony routing strategy in an ATM network, one must first superimpose a virtual topology over the physical topology to emulate telephone network connectivity.

2.1   INTRODUCTION

The increasing demand for multimedia and video services has motivated development of *broadband integrated services digital networks* (B-ISDNs), which are public, switched telecommunication networks capable of supporting both narrowband and broadband services on a single network platform and providing customer access over a single interface. CCITT has chosen *asynchronous transfer mode* (ATM) as the multiplexing and switching technique for B-ISDN. ATM is sufficiently versatile to provide a bearer service capable of integrating a wide spectrum of traffic sources. ATM technology is also well suited to corporate networks, campus backbone networks, and high-speed LAN environments.

Specifically, ATM is a *high-speed, virtual-circuit-oriented packet-switching technique* that uses short, fixed-length packets called *cells*.[14] A *virtual circuit* in ATM is a contract between the network and the customer to deliver traffic of specified statistical characteristics to the destination with a specified *quality of service* (QOS), which is typically defined by limits on cell loss, cell delay, and cell jitter, which the routing algorithm must take into account to optimize performance. Each cell is 53 bytes long, of which 5 bytes are reserved for the header and the remaining 48 bytes for user data.

But before ATM can be employed as a means for offering a wider range of services, numerous connection-management issues first need to be studied. In this chapter we study two important and closely related connection-management issues—VC acceptance and VC routing.

Alternative routing of calls has long been regarded in the telephone industry as a way to increase call throughput and robustness in the telephone network. Call throughput is increased when all circuits are occupied on the direct path by setting up calls on alternative paths. Robustness, measured as the network's ability to respond to equipment failure and to unexpected surges of traffic, is made available by transferring flows to alternative routes.

Since early in the 1980s, the trend in the telephone industry has been to implement *dynamic alternative routing* within *nonhierarchical networks.* A nonhierarchical network consists of a set of switches and (logical) direct links for each pair of switches. With dynamic alternative routing, a call requesting a connection between a pair of switches may be established along the direct link or along any of the two-link alternative routes, the selected route depending on link occupancies. Several dynamic routing schemes have been proposed and implemented in nonhierarchical telephone networks; they have been shown to offer excellent performance throughput and robustness.

For a dynamic routing algorithm to function properly in a telephone network, it is crucial that the network be able to gather and process up-to-date link-occupancy information. This capacity has been made possible by advances in switch technology, enabling switches to track local link occupancies, and *common channel signaling* (CCS) networks (refer to Chapter 12 in reference 22 for further detail), enabling switches to exchange link-occupancy information.

The great gains in performance offered by dynamic nonhierarchical routing in telephone networks make it natural to consider dynamic routing of VCs in ATM networks. Unlike telephone networks, however, VCs have heterogeneous bandwidth characteristics and QOS requirements. Moreover, as we demonstrate in the body of this chapter, the proper choice of routing algorithm strongly depends on the underlying nonstandardized ATM technology, such as the size of the buffers in the switches.

Here we attempt to classify ATM networks according to the network characteristics that have greatest bearing on the performance of dynamic routing algorithms; we also discuss appropriate routing algorithms for each class of ATM network. We classify networks according to whether or not they have these two properties:

1   *Calls are homogeneous in bandwidth characteristics and QOS requirements.* Calls can be considered homogeneous if the various types of traffic (such as voice, video) are segregated into separate logical networks defined by *virtual paths* (VPs). If traffic segregation is not performed, then calls must be treated as heterogeneous.

2   *Statistical multiplexing is not performed in the interior of the network.* This occurs, for example, if calls are admitted according to their peak bandwidth requirements, in which case buffers in the switches can be made small. On the other hand, if the sum of the peak rates for all VCs employing a particular VP exceeds the bandwidth of that link, then the network operates in the statistical-multiplexing mode and larger buffers are needed to prevent excessive cell loss.

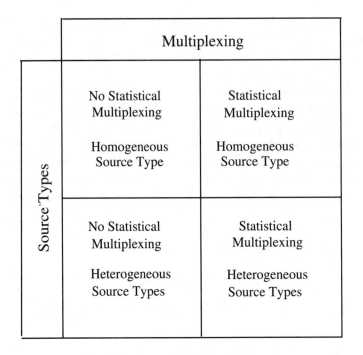

Table 2.1   Classification of ATM networks

Because an ATM network can conceivably be operated with or without either of these two properties, the combinations lead to the four classes of ATM networks summarized in Table 2.1.

From the perspective of accepting and routing VCs, homogeneous traffic with nonstatistical multiplexing is equivalent to single-rate circuit switching; it is therefore not considered in this chapter. Further, statistical multiplexing offers insignificant gains in performance when traffic types have greatly different QOS requirements or have greatly different cell-generation properties.[10,24] If traffic types demanding vastly different QOS are statistically multiplexed, then an overall QOS that is at least as good as the most stringent QOS has to be guaranteed, and therefore some traffic types are provided a QOS that is much better than they demand, leading to inefficient use of resources. Similarly, if traffic types with substantially different traffic characteristics are multiplexed, then the cell-loss probabilities for individual traffic streams can differ by more than an order of magnitude.[4] Hence the system has to be engineered for a QOS that is more stringent than the QOS requirements of the traffic types being multiplexed. For this reason, we also do not consider heterogeneous traffic types and statistical multiplexing.

In Section 2.2 we briefly survey some of the dynamic routing algorithms that have been proposed for and implemented in telephone networks. In Section 2.3 we describe VP-based ATM networks and motivate our classification. In Section 2.4 we propose and compare several routing algorithms for homogeneous traffic and statistical multiplexing, with a QOS requirement based on cell-loss probability. The same possibility is considered in Section 2.5, except with a delay-based QOS requirement. In Section 2.6, we propose a routing algorithm for heterogeneous traffic requirements and nonstatistical multiplexing. Our findings are summarized in Section 2.7.

2.2 DYNAMIC ROUTING IN TELEPHONE NETWORKS

As mentioned in Section 2.1, numerous dynamic routing algorithms have been proposed for and implemented in telephone networks in recent years. We feel that the knowledge acquired from their development and implementation should be exploited by the ATM community. In this section we briefly review some dynamic routing algorithms for telephone networks.

We discuss the routing algorithms in the context of a (logically) fully connected network with N switches and $J = N(N-1)/2$ links. The capacity of link j (equivalently, the number of calls that can be in progress on link j) is denoted C_j and is in units of *circuits*. Each pair of switches has one direct route and $N-2$ two-link alternative routes. Associate with each link j a *trunk reservation* (TR) value, denoted by r_j. A two-link alternative route is said to be *TR-permissible* if, for each of its links, the number of free circuits exceeds the corresponding trunk-reservation level. Most of the routing algorithms discussed below have these properties: when a new call requests establishment between a pair of switches, it is set up in the direct route if at least one free circuit is available; otherwise, the call is set up in a TR-permissible alternative route when at least one such route is available; if the direct route and all the two-link alternative routes are unavailable, the call is blocked. The routing algorithms differ in their way of choosing from the set of TR-permissible alternative routes.

The first routing algorithm that we discuss is *dynamic nonhierarchical routing* (DNHR), employed in AT&T's long-distance network late in the 1980s.[3] The essence of this algorithm is to sequentially examine a subset of the possible alternative routes when the direct route is full. More specifically, an ordered subset of the alternative routes is associated with each pair of switches; the number of routes in a subset is a small proportion of the alternative routes available to the switch pair. When a call arrives and the direct route is full, it is set up in the first TR-permissible alternative route in the ordered list; if no such route is available, the call is blocked. The subsets associated with the node, the ordering of the elements within the subsets, the capacities of the links, and the trunk-reservation parameters vary over time periods, ten in each day. These routing parameters are determined for each time period by performing sophisticated, off-line, centralized computations that rely on traffic forecasts.

Implementing DNHR, as well as the other dynamic routing algorithms, is possible because of switches with stored-program control interconnected through a CCS network. For example, the subset of alternative routes for a switch pair is maintained in the software of the switches, and modifications to the subset are made over the CCS network. Another example occurs when an alternative route is tried and the second link of the route is full; the CCS network performs "crankback" by sending a signal to the originating switch so that another alternative route can be tried.

Implemented in British Telecom's domestic network, *dynamic alternative routing* (DAR) is an algorithm meant to adapt to unforeseen changes in traffic patterns with a minimum of signaling between the switches[12] (see also Chapter 1 in this volume). DAR associates with each pair of switches *one* alternative route. If, when a call arrives the direct route is full, the call is set up in the associated alternative route when it is TR-permissible; otherwise, the call is blocked and a new associated alternative route is chosen for use by subsequent calls. The new route is chosen at random, according to a uniform distribution, from the remaining $N - 3$ alternative routes.

Unlike DNHR, the DAR algorithm does not need to keep track of an ordered list of routes; hence, forecasting information is needed only for determining the capacity of the logical links and to set the trunk-reservation parameters. It also has all $N - 2$ alternative routes available, not just a subset of routes as does DNHR. The signaling needed for implementing DAR is minimal, for at most one alternative route is considered and crankback is not performed.

The *least loaded routing* (LLR) algorithm typically has better performance than DNHR and DAR, but requires a greater exchange of signaling information between the switches. The LLR algorithm keeps track of the *availabilities* of all the alternative routes, where the availability of a route is its number of end-to-end free circuits beyond trunk reservation. (For example, if both links in a route have capacity 100 circuits and trunk-reservation value 10, and 70 circuits of one link and 80 circuits of the other link are busy, then the availability of the route is

$$\min\{100 - 10 - 70, 100 - 10 - 80\} = 10$$

The LLR algorithm operates as follows. When the direct route is full, the most available alternative route (also referred to as the least-loaded alternative route) is selected from the set of TR-permissible routes; if none of the alternative routes is TR-permissible, the call is blocked. Thus, LLR attempts to evenly distribute traffic among its alternative routes.

LLR forms the basis of the *real-time network routing* (RTNR) algorithm, which has been operational in AT&T's long-distance domestic network since early in the 1990s.[2] In the RTNR implementation, when the direct route is full, the originating switch queries the terminating switch through the common-channel signaling network for the busy-idle status of all the links connected to the terminating switch. The originating switch then compares its own link busy-idle status information to that received from the terminating switch, to find the least-loaded alternative route. RTNR also classifies the busy states of each link into a few aggregate states, and the least-loaded route is determined with respect to the aggregate states.[2,15]

Dynamically controlled routing (DCR), developed by Bell Northern Research and planned for the Trans-Canadian Network, uses a central processor to track the busy-idle status of the links and to determine appropriate alternative routes based on status data every 15 seconds.[5]

State-dependent routing (SDR), developed at Bellcore,[16] chooses routes on the basis of "costs" associated with the states of the admissible routes at the time of the call. The cost of a route is an estimate of the expected increase in future call blockings that would result in accepting an additional call on the route in its current state. The costs are determined from the off-line solution of a large nonlinear program that requires forecasts of all traffic demands on the network. A version of SDR has been implemented in local telephone (metropolitan) networks for which link busy-idle information is reported only at five-minute intervals.[6]

2.3 ATM NETWORKS WITH VIRTUAL PATHS

Consider the network shown in Figure 2.1, which consists of ATM switches, inter-connected by (high-speed) backbone links, and multiplexers with access links to the switches. Terminals, which are not shown in the diagram, hang off the multiplexers. Observe that not all pairs of switches in the physical network are directly connected.

In order to facilitate network management and to increase the apparent direct connectedness of the network, *virtual paths* (VPs) are embedded in the network. A VP is defined as a set of adjacent backbone links and a bandwidth allocation. A VP is embedded in the physical network with the aid of the *virtual path identifier* (VPI) in the ATM cell header. An ATM switch reads the VPI of an incoming cell to direct the cell to the appropriate output port of the switch; VPI translation may also be necessary. The collection of VPs naturally defines a VP network (see Figure 2.1) with the switches as nodes and an edge between two nodes if and only if at least one VP lies between the corresponding switches. We do not preclude the possibility of having more than one VP assigned to the same set of physical links; this feature can be used to build virtual private networks or to separate disparate traffic in independent VP networks, as discussed below.

A physical link will typically be shared by many VPs, each having a different bandwidth allocation; we assume that the sum of the VP bandwidth allocations does not exceed the link's capacity. We also assume that the instantaneous, or peak bit rate *transmitted* on a VP never exceeds the VP's bandwidth allocation.

Although the transmitted peak rate may never exceed a VP's bandwidth allocation, the *offered peak rate* may exceed the allocation over short periods when statistical multiplexing is used. To deal with these periods of excessive offered peak rates, buffers are placed at the input of each link, one buffer for each VP that employs the link. We assume that the buffers are served by the link in a weighted, round-robin fashion, the

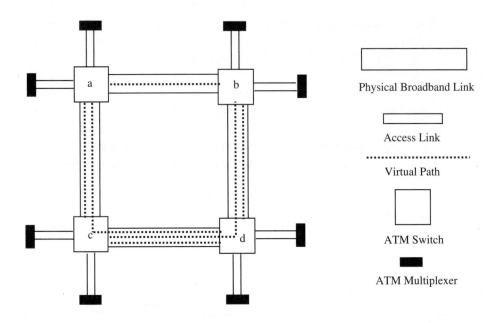

Physical Network With VPs

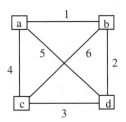

VP Subnetwork

Figure 2.1   Example of an ATM network

weights being proportional to the VP's assigned bandwidths. (For example, if two VPs with assigned bandwidths 50 Mbps and 100 Mbps share a link of 150 Mbps, then in one cycle of three cells, one VP will be served once and the other twice; see Takagi et al.[24] for more details.) Because a VP is allocated the same bandwidth on each link it traverses and no cells join (or leave) a VP at intermediate nodes, cells belonging to a VP do not queue at the intermediate nodes. Thus the VP's buffer space at the inputs of these subsequent links can be made very small; it is used only when cells from different inputs arrive to a link simultaneously, causing *cell-scale congestion* (see Roberts[19]).

When establishing a VC so that a pair of terminals can communicate, a route consisting of a set of VPs is selected. For example, to establish a VC between switches *a* and *b* in Figure 2.1, three possible routes are: {1}, {5, 2}, and {4, 6}. If a route consists of one VP, it is a *direct route*; otherwise, it is an *alternative route*. Following the practices of dynamic routing in telephone networks, we exclude routes that consist of more than two VPs. Thus, every pair of terminals has an associated set of routes, where each route consists of one or two VPs. The route selected for a VC is determined by the routing algorithm.

Throughout this study we assume that the route of a VC is not permitted to be rearranged before call completion. We further assume that VPs are fixed in the network, because the time scales pertaining to routing VCs are significantly smaller than those involving modification of the VP network. Finally, we assume that routing decisions are based only on the knowledge of which VCs are currently in progress, and not on the current buffer contents.

When routing a VC in the VP network, the routing algorithm needs to take into account the traffic characteristics of the VC (peak rate, mean rate, burstiness, etc.) as well as the characteristics of the VCs in progress. The routing algorithm must also take into account the VC's QOS requirements.

In this chapter we distinguish between ATM networks supporting *heterogeneous sources* and ATM networks supporting *homogeneous sources*. If at least one VP supports VCs that have different traffic characteristics and/or QOS requirements, then the sources are said to be heterogeneous. On the other hand, if the various traffic types are segregated into classes so that VCs in a class have the same traffic characteristics and QOS requirements, and if these classes are transported over separate *VP subnetworks*,* then the sources employing a VP subnetwork are homogeneous.

We also distinguish between ATM networks operating in the *statistical* and *nonstatistical multiplexing modes*. An ATM network operates in the statistical multiplexing mode if, for any VP, the VCs routed over the VP are permitted to have an aggregate offered bit rate that exceeds the bandwidth allocation of the VP. During these excess periods, the buffer before the first link of the VP will accumulate with cells and perhaps overflow. The ATM network is operated in the nonstatistical multiplexing mode if, for each VP, the aggregate instantaneous bit rate offered by the VCs does not exceed the VP's bandwidth allocation.†

An ATM network will operate in the nonstatistical mode if VC bandwidth is allocated according to peak rate. Then a VC may be routed through a VP only if its peak

---

* A VP subnetwork is a collection of VPs transporting identical sets of traffic sources.

† The wording *nonstatistical multiplexing* is chosen for consistency with the terminology in the ATM literature. We stress, however, that even for nonstatistical multiplexing the cells propagating on a VP are "randomly" allocated to the various VCs established over the VP.

rate added to the peak rates of the VCs in progress is less than the VP's bandwidth allocation. Such a scheme, of course, does not permit bandwidth to be shared between the VCs. Nevertheless, its management and control are relatively easy compared with the statistical-multiplexing mode.

The two properties discussed above, homogeneous or heterogeneous sources and nonstatistical or statistical multiplexing, lead to four classes of ATM networks, as presented in Table 2.1 in the introduction. As mentioned, we do not consider the cases of (1) homogeneous traffic with nonstatistical multiplexing because it is equivalent to single-rate circuit switching; and (2) statistical multiplexing with heterogeneous sources as the network resources are not utilized efficiently. We now address the remaining two cases.

2.4 STATISTICAL MULTIPLEXING AND HOMOGENEOUS SOURCES

In this section we assume that all sources have the same traffic characteristics and QOS requirements, and that the VCs are statistically multiplexed at the inputs to the VPs. The presence of statistical multiplexing significantly complicates operation and analysis of dynamic routing algorithms: we now have to ensure, for each VC in progress, that the cell-level QOS requirements are met.

The QOS requirement at the cell level should take into account cell loss, cell delay, and cell jitter. To simplify the discussion and to shed some light on this complex problem, however, we assume in this section that the QOS requirement involves only cell loss. Specifically, for each VC in progress we suppose that the fraction of cells lost is not permitted to exceed a given ε.* Notice that for an alternatively routed VC, cell loss can occur at either of the two VP input buffers along the route.

We now introduce some notations and definitions. Let $p_j(l)$ be the fraction of cells lost at the input buffer of VP_j when l VCs are being routed through VP_j. We assume that these probabilities can be determined by a cell-level analysis; for example, see reference 1. We classify a VC as either a VC_j or a VC_{ij} if the VC is assigned route $\{j\}$ or route $\{i, j\}$, respectively. Notice that

$$P(\text{"cell lost on a } VC_{ij}\text{"}|l_i, l_j) \le p_i(l_i) + p_j(l_j) \tag{1}$$

that is, the probability that a cell of a VC_{ij} is lost when there are l_i VCs using VP_i and l_j VCs using VP_j is less than the sum of the two VP loss probabilities. The inequality above will be close to an equality when loss in the buffers is small and almost independent from buffer to buffer. In any case, it follows from equation 1 that

---

* A typical value of ε ranges from 10^{-6} to 10^{-9}.

$$p_i(l_i) + p_j(l_j) \le \varepsilon$$

implies that

$$P(\text{"cell lost on a VC}_{ij}\text{"}|l_i, l_j) \le \varepsilon$$

Consider setting up a directly routed VC_j. The QOS requirement will permit this arrangement if these conditions are satisfied:

QOS-permissibility conditions for direct route $\{j\}$:

1   $p_j(l_j + 1) \le \varepsilon$

2   For every VP_k such that a VC_{jk} is in progress, $p_j(l_j + 1) + p_k(l_k) \le \varepsilon$

Notice that the first of these conditions ensures that the additional VC will not cause cell loss to be excessive for any of the directly routed VCs on VP_j. The second condition ensures that cell loss will not be excessive for any of the "overlapping VCs," that is, the alternatively routed VCs employing VP_j.

Now consider setting up an indirectly routed VC_{ij}. Analogously, the QOS requirement will permit this technique if these conditions are satisfied:

QOS-permissibility conditions for alternative route $\{i, j\}$:

1   $p_i(l_i + 1) + p_j(l_j + 1) \le \varepsilon$

2   For every VP_k such that a VC_{ik} is in progress, $p_i(l_i + 1) + p_k(l_k) \le \varepsilon$; and for every VP_k such that a VC_{jk} is in progress $p_j(l_j + 1) + p_k(l_k) \le \varepsilon$

Notice that determining QOS-permissibility of any route involves examining VPs that are not on the route under consideration. Thus, determining whether a VC is QOS-permissible is more difficult than it is for the nonstatistical multiplexing mode, for which it is not necessary to check the conditions for the overlapping VCs. Let

$$C_j := \max\{l : p_j(l) \le \varepsilon\}$$

so that C_j is the maximum number of direct VCs that can be established in VP_j.

It may be undesirable to set up an alternatively routed VC—even when it is QOS-permissible—for it utilizes more network resources than does a directly routed VC. To discourage alternatively routed VCs and save network resources for directly routed calls, we introduce an $\varepsilon' \le \varepsilon / 2$ and say that an alternatively routed VC_{ij} is TR-permissible if this condition is satisfied:

TR-permissibility condition for alternative route $\{i, j\}$:

• $p_i(l_i + 1) \le \varepsilon'$ and $p_j(l_j + 1) \le \varepsilon'$

The reader should view the parameter ε' as analogous to the trunk-reservation parameter for single-rate circuit-switched networks; its value should be chosen as a function of the arrival rate of calls and of the source's traffic characteristics.*

We now proceed to discuss three routing algorithms for ATM networks with homogeneous sources and statistical multiplexing. The three algorithms share several features: a VC is always established on its direct route when it is QOS-permissible; and, if the direct route is unavailable, alternative routes being both QOS-permissible and TR-permissible are considered. The algorithms differ in how they select an alternative route from the set of permissible routes.

2.4.1 Unrestricted LLR

Before discussing unrestricted LLR, it is convenient to define the load of an alternative route. Consider setting up a new VC on the alternative route $R = \{i, j\}$. Because of the TR-permissibility condition, this step can be done only if $p_i(n_i + 1) \leq \varepsilon'$ and $p_j(n_j + 1) \leq \varepsilon'$. Therefore, one natural definition for the (augmented) load of route R is

$$\text{load}_{\text{TR}}(R) := \max\{p_i(l_i + 1), p_j(l_j + 1)\}$$

The unrestricted LLR algorithm chooses, from the set of QOS-permissible alternative routes, the one that is most TR-permissible, that is, one that has the smallest value of $\text{load}_{\text{TR}}(R)$.

Unrestricted LLR Algorithm

1   First, attempt to set up the VC along the direct route, which is done if the direct route is QOS-permissible. Otherwise, proceed to Step 2.

2   Let $\mathcal{R}$ be the set of alternative routes that are both QOS-permissible and TR-permissible. If $\mathcal{R}$ is empty, then the VC request is rejected. Otherwise, set up the VC on the route in $\mathcal{R}$ that has the smallest value of $\text{load}_{\text{TR}}(R)$.

Although $\text{load}_{\text{TR}}(R)$ is an acceptable definition for load, another definition is equally natural. Indeed, an alternative route that is the most TR-permissible may be barely QOS-permissible, for either of the QOS-permissibility equalities may be close to being violated. Thus, $\text{load}_{\text{TR}}(R)$ ignores the additional burden placed on the overlapping VCs of R. To account for this additional burden, we introduce a second notion of load, $\text{load}_{\text{QOS}}(R)$, which is defined as follows. Let

---

*   The parameter ε' can be set to any value in $(0, \varepsilon)$, but in almost all practical circumstances the optimal value will be less than $\varepsilon / 2$. This restriction will simplify the notation in the subsequent subsection.

$$\text{load}(i) := \max_{k} \ \{p_i(l_i + 1) + p_k(l_k)\}$$

where the maximum is taken over all the ks such that a VC_{ik} is in progress. In an analogous manner, define load(j). Finally, define

$$\text{load}_{QOS}(R) := \max\{\text{load}(i), \text{load}(j), p_i(n_i + 1) + p_j(n_j + 1)\}$$

Notice that route R is QOS-permissible if and only if $\text{load}_{QOS}(R) \leq \varepsilon$; furthermore, we always have $\text{load}_1(R) \leq \text{load}_{QOS}(R)$.

A second unrestricted LLR algorithm can now be defined by replacing $\text{load}_{TR}(R)$ with $\text{load}_{QOS}(R)$ in Step 3. This second algorithm will choose, from the set of TR-permissible alternative routes, the one that is most QOS-permissible. But we now have the problem that the most QOS-permissible alternative route may be barely TR-permissible. It is therefore desirable to develop an algorithm that chooses alternative routes that are both QOS-permissible and TR-permissible with some margin. To this end, let α be fixed such that $0 < \alpha < 1$, and define

$$\text{load}(R) := \alpha\text{load}_{TR}(R) + (1 - \alpha)\text{load}_{QOS}(R)$$

This definition of load gives a third algorithm, parameterized by α, with the desired properties.

To analyze the effort required to implement unrestricted LLR, let N be the number of nodes, and suppose that there is a VP for each pair of switches. Thus, the number of VPs is $J = N(N-1)/2$. If the VC request cannot be established in the direct route, then the load must be determined for each of the $N-2$ alternative routes. In addition, for each alternative route, to determine whether it is QOS-permissible, $1 + 4(N-2)$ alternative routes must be examined. Thus, when the direct route is unavailable, $O(N^2)$ alternative routes must be examined. Performance evaluation of unrestricted LLR by simulation or by the reduced load approximation is also difficult because of the many overlapping routes.[7,17]

2.4.2   Restricted LLR

We now propose an algorithm that reduces the implementation effort at the risk of rejecting more VC establishment requests. An additional definition is needed to define the algorithm. We say that the direct route $\{j\}$ is *restricted QOS-permissible* if $p_j(l_j + 1) \leq \varepsilon/2$.

If the routing algorithm establishes directly routed VCs only when they are restricted QOS-permissible and alternatively routed VCs when they are TR-permissible, then the loss probability on a VP never exceeds $\varepsilon/2$. Hence the loss probability on any pair of VPs never exceeds ε, implying that the QOS requirement is satisfied. These observations motivate the following routing algorithm.

Restricted LLR Algorithm

1   First, attempt to set up the VC along the direct route, which is done if the direct route is restricted QOS-permissible. Otherwise, proceed to Step 2.

2   Determine the alternative route R that minimizes $\text{load}_{TR}(R)$. If R is TR-permissible, set up the VC on R; otherwise, reject the VC request.

Notice that restricted LLR blocks some requests that would be accepted by unrestricted LLR. It is relatively easy to implement, however, because overlapping VPs need not be considered—the implementation effort is now $O(N)$. In fact, restricted LLR is equivalent to LLR for single-rate circuit-switched networks with capacities C_j', $j = 1, \ldots, J$, and trunk-reservation values r_j, $j = 1, \ldots, J$, where

$$C_j' := \max\{l : p_j(l) \leq \varepsilon / 2\}$$

and

$$r_j := C_j' - \max\{l : p_j(l) \leq \varepsilon'\}$$

Notice that $C_j' \leq C_j$, and the inequality normally is strict.

2.4.3   Partially Restricted LLR

We now propose a routing algorithm that, compared with restricted LLR, has comparable implementation complexity but better performance. We say a direct route $\{j\}$ is *partially QOS-permissible* if $p_j(l_j + 1) \leq \varepsilon / 2$ when an alternatively routed VC is present on VP_j and if $p_j(l_j + 1) \leq \varepsilon$ when no alternatively routed VC is present on VP_j.

  If the routing algorithm establishes VCs only on partially QOS-permissible direct routes and TR-permissible alternative routes, then the loss probability for a VP does not exceed $\varepsilon / 2$ when it carries alternatively routed VCs. This observation implies that the cell loss associated with the following algorithm satisfies the QOS requirements.

Partially Restricted LLR Algorithm

1   First, attempt to set up the VC along the direct route, which is done if the direct route is partially restricted QOS-permissible. Otherwise, proceed to Step 2.

2   Determine the set of $\mathcal{R}$ alternative routes that are TR-permissible and have at least one alternatively routed VC on each of its two VPs. The VC is routed on the alternative route $R \in \mathcal{R}$ that minimizes $\text{load}_{TR}(R)$. If $\mathcal{R}$ is empty proceed to Step 3.

3 Determine the alternative route R that minimizes $\text{load}_{TR}(R)$. If R is TR-permissible, set up the VC on R; otherwise, reject the VC request.

With partially restricted LLR, the number of direct VCs established on a VP_j can be as high as $C_j > C_j'$. Notice that the algorithm is an attempt to maximize the number of VPs that do not support alternatively routed VCs. This goal is desirable because the number of VCs that can be accepted on a VP is larger when it is void of alternatively routed VCs.

We would expect the VC-blocking performance of partially restricted LLR to fall between that of unrestricted LLR and of restricted LLR. Indeed, it can carry up to C_j directly routed VCs on VP_j, but it does not carry more than C_j' when one or more alternatively routed VCs is present. Its implementation effort is only $O(N)$. For further details on partially restricted LLR, see reference 9.

2.4.4 Comparing Performance of Algorithms

We conducted extensive simulation studies to evaluate the performance of the various routing algorithms proposed in this section. Before we discuss the simulation results it is instructive to take a look at the model used for cell generation from a single VC.

We suppose that VCs alternate between *On* and *Off periods*. During an On period the VC generates cells at peak rate; no cells are generated during an Off period. For notational simplicity, the unit of time selected is the average On period and the buffer content is characterized in units of data volume generated during an On period. The durations of On and Off periods are assumed to be exponentially distributed with mean 1 and $1/\delta$, respectively. Thus, during an On period, a VC transmits at a constant rate of one unit of information per unit of time. Let F be the ratio of the channel capacity to the peak rate of a VC.

To estimate the loss probability we use the approach in Guérin et al.[8]* Let P_1 be the cell-loss probability computed from fluid approximation developed by Anick et al.[1] From the results in reference 1 it follows that

$$P_1 = e^{-rb}$$

where

$$r = \left(1 + \delta - \frac{l\delta}{F}\right) \Big/ \left(1 - \frac{F}{l}\right)$$

and l is the number of VCs present. Let P_2 be the cell-loss probability as given by the stationary approximation developed in reference 8, which approximates the cell-loss probability as

---

* We emphasize that other approaches are equally acceptable.

$$P_2 = \exp\left(-\frac{\left(F - \frac{l\delta}{1+\delta}\right)^2}{2l\sigma^2} + 0.5\ln 2\pi\right)$$

where σ^2 is the variance in the bit rate due to a single source. Because both approximations are conservative in approach, as in reference 8 we approximate the cell-loss probability as

$$P = \min\{P_1, P_2\} \tag{2}$$

Returning to the simulation study, we consider a fully connected VP subnetwork with 6 nodes. Each VP has a capacity of 150 Mbps. We consider two source types for the cell-generation process from a single VC. Each VC is assumed to generate cells at a peak rate of 3 Mbps, that is, $F = 50$. We assume that $b = 8$, that is, the buffer at the input of each VP can hold 8 times the expected number of cells generated by a single VC during an On period. For source type 1 we assume that $\delta = 0.125$, and for source type 2 we assume that $\delta = 0.25$. For both source types the QOS requirement is that no more than one in 10^6 cells are lost for each VC, that is, $\varepsilon = 10^{-6}$. For simplicity we assume that the arrival processes of VCs (i.e., the connection-request processes) are independent and identically distributed Poisson processes with rate λ, and that the holding time for a VC is exponentially distributed with rate μ. Denote by $\rho = \lambda/\mu$ the offered load to each VP. For each set of parameters the simulation was run for 400,000 VC arrivals to the system; the initial 10 percent were discarded for each.

Given the offered load ρ, the blocking probabilities for each routing algorithm depend on the choice of ε' (the trunk reservation parameter); hence to obtain the best performance we need to fine-tune ε'. Unless otherwise mentioned, we use $\alpha = 1$ for all numerical results in this section. Simulation results are presented in Figure 2.2 and Table 2.2 for source type 1, and Figure 2.3 and Table 2.3 for source type 2. For a given ρ and routing algorithm, we present the least-blocking probability observed as ε' was varied.* It was observed that when the loading is light ($\rho < 80$ for source type 1 or $\rho < 72$ for source type 2) no VC requests are blocked by all routing algorithms. Similarly, when the loading is heavy (i.e., $\rho > 100$ for source type 1 or $\rho > 90$ for source type 2), few VCs are alternatively routed; hence all algorithms except restricted least-loaded routing give similar performance.

Tables 2.2 and 2.3 compare the blocking performance of unrestricted LLR with the various definitions of load (parameterized by α). We observe, for the cases considered, that the load value has little effect on the performance of unrestricted LLR.

Figures 2.2 and 2.3 compare the blocking performance of unrestricted LLR (with $\alpha = 1$), restricted LLR, and partially restricted LLR. As expected, unrestricted LLR

---

* For example, for ULLR with $\alpha = 1$ and source type 1, the optimal choice of ε' for $\rho = 82$, 88, and 92 was seen to be 0.4ε, 0.1ε, and 0.01ε, respectively.

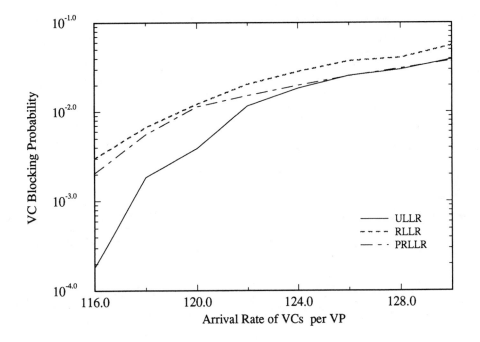

Figure 2.2 Source type 1 ($C = 137$, $C' = 132$)

gives the lowest blocking and restricted LLR gives the highest blocking. We also observe:

	Blocking (ULLR) (%)		
Arrival Rate	**$\alpha = 0$**	**$\alpha = 0.5$**	**$\alpha = 1$**
116	.018 ± .005	.014 ± .006	.020 ± .008
118	.211 ± .013	.215 ± .003	.255 ± .020
120	.382 ± .070	.432 ± .066	.464 ± .059
122	1.17 ± .010	1.16 ± .012	1.17 ± .003
124	1.85 ± .021	1.87 ± .032	1.80 ± .013
126	2.57 ± .067	2.69 ± .068	2.42 ± .061
128	3.02 ± .020	3.02 ± .025	3.00 ± .010
130	3.92 ± .023	3.90 ± .047	3.90 ± .044

Table 2.2 Source type 1 ($C = 137$, $C' = 132$)

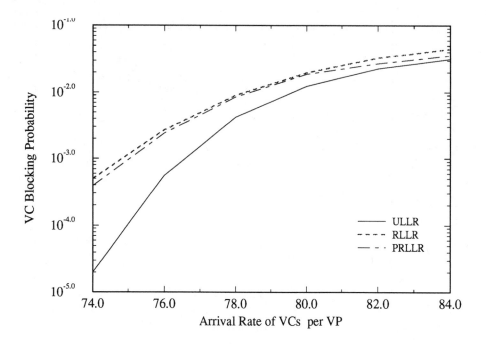

Figure 2.3   Source type 2 ($C = 92$, $C' = 89$)

- Unrestricted LLR gives significantly lower blocking probabilities than restricted LLR and partially restricted LLR when the VC loads are light.

- Partially restricted LLR has blocking comparable to unrestricted LLR and significantly lower than restricted LLR when the loads are low to moderate.

	Blocking (ULLR) (%)		
Arrival Rate	$\alpha = 0$	$\alpha = 0.5$	$\alpha = 1$
74	$.002 \pm .0001$	$.002 \pm .0001$	$.002 \pm .0001$
76	$.056 \pm .004$	$.070 \pm .001$	$.076 \pm .002$
78	$.422 \pm .025$	$.429 \pm .003$	$.419 \pm .049$
80	$1.24 \pm .022$	$1.27 \pm .042$	$1.26 \pm .031$
82	$2.28 \pm .027$	$2.27 \pm .040$	$2.27 \pm .036$
84	$3.17 \pm .037$	$3.15 \pm .033$	$3.13 \pm .031$

Table 2.3   Source type 2 ($C = 92$, $C' = 89$)

We stress that the performance gains of unrestricted LLR come with an implementation cost. Furthermore, if the QOS requirement includes delay, then partially restricted LLR can give significantly better performance than restricted LLR, as shown in the following section and in reference 9.

2.5 DELAY GUARANTEES

In this section we again assume that the traffic types and QOS requirements are homogeneous. But we now consider the following more general QOS requirement: A newly arriving VC can be accepted only if the fraction $1 - \varepsilon$ of cells of each VC in progress reach their destination before a delay D. In this case we denote the QOS requested by the 2-tuple (D, ε). For an application where end-to-end delays have to be bounded, the delay bound D includes the fixed propagation delay D_p. For applications requiring only that the delay jitter be bounded, D should include only the random queuing delays in the network. (Since we assume cells are served in accordance with the first come, first served (FCFS) discipline, the maximum jitter is bounded by maximum queuing delay.[13,25])

We now demonstrate that the routing algorithms proposed earlier in the section can be extended to this delay-based QOS requirement. Before presenting the routing algorithms, we introduce the following notation. Denote by the random variable X_{l_j} the delay of a cell on VP_j when it is carrying l_j VCs. Let $H_{l_j}(\cdot)$ and $H_{l_i l_j}(\cdot)$ be the complementary distribution functions of the random variables X_{l_j} and $X_{l_i} + X_{l_j}$, respectively.* Thus $H_{l_i l_j}(D) \leq \varepsilon$ is equivalent to

$P(\text{"cell exceeds delay on a } VC_{ij}\text{"} \mid l_i, l_j) \leq \varepsilon$

We now say that a direct VC_j is QOS-permissible if: (1) $H_{l_j + 1}(D) \leq \varepsilon$ and (2) for every VP_k such that a VC_{jk} is in progress, $H_{l_j + 1 l_k}(D) \leq \varepsilon$. Similarly, we refer to the setting up of an alternatively routed VC_{ij} as QOS-permissible if: (1) $H_{l_i + 1 l_j + 1}(D) \leq \varepsilon$; and (2) for every VP_k such that a VC_{ik} is in progress, $H_{l_i + 1 l_k}(D) \leq \varepsilon$, and for every VP_k such that a VC_{jk} is in progress, $H_{l_j + 1 l_k}(D) \leq \varepsilon$.

---

* $H_{l_j}(\cdot)$ and $H_{l_i l_j}(\cdot)$ can be obtained either by analytical techniques or by estimating from the cell-level statistics.

Introduce $D' \leq D$ and $\varepsilon' \leq \varepsilon/2$ such that setting up of an alternatively routed VC$_{ij}$ is TR-permissible if $H_{l_i+1}(D') \leq \varepsilon'$ and $H_{l_j+1}(D') \leq \varepsilon'$. Observe that 2-tuple (D', ε') can now be viewed as the trunk-reservation parameter.

Unrestricted LLR Algorithm

We define the load of a route $R = \{i, j\}$ as:

$$\text{load}_{TR}(R) := \max\{H_{l_i+1}(D'), H_{l_j+1}(D')\}$$

As in the preceding section, alternative definitions of load are possible. The unrestricted LLR algorithm introduced in the preceding section can now be employed for the delay-based QOS requirement with loads defined as above.

Restricted LLR Algorithm

Compared with the cell-loss QOS requirements, the implementation complexity of unrestricted LLR is now substantially higher due to the computational effort required to determine each $H_{l_i+l_j}(\cdot)$, which is the convolution of two distributions. In addition, there remains the problem of estimating the distributions $H_{l_j}(\cdot)$ and communicating it to the other nodes, either periodically or when queried.

As before, the implementation effort can be reduced significantly at the risk of rejecting more VC requests. We leave it to the reader to show that defining a direct route $\{j\}$ to be *restricted QOS-permissible* if $H_{l_j+1}(D') \leq \varepsilon/2$, with $D' \leq D/2$, leads to a routing algorithm analogous to restricted LLR.

Partially Restricted LLR Algorithm

A partially restricted LLR routing algorithm proposed before can also be developed for the case at hand by defining a direct route $\{j\}$ to be *partially restricted QOS-permissible* if $H_{l_j+1}(D/2) \leq \varepsilon/2$ when an alternatively routed VC is present on VP$_j$ and if $H_{l_j+1}(D) \leq \varepsilon$ when no alternatively routed VC is present on VP$_j$.

Comparing Performance of Algorithms

As before, we conducted simulation studies to evaluate the performance of the proposed routing algorithms. Due to difficulty in analytically estimating the delay distributions on a VP as a function of the number of VCs that it carries, we do not simulate unrestricted LLR. We also feel that the computational and implementation

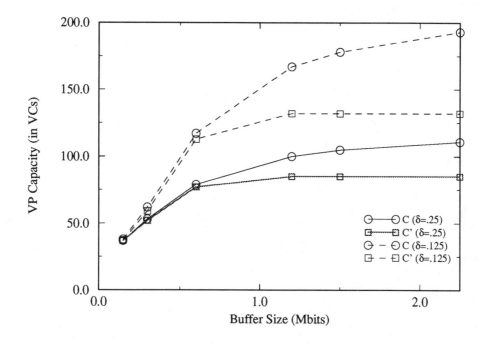

Figure 2.4 VP capacity = 150 Mbps, peak rate = 6 Mbps, D = 30 msec, D_p = 10 msec

complexity of unrestricted LLR, when delay bounds also have to be met, make it difficult to implement.

Once again we consider a symmetrical network with 6 nodes. Each VP has a propagation delay of 10 msec and is allocated 150 Mbps of bandwidth. Each VC generates cells at a peak rate of 6 Mbps and the QOS requirements dictate that D = 30 msec and $\varepsilon = 10^{-6}$. For source type 1 we have δ = 0.25 and for source type 2 we have δ = 0.125. Before considering the simulation results it is instructive to examine the effect of buffer size on C and C', the maximum number of VCs that can be accepted on a VP when there are no alternatively routed VCs and when there are, respectively. Figure 2.4 shows the capacity of a VP for the two sources under consideration as a function of the buffer size at the input of the VP. For a buffer size of 0.6 Mbit, the maximum delay in the buffer at the input of each VP is 4 msec. In this case for source type 1 we have C = 79 and C' = 77. On the other hand if a 1.5 Mbits buffer is used (the maximum delay in the buffer is 10 msec) we have C = 105 and C' = 85. Similarly, for source type 2 we have C = 117, C' = 113, and C = 178, C' = 132 for a buffer of 0.6 Mbit and 1.5 Mbits, respectively. Notice that, as expected, an increase in buffer size leads to an increase in both C and C'. Further, $C - C'$ increases as the buffer size at the input of the VPs increases.

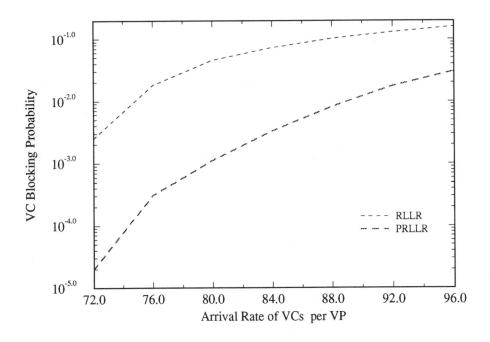

Figure 2.5   Source type 1 ($C = 105$, $C' = 85$)

For both source types we simulated the case where a buffer size of 1.5 Mbits is used at the input of each VP. Figure 2.5 shows the results when each VC generates according to source type 1 and a buffer of 1.5 Mbits is used at the input of each VP. Since the difference between C and C' is much larger now (compared to the case with cell-loss QOS requirement), the blocking probabilities for partially restricted LLR are significantly smaller than those for restricted LLR.

2.6   NO STATISTICAL MULTIPLEXING, HETEROGENEOUS SOURCES

We now assume that the VC bandwidth is allocated according to peak rate, but that peak rates vary from VC to VC. This multiplexing scheme is not to be confused with multirate circuit switching: it does not require that VC peak rates be restricted to a fixed set of rates, or that the VC slots be confined to contiguous regions of TDM frames (see references 2 and 18).

Routing of multirate traffic is a complex problem that should take into account several incongruencies. On one hand, routes should be chosen so that traffic is evenly "spread" throughout the network, thereby setting aside bandwidth for all node pairs as much as possible. On the other hand, it may be desirable to "pack" narrowband VCs within certain routes so that the remaining routes have enough capacity to support additional wideband calls. For example, packing would clearly be desirable for the following scenario: (1) all the VPs have the same bandwidth; and (2) two classes of service are supported—one whose peak rate equals the bandwidth of a VP, another whose peak rate is a small part of the bandwidth of a VP. Further complicating the design of a routing algorithm, it may be necessary to "protect" some services from being dominated by others. For example, it may be desirable to limit admission of one service type once it begins to monopolize network resources.

To gain initial insight into the routing of heterogeneous traffic, of the three difficulties mentioned above—spreading, packing, and protecting—we concentrate on the first. The need for packing is greatly diminished when the wideband services have peak rates that are small compared to the VP bandwidth. And protection, although greatly important from a user's perspective, is not fundamentally a routing issue, for it is equally a problem for single-link systems.[20,21] Our focus in this section therefore is the design of multirate routing algorithms that are easy to implement, require a minimum of forecasting information, and attempt to spread traffic evenly throughout the network. Nevertheless, the actual implementation of a routing algorithm should involve an appropriate blend of algorithms that respond to all three goals.[11]

The algorithm that we introduce here is a multirate version of LLR. We need to define some notation. Let C_j now be the transmission rate of VP_j. The peak rate of a VC, denoted b, is required to satisfy $0 < b \leq C_j$ for each VP_j in the VC's route. Since there is no statistical multiplexing, there is actually a stronger constraint: we must have $B_j \leq C_j$ for each VP_j, where B_j is the sum of the peak rates over all VCs in progress on VP_j. For each peak rate b and VP_j, let $r_j(b)$ be an associated *trunk-reservation value*. For an alternative route $\{j, k\}$ we define its *availability* as

$$\text{avail}(j, k) := \min\{C_j - B_j - r_j(b), \; C_k - B_k - r_k(b)\}$$

which is the amount of end-to-end bandwidth beyond trunk reservation available to route $\{j, k\}$.

Multirate LLR Algorithm

When a VC with peak bit rate b and with direct VP_i requests establishment:

1 First, attempt to set up the VC along the direct route, which is done if $B_i + b \leq C_i$; otherwise, proceed to Step 2.

2 Find the alternative route $\{j, k\}$ that maximizes avail(j, k). If avail$(j, k) \leq b$, set up the VC on route $\{j, k\}$; otherwise, reject the VC request.

Efficient simulation code can be developed to determine the performance of Multirate LLR.[17] If the peak rates belong to a finite set, then the approximation technique outlined in Section 5 of reference 7 can also be used.

2.7   CONCLUSIONS

In this chapter we study two important and closely related connection-management issues in ATM-based broadband networks—namely, VC acceptance and VC routing. We observe that in an ATM environment VCs have heterogeneous traffic characteristics and QOS requirements that must be taken into account to optimize performance. We classify ATM networks (for purposes of routing) according to whether or not they have these two properties: (1) VCs are homogeneous in traffic characteristics and QOS requirements; and (2) statistical multiplexing is performed in the interior of the network. The two properties above lead to four classes of ATM networks.

We have argued that the case of homogeneous sources with nonstatistical multiplexing is equivalent to single-rate circuit switching, and therefore that routing algorithms currently in use in the telephone networks can be employed. For homogeneous sources with statistical multiplexing, we propose three routing algorithms: unrestricted LLR, restricted LLR, and partially restricted LLR. The routing algorithms differ in their implementation costs and overall VC blocking probabilities. As expected, algorithms with higher implementation cost provide the lowest blocking probabilities. We argue that partially restricted LLR may be the most attractive solution because it provides VC blocking probabilities that are marginally smaller than those given by unrestricted LLR with minimal implementation costs. For heterogeneous sources with nonstatistical multiplexing, we highlight the key issues and suggest a routing algorithm. We exclude from our discussion heterogeneous sources with statistical multiplexing, because such sources should be segregated over different VP subnetworks when statistical multiplexing is used.

Many of the ideas in this chapter are further developed in Ross.[26] In particular, admission and scheduling policies for a variety of service and route separation schemes are explored.

2.8   ACKNOWLEDGMENTS

We thank Jim Roberts for discussing the problem with us during the early stages of the research.

REFERENCES

1   D. Anick, D. Mitra, and M. M. Sondhi, "Stochastic Theory of a Data-Handling System with Multiple Sources," *Bell Systems Technical Journal*, Vol. 61, No. 8, 1982, pp. 1871–1894.

2 G. R. Ash, J. S. Chen, A. E. Frey, and B. D. Huang, "Real-Time Network Routing in a Dynamic Class-of-Service Network," *Proceedings of the Thirteenth International Teletraffic Congress,* Copenhagen, June 1991, pp. 187–194.

3 G. R. Ash, R. H. Cardwell, and R. P. Murray, "Design and Optimization of Networks with Dynamic Routing," *Bell Systems Technical Journal,* Vol. 60, No. 8, 1981, pp. 1787–1820.

4 J. J. Bae, T. Suda, and R. Simha, "Analysis of a Finite Buffer Queue with Heterogeneous Markov Modulated Arrival Process: A Study of the Effects of Traffic Burstiness on Individual Packet Loss," *Proceedings of the IEEE INFOCOM,* 1992, pp. 219–230.

5 W. H. Cameron, J. Regnier, P. Galloy, and A. A. Savoie, "Dynamic Routing for Intercity Telephone Networks," *Proceedings of the Tenth International Teletraffic Congress,* Montreal, June 1983.

6 V. P. Chaudhary, K. R. Krishnan, and C. D. Pack, "Implementing Dynamic Routing in Local Telephone Companies of USA," *Proceedings of the Thirteenth International Teletraffic Congress,* Copenhagen, June 1991, pp. 87–91.

7 S-P. Chung, A. Kashper, and K. W. Ross, "Computing Approximate Blocking Probabilities for Large Loss Networks with State-Dependent Routing," *IEEE/ACM Transactions on Networking,* Vol. 1, No. 1, February 1993, pp. 105–115.

8 R. Guérin, H. Ahmadi, and M. Naghshineh, "Equivalent Capacity and Its Application to Bandwidth Allocation in High-Speed Networks," *IEEE Journal on Selected Areas in Communications,* Vol. 9, No. 7, 1991, pp. 968–981.

9 S. Gupta, K. W. Ross, and M. El Zarki, "Routing in Virtual Path-Based ATM Networks," *Proceedings of the GLOBECOM 1992,* 1992, pp. 571–575.

10 S. Gupta and M. El Zarki, "Traffic Classification for Round-Robin Scheduling Schemes in ATM Networks," *Proceedings of the IEEE INFOCOM,* 1993, pp. 820–827.

11 R. Hwang, J. F. Kurose, and D. Towsley, "State-Dependent Routing for Multirate Loss Networks," *Proceedings of the GLOBECOM 1992,* 1992, pp. 565–570.

12 P. B. Key and G. A. Cope, "Distributed Dynamic Routing Schemes," *IEEE Communications Magazine,* Vol. 28, No. 10, October 1990, pp. 54–64.

13 T. D. C. Little and A. Ghafoor, "Network Considerations for Distributed Multimedia Object Composition and Communication," *IEEE Network Magazine,* Vol. 4, No. 6, November 1990, pp. 32–49.

14 J. B. Lyles and D. C. Swinehart, "The Emerging Gigabit Environment and the Role of Local ATM," *IEEE Communications Magazine,* Vol. 30, No. 4, April 1992, pp. 52–58.

15 D. Mitra, R. J. Gibbens, and B. D. Huang, "State-Dependent Routing on Symmetric-Loss Networks with Trunk Reservations, I," *IEEE Transactions on Communications,* February 1993, pp. 400–411.

16 T. J. Ott and K. R. Krishnan, "State-Dependent Routing of Telephone Schemes and the Use of Separable Routing Schemes," *Proceedings of the Eleventh International Teletraffic Congress,* Kyoto, 1985.

17 M. Prindiville, M. Rajasekaren, and K. W. Ross, "Efficient Sequential Simulation of Large-Scale Loss Networks," Technical Report, Dept. of Computer and Information Science, University of Pennsylvania, 1991.

18 V. Ramaswami and K. A. Rao, "Flexible Time Slot Assignment—A Performance Study for the Integrated Services Digital Network," *Proceedings of the Eleventh International Teletraffic Congress,* Kyoto, 1986, pp. 2.1A–3.

19 J. W. Roberts, "A Service System with Heterogeneous User Requirements," in G. Pujolle, ed., *Performance of Data Communications Systems and Their Applications,* Amsterdam, North-Holland, 1981, pp. 423–431.

20 K. W. Ross and D. Tsang, "Optimal Circuit Access Policies in an ISDN Environment: A Markov Decision Approach," *IEEE Transactions on Communications,* Vol. 37, No. 9, 1989, pp. 934–939.

21 K. W. Ross and D. Tsang, "The Stochastic Knapsack Problem," *IEEE Transactions on Communications,* Vol. 37, No. 7, 1989, pp. 740–747.

22 M. Schwartz, *Telecommunication Networks: Protocols, Modeling and Analysis,* Reading: Addison-Wesley, 1987.

23 H. Takagi, *Analysis of Polling Systems,* Cambridge, MA: MIT Press, 1986.

24 Y. Takagi, S. Hino, and T. Takahashi, "Priority Assignment Control of ATM Line Buffers with Multiple QOS Classes," *IEEE Journal on Selected Areas in Communications,* Vol. 9, No. 7, 1991, pp. 1078–1092.

25 D. J. Wright and M. To, "Telecommunication Applications of the 1990s and Their Transport Requirements," *IEEE Network Magazine,* Vol. 4, No. 2, March 1990, pp. 34–40.

26 K. W. Ross, *Multiservice Loss Models for Broadband Telecommunication Networks,* London: Springer-Verlag, to appear 1995.

PART II   ❖   ❖   ❖   ❖

PACKET-SWITCHED NETWORKS

Packet switching, a technology more recent than circuit switching, was first conceived in the 1960s as a means for providing efficient and cost-effective data communication between large "host" computers and remote users. In a packet-switched network, data traffic from multiple users contends for switching and transmission resources. Statistical multiplexing of traffic flows over network resources is the principal means of enabling competing traffic to share these resources.

The evolution of packet switching has been driven primarily by advances in computer technology. Over the years, increases in the processing speed and memory capacity of computers, coupled with reductions in their cost and size, have dramatically increased the availability and distribution of computing resources. Initially, these resources consisted of large and expensive central computers shared by many users who accessed them through specialized peripheral devices directly connected to the central computer via dedicated links. This approach became impractical, however, when remote users wanted to access multiple computers, and as a consequence packet-switched networks were created.

Three independent, concurrent efforts contributed to the rapid development of packet-switching technology. Computer time-sharing companies, eager to expand their customer base, developed their own packet-switched networks and protocols (e.g., Tymshare's TYMNET[1,2]) to provide remote user access to their geographically distributed host computers. Computer manufacturers, eager to increase customer demand for their computers and peripherals, developed integrated systems for data communications, including special-purpose communications processors and protocols (e.g., IBM's SNA[1,2]). The Advanced Research Projects Agency (ARPA) of the U.S. Department of Defense, envisioning future need for wide-area user access to computers capable of performing specialized functions (e.g., maintaining large distributed databases or performing complicated numerical calculations), funded development of the ARPANET,[1,2] which interconnected users and host computers across the United States.

The widely varied routing strategies employed in packet-switched networks reflect the diverse purposes for which these networks are designed. Individual packet-switched networks vary greatly in terms of packet forwarding techniques, route generation and selection algorithms, and decentralization and dynamism of routing control.

Packet forwarding techniques cover the range from connection-oriented to connectionless and include *virtual-circuit, source-specified,* and *datagram* forwarding. Both virtual-circuit forwarding and source-specified forwarding constrain packets to specific paths. With virtual-circuit forwarding, a "virtual circuit" is established for the duration of a traffic session in intermediate switches along a path. Each of these switches directs a data packet toward its destination according to its associated virtual circuit. With source-specified routing, each data packet carries routing directives to be followed by intermediate switches along the path. Datagram forwarding allows each switch to forward a data packet according to that switch's preference. Although flexible, datagram forwarding requires forwarding consistency among individual switches to enable packets to reach their intended destinations.

Most packet-switched networks operate in a *store-and-forward* mode, independent of forwarding technique. Each switch must receive and store an entire packet prior to forwarding the packet toward its destination. An alternative mode, *virtual cut-through,*[6] has been proposed to reduce buffering delays associated with store-and-forward switching. With virtual cut-through, a switch may begin to forward a packet as soon as it has received enough of the packet to make a correct forwarding decision.

Route generation and selection algorithms for packet-switched networks may be broadly categorized as either *optimal routing* algorithms or *shortest-path* algorithms, both of which are amenable to centralized and decentralized implementations. The objective of optimal routing is to determine an allocation of traffic flows over paths that minimizes a network-wide cost (e.g., delay), represented as the sum of individual link costs that depend on link traffic. Optimal routing often results in the use of multiple paths for an individual traffic flow between a source and destination. Existing approaches to optimal routing involve computationally intensive iterative algorithms, and hence optimal routing has been used primarily for the static routing portion of network design. Nevertheless, decentralized optimal routing algorithms[7,8] have been proposed for quasi-static routing within a packet-switched network.

Optimal routing may be characterized as a multicommodity flow problem, where the commodities are the traffic flows between the sources and destinations. The objective is to minimize the value of a cost function of the flows, subject to the constraints of flow conservation at each switch and flow nonnegativity over each link. Constraints on link capacity are usually captured as interior penalties within the objective function. Solutions to this problem include heuristic approaches[9] as well as exact methods such as *flow deviation*[10] and *gradient projection*.[11,12] Both flow deviation and gradient projection techniques iteratively select flow allocations so that successive changes reflect movement in a feasible and cost-reducing direction toward the optimal flow allocation over paths. Gradient projection methods converge more quickly than flow deviation, by permitting a different incremental change in flow for each path and obtaining a feasible descent direction by projecting to zero the gradient components resulting in nonfeasible (i.e., negative) flows.

The objective of shortest-path routing is to determine a least-cost (e.g., minimum-delay) path between a source and destination. Most packet-switched networks employ some type of shortest-path algorithm for dynamically generating and selecting routes according to current user and network state. Shortest-path algorithms are divided into two classes: *distance vector* and *link state*. Distance-vector algorithms, derived from dynamic programming, are usually implemented in a distributed, asynchronous fashion and base their route selections on local estimates of route costs. Link-state algorithms are usually implemented in a replicated fashion (each switch performs an independent route computation) and construct routes based on global estimates of individual link costs. Each of these shortest-path algorithms generates least-cost paths in polynomial time. Finding a path that meets multiple user-imposed service constraints (e.g., specific bounds on delay and packet error rate) is an NP-complete problem, however. Approximate but not necessarily feasible solutions to this problem may be obtained using shortest-path and other polynomial-time algorithms.[13]

Although a traffic session normally requires only a single path, multiple paths may be required under certain circumstances. A session demanding high reliability may require multiple secondary paths to be available for use in case of failure of a link or switch on the primary path. A session demanding high throughput may require the resources of multiple paths for simultaneous use. Secondary paths that are maximally disjoint from the primary path provide maximum fault tolerance for the session. Distributing session packets over multiple paths can help reduce the potential for network congestion, but delay differences among the paths may require introduction of mechanisms for maintaining packet ordering during delivery to the destination. Several shortest-path algorithms[14–18] have been proposed to generate multiple disjoint paths for a session.

Multipoint (one-to-many, many-to-one, and many-to-many) communication is a necessary component of today's distributed applications (e.g., videoconferencing and data fusion). The objective of *multicast* routing is to provide efficient, low-cost multipoint distribution of user traffic according to user service requirements. Proposed solutions to the multicast routing problem for packet-switched networks have focused on forwarding techniques and distribution tree construction.

Reverse path forwarding (RPF)[19] was originally developed for efficiently broadcasting a packet to all destinations. With RPF, a switch forwards a broadcast packet to its neighbors, only if that packet arrives on the path that the switch considers the shortest one to the packet's source. Enhanced versions of RPF include pruning mechanisms[20] that restrict packet distribution to a subset of network destinations, making it applicable to multicast routing.

Constructing multicast distribution trees is, in general, an NP-complete problem. Generating a minimum-cost tree that spans all network destinations can be accomplished in polynomial time with any of several minimum spanning tree algorithms. However, the problem of generating a minimum-cost tree that spans a subset of network destinations (also called the Steiner problem) is NP-complete. Efficient heuristic approaches and close approximations exist for the Steiner problem.[21,22] Accounting for user service requirements (e.g., delay, throughput) in addition to solving the Steiner problem further complicates multicast tree construction, and heuristic approaches have been proposed for this case.[23]

Packet switching's success is evidenced by the many private packet-switched networks currently in existence and by expansion of the Internet as a global data-communications substrate. As packet-switched networks grow to accommodate their increasing population of users, the amount of routing information that must be distributed, stored, and manipulated in these networks also grows. Research on routing in large packet-switched networks has focused on ways of reducing the quantity of routing information without sacrificing the quality of routes selected. The majority of proposed solutions[24-30] provide algorithms for hierarchical clustering of network entities, abstraction of routing information relating to these clusters, and packet forwarding within the hierarchy.

The four chapters in this section—"Distance-Vector Routing" by G. S. Malkin and M. E. Steenstrup, "Inter-Domain Routing: EGP, BGP, and IDRP" by Y. Rekhter, "Link-State Routing" by J. Moy, and "AppleTalk Routing" by A. B. Oppenheimer and F. Kuang—describe the principal dynamic routing strategies employed within the packet-switched networks constituting today's internetworks. *Bridging*, a popular method for routing packets among individual local area networks interconnected in simple topologies, is not covered in this section. The interested reader may consult reference 31 for a comprehensive treatment of bridging techniques.

SELECTED SUGGESTIONS FOR FURTHER READING

1 D. Bertsekas and R. Gallager, *Data Networks,* Englewood Cliffs: Prentice Hall, 1991.

2 M. Schwartz, *Telecommunication Networks: Protocols, Modeling and Analysis,* Reading: Addison-Wesley, 1987.

3 M. Schwartz and T. E. Stern, "Routing Techniques Used in Computer Communications Networks," *IEEE Transactions on Communications,* Vol. COM-28, No. 4, April 1980, pp. 539–552.

4 H. Rudin, "On Routing and 'Delta Routing': A Taxonomy and Performance Comparison of Techniques for Packet-Switched Networks," *IEEE Transactions on Communications,* Vol. COM-24, No. 1, January 1976, pp. 43–59.

5 A. Segall, "The Modelling of Adaptive Routing in Data-Communications Networks," *IEEE Transactions on Communications,* Vol. COM-25, No. 1, January 1977, pp. 85–95.

6 P. Kermani and L. Kleinrock, "Virtual Cut-Through: A New Computer Communication Switching Technique," *Computer Networks,* Vol. 3, 1979, pp. 267–286.

7 R. G. Gallager, "A Minimum Delay Routing Algorithm Using Distributed Computation," *IEEE Transactions on Communications,* Vol. COM-25, No. 1, January 1977, pp. 73–85.

8 T. E. Stern, "A Class of Decentralized Routing Algorithms Using Relaxation," *IEEE Transactions on Communications,* Vol. COM-25, No. 10, October 1977, pp. 1092–1102.

9 H. Frank and W. Chou, "Routing in Computer Networks," *Networks,* Vol. 1, 1971, pp. 99–122.

10 L. Fratta, M. Gerla, and L. Kleinrock, "The Flow Deviation Method: An Approach to Store-and-Forward Communication Network Design," *Networks,* Vol. 3, 1973, pp. 97–133.

11 D. G. Cantor and M. Gerla, "Optimal Routing in a Packet-Switched Computer Network," *IEEE Transactions on Computers,* Vol. C-23, October 1974, pp. 1062–1069.

12 M. Schwartz and C. K. Cheung, "The Gradient Projection Algorithm for Multiple Routing in Message-Switched Networks," *IEEE Transactions on Communications,* Vol. COM-24, No. 4, April 1976, pp. 449–456.

13 J. M. Jaffe, "Algorithms for Finding Paths with Multiple Constraints," *Networks,* Vol. 14, 1984, pp. 95–116.

14 J. W. Suurballe, "Disjoint Paths in a Network," *Networks,* Vol. 4, 1974, pp. 125–145.

15 D. M. Topkis, "A Shortest Path Algorithm for Adaptive Routing in Communications Networks," *IEEE Transactions on Communications,* Vol. 36, No. 7, July 1988, pp. 855–859.

16 R. Ogier and N. Shacham, "A Distributed Algorithm for Finding Shortest Pairs of Disjoint Paths," *Proceedings of the IEEE INFOCOM '89,* Ottawa, April 1989, pp. 173–182.

17 D. Torrieri, "Algorithms for Finding an Optimal Set of Short Disjoint Paths in a Communications Network," *IEEE Transactions on Communications,* Vol. 40, No. 11, November 1992, pp. 1698–1702.

18 M. L. Gardner, I. S. Loobeek, and S. N. Cohn, "Type-of-Service Routing with Loadsharing," *Proceedings of the GLOBECOM '87,* Tokyo, 1987.

19 Y. K. Dalal and R. M. Metcalfe, "Reverse Path Forwarding of Broadcast Packets," *Communications of the ACM,* Vol. 21, December 1978, pp. 1040–1048.

20 S. E. Deering, "Multicast Routing in Internetworks and Extended LANs," *Computer Communications Review,* Vol. 18, No. 4, August 1988, pp. 55–64.

21 K. B. Kumar and J. M. Jaffe, "Routing to Multiple Destinations in Computer Networks," *IEEE Transactions on Communications,* Vol. COM-31, No. 3, March 1983, pp. 343–351.

22 A. Z. Zelikovsky, "An 11/6-Approximation Algorithm for the Network Steiner Problem," *Algorithmic,* Vol. 9, 1993, pp. 463–470.

23 D. C. Verma and P. M. Gopal, "Routing Reserved Bandwidth Multi-Point Connections," *Computer Communication Review,* Vol. 23, No. 4, October 1993, pp. 96–105.

24 J. McQuillan, "Adaptive Routing Algorithms for Distributed Computer Networks," *BBN Report No. 2831,* Bolt Beranek and Newman, May 1974.

25 L. Kleinrock and F. Kamoun, "Hierarchical Routing for Large Networks," *Computer Networks,* Vol. 1, 1977, pp. 155–174.

26 J. Hagouel, "Issues in Routing for Large and Dynamic Networks," Ph.D. dissertation, Columbia University, 1983.

27 A. E. Baratz and J. M. Jaffe, "Establishing Virtual Circuits in Large Computer Networks," *Computer Networks and ISDN Systems,* Vol. 12, 1986, pp. 27–37.

28 P. F. Tsuchiya, "The Landmark Hierarchy: A New Hierarchy for Routing in Very Large Networks," *Computer Communication Reviews,* Vol. 18, No. 4, August 1988, pp. 35–42.

29 J. J. Garcia-Luna-Aceves, "Routing Management in Very Large-Scale Networks," *Future Generations Computer Systems,* Vol. 4, 1988, pp. 81–93.

30 W. T. Tsai, C. V. Ramamoorthy, W. K. Tsai, and O. Nishiguchi, "An Adaptive Hierarchical Routing Protocol," *IEEE Transactions on Computers,* Vol. 38, No. 8, August 1989, pp. 1059–1075.

31 R. Perlman, *Interconnections: Bridges and Routers,* Reading: Addison-Wesley, 1992.

CHAPTER 3 ❖ ❖ ❖ ❖

Distance-Vector Routing

GARY SCOTT MALKIN AND MARTHA E. STEENSTRUP

CONTENTS

Shortest-path algorithms, those producing least-cost paths between network sources and destinations, are the most widely used route-generation algorithms for packet-switched networks. Among the shortest-path algorithms, the distance-vector class constituting algorithms based on the concepts of dynamic programming is the largest. Distance-vector algorithms were employed in the ARPANET at its inception and continue to function in the Internet today. Their popularity can be attributed to their amenability to simple implementations that admit distributed, asynchronous operation and use only locally available cost information to generate and select routes. This chapter presents the basic distance-vector algorithm, together with several of the enhancements developed to improve its performance in networks with frequently changing link connectivity and costs.

3.1   INTRODUCTION

Distance-vector routing algorithms have been employed in packet-switched networks for more than two decades, beginning with the ARPANET.[1,2] They determine minimum-cost routes using a simple, iterative cost refinement procedure which is usually distributed over the switches in a network. A source switch estimates the cost of a route to a destination switch, based on the corresponding cost estimates obtained from its neighboring switches. Thus, switches need only exchange local cost estimates with their neighbors when computing minimum-cost routes to distant destinations.

Distance-vector algorithms today enjoy widespread deployment, forming the basis for many of the standard routing procedures used in internetworks. In this chapter, we focus on the behavior of distance-vector routing in practice. We have selected a popular family of internetwork routing procedures, referred to as Routing Information Protocols (RIPs), to illustrate the advantages and limitations of distance-vector routing algorithms.

3.2   BASIC DISTANCE-VECTOR ALGORITHM

Distance-vector algorithms generate routes that are optimal with respect to a specific metric. Example routing metrics include delay, throughput, error rate, monetary cost, or a function of several such metrics. We focus on the case in which *optimal* means *minimum cost*, and *route cost* is an additive function of *link costs* (e.g., route delay). Distance-vector algorithms can also find minimum-cost routes, however, in which link costs are not additive (e.g., route error rate is a multiplicative function of link error rates). Moreover, distance-vector algorithms can also find maximum-capacity routes; in this case, route capacity is the minimum of the link capacities.

The basic distance-vector routing algorithm is often referred to as the Ford-Fulkerson method.[3] It is also known as the Bellman-Ford algorithm[4] because from the perspective of dynamic programming,[5] it may be expressed in terms of Bellman's equation.

Consider a communications network as a graph comprising nodes and links, where nodes represent switching elements (e.g., routers and hosts) and links represent connections between switches (e.g., point-to-point links and multiaccess networks). Let D_{ij} represent the cost of the minimum-cost route from source node i to destination node j, and let it be defined for every pair of nodes i and j. If i and j are neighbors and thus have a direct link, let d_{ij} be the cost of that link; otherwise, let $d_{ij} = \infty$. Assuming that link costs are additive, the minimum-cost route between i and j can be obtained by solving Bellman's equation:

$$D_{ii} = 0, \text{ for all } i$$

$$D_{ij} = \min_{k} \ (d_{ik} + D_{kj}), \text{ for } i \neq j$$

using the Bellman-Ford algorithm, an iterative algorithm on the number of hops h, given by:

$$D_{ii}(h+1) = 0, \text{ for all } i$$

$$D_{ij}(h+1) = \min_{k} \ (d_{ik} + D_{kj}(h)), \text{ for } i \neq j$$

with initial conditions:

$$D_{ii}(0) = 0, \text{ for all } i$$

$$D_{ij}(0) = \infty, \text{ for } i \neq j$$

The computational complexity of the Bellman-Ford algorithm for solving the problem of finding the minimum-cost routes from a given source node to all destination nodes is $O(N^3)$, where N is the number of nodes in the network graph. In the worst case, the algorithm requires $h \leq N-1$ iterations for each of $N-1$ destination nodes, and for each node, the algorithm must consider at most $N-1$ alternatives when choosing a minimum-cost route. For convergence, link costs need not be positive, but there must be no network cycles with negative cost.[3] Practical link costs, such as delay or distance, are normally nonnegative quantities.

The Bellman-Ford algorithm readily lends itself to distributed execution in nodes throughout a network. Each node i estimates the cost to each destination node j by executing the following procedure. For each neighbor node k, node i collects k's estimate of the cost of the route to j and then adds d_{ik} to it. Node i then compares all these newly computed estimates and selects the smallest one.

The distributed Bellman-Ford algorithm may execute synchronously or asynchronously. Both versions of the algorithm converge to the correct minimum-cost routes, but in some cases the asynchronous version may exchange more cost estimates among nodes and may converge more slowly than the synchronous version. For the asynchronous version, the number of cost estimates exchanged and the convergence time depend upon the order in which nodes generate, distribute, and receive cost estimates. The asynchronous distributed Bellman-Ford algorithm is given by:

$$D_{ii}(t) = 0, \text{ for all } i$$

$$D_{ij}(t) = \min_k \ (d_{ik} + D^i_{kj}(t)), \text{ for } i \neq j$$

where $D_{ij}(t)$ is i's estimate of the cost to j available to node i at time t and $D^i_{kj}(t)$ is k's estimate of the cost to j available to node i at time t.

The asynchronous distributed Bellman-Ford algorithm will converge to the correct minimum-cost routes in finite time, provided there are no link cost changes after a given time t_0. The proof[4] relies on these assumptions:

1   Nodes must never stop recomputing cost estimates or receiving cost estimates from their neighbors.

2   All cost estimates made at time t_0 by node i must be nonnegative, and all cost estimates exchanged with neighbors before and after time t_0 must be nonnegative.

3   Old cost estimates do not remain indefinitely within the network.

These assumptions imply that nodes must never stop distributing cost estimates, and networks must not delay indefinitely the propagation of such estimates. Moreover, the convergence proof does not rely on any assumptions about synchronization of cost-estimate calculation or distribution. Each node may calculate cost estimates and distribute them according to its own timing. Cost estimates may even be lost during distribution, as long as they are not all lost, without affecting eventual convergence.

3.2.1   RIP Implementations

When using a RIP implementation, each router maintains a *routing table* of information about routes from itself to each destination. In general, a router initializes its routing table by inserting routes for each of the destinations to which it is directly connected. Each entry in a router's routing table includes the address of the *next-hop* router on the way to the destination, the *distance* (or cost) from the router to the destination (hence the name *distance vector*), and the *age* of the entry itself. For most RIP implementations, the distance refers to the number of routers through which a packet must pass on the way to the destination (i.e., the hop count of the route).

With a RIP implementation, a router normally represents the routes to all destinations on a given network, with a single entry in its routing tables. Hence, the network becomes the referrant for all individual destinations on that network. The router usually assigns a single link cost to a network, so that the cost of going between any two nodes (routers or hosts) on that network is the same. Routers, however, may also distinguish routes to specific destinations when desired.

RIP implementations differ from the basic distance-vector algorithm in two respects. Instead of retaining cost estimates, for a given destination, from all its neighbors and occasionally choosing the minimum-cost route from among them, a router retains only the current minimum-cost route and the identity of the neighbor associated with it. The router replaces this information whenever it finds a route with a lower cost to the destination. Thus, a router may compute minimum-cost routes without having to store information from all its neighbors, as in the basic Bellman-Ford algorithm. Nevertheless, with RIP, routers must periodically distribute cost estimates to discover lower-cost routes.

The second difference between the basic distance-vector algorithm and the RIP implementations is that with RIP, a router need not include a routing table entry with distance 0 for itself. Consider the situation of a host or router G that is connected to network A. Let c represent the cost of using network A, between any two nodes on A. Instead of getting an update message from every other node H on network A, showing a cost of 0 to get from H to itself, and then computing $c + 0$ as the distance to H, G simply starts out by making a single routing table entry for network A with cost c. The only node on A that cannot be summarized by that common entry is G itself, because the cost of going from G to G is 0, not c. This 0 entry is never needed, however, and so G requires only the single entry for network A.

3.3 RESPONDING TO CHANGES IN LINK COSTS

Thus far we have considered only the behavior of distance-vector algorithms and their RIP implementations in stationary networks—those in which there are no changes in link costs. In practice, changes in link costs are common events in networks. There are two types of link cost changes: those caused by node or link failures and those resulting from a cost increase or reduction for an active link. We begin by describing how protocols in the RIP family recalculate routes following a change in link cost, and then we describe several mechanisms for accelerating convergence following a change in link cost.

3.3.1 Recalculating Costs

The RIP implementations, as described thus far, select a new route to a given destination only if the new cost estimate is less than the currently stored cost estimate. Following a link cost increase, however, the currently stored cost estimate may be lower than the new cost estimate. Therefore, there must be a way to select a route with a higher cost.

RIP implementations use the following rules to accommodate an increase in link cost. Given the current route to destination Z, with distance D and next hop G, a router replaces that route with any route to Z learned from a neighbor G', only if the associated distance $D' < D$. However, if a new route to Z learned from G has distance $D' > D$, the router replaces the current route with the new route. These route selection rules produce the same routes as the basic distance-vector algorithm.

In practice, nodes and links fail. RIP implementations must be able to handle the situation in which the next-hop router for a destination becomes unreachable (i.e., it fails or the link to it fails). With the RIP implementation as described thus far, a neighboring router would not detect the connectivity failure, because new route selection depends upon receiving notification of a change in a neighbor's cost estimate for a given destination. A router does not update its routing table without a positive indication of link cost change, and an unreachable next-hop router would not be able to provide that indication.

To handle these kinds of problems, RIP implementations provide for aging and invalidating entries in routing tables. The rules and timeout values depend on the specific protocol, but all routers executing a given protocol must use the same rules and timeout values for proper operation. For example, in one RIP implementation, every participating router sends an update message to all its neighbors every 30 seconds. Suppose a router uses neighbor G as the next hop for a set of routes to a set of destinations. If the router receives no update messages from G for 180 seconds (i.e., six successive update messages have not been received), it can assume that G is no longer reachable. Therefore, the router marks as invalid all the routes in its routing table that used G as a next hop. It does so by setting the associated costs to "infinity." The next time an update from a neighbor arrives with valid routes to the affected destinations, the router replaces the invalid routes with the valid ones.

3.3.2 Accelerating Convergence

The basic distance-vector algorithm is guaranteed to converge to the correct minimum-cost routes in finite time, provided there are no changes in link costs after a certain point in time. Any distance-vector algorithm applied in practice must at least be able to accommodate the occasional link cost changes likely to occur in a network. In the worst case, however, a distance-vector algorithm will fail to converge, if changes in link costs are continual and if its convergence time following such a change is longer than the time interval between successive changes.

When link costs increase, the basic distance-vector algorithm may spawn inconsistencies in the routes computed by different nodes. These inconsistencies arise because of the asynchronous, distributed nature of the algorithm and may persist for some time. Often, such inconsistencies result in *routing loops* (see examples in Sections 3.3.2.1 and 3.3.2.2 below) which must be eliminated to achieve convergence of the algorithm. Mechanisms have been developed for terminating (and in some cases, preventing the formation of) such routing loops, thus improving the performance of the network following an increase in link cost. Many of these mechanisms have been incorporated into the RIP implementations.

3.3.2.1 *Counting to Infinity*

RIP implementations handle inaccessible destinations by assigning an "infinite" route cost to such destinations. This cost must be larger than the maximum cost of a minimum-cost route in the network. Many RIP implementations use the value of 16 hops to represent infinite cost.

Given infinity equal to 16, consider a destination that becomes inaccessible. All the neighboring routers invalidate the routes to that destination and set the associated route costs to 16. These neighbors are the only ones connected to the vanished destination, and so all the other routers will converge to new routes that traverse one of these neighbors. Once convergence occurs, all routers will have costs of at least 16 for routes to the vanished destination. Routers one hop away from the original neighbors will end up with costs of at least 17 to that destination, routers two hops away will end up with costs of at least 18, and so on. These costs are larger than the maximum permitted value of 16, and thus they will all be set to 16. Hence, all routers converge to costs of 16 for the routes to the vanished destination.

Unfortunately, the question of how long convergence will take is not a simple one. Consider the example shown in Figure 3.1, with routers connected by links. All links have a cost of 1 except the link from C to D, which has a cost of 10.

In practice, each router will have a routing table containing a route to each destination. For illustration, though, only the routes from each router to the destination network are shown:

D: directly connected, distance 1
B: route via D, distance 2
C: route via B, distance 3
A: route via B, distance 3

Now, suppose that the link from B to D fails. The routes should now adjust to use the link from C to D, but it will take a while for this adjustment to happen. Routing changes start when B discovers that the direct route to D is no longer usable. For simplicity, the chart below shows all routers sending cost updates simultaneously at times t_i. It also shows the cost to the destination network, as it appears in the routing table

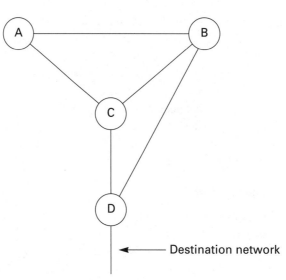

Figure 3.1   Convergence example

of each router, after each router recalculates its cost estimate. Note: "*" indicates directly connected and "—" indicates unreachable.

	t_1	t_2	t_3	t_4	...	t_9	t_{10}
D:	*, 1	*, 1	*, 1	*, 1		*, 1	*, 1
B:	—	C, 4	C, 5	C, 6		C, 11	C, 12
C:	B, 3	A, 4	A, 5	A, 6		A, 11	D, 11
A:	B, 3	C, 4	C, 5	C, 6		C, 11	C, 12

B is able to get rid of the failed route in its routing table using the timeout mechanism, but vestiges of that route persist in other routers for a long time. Initially, A and C still believe they can get to D via B for a cost of 3. In the next iteration, B claims that it can get to D via C for a cost of 4. The routes and costs claimed by A and C are nonexistent, but A and C have no way of knowing that yet. Even when they discover that their routes via B have disappeared, each thinks a route is available via the other. Eventually the routes converge, but not until the cost of the old route exceeds that of the route through C. The worst case occurs when a destination becomes completely inaccessible from some part of the network. Then the routers' cost estimates may increase slowly in a pattern like the one above until all finally reach infinity. For this reason, the problem is called *counting to infinity*.

3.3.2.2 *Split Horizon*

In the counting-to-infinity example above, part of the problem is caused by A and C engaging in a pattern of mutual deception. Each claims to be able to get to D via the other. *Split horizon* and split horizon with *poisoned reverse* are two techniques for preventing such routing loops. Split horizon selectively excludes a destination from advertisement to a neighbor, if the next hop to that destination is that neighbor. This technique was first employed in the TIDAS[20] and Datapac networks.[21] Split horizon with poisoned reverse advertises the destination to the neighbor, but with a cost of infinity. In other words, poisoned reverse explicitly advertises the destination as unreachable.

A can guard against the possibility of confusing C by using either pure split horizon (not telling C that D is reachable through A) or split horizon with poisoned reverse (telling C that D is unreachable through A). These techniques work not only when A and C are connected by a point-to-point link but also when they are connected by a multiaccess network containing other routers as well. In the multiaccess case, suppose that A's best route to D is through the multiaccess network via C. No other routers connected to that network need to know this information. They can all reach C directly and hence would never travel through the network via A to reach C. Thus, A can treat all such routers in the same fashion, with respect to distributing cost update messages. If A applies either split horizon or split horizon with poisoned reverse when distributing cost updates to C concerning D, it can also distribute the same messages to all other routers connected to the network. Therefore, A may safely broadcast all of its cost updates over the network.

Split horizon with poisoned reverse offers faster convergence than pure split horizon, for the following reason. Suppose that erroneous routes form so that two routers have each other as the next hop on their respective routes to a given destination. The routers can break their routing loop immediately by advertising to each other infinite costs for routes to the destination. Without explicit advertisement of infinite costs, the erroneous routes will be eliminated from the routing tables only after the routers time them out. The disadvantage of poisoned reverse, however, is that it increases the size of cost update messages. In a network with infrequent link cost changes, advertising the extra infinite costs wastes network resources. Hybrid RIP implementations also exist that use split horizon with poisoned reverse for some time after a change in network topology or link cost and then revert back to pure split horizon.

Split horizon with poisoned reverse will prevent any routing loops involving only two routers. It is possible, however, to encounter routing loops in which three or more routers are engaged in mutual deception. Referring to the example network depicted in Figure 3.1, suppose that each link has a cost of 1 except the link between A and C, which has a cost of 5. Thus, A's best route to D is via B. A advertises this route to C but not to B, because A uses split horizon. B and D both have direct routes to D. Suppose the link between B and D fails. B's best route to D is now via C, and

A's best route to *D* is via *B* and *C*. Suppose the link between *C* and *D* fails. Although *C* can no longer reach *D*, it believes that it has a route to *D* via *A*, because it has been receiving advertisements from *A*. Thus, although *A*, *B*, and *C* can no longer reach *D*, each believes that *D* is reachable via the next. Any routing loop involving three or more routers, such as the example described, can be eliminated by counting to infinity but cannot be eliminated by using split horizon.

3.3.2.3   *Triggered Updates*

Triggered updates are a mechanism to speed up convergence in RIP implementations in which cost update distribution is normally periodic. A triggered update is a cost update distributed immediately in response to a detected change in the cost estimate for a route to a destination. In most RIP implementations, the triggered update contains information about only those destinations whose route costs have changed, in order to conserve network resources. Moreover, most of these implementations delay triggered updates for a short time, to be able to combine cost information for several affected destinations in a single update message and hence reduce the amount of network resources consumed. Also, if a periodic update is scheduled to occur before the delayed triggered update, the triggered update need not be sent.

Triggered updates result in a cascade of triggered updates as follows. Suppose a router *G* times out a route to a destination *Z* and declares the destination unreachable. *G* then sends a triggered update indicating this fact to all its neighbors. According to the rules for updating cost estimates (described in Section 3.3.1), only those neighbors whose routes to *Z* have next hop *G* will react to the triggered update; all other neighbors will ignore it. The neighbors that heed the triggered update calculate new cost estimates for routes to *Z* and then generate their own triggered updates. This cascade of triggered updates will propagate backward from *G* along all routes to *Z* that include *G*.

With the triggered update mechanism, counting to infinity will not occur after a link cost change, provided there are no new routing table changes for the affected destinations, until all triggered updates have reached the routers affected by the original change. In practice, however, such routing table changes may occur. Routers may distribute periodic updates during the time triggered updates are being distributed. Any router which has yet to receive a triggered update and which has routes that will be affected by the link cost change will continue to advertise old cost information for those routes. Thus, an unfortunate sequence of update receptions in which a router receives a triggered update containing new cost information from one neighbor followed by a periodic update containing old cost information from another neighbor may reinstate an old route.

Holddowns help to prevent the reinstatement of old routes. When a router removes from its routing table a route to a particular destination, it invokes a holddown that disables acceptance of new routes to this destination for a specified time interval. The holddown interval should be long enough to enable triggered updates to propagate to all affected routers. It may also be desirable for the holddown to persist for a few periodic update cycles to allow for lost update messages. Although holddowns do help to reduce the chances of reinstating old routes following triggered updates, they also increase the time it takes for routers to learn the correct new routes.

3.3.2.4 Loop-Free Distance-Vector Routing

In the previous sections, we described a set of mechanisms designed to improve the performance of distance-vector algorithms in the presence of link cost increases. Each of these mechanisms has been implemented as an integral part of one or more routing procedures in the RIP family. The emphasis is on hastening convergence by terminating routing loops or better yet preventing their formation in the first place. None of these mechanisms can prevent routing loops under all conditions, however.

Distance-vector algorithms that offer loop freedom under a variety of conditions do exist, mostly in the context of networking research rather than practice. Each possesses special features not present in the RIP implementations and requires one or more of the following: additional control message exchanges, additional information contained in update messages, or additional computations to detect routing loops.

These algorithms may be divided into two categories. The first category contains those that attempt to prevent routing loops by distributing enough information in update messages to enable recipient nodes to reconstruct entire routes. Such algorithms may not always prevent routing loops but can detect them quickly should they occur. Representative examples include the algorithms given in references 8, 10, and 11. The second category contains those that attempt to prevent routing loops by controlling the order in which nodes distribute update messages and compute routes in response to an increase in link cost. Nodes coordinate computations by exchanging control messages. Many of the algorithms in this category can actually guarantee loop freedom, but require a significant number of message exchanges and tend to converge slowly. Representative examples include the algorithms given in references 6, 7, 9, and 12.

3.4 RIP PROTOCOL DESCRIPTIONS

In the next sections we briefly describe each of the distance-vector routing protocols in the RIP family. This family originated with the Xerox network protocols. The PARC Universal Packet (PUP) Gateway Information Protocol (GIP)[13] was the basis for the first routing protocol to be named RIP, subsequently used within the Xerox Networking Systems (XNS) Internet Transport Protocols.[14] XNS RIP was the starting point for the RIP implementations used with the Internet Protocol (IP)[15] and with Novell's Internetwork Packet Exchange (IPX) protocol.[18] In turn, IP RIP[16] provided the starting point for the Inter-Gateway Routing Protocol (IGRP), cisco System's proprietary version of RIP.

3.4.1 XNS RIP

XNS RIP is the most direct implementation of the basic distance-vector algorithm. The protocol has no features that are not required to correctly implement the basic algorithm. Optimal routes are those with the fewest hops.

During initialization, a router broadcasts a request for routing table entries. All routers that act as information suppliers send responses containing complete routing table information directly to the requestor. Information suppliers also gratuitously broadcast routing table updates approximately once every 30 seconds. Routers that are only information requestors gather the routing table updates but never advertise any.

In XNS RIP, aging of routing table entries works as follows. Routes age out in 90 seconds. Every time a router receives a routing table update, it resets the timers for the associated routes. If a route's timer expires, the router marks the destination as unreachable by setting the distance to 16. Following a 60-second interval, the router deletes the route from its routing table. These time intervals are chosen so that three update messages will have to be lost before a route is timed out and so that two update messages indicating that a destination is unreachable will have to be sent before the route is deleted from the routing table. The timer values represent a tradeoff between rapid recognition of connectivity failures within the internetwork and prevention of spurious failure indications.

The design of XNS RIP was based on the assumption that the size of the internetwork in which the protocol would be deployed would contain, at most, a few hundred networks. As long as an internetwork does not violate this assumption, XNS RIP is a very efficient protocol with respect to computational overhead and bandwidth usage.

There are four reasons why XNS RIP is not suitable for large, complicated network topologies. First, the memory required for maintaining a routing table with more than a few hundred entries is considerable. Second, the bandwidth required to exchange routing tables can become prohibitive, especially because a large internetwork is likely to have more frequent link cost changes. Third, minimum-hop routes are not always equivalent to minimum-delay routes in a large, heterogenous internetwork, because component routers, networks, and links are likely to have varied delay characteristics. Fourth, infinity is equal to 16, implying that shortest paths with costs greater than 15 cannot be accommodated. This value was chosen as a compromise between the need for flexibility in network design and the need to limit the overhead caused by temporary routing loops.

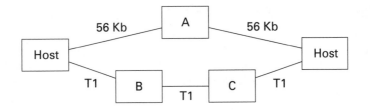

Figure 3.2 IPX example

3.4.2 IPX RIP

IPX RIP differs from XNS RIP in two respects. It employs the split horizon mechanism, and it includes a delay metric (ticks, where a tick is approximately 1/18 second) in addition to a distance metric (hops).

Selecting the optimal route is more complicated in IPX RIP because of the number of ticks. The route with the fewest ticks is considered to be the optimal one. When two routes have the same number of ticks, the route with the fewest hops is selected. This extension to the protocol has the advantage of taking into account the speed of the links between routers. For example, consider the network shown in Figure 3.2. With XNS, the host on the left would choose the path through router *A* to communicate with the host on the right. With IPX, however, the host on the left would choose the path through *B* and *C,* because that path has lower delay (provided the queueing delays are similar in all routers).

3.4.3 IP RIP

IP RIP version 1 (RIP-1) is based on XNS RIP and selects minimum-hop routes as optimal. Moreover, it extends the split horizon mechanism introduced with IPX RIP to include the poisoned reverse mechanism.

Improvements continue to be added to IP RIP implementations. In particular, the recent version of RIP[17] incorporates a loop control algorithm based on diffusing computations[12] which prevents temporary loops from forming while routes converge after a link cost change. Also, the value of infinity has been increased from 16 to 32, to accommodate larger networks.

3.4.4 IGRP

IGRP is a proprietary form of RIP developed by cisco Systems. The major differences between IGRP and the other members of the RIP family are:

1   A composite metric that accounts for multiple types of link costs.

2   The ability to select routes according to type of service.

3   Traffic load splitting among multiple routes.

4   Route poisoning.

IGRP's route metric is a weighted combination of delay, capacity, and reliability. Specifically, the metric function is defined as

$$\left(\frac{k_1}{C} + \frac{k_2}{D} \right) / R$$

C is the effective route capacity computed as the product of the bandwidth of the route (equal to the minimum bandwidth over all links in the route) and the percentage of available capacity based on load. D is the route delay and may include switching delay, transmission delay, and propagation delay. R is the reliability of the route in terms of the percentage of successful transmissions. The parameters k_1 and k_2 are configurable coefficients that determine the relative importance of delay and bandwidth in the metric function. By carefully configuring values of k_1 and k_2, network managers can enable IGRP to select routes that provide a particular type of service. Using IP, data packets indicate their requested type of service; IP types of service include low delay, high throughput, and high reliability.

IGRP permits traffic load splitting across similar routes to the same destination. A route is eligible for membership in the set of load-splitting routes if the cost of the route is within a specified range of the minimum cost to the destination. Specifically, the acceptable routes must have costs less than or equal to a coefficient v times the minimum cost. Care must be taken in configuring v. If v is too large, routes that are actually "in the wrong direction" may be selected as candidates for load splitting. In practice, v is usually set to 1.

IGRP uses route poisoning to help eliminate larger loops that split horizon cannot eliminate. With route poisoning, a router assumes that a loop has formed, if it calculates a new cost for a route and that cost is significantly larger than the previously calculated one. The router then eliminates the route from its routing table and imposes a holddown. Not all increases in route costs result from loop formation, however; small changes in individual link costs along the route may result in an increase in route cost. Care must be exercised in selecting the size of the parameter that represents a significant increase in route cost. In practice, this multiplicative parameter is set to 1.1.

3.5   CONCLUSION

Distance-vector algorithms have been widely deployed to provide shortest-path routing in packet-switched networks. They are simple to implement and are amenable to distributed, asynchronous operation. Moreover, they only require routing information exchanges among neighboring switches. Their major drawback is that they are susceptible to convergence problems in networks with fluctuating link costs. Over the years, a number of extensions have been developed to improve the performance of distance-vector algorithms in large, dynamic networks.

REFERENCES

1 J. McQuillan, *Adaptive Routing Algorithms for Distributed Computer Networks, BBN Report No. 2831,* Cambridge, MA: Bolt Beranek & Newman Inc., May 1974.

2 D. C. Walden and J. McQuillan, "The ARPANET Design Decisions," *Computer Networks*, Vol. 1, August 1977.

3 L. R. Ford Jr. and D. R. Fulkerson, *Flows in Networks,* Princeton, NJ: Princeton University Press, 1962.

4 D. P. Bertsekas and R. G. Gallager, *Data Networks,* Englewood Cliffs, NJ: Prentice-Hall, 1987.

5 R. E. Bellman, *Dynamic Programming,* Princeton, NJ: Princeton University Press, 1957.

6 P. M. Merlin and A. Segall, "A Failsafe Distributed Routing Protocol," *IEEE Transactions on Communications,* Vol. COM-27, No. 9, September 1979.

7 J. M. Jaffe and F. H. Moss, "A Responsive Distributed Routing Algorithm for Computer Networks," *IEEE Transactions on Communications,* Vol. COM-30, No. 7, July 1982.

8 K. G. Shin and M. Chen, "Performance Analysis of Distributed Routing Strategies Free of Ping-Pong-Type Looping," *IEEE Transactions on Computers,* Vol. 36, No. 2, February 1987.

9 J. J. Garcia-Luna-Aceves, "A Minimum-Hop Routing Algorithm Based on Distributed Information," *Computer Networks and ISDN Systems,* Vol. 16, No. 5, May 1989.

10 C. Cheng, R. Riley, S. Kumar, J. J. Garcia-Luna-Aceves, "A Loop-Free Extended Bellman-Ford Routing Protocol without Bouncing Effect," *ACM Computer Communications Review,* Vol. 19, No. 4, September 1989.

11 B. Rajagopalan and M. Faiman, "A New Responsive Distributed Shortest-Path Routing Algorithm," *ACM Computer Communications Review,* Vol. 19, No. 4, September 1989.

12 J. J. Garcia-Luna-Aceves, "Loop-Free Routing Using Diffusing Computations," *IEEE/ACM Transactions on Networking,* Vol. 1, No. 1, February 1993.

13 D. R. Boggs, J. F. Shoch, E. A. Taft, and R. M. Metcalfe, "PUP: An Internetwork Architecture," *IEEE Transactions on Communications,* Vol. COM-28, No. 4, April 1980.

14 Xerox Corporation, "Internet Transport Protocols," *Xerox System Integration Standard XSIS 028112,* Stamford, CT: Xerox Corporation, December 1981.

15 J. Postel, "Internet Protocol," *Internet Request for Comments 791,* September 1981.

16 C. Hedrick, "Routing Information Protocol," *Internet Request for Comments 1058,* Rutgers University, June 1988.

17 G. Malkin, "RIP Version 2—Carrying Additional Information," *Internet Request for Comments 1388,* Xylogics Inc., January 1993.

18 Novell, Inc., *IPX Router Specification, Revision A,* Provo: Novell Inc., 1992.

19 C. Hedrick, *An Introduction to IGRP,* New Brunswick, NJ: Rutgers University, August 1991.

20 T. Cegrell, "A Routing Procedure for the TIDAS Message-Switching Network," *IEEE Transactions on Communications,* Vol. COM-23, No. 6, June 1975.

21 D. E. Sproule and F. Mellor, "Routing, Flow Control, and Congestion Control in the Datapac Network," *IEEE Transactions on Communications,* Vol. COM-29, No. 4, April 1981.

CHAPTER 4 ❖ ❖ ❖ ❖

Inter-Domain Routing: EGP, BGP, and IDRP

YAKOV REKHTER

CONTENTS

Internetworks are inherently heterogeneous entities. Their interconnected component networks are owned and operated by different organizations, provide different services, impose different restrictions on access to these services, and use different protocols to distribute routing information and forward packets internally. Thus, internetwork routing requires extensive cooperation among these disparate constituent networks. This chapter traces three major developments in the evolution of internetwork routing, each of which is a routing procedure based on the distance-vector paradigm. The three procedures are the Exterior Gateway Protocol (deployed when the ARPANET functioned as the core of the Internet), the Border Gateway Protocol (developed to handle arbitrary network interconnectivity), and the Inter-Domain Routing Protocol (designed to accommodate growth in the number of networks and users and diversification of service offerings).

4.1   INTRODUCTION

In this chapter we describe three inter-domain routing protocols—the Exterior Gateway Protocol (EGP), the Border Gateway Protocol (BGP), and the Inter-Domain Routing Protocol (IDRP)—which are intended for use in heterogeneous internets comprising multiple organizations.

4.1.1   Internet Evolution

The design of all the protocols that are described in this chapter was strongly influenced by the practical requirements and operational experience in the Internet. Therefore, understanding the Internet, its evolution, and its requirements is essential if we want to understand the rationale behind the design choices for the protocols.

The system known today as the Internet had its origin in the ARPANET. The ARPANET was formed in the late 1970s. At that time it represented a single community of interest, comprising mostly researchers studying aspects of computer networks. The ARPANET was used primarily as an experimental network.

Until 1983 the ARPANET was the sole network that interconnected various sites. The sites attached to the ARPANET had no direct connectivity with each other. Thus, the Internet topology was restricted to a strict two-level hierarchy (treelike topology), with the ARPANET at the top level.

Even at that early stage of the Internet, expansion became one of the key problems. Specifically, it was necessary to deal with such issues as the overhead associated with handling routing information (e.g., storage overhead, CPU overhead), fault isolation in the presence of heterogeneous hardware and software, and complexity associated with upgrading equipment due to changes in software and algorithms.

In 1983 a portion of the ARPANET was split into a separate network, the MILNET. The MILNET was intended to provide operational service to military installations, and the ARPANET continued its function as primarily an experimental network. Some of the sites that were previously connected only to the ARPANET acquired additional connectivity to the MILNET. As a consequence of the split, the single network was replaced by two networks, ARPANET and MILNET, directly connected to each other.

In 1984 the National Science Foundation (NSF) established the NSFNET Backbone, whose purpose was to provide connectivity among various research institutions in the U.S. and to form the foundation for a nationwide academic research network. Individual sites (e.g., campuses) were attached to the Backbone via one or more Regional Networks (e.g., New York State Educational and Research Network—NYSERNET); the Backbone itself was directly connected to the ARPANET at several points. Thus, all the networks—ARPANET, MILNET, and NSFNET—were directly connected to each other. The original strict hierarchy of the ARPANET gave way to a less constrained topology, where some of the Regional Networks had multiple attachment points to the NSFNET Backbone. Direct connections between Regional Networks were used to supplement the connectivity provided by the Backbone itself, and sites were connected to one or more Regional Networks, and in some cases also to ARPANET or MILNET or both.

By the late 1980s the Internet had undergone significant changes. Rapid geographic expansion resulted in evolution from a U.S.-centric to a worldwide communications infrastructure. By the end of 1993 the Internet provided connectivity among more than 2 million computers in more than 100 countries in the Americas, Europe, Asia, Africa, and Australia. Although the original simple topology of the Internet was superseded by a much less constrained topology, the overall structure still preserves the hierarchical nature (e.g., sites, regionals). The focus of the Internet shifted from being primarily a research network for researchers to an infrastructure that provides production-quality service to a large and diverse user population (e.g., schools, private industry, universities, libraries). The Internet evolved from a single homogeneous environment into the infrastructure that consists of a multivendor collection of diverse networking technologies connected with one another, whose operations are controlled by multiple organizations with heterogeneous goals and objectives. Increased heterogeneity is also reflected in the network-layer protocols directly supported in the Internet. From a pure IP environment, the Internet evolved into a multiprotocol environment that presently supports IP[26] and CLNP.[12] It is quite realistic to expect that in the not too distant future support for other network layer protocols, like IPX,[23] will be fully integrated into the Internet.

4.1.2 Service Providers and Service Subscribers

Resources that compose today's Internet infrastructure (e.g., switches, subnetworks) belong to various organizations (e.g., MERIT controls switches and subnetworks that form the NSFNET Backbone, but it has no control over switches and subnetworks of any of the Regional Networks, like NYSERNET, attached to the Backbone). As a consequence, providing ubiquitous connectivity within the Internet implies resource sharing across organizational boundaries. To cover expenses associated with acquiring and maintaining resources, as well as to gain some profit, organizations need to be able to exercise control over resource sharing. Moreover, the need to exercise control has to be carefully balanced against the cost of the mechanisms for providing such control. It would make little or no sense to employ a cost-recovery mechanism whose cost would be greater than that recovered by the mechanism.

To facilitate further discussion we introduce two concepts, *service providers* and *service subscribers*. Organizations that share their resources with other organizations are called service providers (or just providers). Organizations that use other organizations' resources are called service subscribers (or just subscribers). Using the notion of service provider and service subscriber, we can model the Internet as a collection of interconnected service providers and service subscribers.

The basic service offered by a provider at the network layer is the set of destinations (hosts) that can be reached through the provider. Once a subscriber establishes direct connectivity to a provider, the subscriber can reach all the destinations reachable through the provider. Because the value of the service offered by a provider increases with the number of destinations reachable through the provider, providers are motivated to interconnect with each other. Thus, a given organization may act as both a provider and a subscriber. For example, a Regional Network such as NYSER-NET acts as a provider to a campus network (e.g., Columbia University) but acts as a subscriber to the NSFNET Backbone.

Service providers differ from each other in several aspects. Some of the providers cover a limited geographical area (e.g., one state or a group of neighboring states), but coverage of other providers spans multiple countries or even multiple continents. Examples of the former are such Regional Networks as OARNet (Ohio Academic and Research Network) which covers subscribers within the state of Ohio. Examples of the latter are Alternet and SprintLink. Some of the providers place no restrictions on the types of subscribers that the providers can offer their service to, but others place constraints on their potential subscribers. An example of the former is Alternet. An example of the latter is the NASA Sciences Internet (NSI), where only subscribers associated with NASA-related activities are allowed to connect to the NSI.

4.1.3 Internet Routing Framework

The protocols covered in this chapter are designed to operate in conjunction with connectionless network-layer protocols, like IP[26] or CLNP.[12] Information exchanged between hosts via a connectionless network-layer protocol is partitioned into segments (packets), called *network-layer protocol data units* (NPDUs). Throughout this chapter we use ISO (International Standards Organization) terminology when referring to networking concepts.

Forwarding of NPDUs across the Internet is governed by routing protocols. Entities that participate in NPDU forwarding are called *intermediate systems* (ISs). With a *hop-by-hop* forwarding mechanism, when an IS receives an NPDU, the IS makes its forwarding decision (determines the next hop) using the information carried in the NPDU header (e.g., destination address) and local forwarding table, called the *forwarding information base* (FIB). Conceptually, each FIB entry consists of a destination address, some other parameters that can be carried in the NPDU header (e.g., Quality of Service), and the network address of the next hop IS on a path to the destination. An IS constructs its FIB using routing information it receives as a result of its participating in one or more routing protocols. An IS stores the routing information in its *routing information base* (RIB).

To facilitate dealing with the diversity and heterogeneity of the Internet, routing in the Internet is partitioned into two components, intra-domain and inter-domain. Intra-domain routing handles routing procedures within a single provider/subscriber. Inter-domain routing handles routing procedures that span multiple providers/subscribers. Thus, intra-domain routing handles the exchange of routing information within a single provider or subscriber, and inter-domain routing handles the exchange of routing information across provider/subscriber boundaries.

Recast in routing terminology: a single provider or subscriber that spans a contiguous segment of an internet topology forms an *administrative domain* (AD).* The concept of an AD provides inter-domain routing with a convenient model upon which organizations that contribute their resources to the Internet can establish boundaries to protect and control access to their resources. A connected set of ISs that participate in a single instance of a particular intra-domain routing protocol forms a *routing domain* (RD).† ISs that participate in inter-domain routing are called *boundary intermediate systems* (BISs). Because in certain cases a single administration may employ several intra-domain routing protocols, an AD may consist of several interconnected RDs. Exchange of routing information across RD boundaries in such cases may be accommodated either via inter-domain routing (even if the RDs are within the same

---

* Notice that the notion of an AD is quite similar to that of an autonomous system (see reference 37).

† This is a rather informal definition. For a more formal description of routing domain see reference 14.

AD) or via mechanisms specific to an intra-domain routing protocol used by the corresponding RDs.

Quite often, inter-domain routing is associated with the term *policy-based routing*. Constraints and rules on who can use whose resources are often referred to as *routing policies* or just *policies*.* A service provider uses *transit policies* to govern the use of its resources by service subscribers. A service subscriber uses *source policies* to govern its choices with respect to the service providers whose services the subscriber uses to reach destinations outside the subscriber. Likewise, a service subscriber uses *destination policies* to govern its choices about the service providers whose services the subscriber uses when other subscribers want to reach destinations within the subscriber.

The need to have distinct intra-domain and inter-domain routing is motivated by the inherent differences in the objectives and design constraints. Although issues such as providing mechanisms for controlling resource sharing (routing policies) and for dealing with autonomy and distribution of such control dominate inter-domain routing design, they are of peripheral importance to intra-domain routing, due to the relative homogeneity and centralized control associated with routing within a single domain. Likewise, though the issue of scaling is important for intra-domain routing only to a certain extent, it becomes one of the primary design goals for inter-domain routing.† After all, one can always compensate for inadequate scaling in intra-domain routing by making individual domains smaller and interconnecting them via inter-domain routing, but there is no such fallback for inter-domain routing. Inter-domain routing is also intended to provide sufficient fault isolation between domains, so that problems within one domain will not adversely affect intra-domain routing within any other domain, and inter-domain routing will not adversely influence intra-domain routing. Routing efficiency (route optimality with respect to a given performance metric, such as throughput or delay), which is one of the primary design objectives in intra-domain routing, is a tertiary objective, after autonomy and fault isolation, in inter-domain routing.

A reader may wonder if a single protocol can accommodate both intra-domain and inter-domain routing or if more than one protocol is needed. (To shed some light on this issue we observe that even if it were conceptually possible to come up with a single routing protocol that would provide all the functionality needed for both intra-domain and inter-domain routing, such a protocol would strongly resemble a "kitchen sink." Having two protocols, one for intra-domain and one for inter-domain, provides a less complex and more modular design alternative.)

---

*   The reader may notice that the term *policies* is underspecified. We have said nothing specific about the type and the nature of constraints or rules that form the policies. This observation suggests that *policy-based routing* may be viewed as an instance of an *arbitrary internet* (AI) problem. One may wonder whether the acronym AI may be used as a reliable indicator of the complexity associated with policy-based routing.

†   Current design requirements assume that a single instance of an inter-domain routing protocol should be able to handle an internet that interconnects from 10^9 to 10^{12} hosts.

Although the routing architecture of the Internet consists of two components, inter-domain routing and intra-domain routing, these components are not completely independent—only combined do they provide sufficient functionality to support Internet-wide routing. To see why, realize that although carrying NPDUs across a domain's boundary can be accomplished solely by inter-domain routing, carrying NPDUs through a domain assumes some assistance from intra-domain routing. This assistance is realized via exchange of routing information between inter-domain and intra-domain routing. At one extreme enough inter-domain routing information is *leaked* into intra-domain routing. Within a domain this information is first leaked from inter-domain routing to intra-domain routing at the BISs of the domain that participate in both inter- and intra-domain routing protocols, and then disseminated within the domain via intra-domain routing. In this way, even if the ISs within a domain don't explicitly participate in inter-domain routing, they have sufficient routing information about destinations outside the domain to correctly forward NPDUs destined for hosts outside the domain. At the other extreme, carrying NPDUs across a domain is accomplished via encapsulation, so that no leakage is needed. Interaction between inter-domain and intra-domain routing is an interesting subject on its own. Readers may find more details on this topic in references 17, 30, 32, and 43.

4.2 EXTERIOR GATEWAY PROTOCOL (EGP)

The Exterior Gateway Protocol (EGP),[22,40,41] was the first inter-domain routing protocol introduced in the Internet. It was developed in the early 1980s to deal with routing between the ARPANET and the sites attached to it. EGP was intended to be used in conjunction with IP. The primary goals of EGP were to provide fault isolation in the presence of heterogeneous hardware and software and to simplify deployment of equipment running new software that was not necessarily backward compatible.

4.2.1 EGP Topological Model

At the time EGP was introduced (see Section 4.1.1), the Internet topology (at the domain level) was a strict two-level hierarchy (treelike topology). The ARPANET, under the control of a single administration (BBN), formed the top-level domain (level 0), with all the sites attached to the ARPANET forming domains at the next level (level 1) of the hierarchy. EGP explicitly restricts its applicability to such an environment. Thus, from the EGP point of view, the Internet can be modeled at the domain level as a two-level strict hierarchy with no direct links between domains at level 1. In EGP terminology the top-level domain is called the *core*.

EGP was the first protocol that introduced the concept of a domain (in EGP terminology it is called an *autonomous system*). Domains are not allowed to overlap—a given BIS may belong to only one domain. A pair of BISs participating in EGP are called *neighbors* if these BISs have a common subnetwork (they can reach each other in a single network-layer hop). EGP defines a protocol that governs the exchange of routing information between two neighbors. A pair of BISs that are neighbors, but belong to different domains, are called *exterior neighbors*. Two domains are said to be *adjacent* if they have BISs that are exterior neighbors of each other.

The protocol requires each domain to have a globally unique identifier, called an *autonomous system number*. Procedures for assigning and managing autonomous system number space are outside the scope of EGP.* A BIS that participates in EGP is expected to be preconfigured with the autonomous system number of the domain the BIS belongs to.

4.2.2 EGP Routing Algorithm

In the routing information exchanged, EGP closely resembles other routing protocols that are based on the distributed Bellman-Ford (or Distance-Vector) routing algorithm (e.g., RIP,[9] IGRP[10]). (See Chapter 3 for more information.) Routing information (routes) exchanged via EGP consist of *network-layer reachability information* (NLRI, expressed as a list of IP network numbers), the network-layer address of the IS that should be used as the next hop when forwarding to the destinations depicted by the NLRI, and a metric.

The EGP route-selection algorithm consists of a BIS selecting, from multiple routes to a destination (that were received from the BIS's neighbors), one route, and using it to construct an appropriate FIB entry. The selected route may also be advertised (under certain conditions) to other neighbors. In contrast with the EGP routing information exchange, the EGP route-selection algorithm has little in common with the distributed Bellman-Ford algorithm. Specifically, EGP defines how the metric should be used in selecting among multiple routes to a destination *only* if these routes were received from the same adjacent domain. In all other cases, use of the metric is undefined, and each BIS is expected to select among multiple routes to a destination based on some criteria local to the BIS.

Loop-free steady-state NPDU forwarding with EGP requires suppression of routing-information looping. To understand the rationale behind this requirement, we need to observe that an NPDU's flow is determined by the flow of NLRI and that the direction of the NPDU's flow is opposite to the direction of NLRI flow. Therefore, to provide steady-state loop-free NPDU forwarding (at the domain level) with EGP, it is sufficient to guarantee that NLRI doesn't loop. Because NLRI is just a component of

---

*   Assigning and managing the autonomous system number space in the Internet is done by the IANA (Internet Assigned Numbers Authority).

routing information, it follows that steady-state suppression of routing-information looping provides steady-state loop-free NPDU forwarding.

The basic distributed Bellman-Ford algorithm uses a *count-to-infinity* mechanism for suppressing routing-information looping. This mechanism assumes that when presented with multiple routes to a destination, an IS always selects the one with the smallest metric. It also assumes that when an IS advertises a route, it increases the route's metric. Because EGP doesn't define handling of the metric (other than using it to select among routes received from the same adjacent domain), it follows that neither of these two assumptions is correct for EGP. Consequently, EGP has no built-in mechanism for suppressing routing-information looping. Taken out of context, this deficiency may be viewed as a fatal flaw of the protocol, because routing-information looping would result in persistent faulty NPDU forwarding. In the context of EGP, however, lack of such a mechanism turned out to be a nonissue. Because EGP requires that the inter-domain topology be constrained to a two-level strict hierarchy, this absence makes routing-information looping impossible—only BISs that belong to the *core* (level 0 domain) are allowed to propagate nonlocal routing information (information received from other domains—level 1 domains) to other domains. Moreover, due to the topology constraint it becomes impossible for a BIS to receive more than one route to a particular destination from different adjacent domains. Hence, the use of the metric to select among multiple routes to a given destination, received from different adjacent domains, is undefined in EGP and becomes a nonissue as well.

4.2.3 Basic Functionality

EGP operations consist of three distinct components: neighbor acquisition, neighbor reachability, and exchange of routing information.

Before starting to exchange routing information with a neighbor, a BIS needs to *acquire* this neighbor. The acquisition component consists of a simple two-way handshake. A BIS that wants to acquire a neighbor sends to that neighbor a Neighbor Acquisition message carrying a REQUEST command. The message may be retransmitted until the BIS receives a matching Neighbor Acquisition message carrying either a CONFIRM response or a REFUSAL response. To facilitate matching, messages carry a SEQUENCE number. A BIS is said to acquire a neighbor either when it receives a Neighbor Acquisition message carrying a REQUEST command and replies to it with a Neighbor Acquisition message carrying a CONFIRM response, or when it sends a Neighbor Acquisition message carrying a REQUEST command and receives a matching Neighbor Acquisition message carrying a CONFIRM response. A BIS may refuse to be acquired by another BIS by sending a Neighbor Acquisition message carrying a REFUSE response in response to a Neighbor Acquisition message carrying a REQUEST command received from the other BIS.

Once a pair of BISs acquire each other, it is important for each BIS to maintain timely information about the operational status of its peer. This is done via the neighbor-reachability component of EGP. A BIS can participate in neighbor reachability in either *active* or *passive* mode. An active BIS periodically transmits Neighbor Reachability messages carrying a HELLO command and expects its peer to reply with Neighbor Reachability messages carrying an I-HEARD-YOU response. A passive BIS doesn't transmit Neighbor Reachability messages carrying a HELLO command; instead it replies only to incoming Neighbor Reachability messages that are carrying a HELLO command with Neighbor Reachability messages that are carrying an I-HEARD-YOU response. Neighbor Reachability messages carry a STATUS field. This field is used by the sender of a message to indicate whether it thinks the receiver of the message is reachable or not. Thus, a BIS that is passive declares its neighbor reachable when the STATUS field of a Neighbor Reachability message received from the neighbor indicates that the neighbor thinks the BIS is reachable. EGP requires at least one of the neighbors to be active; however, both neighbors may be active. Notice that when only one neighbor is active, the volume of traffic associated with the neighbor-reachability component is half the volume of traffic when both neighbors are active.

To dampen routing instabilities, EGP introduces hysteresis into neighbor reachability. An active BIS changes the status of its neighbor from reachable to unreachable if, in response to the last n Neighbor Reachability messages carrying a HELLO command the BIS sent to the neighbor, the BIS received fewer than k Neighbor Reachability messages carrying an I-HEARD-YOU response (of course, $n \geq k$). Likewise, an active BIS changes the status of its neighbor from unreachable to reachable if, during the time the BIS sent its last n Neighbor Reachability messages carrying a HELLO command, it received at least j Neighbor Reachability messages carrying an I-HEARD-YOU response from the neighbor. A similar technique is used for a passive BIS. To ensure correct operation EGP requires a BIS to be able to generate a Neighbor Reachability message carrying an I-HEARD-YOU response within several seconds from receipt of a Neighbor Reachability message carrying a HELLO command.

A pair of BISs that have acquired each other and are reachable (in the EGP sense) can exchange routing information via Network Reachability messages. Each Network Reachability message includes the NLRI, the metric, and the network-layer address of an appropriate next-hop IS. A BIS uses information received via Network Reachability messages to construct its FIB. Usually a BIS sends a Network Reachability message to its neighbor in response to a Poll message received from the neighbor. Network Reachability messages are matched with Poll messages via a SEQUENCE number carried by both types of messages. In addition to solicited updates (via Poll messages), EGP provides a limited form of unsolicited updates. However, the frequency of unsolicited updates is constrained by the protocol—between two consecutive polls a BIS is allowed to send at most one unsolicited Network Reachability message to its neighbor. To control the overhead associated with sending and receiving Network Reachability messages, EGP allows each BIS to impose an upper bound on the frequency with which it can be polled by its neighbor. To ensure correct operation, EGP requires that a BIS be able to generate a Network Reachability message within several seconds from receipt of a Poll message.

Whenever a BIS advertises to its neighbor a route with metric 255, such an advertisement serves to indicate that the destinations covered by the NLRI of the route are unreachable through the BIS. Whenever a BIS receives several successive Network Reachability messages from its neighbor, such that these messages don't contain some NLRI that was advertised by the neighbor in some previous Network Reachability message, this lack should be taken as an indication that the destinations depicted by the NLRI are unreachable through the neighbor. As a consequence, EGP requires frequent periodic updates of complete routing information maintained by a BIS.

In certain cases it might be desirable for a BIS to advertise to its neighbor some other IS as the next hop to a particular destination. This feature may be especially useful when a domain is built around a nonbroadcast multiple-access subnetwork technology, like X.25. To accommodate this requirement, EGP allows a BIS to advertise, in the Network Reachability message, the network-layer address of some other IS (as the next hop), so that the BIS's neighbor would forward NPDUs to that IS rather than to the BIS. To enforce the strict hierarchy constraint, however, only BISs in the core are allowed to advertise, as the next hop, network-layer addresses of ISs that belong to other than core domains. A BIS in any other domain may advertise as the next hop only network-layer addresses of the ISs within its own domain.

A BIS can unilaterally terminate routing-information exchange and deacquire its neighbor by sending to it a Neighbor Acquisition message carrying a CEASE command. The neighbor is expected to respond with a Neighbor Acquisition message carrying a CEASE-ACK response. A BIS also terminates routing-information exchange with its neighbor if the BIS changes the neighbor's status from reachable to unreachable. Other reasons for terminating routing-information exchange and declaring a neighbor unreachable include link-layer notifications about the status of the subnetwork that interconnects a BIS to its neighbor (e.g., a link-down indication). Once a BIS terminates routing-information exchange with its neighbor, all the routes received from the neighbor must be deleted from the local RIB, and the FIB must be adjusted accordingly.

All EGP messages are carried directly over IP with no intervening transport protocol. When the size of an EGP message is larger than the maximum size that can be transmitted over a particular subnetwork, the message is fragmented by a sender and reassembled by a receiver using the IP fragmentation/reassembly mechanism.

4.2.4 Problems with EGP

Although EGP was sufficient for the environment for which it was designed, EGP suitability deteriorated with the changes in the Internet.

The first major problem with EGP was its failure to cope with the transition of the Internet from a strict two-level hierarchy (at the domain level) with a single-service provider to a less constrained topology with multiple-service providers. Since EGP provides no routing-information loop-suppression mechanisms, use of EGP in such a topology requires some means outside the protocol to constrain inter-domain routing information flow to a treelike topology, even if the actual physical topology (at the domain level) is less constrained. A scheme that satisfies this requirement was developed and implemented in the NSFNET Backbone Phase II.[1,29] It employs tight administrative control over the distribution of routing information via EGP, combined with support from the intra-domain routing protocol employed within the NSFNET Backbone.[28] Acceptance and announcement of inter-domain routing information exchanged via EGP between the Backbone and Regional Networks is controlled via configuration files installed on all the BISs in the Backbone. Although the scheme used in the NSFNET Backbone addressed the issue of suppressing routing-information looping, it also resulted in artificially restricted routing choices. These restrictions became an increasing problem on their own. The approach used in the NSFNET Backbone also requires a fair amount of configured information needed to control distribution of routing information. The configuration information needs to be collected and updated in a timely fashion, which also tends to be somewhat of an issue.

The second major problem with EGP was caused by the semistatelessness of the protocol. On the positive side, the semistatelessness simplifies the protocol. However, this simplification has one significant drawback—it requires periodic full updates of routing information. With the growth of the Internet the resources needed to exchange and process periodic full updates became more and more of a problem. In an attempt to reduce the amount of resources needed to transmit and process periodic full updates, certain implementations reduced the frequency of polling. Although this tactic alleviated one problem (resource utilization), it created another by so adversely affecting routing convergence that users experienced disruption of transport-layer connections (TCP[27]).

The third major problem was caused by the size of Network Reachability messages that, due to the growth of the Internet, exceeded the maximum size that can be transmitted over an Ethernet. Because most of the domains in the Internet are connected with each other via Ethernet subnetworks, this crowding causes fragmentation and reassembly of these messages at the network layer (IP). Loss of fragments at the receiving end (e.g., due to congestion) with no retransmission of missing fragments by the sender (because IP is connectionless) causes the inability to reassemble Network Reachability messages. That, in turn, results in excessive polling and quite often in large-scale routing instabilities due to failures to perform, in a timely fashion, periodic full updates needed to retain routes.

Clearly, all these factors were quite detrimental to the stability of the Internet and its growth. In the late 1980s it became clear that EGP turned into one of the major stumbling blocks in the evolution of the Internet. In retrospect one may also observe that for the set of functions provided by EGP, as well as for all of its shortcomings, the protocol may be viewed as unjustifiably complex.

4.3 BORDER GATEWAY PROTOCOL (BGP)

The Border Gateway Protocol (BGP) is an inter-domain routing protocol designed to be used in conjunction with IP. It was introduced in the Internet late in the 1980s to address all the shortcomings of EGP. Over the past few years the protocol evolved significantly beyond its original design goals. In this chapter we present the most recent version of the protocol—BGP-4.[37,38] *

4.3.1 BGP Topological Model

In contrast with EGP, which is intended to operate only within a strictly hierarchical inter-domain topology, BGP places no such restrictions—it is designed to operate in the presence of an arbitrary inter-domain topology. Like EGP, BGP disallows overlapping domains—a given BIS may belong to only one domain. A pair of BISs are called *external neighbors* if these BISs belong to different domains but have a common subnetwork (i.e., a BIS can reach its external neighbor in a single network-layer hop). Two domains are said to be *adjacent* if they have BISs that are external neighbors of each other. A pair of BISs are called *internal neighbors* if these BISs belong to the same domain. In contrast with external neighbors, internal neighbors don't have to share a subnetwork—BGP assumes that a BIS should be able to exchange NPDUs with any of its internal neighbors by relying solely on intra-domain routing procedures.

Like EGP, BGP governs the exchange of routing information between a pair of neighbors, either external or internal. BGP is self-contained in exchange of information between external neighbors. Exchange of information between internal neighbors relies on additional support provided by intra-domain routing (unless internal neighbors share a subnetwork).

Like EGP, BGP requires that each domain be assigned a unique identifier, the autonomous system number. A BIS participating in BGP is expected to be preconfigured with the autonomous system number of the domain to which the BIS belongs.

---

*   The reader who is interested in the evolution of the protocol should consult BGP-1,[19] BGP-2,[11,20] and BGP-3[21,31] specifications.

4.3.2 BGP Routing Information

In routing information exchanged, BGP, like EGP, carries NLRI and the network-layer address of the IS that should be used as the next hop when forwarding to the destinations depicted by the NLRI. However, BGP introduces a new type of routing information—the list of domains that the routing information traversed so far. One may think about this list as a domain-level description of the path traversed by the routing information. This property causes BGP to be labeled a *path-vector* protocol, where routing information exchanged between neighbors consists of a *vector* of destinations (each expressed as NLRI) and domain-level *paths* associated with each destination. As we'll see in Section 4.3.3, the presence of domain-level path information strongly influences the overall functionality of BGP.

To formalize the type of routing information exchanged, BGP introduces the concept of *path attributes*. Routing information (routes) exchanged via BGP consists of NLRI and a set of attributes of a path toward the destinations depicted by the NLRI. To phrase it differently, a *route* in the context of BGP is defined as a pairing of NLRI and path attributes.

Information carried via path attributes may be partitioned into these categories:

- Information that always has to be present and must be understood by all BISs to ensure correct operation of the protocol

- Information that may not always be present, but if present must be understood by all BISs to ensure correct operation of the protocol

- Information that may not always be present; moreover, correctness of the protocol is not affected by a BIS that doesn't understand this information

The last category may be further subdivided into two cases depending on whether it makes sense for a BIS to propagate information that it doesn't understand. Corresponding to this taxonomy, BGP groups all path attributes into four separate categories: *well-known mandatory, well-known discretionary, optional transitive,* and *optional nontransitive.* A mandatory attribute must be present in every route, but discretionary and optional attributes need not be present in every route. A BIS is required to understand the semantics of every well-known attribute but not every optional attribute. If a BIS doesn't understand the semantics of an optional attribute of a route, then the BIS may propagate this attribute (as part of the route) only if the attribute is transitive. When propagating the route to other BISs, the BIS marks the attribute indicating that the BIS didn't understand its semantics. If an attribute is optional but nontransitive, and a BIS doesn't understand the semantics of the attribute, then the BIS may propagate the route, but the attribute should be stripped from the route prior to propagation.

Encoding of the attributes is based on a rather general type-length-value (TLV) scheme, where each attribute is encoded as a triplet consisting of the attribute type, the attribute length, and the value of the attribute. Part of the attribute-type field encodes whether an attribute is well known or optional, so that a BIS can determine an attribute's category without understanding the attribute's semantics. For optional attributes the attribute-type field also specifies whether an attribute is transitive or nontransitive. Taxonomy and encoding of path attributes provides enough extensibility of the protocol that new optional attributes can be added incrementally.

BGP specifies a total of 7 path attributes: 3 well-known mandatory (ORIGIN, AS-PATH, and NEXT-HOP), 2 well-known discretionary (LOCALPREF and ATOMIC-AGGREGATE), 1 optional transitive (AGGREGATOR), and 1 optional nontransitive (MULTI-EXIT-DISC). We describe some of these below.

4.3.3 Basic Functionality

Like EGP, BGP operations may be partitioned into three components: neighbor acquisition, neighbor reachability, and exchange of routing information.

Acquisition begins with establishing a reliable transport-layer connection between two neighbors. Once the connection is established, a BIS sends to its neighbor an Open message. If the neighbor is willing to be acquired, it replies with a KEEPALIVE message. The acquisition component is completed once a BIS sends an Open message to its neighbor, receives a KEEPALIVE message from that neighbor, receives an Open message from that neighbor, and sends a KEEPALIVE message to that neighbor.

To monitor operational status of an acquired neighbor, BGP uses KEEPALIVE messages. A BIS is required to periodically send KEEPALIVE messages to all its acquired neighbors. If a BIS doesn't receive a KEEPALIVE message from its neighbor within more than Holding Time, as specified by the BIS in its Open message sent to the neighbor, the BIS declares the neighbor unreachable.

Two neighbors that are reachable (in the sense of BGP) can exchange routing information (routes) with each other. The information is carried in Update messages. A single Update message may carry one or more routes; however, if more than one route is present, all the routes have to have all their path attributes the same. An Update message is also used to indicate that some of the previously advertised routes can no longer be used.

The exchange of routing information is incremental—after the initial exchange of complete routing information, only changes to that information are exchanged. Incremental updates provide a clear savings in bandwidth and processing, compared to the periodic full updates used by EGP. However, incremental updates require reliable delivery of these updates. Rather than reinventing its own protocol, BGP uses an existing reliable transport protocol—TCP.[27] Use of TCP also eliminates the problem associated with network-layer fragmentation and reassembly of messages that is needed by EGP.

To help better understand the protocol, we introduce this model of the Routing Information Base (RIB) maintained by a BIS:*

- Adj-RIB-In (Adjacency Routing Information Base Input)—this database stores routing information that a BIS receives from its neighbor. A BIS maintains a separate Adj-RIB-In for each of its neighbors (either internal or external).

- Loc-RIB (Local Routing Information Base)—this database is created by applying the BGP route-selection algorithm to the set of routes present in all the Adj-RIBs-In of the BIS.

- Adj-RIB-Out (Adjacency Routing Information Base Output)—this database stores routing information that a BIS advertises to its neighbor. A BIS maintains separate Adj-RIB-Out for each of its neighbors (either internal or external).

Using this model, we can describe the routing-information-exchange component of BGP in more detail. A BIS receives routes from its neighbors (via Update messages) and stores them in the appropriate Adj-RIBs-In. These routes are used as input to the BGP route selection algorithm. The algorithm is modeled as requiring a BIS to assign a nonnegative integer, called the *Degree of Preference,* to each route received from the BIS's external neighbors. A BIS selects among all the routes to a given destination received from all its external neighbors the one with the highest Degree of Preference and sends this route to all its internal neighbors. When sending a route to an internal neighbor, the route carries the Degree of Preference assigned to it by the sending BIS in the LOCAL-PREF path attribute. Among all the routes to a destination received from all its neighbors (both internal and external), the BIS selects the one with the highest Degree of Preference and installs this route in its Loc-RIB. Once a route is placed in the Loc-RIB, the BIS also adjusts its FIB according to this route. A BIS may advertise to any of its external neighbors any route (after appropriately updating path attributes of the route) that is installed in the BIS's Loc-RIB.

Providing loop-free steady-state NPDU forwarding with BGP, as with EGP, requires suppressing routing-information looping. However, in sharp contrast with EGP, which relies on mechanisms external to the protocol for loop suppression (see Section 4.2.2), BGP has an internal mechanism to deal with this issue. The mechanism allows BGP to completely remove the strict two-level hierarchy topology restriction that is essential for correct operation of EGP. To prevent looping of routing information, BGP uses information carried in the AS-PATH attribute. This attribute contains the list of domains (expressed in autonomous system numbers) that the route has traversed so far. Whenever a BIS sends a route to an external neigh-

---

* The reader is strongly cautioned that this model is purely conceptual and need not bear any relationship to how a particular implementation of BGP handles a RIB.

bor, the BIS updates the AS-PATH attribute with the autonomous system number of the domain the BIS belongs to. When a BIS receives a route from its external neighbor, the BIS checks whether the AS-PATH attribute of the route includes the autonomous system number of the domain the BIS belongs to. If it does, the route can be retained in the appropriate Adj-RIB-In but cannot be passed as input to the BGP route-selection algorithm. Thus the AS-PATH attribute provides a simple but powerful mechanism to suppress routing-information looping and thus ensures steady-state loop-free NPDU forwarding.

BGP doesn't specify the criteria a BIS should use in assigning a Degree of Preference to a route—it is left as a local decision. Thus, in contrast with other routing protocols, BGP has no globally agreed-upon metric—the significance of the metric, as expressed by the Degree of Preference and exchanged between BISs via the LOCAL-PREF path attribute, is confined to a single domain. Absence of a globally agreed-upon metric allows a significant degree of autonomy in how a domain selects its routes; each domain can employ whatever criteria it chooses. Though not mandating any global criteria, BGP carries varied information that facilitates selection of the route. For example, a BIS may establish its preferences using the information carried in the AS-PATH attribute, like the number of domains in the attribute or the presence or absence of particular domains. Thus, in addition to suppression of routing-information looping, the AS-PATH powerfully affects the BGP route-selection algorithm.

Because suppression of routing-information looping is done via the AS-PATH attribute, lack of a globally agreed-upon metric has no implications for the correct operation of the protocol. Therefore, the only thing that is needed to provide consistent operation across multiple domains is to standardize on the mechanism for exchanging the results of the route-selection procedure (results of route computation), while allowing the selection procedures (criteria) that affect the route selection to be locally significant and private.*

As with EGP, in certain cases it might be desirable for a BIS participating in BGP to advertise to its neighbor some other IS as the next hop to a destination. Unlike EGP, however, BGP doesn't restrict this functionality to a particular domain—a BIS in any domain can perform the function. The network-layer address of the next hop is carried in the well-known mandatory NEXT-HOP path attribute.

Using capabilities provided by the NEXT-HOP path attribute allows significant simplification of operations when a domain is fully contained within one multiaccess subnetwork (e.g., X.25, SMDS, ATM). Then it is sufficient to deploy a few BISs within the domain (one may need more than one BIS for redundancy). These BISs, usually referred to as *route servers,* would maintain BGP peering with BISs in adjacent domains that are connected to the subnetwork forming the domain itself. Routing information would flow from one adjacent domain through route servers to other

---

* Ross Callon (Wellfleet) provided this succinct characterization.[25]

adjacent domains. No routing information needs to be exchanged directly between any adjacent domains. However, NPDU flow would completely bypass route servers—NPDUs will be forwarded directly between BISs in adjacent domains.

A BIS can unilaterally terminate routing-information exchange and deacquire its neighbor by sending to it a Notification message and terminating the transport connection used by BGP. A BIS can also terminate routing information exchange and deacquire its neighbor when it determines that the neighbor is unreachable, or when the BIS detects termination of the transport connection with the neighbor. Whenever a BIS terminates routing exchange and deacquires its neighbor, all the routes received from the neighbor should be removed from the Adj-RIB-In associated with that neighbor, and the BIS should rerun its route-selection algorithm.

BGP requires all the internal neighbors within a domain to exchange BGP routing information with one another. One way to satisfy this requirement is by maintaining a full-mesh BGP relationship among all the BISs within a domain. A possible alternative to a full mesh is to use intra-domain routing procedures to disseminate BGP information among internal neighbors. LinkState protocols that use flooding (e.g., OSPF, IS-IS) are especially well suited for this purpose. Each of the choices above has its pros and cons. For a domain where the number of BISs constitutes a relatively small percentage of the number of ISs, a full-mesh approach may be preferred. For a domain where most of the ISs are BISs, using intra-domain routing procedures may be a better alternative.

4.3.4   Scaling Mechanisms: Route Aggregation

To deal with a large and rapidly growing Internet, BGP provides a mechanism that allows reduction of the volume of routing information that needs to be handled by BISs. Essential to this mechanism is the technique of hierarchical routing first introduced by Kleinrock.[18] This technique assumes that the topology is more or less hierarchical. If network-layer address assignment is done in such a way as to reflect the underlying hierarchical topology, and NLRI can be expressed as variable length address prefixes, then NLRI can be aggregated by NLRI summarization. Summarization reduces the volume of NLRI by allowing aggregation of a set of topologically close destinations, depicted by a pair of address prefixes of length n that have the first $(n-1)$ bits in common, into a single address prefix of length $(n-1)$. The process may be applied recursively, and so the number of destinations covered by a single address prefix is limited only by the network-layer address space. As an extreme case, an address prefix of length 0 covers all destinations.

The current Internet exhibits a natural hierarchy along the service-provider/service-subscriber lines. A single service provider interconnects a large number of service subscribers. The providers themselves are often interconnected indirectly via other providers (e.g., the NSFNET Backbone interconnects several regional providers, like

NYSERNET, BarrNet, and NEARNET). Continental boundaries provide yet another natural level of hierarchy. These factors make a hierarchical routing technique well suited to the Internet. Addressing plans that exploit the Internet's hierarchy and make hierarchical routing possible are being developed both for IP[7,34] and CLNP.[3]

Contrary to a popular misconception, hierarchical address assignment does not imply that routing must follow a strict hierarchy. A BIS may maintain multiple FIB entries whose destination addresses exhibit a subset relation. When forwarding an NPDU, a BIS matches the destination address of the NPDU against all the entries in its FIB. The FIB entry with the prefix that provides the longest match is used for forwarding. Thus, within one FIB a more specific route (the one with the longer address prefix) always takes precedence over a less specific route (the one with the shorter address prefix). Propagating a more specific route allows overriding of strict hierarchical routing when necessary.

Providing NLRI summarization in the context of BGP implies that two routes (whose NLRI can be summarized) could be combined into one—a process known as *route aggregation*. However, in addition to NLRI summarization, route aggregation requires the ability to combine path attributes. Rules for combining path attributes are specific to individual attributes. For example, to allow combination of AS-PATH attributes, the attribute is defined as a sequence of *path segments*. Each segment may be of type AS-SEQUENCE or AS-SET. An AS-SEQUENCE path segment carries a sequence of domains that a route has traversed so far. An AS-SET path segment carries a set of domains that a route has traversed so far. AS-SEQUENCE path segments associated with several routes that need to be aggregated may be combined into a single AS-SET path segment of the aggregated route by applying the set union operation to the set of autonomous system numbers in each AS-SEQUENCE path segment.

4.3.5 Support for Controlled Resource Sharing

One of the key functions that needs to be supported in an internet comprising multiple administrations is the ability of a domain to control the use of its resources. In the context of inter-domain routing this control can be accomplished by providing a mechanism that allows a domain to control its *transit traffic*—traffic that is neither destined for nor originated within the domain. To support this functionality, BGP uses the technique of *controlled distribution* of NLRI. This technique was first pioneered in the NSFNET Backbone[1,2,29] and is based on the rather simple observation that an NPDU's flow is determined by the flow of NLRI and that the direction of the NPDU's flow is opposite to the direction of NLRI flow. In other words, choices a BIS may have when forwarding NPDUs are constrained by the routing information and more specifically by the NLRI the BIS receives from its neighbors.

BGP supports controlled distribution of routing information by allowing a BIS to advertise to its external neighbor some, all, or none of the routes stored in the BIS's Loc-FIB. Decisions about what routes to advertise are local to the BIS but may take into account various path attributes of a route. A BIS can make different decisions for different external neighbors.

In addition to providing support for controlled resource sharing, the controlled distribution of routing information used by BGP also makes it possible to provide each BIS with only the information it needs—a BIS doesn't maintain routing information that is of no use to the BIS. This property should not be underestimated in view of the need to maintain mutual autonomy about the amount of routing-information overhead one domain can impose on others.

4.3.6   Selecting among Multiple Entry/Exit Points

Although inter-domain routing in general, and BGP in particular, are intended to separate intra-domain routing in different domains, in some cases it may be beneficial to be able to leak certain intra-domain routing information across a domain's boundaries. For example, when two domains are interconnected via multiple external neighbors, it may be beneficial for one domain to be aware of certain aspects of the internal topology of the other domain. In this way, when ISs within a domain forward NPDUs to destinations reachable through an adjacent domain, such forwarding will result in picking up the most appropriate exit/entry BISs.

To provide this functionality, BGP uses the MULTI-EXIT-DISC path attribute. The value of this attribute is a nonnegative number. When a BIS receives multiple routes to a destination, and the routes carry the MULTI-EXIT-DISC attribute, the BIS may use the value of the attribute in its route-selection algorithm, provided that the AS-PATH attribute of all these routes is the same. The choice to use, or not to use, MULTI-EXIT-DISC for route selection is left to an individual BIS and is controlled via system management.

As an example of possible use of the MULTI-EXIT-DISC attribute, a BIS that originates a BGP route to some of the destinations within its own domain may take the metric of the intra-domain path to these destinations and use it to construct the MULTI-EXIT-DISC attribute of the route. As a result, intra-domain routing information (the metric of the intra-domain path) will be carried across a domain's boundary and may influence route selection in an adjacent domain. This arrangement may be further generalized to support a limited form of load splitting, where traffic between a given source and a given destination may take different paths, as long as all these paths are confined to the same sequence of domains. The value carried by the MULTI-EXIT-DISC attribute also can be used when injecting BGP routes into intra-domain routing. This approach, in effect, would result in importing intra-domain routing information from one domain into another.

4.3.7 BGP Shortcomings

Although BGP is a significant improvement over EGP, the protocol has its own shortcomings.

To begin with, BGP provides a scalable mechanism for aggregating/abstracting NLRI via a combination of address prefixes and route-aggregation procedures; the protocol is rather weak in aggregating/abstracting topology information carried in the AS-PATH attribute. For example, a route with an extreme case of NLRI aggregation (a prefix of length 0) should have in its AS-PATH attribute autonomous system numbers of all the domains in the Internet.

BGP identifies domains using autonomous system numbers. Because autonomous system numbers are 16-bit entities, the number of domains within a single internet is limited to 65,536. This total is likely to be insufficient for very large internets (10^9 to 10^{12} hosts).

Control over distribution of routing information provided by BGP is limited to adjacent domains. A domain has no mechanism within the protocol to control how other domains (e.g., adjacent domains) redistribute routes received from the domain. That lack limits a domain's flexibility in controlling resource sharing.

BGP provides at most one route to a destination. That constraint immediately rules out any ability to support multiple routes with different performance characteristics and/or administrative restrictions attached to them.

Finally, BGP is designed to be used as an inter-domain routing protocol in conjunction with IP. Today's Internet is multiprotocol and is likely to stay that way. Therefore, it might be beneficial to have a single inter-domain routing protocol that could accommodate multiple network-layer protocols (e.g., IP, CLNP, IPX). BGP has no mechanism for multiprotocol routing support. BGP's dependency on the IP-specific transport protocol, TCP, further complicates any attempts to add multiprotocol support features.

4.4 INTER-DOMAIN ROUTING PROTOCOL (IDRP)

The last protocol we describe in this chapter is the Inter-Domain Routing Protocol—IDRP.[16] It is built on some of the key ideas that formed the foundation of BGP—path-vector routing, scalability via information abstraction/aggregation, and controlled resource sharing via controlled distribution of routing information. Using these ideas, IDRP evolved into an inter-domain routing protocol that can accommodate many routing requirements and support flexible routing in fairly heterogeneous, multiprotocol (e.g., IP, CLNP) internets of practically unlimited size.

Because IDRP includes all the BGP-4 functionality as a proper subset, we just briefly cover IDRP features that are common with BGP, and focus more on the new functionality. Therefore, we strongly encourage the reader to thoroughly read Section 4.3 before reading this section.*

4.4.1 IDRP Topological Model

Like BGP, IDRP places no restrictions on the inter-domain topology. As with BGP, domains that participate in IDRP are not allowed to overlap—a BIS may belong to only one domain. To facilitate information aggregation/abstraction, IDRP added a new feature—it allows grouping of a set of connected domains into a *routing domain confederation* (RDC). A given domain may belong to more than one RDC. There are no restrictions on the number of RDCs to which a domain may simultaneously belong, and no preconditions on how RDCs should be formed—RDCs may be *nested,* may be *disjoint,* or may *overlap.* One RDC is nested within another RDC if all members (RDs) of the former are also members of the latter, but not vice versa. Two RDCs overlap if both of them have members in common, but also each of them has members that are not in the other. Two RDCs are disjoint if they have no members in common.

It is interesting that although IDRP allows RDCs to overlap, it prohibits overlap of individual domains. The reason is that when RDCs overlap, routing both within RDCs and between RDCs is determined solely by IDRP and therefore correct routing can be ensured by IDRP alone. In contrast, when individual domains overlap, routing within domains is determined by intra-domain routing, but routing between domains is determined by IDRP. Therefore, correct routing can't be ensured by IDRP alone. Moreover, Link-State based intra-domain routing protocols (e.g., OSPF, IS-IS) can't guarantee loop-free NPDU hop-by-hop forwarding in the presence of overlapping domains.[36]

Each domain participating in IDRP is assigned a unique *routing domain identifier* (RDI). Syntactically, an RDI is represented as an OSI network-layer address. Because these addresses have variable length, it follows that using them for RDIs allows for a practically unlimited number of domains within one internet. For example, using RDIs of up to 20 octets allows for up to 2^{160} domains—in contrast, BGP allows only up to 2^{16} domains. Each RDC is assigned a unique *routing domain confederation identifier* (RDCI). RDCIs are assigned out of the address space allocated for RDIs—RDCIs and RDIs are syntactically indistinguishable. Procedures for assigning and managing RDIs and RDCIs are outside the scope of the protocol. But because RDIs are syntactically nothing more than network-layer addresses, and RDCIs are syntactically nothing more than RDIs, it is expected that RDI and RDCI assignment and management would be part of the network-layer assignment and management procedures.

---

*   For more information, see Y. Rekhter, "Inter-Domain Routing Protocol (IDRP)," *Internet-working: Research and Experience,* Vol. 4, No. 2, pp. 61–80, John Wiley & Sons, Ltd., June 1993.

IDRP requires a BIS to be preconfigured with the RDI of the domain the BIS belongs to. If a BIS belongs to a domain that is a member of one or more RDCs, then the BIS has to be preconfigured with RDCIs of all the RDCs containing the domain, and with information about the relations between the RDCs (nested or overlapped).

Like BGP, IDRP distinguishes between *internal* and *external* neighbors. Domains are said to be *adjacent* if they have BISs that are external neighbors of each other.

4.4.2 IDRP Routing Information

Like BGP, IDRP defines a *route* as a pairing between NLRI and a set of attributes of a path toward the destinations depicted by the NLRI. IDRP incorporates BGP's path attribute taxonomy—it defines *well-known mandatory, well-known discretionary, optional-transitive,* and *optional-nontransitive* attributes. In addition, IDRP introduces a separate category of well-known discretionary path attributes—*distinguishing* path attributes. One may conceptually think of such attributes as tags. Tagging routes with distinguishing attributes is used in IDRP to support multiple routes to a destination. These routes may differ in some performance characteristics (e.g., delay, residual error rate), administrative constraints, or security, or a combination of these.

Each route has associated with it a set of distinguishing path attributes. The set may be empty or may include one or more attributes. IDRP places certain restrictions on the permissible combination of distinguishing attributes that can be present within a set. However, these restrictions are not inherent in IDRP, but rather reflect constraints imposed by a network-layer protocol, like CLNP, on the possible combination of optional network-layer parameters (e.g., Quality of Service, Security) that are allowed within a single NPDU. For example, a route can't have a set of distinguishing attributes that contains both EXPENSE and DELAY. The reason is CLNP disallows EXPENSE and DELAY Quality of Service maintenance parameters to be present simultaneously within the same NPDU.

4.4.3 Basic Functionality

Like EGP and BGP, IDRP operations may be partitioned into three components: neighbor acquisition, neighbor reachability, and exchange of routing information.

Neighbor acquisition in IDRP is based on a conventional *three-way handshake* algorithm. A BIS begins the acquisition by sending an Open message to a neighbor. The neighbor may either decide to be acquired, so that it responds with its own Open message, or it may reject the acquisition by responding with an IDRP Error message. If a BIS receives an Open message from its neighbor that was sent in response to the Open message sent by the BIS, then the BIS completes the acquisition by sending a Keepalive message to the neighbor. IDRP allows a pair of neighbors to independently send Open messages to each other—one of the BISs will resend an Open message acknowledging the Open message received from its neighbor.

To monitor the operational status of an acquired neighbor, IDRP uses Keepalive messages. A BIS is required to periodically transmit Keepalive messages to all its acquired neighbors. If a BIS doesn't receive a Keepalive message from its neighbor within more than Holding Time, as specified by the neighbor in its Open message, the BIS declares its neighbor to be unreachable.

Two neighbors that have acquired each other and are mutually reachable can exchange routing information (routes). The information is carried in the Update messages. A single Update message may carry more than one route; however, if multiple routes are carried, all the nondistinguishing path attributes of these routes must be identical, but each route may have its own set of distinguishing attributes. To separate distinguishing attributes of multiple routes carried within a single Update message into sets associated with individual routes, IDRP uses a well-known mandatory-path attribute, called the ROUTE-SEPARATOR. Each route exchanged between a pair of BISs carries as part of its ROUTE-SEPARATOR attribute a 32-bit entity associated with the route, called the ROUTE-ID. The protocol requires the ROUTE-ID to be unambiguous within a given pair of neighboring BISs. The ROUTE-ID is used as a shorthand for exchanging information about unfeasible routes—when a previously advertised route has to be withdrawn, the BIS that advertised the route indicates its unfeasibility by just sending its ROUTE-ID in an Update message.

Like BGP, IDRP provides support for incremental exchange of routing information. However, in contrast with BGP that operates over a reliable transport-layer protocol—TCP—IDRP operates directly over a connectionless network protocol—CLNP. Therefore, IDRP provides its own mechanism for reliable delivery of routing information. The reliable-delivery mechanism is based on a combination of sequence numbers carried by each individual Update message, acknowledgments usually carried by Keepalive messages, and retransmission of unacknowledged Update messages.

When the internet topology is relatively stable, using incremental exchange of routing information imposes lower overhead, compared to using full updates (like the one used by EGP). However, during large instabilities incremental exchange of routing information may generate more overhead than full updates do. If we describe routing information as a function of time, then the overhead associated with using incremental exchange is proportional to the first derivative of this function. Thus, the decision on which of the two techniques for exchanging routing information (incremental versus full) generates less overhead boils down to whether the first derivative of the routing information is less than or greater than the routing information itself. To minimize overhead in both cases (either in a stable or unstable topology) IDRP, in addition to the incremental exchange of routing information, also provides support for a full update of routing information. This feature is implemented by using RIB

Refresh messages. These messages have three flavors: REFRESH-REQUEST, REFRESH-START, and REFRESH-END. A BIS may update its Adj-RIB-In associated with a particular neighbor by sending to that neighbor a RIB Refresh message indicating a REFRESH-REQUEST. The neighbor replies with a RIB REFRESH message indicating a REFRESH-START, followed by a complete set of routing information passed in one or more Update messages, followed by a RIB Refresh message indicating a REFRESH-END. Alternatively a BIS may force its neighbor to update an Adj-RIB-In associated with the BIS by sending to that neighbor a RIB Refresh message indicating a REFRESH-START, followed by a complete set of routing information passed in one or more Update messages, followed by a RIB Refresh message indicating a REFRESH-END.

To reflect IDRP capabilities for supporting multiple routes to a destination, we augment the model of the routing information base (RIB) we used for BGP (see Section 4.3.3) as follows. Instead of a single Loc-RIB, a BIS maintains multiple Loc-RIBs. Associated with each Loc-RIB is a permissible set of distinguishing attributes, called RIB-Atts (routing information base attributes). As we have mentioned (see Section 4.4.2), the decision of what constitutes a *permissible set* has to be made in the context of a particular network-layer protocol. Instead of a single Adj-RIB-In per neighbor, a BIS maintains multiple Adj-RIBs-In per neighbor; each Adj-RIB-In has RIB-Atts of a particular Loc-RIB. Similarly, a BIS maintains multiple Adj-RIBs-Out per neighbor, with each Adj-RIB-Out having the RIB-Atts of a particular Loc-RIB.

Each BIS is preconfigured (via system management) with a set of RIB-Atts, each consisting of a set of distinguishing attributes that the BIS is willing to support. A pair of neighboring BISs, as part of the neighbor-acquisition component, exchange in the Open message the set of all the RIB-Atts each BIS is willing to support. This information is used by the routing-information exchange component to decide whether a BIS may pass a route to an external neighbor—if a neighbor doesn't support a particular combination of distinguishing attributes, there is no reason to send a route with such a combination of the attributes to the neighbor. IDRP expects that within a domain all the BISs will support the same set of RIB-Atts; different domains may support different RIB-Atts.

Whenever a BIS receives a route from its neighbor, the BIS checks whether the set of distinguishing attributes of the route matches the set of distinguishing attributes in one of its RIB-Atts. If it does, the route is placed in the appropriate Adj-RIB-In (the one that is associated with the neighbor and has RIB-Atts that contain all the distinguishing attributes of the route). Like BGP, the IDRP route-selection algorithm is modeled as requiring a BIS to assign a nonnegative integer, called a *Degree of Preference,* to each route received from the BIS's external neighbors. A BIS selects among all the routes to a given destination with the same set of distinguishing attributes received from all its external neighbors the one with the highest Degree of Preference and sends it to all its internal neighbors. When sending a route to an internal neighbor, the Degree of Preference assigned to the route by the sending BIS is carried as part of the ROUTE-SEPARATOR path attribute. Among all the routes to a given set of destinations, with the same set of distinguishing attributes received from all the neighbors (both external and internal), the BIS selects the one with the highest Degree of Preference and installs it in its Loc-RIB with RIB-Atts that consist of all the distinguishing attributes of the route. Once a route is placed in one of the Loc-RIBs, the BIS also adjusts its FIB. The BIS may advertise to its external neighbor any route (after appropriately updating the path attributes of the route) that is installed in one of the Loc-RIBs, provided that the neighbor supports the set of distinguishing attributes of the route.

Providing loop-free steady-state NPDU forwarding with IDRP, as with EGP and BGP, requires suppression of routing-information looping. Like BGP, IDRP records the domains the routing information has traversed so far and uses this information to suppress routing-information looping. The information is carried in the RD-PATH attribute. If we ignore the ability of IDRP to group domains into confederations, then the handling of this attribute is quite similar to the way the AS-PATH attribute is handled in BGP. Whenever a BIS sends a route to its external neighbor, the BIS updates the RD-PATH attribute with the RDI of the domain the BIS belongs to. Whenever a BIS receives a route from an external neighbor, the BIS checks whether the RD-PATH attribute contains the RDI of the domain the BIS belongs to. If it does, the route may be stored in the appropriate Adj-RIB-In but can't be used as input to the route-selection algorithm.

Like BGP, IDRP doesn't specify what criteria a BIS should use when assigning a Degree of Preference to a route. IDRP doesn't have a globally agreed-upon metric—significance of the metric (expressed as the Degree of Preference) is confined to a single domain. To facilitate route selection, IDRP provides two new, well-known mandatory attributes that are not present in BGP: CAPACITY and RD-HOP-COUNT. The CAPACITY attribute provides information about capacity of the route. The RD-HOP-COUNT attribute provides an upper bound on the number of domains the routing information has traversed so far. Furthermore, for routes with a non-empty set of distinguishing attributes, the route-selection procedure can be facilitated by taking into account information carried by the distinguishing attributes (e.g., the DELAY distinguishing attribute carries information about delay associated with a route).

Like BGP, IDRP provides limited support for exporting intra-domain routing information across domain boundaries. The support is realized via an optional non-transitive attribute, called MULTI-EXIT-DISC. Its purpose and use are precisely the same as in BGP (see Section 4.3.6).

Like BGP, IDRP provides special mechanisms to facilitate inter-domain routing in the presence of domains constructed out of multiaccess subnetworks. A BIS may pass to its neighbor a route that specifies the network-layer address of some other IS as the next hop to destinations depicted by the NLRI of the route. The information about the next-hop network-layer address is passed in the NEXT-HOP path attribute. In contrast with BGP, where NEXT-HOP is a well-known mandatory-path attribute, in IDRP this attribute is well-known discretionary. Whenever a route doesn't carry this attribute, it is assumed that the BIS that sends the route should be used as the next hop. In addition to the network layer address of the next hop, IDRP provides the link layer address of the next hop. This feature facilitates operations by eliminating the need to perform a separate mapping between network-layer and link-layer addresses of the next-hop BIS.

A BIS can unilaterally terminate routing-information exchange with its neighbor by sending to it a Cease message. A BIS is also required to terminate routing-information exchange whenever it detects IDRP protocol errors. Then the BIS sends an IDRP Error message to the neighbor. Whenever a BIS terminates routing-information exchange with its neighbor, the BIS removes all the routes received from that neighbor from all the Adj-RIBs-In associated with that neighbor and reruns its route-selection algorithm.

Like BGP, IDRP requires all the internal neighbors within a domain to exchange IDRP routing information with one another. The choices to satisfy this requirement are the same as with BGP: either full-mesh IDRP sessions among all the BISs within a domain or use of an intra-domain routing protocol to flood IDRP information throughout a domain.

IDRP provides mandatory support for data integrity and optional support for data-origin authentication for all its messages. Each message carries a 16-octet *digital signature,* called the VALIDATION-PATTERN, which is computed by applying the MD-4 algorithm[39] to the context of the message itself. This signature provides support for data integrity. To support data-origin authentication a BIS, when computing a digital signature of a message, may prepend and append additional information to the message. This information is not passed as part of the message but is known to the receiver. Though the scheme is rather simple and involves little overhead, it is shown to be fairly robust.[42]

4.4.4 Scalability—Reducing Routing Information

One of the major design goals of IDRP is to support inter-domain routing in very large internets—at least 10^9 to 10^{12} hosts. Thus the protocol strongly emphasizes the mechanisms for routing information aggregation/abstraction. In the context of IDRP, routing information that depends on the size of an internet, and therefore requires mechanisms for aggregation/abstraction, consists of three components: NLRI, inter-domain topology information (carried by the RD-PATH attribute), and information that controls transit traffic through a domain. All other path attributes are of fixed size and thus introduce fixed overhead, independent of the size of an internet. In this section we describe mechanisms for providing aggregation/abstraction of NLRI and topology information. Mechanisms for providing aggregation/abstraction of information that controls transit traffic are covered in Section 4.4.5.

The mechanism used by IDRP for aggregation/abstraction of NLRI is essentially the same as that used by BGP—a combination of expressing NLRI as address prefixes, hierarchical address assignment, and NLRI summarization. Like BGP, this mechanism doesn't confine the actual NPDU forwarding to a strict hierarchy—a BIS may maintain within its FIB multiple entries whose NLRI exhibits a subset relation. NPDU forwarding is done by performing a longest match of the destination address carried by an NPDU against all the entries in the FIB. Therefore, propagating a more specific route (a route with a longer address prefix) allows support of nonhierarchical routing by overriding a less specific route (a route with a shorter address prefix).

Like BGP, NLRI summarization implies that two or more routes (whose NLRI can be summarized) could be combined into one—a process known as *route aggregation*. One of the mechanisms used by IDRP for route aggregation is the same as the one used by BGP—route aggregation is performed by aggregating individual path attributes and performing NLRI summarization of several routes. To provide aggregation of the RD-PATH attribute, IDRP specifies this attribute as a sequence of *path segments*. Two path segments that are used for aggregation of RD-PATH are RD-SEQ and RD-SET. RD-SEQ is the same as AS-SEQUENCE in BGP; RD-SET is the same as AS-SET in BGP. Rules for aggregating several RD-SEQ path segments into a single RD-SET path segment are the same as in BGP—apply the set union operation to the set of RDIs in each RD-SEQ path segment and place the result in the RD-SET path segment.

The major drawback of the route-aggregation mechanism is its rather limited capability for aggregation/abstraction of topology information—recall that a route with NLRI that consists of a prefix of zero length would have to contain all the RDIs of all the domains within an internet (see Section 4.3.7). IDRP solves this problem by providing a mechanism for aggregating topology information (carried by the RD-PATH attribute) based on the concept of routing domain confederations (RDCs). Whenever a route traverses a set of domains that belongs to a common RDC, the RD-PATH attribute of the route records this set of domains. However, once the route leaves the RDC, the set of domains traversed within the RDC is replaced by a single identifier—the RDCI.

The presence of RDCs complicates the handling of the RD-PATH attribute very little. Recall that each BIS is preconfigured with the set of RDCs that the BIS's own domain belongs to. This information is exchanged between BISs in Open messages as part of the neighbor-acquisition component of IDRP. Given this information, a BIS can determine for each of its external neighbors whether the neighbor's domain is in the same set of RDCs as the BIS's own domain. If the set of RDCs is the same, then the handling of the RD-PATH attribute isn't affected by the presence of RDCs. If the set of RDCs is different, then whenever the BIS belongs to an RDC, such that the neighbor's domain is not in it, we say that a route passed from the BIS to that neighbor *exits* the RDC. Whenever the neighbor's domain belongs to an RDC, such that the BIS's own domain is not in it, we say that a route passed from the BIS to that neighbor *enters* the RDC. The RD-PATH attribute, in addition to the RD-SEQ and RD-SET path segments, may also contain two new types of path segments, ENTRY-SEQ and ENTRY-SET. An ENTRY-SEQ path segment carries the sequence of RDCs (expressed as RDCIs) that a route has entered but not yet exited. An ENTRY-SET path segment carries the set of RDCs (expressed as RDCIs) that a route has entered, but not yet exited. Whenever a route enters an RDC, the first BIS in the RDC updates the RD-PATH attribute of that route with the RDCI of that RDC, indicating that the RDC has been entered. Whenever a route exits an RDC, the last BIS in the RDC replaces the set of RDIs within that RDC with a single RDCI of the RDC. This step, in effect, provides topology information (RD-PATH) abstraction.

In the preceding section we describe how IDRP deals with suppressing routing information looping in the absence of RDCs. To suppress looping of routing information in the presence of RDCs, whenever a BIS receives a route from an external neighbor, the BIS checks the RD-SEQ and RD-SET path segments of the RD-PATH attribute of the route for the presence of either the RDI of the domain the BIS is in or one or more RDCIs associated with the RDCs that the BIS's domain is in. If they are present, the route may be placed in the appropriate Adj-RIB-In but can't be passed as input to the route-selection algorithm.

4.4.5 Support for Controlled Resource Sharing

Like BGP, IDRP supports controlled resource sharing via controlled distribution of routing information. Compared with BGP, however, IDRP significantly enhances mechanisms controlling such distribution. Recall that in BGP, control over the distribution of routing information is limited to adjacent domains. IDRP overcomes this limitation in several ways.

First, IDRP introduces two new, well-known discretionary-path attributes, DIST-LIST-INCL and DIST-LIST-EXCL. The DIST-LIST-INCL path attribute contains the list of RDs or RDCs, expressed as RDIs or RDCIs, to which the route carrying the attribute can be distributed. The DIST-LIST-EXCL path attribute contains the list of RDs or RDCs, expressed as RDIs and RDCIs, to which the route carrying the attribute is not to be distributed. A BIS may update DIST-LIST-INCL by removing RDIs or RDCIs from it; a BIS may update DIST-LIST-EXCL by adding RDIs and RDCIs to it. By using these two attributes IDRP allows a domain to extend control over the distribution of routing information beyond adjacent domains. The ability to specify restrictions on distribution of routing information in terms of RDCs, rather than individual RDs, provides a mechanism for abstracting information that controls distribution of routing information.

The second mechanism that can be used to control distribution of routing information is based on how RDCs are formed. For a set of nested or overlapped RDCs this mechanism allows constraints on the flow of routing information by using a well-known discretionary-path attribute, called HIERARCHICAL-RECORDING. The value of this attribute is initially set to 1. When a BIS passes a route to an external neighbor, so that the neighbor is in an RDC that the BIS's own domain is not in, the value of the attribute is set to 0. IDRP allows a BIS to advertise to an external neighbor a route with the value of the HIERARCHICAL-RECORDING attribute set to 0, only if the RDCs that the neighbor's domain is in form a subset (need not be proper) of the RDCs of the BIS's own domain. If one thinks about entering an RDC as a *down* move and exiting an RDC as an *up* move, then the constraint on the propagation of routing information that can be enforced via the HIERARCHICAL-RECORDING attribute may be thought of as a *two-phase* rule: once routing information starts to go down, it can never go up.

Finally, the third mechanism that can be used to control distribution of routing information is based on using distinguishing attributes. By restricting the set of RIB-Atts supported by BISs within a domain, the domain restricts the flow of NPDUs to those which carry optional parameters (e.g., DELAY) that match the distinguishing attributes defined by the set of RIB-Atts.

4.4.6   Multiprotocol Inter-Domain Routing with IDRP

Although IDRP was originally designed as an inter-domain routing protocol to be used in conjunction with CLNP, the protocol includes capabilities that make it suitable as an inter-domain routing protocol in conjunction with other connectionless network-layer protocols like IP or IPX.

The extensions needed to support multiple network-layer protocols are rather straightforward: IDRP tags NLRI and the network-layer address of the next-hop IS carried in the NEXT-HOP path attribute with a network-layer protocol identifier. This identifier unambiguously specifies the network-layer protocol associated with NLRI or NEXT-HOP information. IDRP provides two mechanisms for specifying the identifiers: using ISO IPI/SPI[15] or using ISO 8802 LSAP.[13]

Support for multiprotocol inter-domain routing with IDRP can be realized in two modes: *integrated* and *ships-in-the-night*. In the integrated mode, a BIS operates a single instance of IDRP, but this instance carries routes whose NLRI and NEXT-HOP information is associated with multiple network-layer protocols. In the ships-in-the-night mode, a BIS operates multiple instances of IDRP, one per network-layer protocol supported by the BIS. Each instance operates over the network-layer protocol supported by that instance. For example, an instance of IDRP that supports inter-domain routing for IP operates over IP. Because IDRP makes minimal assumptions about services provided by a connectionless network-layer protocol, specifying IDRP operations over any of the existing connectionless network-layer protocols is rather straightforward. An example of such a specification for IP is presented in reference 8.

IDRP leaves the choice of using either the integrated or the ships-in-the-night modes of operation to a domain administrator. Within a single multiprotocol internet both of these modes can be intermixed, so that some domains will use IDRP in the integrated mode and some in the ships-in-the-night mode.

4.5 CONCLUSIONS

In this chapter we cover three inter-domain routing protocols: EGP, BGP, and IDRP. We find some commonalities among them. All the protocols belong to a category of distributed routing protocols capable of adapting to topological changes. They all may be viewed as point-to-point protocols because they govern exchange of routing information between a pair of BISs. We find a great deal of similarity among these protocols in the type of information exchanged; it always includes NLRI and the network-layer address of the IS that should be used as the next hop on a path to destinations depicted by the NLRI. In all three protocols, distribution of routing information is preceded by computation over the routing information; only the result of the computation is distributed. Thus the algorithms used for route selection can be kept private outside the scope of the protocols—the protocols govern only exchange of routing information. This exchange in turn provides autonomy needed for inter-domain routing. It also reduces the volume of routing information, which results in improved scaling properties. Two of the protocols described in this chapter, BGP and IDRP, are based on a common routing algorithm—*path-vector*.

Differences among these protocols are also quite noticeable. From EGP, a protocol with very limited applicability and restricted functionality, inter-domain routing evolved first to BGP and then to IDRP. Each successor in this evolutionary chain was developed using the experience gained with its predecessors, as well as the operational requirements for inter-domain routing. Although EGP constrains its use to a strict two-level hierarchy, BGP and IDRP provide correct operation in the presence of an arbitrary inter-domain topology. IDRP provides multiple enhancements over BGP to deal with information aggregation/abstraction, as well as with support for policy-based routing.

The protocols described in this chapter are sufficiently versatile to provide inter-domain routing functionality in a variety of environments. Even if the protocols were designed to be used in conjunction with connectionless network-layer protocols, nothing inherent in these protocols would preclude their use in conjunction with connection-oriented network-layer protocols. For example, it should be possible to use IDRP as an inter-domain routing protocol in conjunction with ATM. Two of the protocols, BGP and IDRP, carry enough information to allow support for both hop-by-hop and source-routing forwarding mechanisms (provided that the source route is expressed in terms of domains).

As we have mentioned (see Section 4.1.3), support for routing policies is essential for inter-domain routing. To be practical, however, such support has to scale to very large internets. These two requirements combined imply that the feasibility of supporting a particular policy needs to be carefully evaluated for the policy's effect on the overall overhead, scalability, and autonomy. Because policies are nothing more than constraints and rules on who can use whose resources, potentially there is a wide variety of factors on which routing policies may depend. If left unconstrained, the list of *conceivable* requirements that one may wish to impose on the set of policies that a solution to inter-domain routing has to support is limited only by the stretch of our imagination. Given our current knowledge about possible alternatives, it is highly unlikely that a solution that meets all the requirements will be found in the foreseeable future. The reason is that scalability always implies ability to reduce the volume of routing information via abstraction. Abstraction, in turn, implies similarity of the information to be abstracted. On the other hand, diverse routing policies imply *dissimilarity* of routing information. In other words, an inherent conflict lies between the requirement to provide a scalable solution and the requirement to support an arbitrary set of routing policies.

IDRP doesn't pretend to claim that it can meet all the requirements for inter-domain routing that one can think of. Realize, however, that IDRP meets most of the requirements, and meets all the essential requirements for inter-domain routing. Rather than try to create a scheme where arbitrary requirements are encouraged at the expense of poor scaling properties, IDRP created a scheme wherein complexities associated with supporting some specialized routing requirements are discouraged, so that a scalable solution can be achieved. IDRP is designed to provide "a minimum of ancillary information, while providing a maximum of routing functionality,"[14] as well as to deal with flexible support for control over resource sharing and heterogeneous routing requirements. Analysis and practical experience show that the *path-vector* routing technology used by IDRP is a promising candidate for scalable and flexible inter-domain routing.[4,33,35] All these factors make IDRP well suited as an inter-domain routing protocol for heterogeneous internets of practically unlimited size.

Recently, additional efforts have emerged to address the need for specialized routing requirements but address them so as to avoid placing a burden on all the domains and instead localize them to the domains that need such requirements. The overall architecture of this scheme is described in reference 5. The architecture consists of two components, one to handle widely used requirements and one to deal with specialized requirements. The first component uses IDRP; the protocol for the second component is described in reference 6.

REFERENCES

1 H-W. Braun, "The NSFNET Routing Architecture," *Internet Request for Comments 1093,* February 1989.

2 H-W. Braun, "Models of Policy Based Routing," *Internet Request for Comments 1104,* June 1989.

3 R. Colella, E. Gardner, and R. Callon, "Guidelines for OSI NSAP Allocation in the Internet," *Internet Request for Comments 1237,* July 1991.

4 D. Estrin, Y. Rekhter, and S. Hotz, "Scalable Inter-Domain Routing Architecture," *SIGCOMM*, Vol. 22, No. 4, pp. 40–52, 1992.

5 D. Estrin, Y. Rekhter, and S. Hotz, "A Unified Approach to Inter-Domain Routing," *Internet Request for Comments 1322,* May 1992.

6 D. Estrin, T. Li, and Y. Rekhter, "Source Demand Routing Protocol: A Component of the Unified Approach to Inter-Domain Routing," *ConneXions,* Vol. 6, No. 11, November 1992, pp. 14–24.

7 V. Fuller, T. Li, and K. Varadhan, "Supernetting: An Address Assignment and Aggregation Strategy," *Internet Request for Comments 1519,* September 1993.

8 S. Hares, "IDRP for IP," *Internet Draft,* March 1993.

9 C. Hedrick, "Routing Information Protocol," *Internet Request for Comments 1058,* June 1988.

10 C. Hedrick, "An Introduction to IGRP," Laboratory for Computer Science Research, Rutgers University, August 1991.

11 J. Honig, D. Katz, M. Mathis, Y. Rekhter, and J. Yu, "Application of the Border Gateway Protocol in the Internet," *Internet Request for Comments 1164,* June 1990.

12 "Protocol for Providing the Connectionless-Mode Network Service," *ISO 8473,* 1988.

13 "Information Processing Systems—Local Area Networks," *ISO 8802,* 1989.

14 "OSI Routing Framework," *ISO/IEC TR 9575,* 1989.

15 "Protocol Identification in the Network Layer," *ISO/IEC TR 9577,* 1992.

16 "Protocol for Exchange of Inter-Domain Routing Information among Intermediate Systems to Support Forwarding of ISO 8473 PDUs," *ISO 10747.*

17 "Interaction and Routing Information Exchange between ISO 10589 (ISIS) and ISO 10747 (IDRP)," *ISO/IEC JTC 1/SC 6 N7535,* July 1992.

18 L. Kleinrock and K. Farouk, "Hierarchical Routing for Large Networks," *Computer Networks,* Vol. 1, 1977.

19 K. Lougheed and Y. Rekhter, "Border Gateway Protocol (BGP)," *Internet Request for Comments 1105,* June 1989.

20 K. Lougheed and Y. Rekhter, "A Border Gateway Protocol," *Internet Request for Comments 1163,* June 1990.

21 K. Lougheed and Y. Rekhter, "A Border Gateway Protocol (BGP-3)," *Internet Request for Comments 1267,* October 1991.

22 D. Mills, "Exterior Gateway Protocol Formal Specification," *Internet Request for Comments 904,* April 1984.

23 "NetWare Application Notes," *Novell Research,* September 1990, pp. 32–33.

24 Novell Inc., "IPX Router Specification," Revision A, Provo, 1992.

25 D. Piscitello and A. L. Chapin, *Open Systems Networking: TCP/IP and OSI,* Reading: Addison-Wesley, 1993.

26 J. Postel, "Internet Protocol," *Internet Request for Comments 791,* September 1981.

27 J. Postel, "Transmission Control Protocol," *Internet Request for Comments 793,* September 1981.

28 Y. Rekhter, "NSFNET Backbone SPF Based Interior Gateway Protocol," *Internet Request for Comments 1074,* October 1988.

29 Y. Rekhter, "EGP and Policy Based Routing in the New NSFNET Backbone," *Internet Request for Comments 1092,* February 1989.

30 Y. Rekhter, "Constructing Intra-AS Path Segments for an Inter-AS Path," *ACM CCR,* Vol. 21, No. 1, 1991, pp. 44–57.

31 Y. Rekhter and P. Gross, "Application of the Border Gateway Protocol in the Internet," *Internet Request for Comments 1268,* October 1991.

32 Y. Rekhter and B. Chinoy, "Injecting Inter-Autonomous System Routes into Intra-Domain System Routing," *Internetworking: Research and Experience,* Vol. 3, 1992, pp. 189–202.

33 Y. Rekhter, "IDRP Protocol Analysis: Storage Overhead," *ACM CCR,* Vol. 22, No. 2, April 1992, pp. 17–28.

34 Y. Rekhter and T. Li, "An Architecture for IP Address Allocation with CIDR," *Internet Request for Comments 1518,* September 1993.

35 Y. Rekhter, "Forwarding Database Overhead for Inter-Domain Routing," *ACM CCR,* Vol. 23, No. 1, January 1993.

36 Y. Rekhter, S. Hotz, and D. Estrin, "Constraints on Forming Clusters with Link-State Hop-by-Hop Routing," *IBM Research Report,* RC 19203 (83635), July 1994.

37 Y. Rekhter and T. Li, "A Border Gateway Protocol 4 (BGP-4)," *Internet Request for Comments 1654,* July 1994.

38 Y. Rekhter and P. Gross, "Application of the Border Gateway Protocol in the Internet," *Internet Request for Comments 1655,* July 1994.

39 R. Rivest, "The MD4 Message Digest Algorithm," *Internet Request for Comments 1186,* October 1990.

40 E. Rosen, "Exterior Gateway Protocol (EGP)," *Internet Request for Comments 827,* October 1982.

41 L. Seamonson and E. Rosen, "Stub Exterior Gateway Protocol," *Internet Request for Comments 888,* January 1984.

42 G. Tsudik, "Message Authentication with One-Way Hash Functions," *ACM CCR,* Vol. 22, No. 5, October 1992, pp. 29–38.

43 K. Varadhan, "BGP OSPF Interaction," *Internet Request for Comments 1403,* January 1993.

Link-State Routing

JOHN MOY

CONTENTS

Link-state routing, a more flexible and robust alternative to distance-vector rout-ing, was originally deployed in the mature ARPANET and continues in use throughout the Internet today. In the link-state context, a network becomes a graph of interconnected nodes and links. Each node forms a local view of the net-work, in terms of the properties of the links connecting it to neighboring nodes, hence the term "link-state." In the most common form of link-state routing, each node acts autonomously, distributing its link-state routing information to all other nodes and computing shortest paths from itself to all destinations based upon the link-state information obtained from other nodes. This chapter presents the basic link-state routing-information distribution and route-generation tech-niques and provides several examples of internetwork routing procedures based on the link-state paradigm.

5.1 INTRODUCTION

Link-state routing has become popular lately, as an alternative to more traditional approaches such as static routing and distance-vector routing. There is now a wide range of link-state routing protocols in use. The core of each of these protocols is a distributed and replicated database. This database is essentially a dynamic map of the network, describing the network's components and their current interconnections. From this database, optimal routes are calculated for the network's data traffic.

The first link-state protocol was developed by Bolt Beranek and Newman in 1979 for the ARPANET.[12] They found that a link-state protocol had significant advan-tages over their previous, Bellman-Ford-based routing protocol (see Chapter 3 for a description of the Bellman-Ford algorithm) in efficiency, reliability, loop freedom, and speed of adaptation. Since then, link-state routing protocols have been developed for a number of protocol stacks, including the OSPF protocol for TCP/IP,[16] the IS-IS protocol for OSI,[7] and NLSP for Novell's NetWare.[19] Link-state technology also forms the base of IBM's APPN network-node routing.[8]

Before delving into the details of link-state protocols, it is helpful to establish some definitions that will be used throughout this chapter. *Switches* denotes the devices that execute the link-state protocol and use the result to make forwarding decisions for application data. For example, in a TCP/IP environment the IP routers are the switches. Each switch is connected to several *network segments* (e.g., point-to-point serial lines, Ethernet segments) through *interfaces* or *links*. The entire set of switches, network segments, and their interconnecting links is called the *routing domain* or *net-work*. It is the purpose of the network to deliver data traffic between *applications*. These data are commonly in the form of *packets* or *datagrams*.

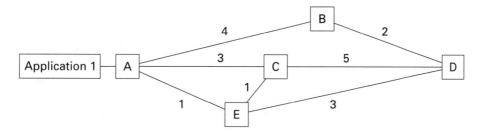

Figure 5.1   A simple routing domain. Boxes indicate switches, which are joined by point-to-point links. Each application is assumed to be attached to a particular switch.

The distributed and replicated database residing at the core of each link-state protocol is called the *link-state database*. Each switch maintains an identical copy of this database, which describes the complete map of the routing domain. The constituent pieces of the link-state database are called *link-state advertisements* or *LSAs*. Each switch is responsible for originating an LSA describing that switch's set of working interfaces. This LSA is then distributed to all other switches in the routing domain.

A procedure called *flooding* is used for distributing the LSAs throughout the routing domain. In flooding, a switch receiving an LSA on one interface sends the LSA out all its other interfaces. Flooding must be reliable and quick. A typical link-state protocol depends on the switches having identical databases to ensure that routing is correct and free from loops. When something in the routing domain changes (for example, a serial line becomes inoperative), a new LSA describing the change must be created and flooded to all switches. During the flooding, not all switches will have identical databases, with some having the new LSA and others not. But a reliable flooding algorithm ensures that the databases will synchronize after some period of convergence. Good flooding algorithms achieve distribution of LSAs quickly, ensuring that the convergence time is small—that is, on the order of the propagation delay across the network.

Once a switch has a synchronized link-state database, it remains for the switch to calculate the best paths for the network's application traffic, using the link-state database as input. This is called the *routing calculation*. Dijkstra's algorithm, also called *shortest path first* (SPF), is the most popular method for calculating best paths (see Chapter 31 in reference 24); for this reason, link-state protocols are also often called SPF-based protocols. However, other algorithms for calculating best paths are possible (see Section 5.4).

In the rest of this chapter we explore the main components of a link-state protocol in more detail. The network map in Figure 5.1 is used for illustration. In this figure, a simple network topology consists of a few switches (boxes labeled A through E) connected by point-to-point links. Each link is assigned a number, which indicates the cost of sending data traffic over the link. Applications are homed off a particular switch, to which they submit their data directly. It is then the job of routing to find the best path to the switch that services the destination of the data.

Various link-state protocols differ slightly in their ways of implementing these main components. In Sections 5.2 through 5.6, we discuss features commonly found in link-state protocols. No one link-state protocol, though, will have all the features described. The chapter ends with a summary of some link-state routing protocols, highlighting the areas where their algorithms provide unique support and/or solutions.

5.2 DESCRIBING THE ROUTING DOMAIN: LSAs

The routing domain is described by its link-state database's LSAs. Each LSA describes one switch's local environment in the routing domain. In particular, the switch's LSA includes:

- The identity of the switch itself

- A list of the switch's operational links (i.e., interfaces)

- The cost of each operational link, when used to forward application traffic

- The identity of the network segment or switch to which each link connects

- An indication of the applications (e.g., electronic mail, file transfer) homed off the switch. An application's location is usually described by its "address." For example, if the switch is an IP router, the IP network numbers of the router's directly connected network segments effectively describes the locations of the applications that will be sending or receiving data to or from the switch.

The link-state database that might result from the routing domain in Figure 5.1 is displayed in Figure 5.2. The database consists of five separate LSAs, one for each switch. Looking at switch A's LSA in detail, one sees that A advertises three active interfaces: one connecting to switch B with a cost of 4, one connecting to switch C with a cost of 3, and one connecting to switch E with a cost of 1. Switch A also indicates that it provides services for Application 1.

Each switch receives and stores these five LSAs. By examining the links described in the LSAs, and recording what the links connect, any given switch can construct a map of the routing domain. This procedure is indicated by the connecting lines in Figure 5.2. It is this map that is used as input to the routing calculation (see Section 5.4).

There is usually more information in an LSA than that listed above. Other fields that can usually be found in an LSA include:

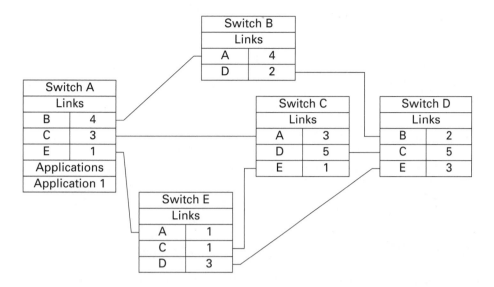

Figure 5.2 The routing domain's link-state database

- *Sequence number* When multiple instances of an LSA exist in the routing domain simultaneously, the sequence number is used to determine the most up-to-date instance.

- *Age of the LSA* This number is used to indicate when defunct LSAs should be discarded. It is also used to indicate when a switch should refresh its LSA, for robustness (see Section 5.6).

- *Checksum of the advertisement's contents* This number can be used to guard against data corruption, both during flooding and while the LSA is held in the switch's link-state database.

In any given link-state protocol, LSAs may also include additional descriptions of the switch and its links. Examples include:

- Separate link costs may be included for each type of service that the network supports, allowing, for example, delay-sensitive traffic to take separate paths from bulk file transfers.[7,16]

- The policies describing what kind of application traffic the switch is willing to forward may be included.[28]

- The location of multicast group members may be advertised in LSAs.[17]

- An indication of switch congestion may also be included.[5]

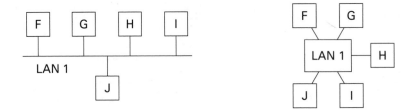

Figure 5.3   Representing a LAN in the link-state database

Adding these types of information to LSAs, and hence to the link-state database, enables more sophisticated routing-table calculations (see Section 5.4).

5.2.1 LAN Abstraction

So far we have considered only switches interconnected by point-to-point links. However, switches can also be connected by other network technologies, such as *local area networks* (LANs). *N* switches connected to a common LAN can be modeled as $N \times (N-1) / 2$ point-to-point connections. This method, however, would be very expensive in size of link-state database. Commonly, therefore, a separate LSA is originated for the LAN, containing links to each of the *N* routers.

This situation is pictured in Figure 5.3. Five switches are connected to a LAN. Rather than model this configuration using 5 LSAs interconnected with 10 links, a sixth LSA representing the LAN is introduced to provide the link-state database's interconnections.

The responsibility for originating the LAN's LSA is given to a distinguished switch, which is elected from among the LAN's connected switches. For example, in OSPF this distinguished switch is called the *designated router.*

5.2.2 Updating LSAs

A switch updates its LSA when its local environment changes. For example, one of the switch's interfaces may become inoperative, or one of the switch's neighbors may go down. The time it takes the switch to notice changes in its local environment greatly affects the responsiveness of a link-state protocol to network changes. Changes in a switch's local environment may be detected by other protocols running in the switch (e.g., point-to-point links may run a separate up–down protocol, such as PPP's line-quality monitoring[26]). Also, many link-state protocols mandate that all switches send periodic "Hello" indications to their neighbors, so that a switch's absence will eventually be detected.

For robustness, most link-state protocols also periodically update all their LSAs, even in the absence of network changes (see Section 5.6).

5.3 RELIABLE FLOODING

A good flooding algorithm is crucial to any link-state protocol. The flooding algorithm ensures that all switches maintain identical link-state databases. This in turn ensures correct, loop-free routing. To maintain database synchronization and ensure quick routing around network failures, the flooding algorithm must be both reliable and fast. Reliability is usually achieved through explicit acknowledgment of all LSAs sent from one switch to a neighboring switch. Speed is usually achieved by giving flooding precedence over application data traffic.

Often most of the complication in a link-state protocol is in the flooding algorithm. Once the flooding algorithm is defined, however, new features are easily introduced to the routing through straightforward extensions to both LSA content and routing calculations. Examples include the extensions made to OSPF to support multicasting (see Section 5.7.5), and the ability to introduce new routing policies in IDPR (see Section 5.7.4).

Before the flooding algorithm even gets started, a switch needs an initial copy of the link-state database. This exchange happens when a switch is powered up, or when a new link becomes operational. The switch then discovers its new neighbors, and they download into the switch the current copy of the database.

After this initial synchronization, flooding activity will occur for one of two reasons. First, something in the network changes (e.g., a link becomes operational), and a new LSA describing the changed piece of the routing domain is flooded. Second, for robustness every LSA is updated at some low-level background rate.

In outline, here is how the flooding algorithm in any link-state protocol works:

1   The switch receives a flooded LSA on one of its links.

2   The switch examines the LSA's sequence number and compares it to the sequence number of the current copy (if any) of the LSA in the switch's link-state database. This examination indicates whether the flooded LSA actually includes new data.

3   If the LSA is new, it is installed in the link-state database, replacing the current copy (if any), and is then sent out all the switch's links save the link the LSA was received on.

4   Regardless of whether the LSA is new, an acknowledgment is sent back out the link on which the LSA was received.

This algorithm is made reliable by continuing to retransmit the LSA over the link until the switch on the other end acknowledges it. To optimize the case where both ends of the link transmit the LSA simultaneously, receiving the LSA is treated as an implicit acknowledgment.

As a flooding example, suppose that switch A in Figure 5.1 needs to update its own LSA. Assuming that most elapsed time during the flooding is accounted for by link-transmission times, the flood might happen in these phases:

- *Phase 1*   Switch A floods the LSA to switches B, C, and E.

- *Phase 2*   Switches B, C, and E accept the LSA as having new information, install the LSA in their databases, and send acknowledgments back to A. B then floods the LSA to D, C floods it to D and E, and E floods it to C and D.

- *Phase 3*   The LSAs crossing between C and E are treated as implicit acknowledgments. Supposing that the LSA from C is received first at D, D sends an acknowledgment back to C, sends the LSA to switches B and E, and then treats the LSAs from B and E as implicit acknowledgments.

- *Phase 4*   The LSAs received by E and B from C are treated as implicit acknowledgments.

Two general facts about flooding can be observed in this example. First, during flooding a new LSA transits each link at least once, and sometimes twice (in implicit acknowledgments). Second, the flooding does not depend on the routing. It thus avoids circular dependencies, for correct routing certainly depends on the flooding.

Some link-state protocols also use flooding to remove LSAs from the link-state database. For example, in OSPF a router may advertise LSAs to import external information learned from other routing protocols. When these other routing protocols indicate that this external information is no longer viable, the OSPF router can indicate via flooding that the imported information should be removed from the routing domain.

Most link-state protocols also limit the rate of flooding by requiring some minimal time interval between successive updates of the same LSA. This rate limiting may need to be invoked when one of a switch's links is rapidly and repeatedly transitioning from up to down. The minimum time interval between updates puts an upper bound on the amount of network bandwidth consumed by flooding, and prevents the LSA's sequence-number space from being exhausted.

Optimizations

Various optimizations can be made in the flooding algorithm to conserve the amount of network bandwidth used by flooding. For example, LSAs can be kept small. In this case, when something in the network changes, only the changed data need be flooded. OSPF has taken this approach, with the result that, even though some pieces of the network may change quite frequently, the overall flooding rate stays very close to the minimum level consisting solely of refreshed LSAs.[14]

Another optimization is to delay acknowledgment of LSAs, in the hope that more LSAs will be received and that multiple LSAs can be acknowledged in a single transaction.

The case of multiple switches attached to a LAN can also be optimized. As in representing LANs in LSAs, treating N routers attached to a common LAN as having $N \times (N-1) / 2$ pairwise connections is very inefficient, resulting in a lot of flooding. Instead, link-state protocols typically elect a distinguished switch and have all other switches on the LAN synchronize with it only. OSPF performs explicit synchronization, specifying that the distinguished switch (called the *designated router*) receive acknowledgments from the other switches during flooding. On the other hand, the IS-IS protocol achieves synchronization by having the distinguished switch (called the *designated intermediate system*) periodically broadcast a summary of the link-state database onto the LAN; other switches, finding that pieces of their database are out of date, will request the needed updates.

5.4 ROUTING CALCULATIONS

From their link-state database, the switches calculate the best routes through the network for the application data. Many algorithms are possible for the routing calculation. As mentioned in Section 5.1, the most popular algorithm is Dijkstra's algorithm (or SPF), popular for its simplicity and efficiency. Dijkstra's algorithm requires that each link be assigned a nonnegative cost. It then produces a set of shortest paths from the calculating switch to all other switches (hence all applications) in the network. Here, the cost of the path is the sum of the costs of the links making up the path.

Dijkstra's algorithm can be described very simply. Of the two disjoint sets of switches, one consists of switches to which shortest paths have already been found. The other set consists of switches to which candidate paths have been found. The algorithm starts by putting the calculating switch on the shortest-path set, and setting the candidate list to empty. The algorithm then iterates. At each iteration, the switch (called Switch X) just added to the shortest-path set is examined and these steps are executed:

1   The neighbors of Switch X not belonging to the shortest-path set are added to the candidate set (if they are not there already); the neighbors' candidate paths are updated if the path through Switch X is shorter than the previously known path (if any).

2   If the candidate list is now empty, the algorithm terminates.

3   The switch in the candidate set that is closest to the calculating switch is moved to the shortest-path set, and the algorithm iterates again.

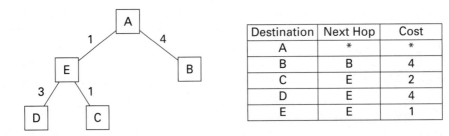

Figure 5.4   The shortest-path tree calculated by Switch A, with A's resulting hop-by-hop routing table

Take the link-state database in Figure 5.2. The Dijkstra calculation in switch A would run:

- *Initial State*   The shortest-path set consists of switch A itself, and the candidate set is empty.

- *Iteration 1*   Switches B, C, and E are added to the candidate set, and E is then moved to the shortest-path set.

- *Iteration 2*   Switch D is added to the candidate set, and switch C's candidate path is changed to go through switch E. Switch C is then moved to the shortest-path set.

- *Iteration 3*   Switch B is moved to the shortest-path set.

- *Iteration 4*   Switch D is moved to the shortest-path set. The algorithm then terminates. Here, A's set of shortest paths to all the other switches in the network is pictured in Figure 5.4. In most link-state algorithms, only the next hop switch needs to be stored instead of the whole path. This is commonly called a *routing table,* and is also pictured in Figure 5.4.

The performance of Dijkstra's algorithm scales as $O((n + l) \times \log(n))$, where l is the number of links in the network and n is the number of switches.[24] The $\log(n)$ term characterizes the complexity of finding the shortest path in the candidate set, when using a heap as the candidate-set data structure. Often it is assumed that as the number of switches grows, the number of interfaces per switch stays constant. If it does, the asymptotic behavior of Dijkstra's algorithm can be given as $O(n \times \log(n))$. To get another perspective on the cost of Dijkstra's algorithm, one implementation of the Dijkstra algorithm, run on a 10 MIPS processor, took 15 milliseconds to run the routing calculation on a 200-switch network.[14]

Link-state protocols do vary the basic Dijkstra calculation. The most common variation is performed when routing is also based on *type of service* (TOS) parameters, such as delay and reliability. In this case, the Dijkstra calculation is run multiple times, once for each TOS, giving a separate set of paths for each TOS parameter.

Some link-state protocols make much more complicated routing calculations. For example, the IDPR protocol (see Section 5.7.4) carries quality-of-service and policy information in its LSAs, and makes routing calculations attempting to minimize cost while satisfying multiple minimum-service guarantees (for example, calculate the path having minimum monetary cost but which has delay of no more than X seconds and a bandwidth of no less than Y bits per second). This kind of calculation cannot be done with the standard Dijkstra algorithm, although modifications to the algorithm can be made to calculate such constrained paths. However, Dijkstra's algorithm when so modified no longer performs as $O(n \times \log(n))$, and in fact certain sets of constraints turn the calculation into an NP-complete problem.

Variation on the Routing Calculation

At this time it is useful to introduce two routing paradigms, *hop-by-hop* routing and *source-specified* routing, either of which can be supported by a link-state protocol. In hop-by-hop routing, data traffic is forwarded using a destination address that is carried along with the data stream. Switches route independently based on this address, which means that their routing calculations must produce compatible routes (or routing loops will ensue). Fortunately, Dijkstra's algorithm does guarantee that each switch will produce compatible routes. In fact, most link-state protocols that use the Dijkstra algorithm employ hop-by-hop routing.

In source-specified routing, data traffic is forwarded according to an exact path specified by the source switch and carried along with the data stream. Source-specified routing is possible in a link-state algorithm, because each switch has a complete map of the network in the form of the link-state database. In fact, source-specified routing is employed in the link-state protocols IDPR and APPN. The advantages of source-specified routing are (1) that freedom from loops is guaranteed by the source and (2) switches can actually use different route-computation algorithms. The latter point is employed by IDPR, which takes the routing policies of the source into effect when computing routes, even though the source's policies are not distributed in LSAs (see Section 5.7.4).

Another difference in link-state protocols is in calculating all their routes at once, or calculating them as needed. When using the basic Dijkstra calculation, paths to all switches are calculated at the same time. However, it may be desirable to divide more complicated routing calculations into pieces, spreading out the computational burden. For example, this is done in the multicast extensions to OSPF (MOSPF; see Section 5.7.5), which requires a switch to make a separate Dijkstra calculation for each multicast source. To avoid doing all these Dijkstra calculations at once, the Dijkstra calculation for a source is delayed until matching application data are actually received.

5.5   AREA ROUTING

Area routing is a way of splitting a network into pieces, called *areas,* to simplify routing decisions and reduce the routing information that must be distributed throughout the routing domain. Typically, most switches belong to a single area. A switch has complete information about its own area, but knows little about other areas. When forwarding to applications homed in different areas, these switches merely forward the data to switches at the area boundaries, which are assumed to have more complete information. This strategy effectively yields a two-level routing hierarchy: the first intra-area, and the second interarea.

When a link-state protocol provides an area capability, each area essentially runs a separate copy of the link-state protocol, complete with its own link-state database, flooding, and routing calculation. Because most routers belong to a single area, they have smaller link-state databases and easier routing calculations than if areas were not used. At the boundary of the area, information about the destinations contained in other areas is summarized and imported. If commonality appears in the application addresses belonging to an area, information about this area can be greatly condensed before exporting to other areas, leading to a reduction in routing-table size.

An example is given in Figure 5.5. A routing domain has been divided into two areas. The first area (consisting of switches A through D) runs one copy of the link-state protocol, while the second area (consisting of switches D through F) runs another. It is the responsibility of switch D to summarize the first area's application addresses to the second, and vice versa.

Various schemes for implementing area routing in link-state algorithms can be found in references 7, 16, and 25.

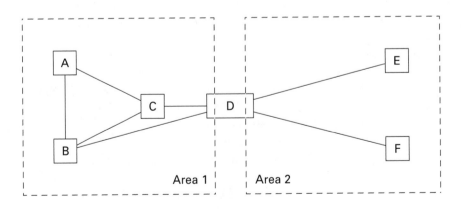

Figure 5.5   Splitting a routing domain into areas

5.6 ROBUSTNESS

A protocol is robust if it can detect and recover from unexpected errors. These errors can include hardware errors in the switches, transmission errors, and even software bugs. Most routing protocols include robustness features, and link-state protocols are no exception. Typical robustness provisions in a link-state protocol include:

- LSAs typically contain a checksum, which is used to detect data corruption that may occur either during flooding or while the LSA is held in the switch's link-state database.

- A background-refresh rate for LSAs. Even if the network is not changing, LSAs will be reflooded every so often. This provision guards against errors in flooding, or LSAs getting mistakenly deleted from the link-state database.

- LSAs are aged during flooding. Even if an error in flooding occurs and an LSA continually circulates throughout the network, eventually its age will hit the maximum value and it will be discarded. This use is similar to the TTL field found in the TCP/IP network-layer packet header.[21]

- A link between two switches will not be used by the routing calculation until the two switches perform an initial synchronization of their databases. This procedure is implemented by delaying report of the link in the two switches' LSAs until synchronization, and ensures that the two switches will perform compatible routing calculations (thereby avoiding routing loops).

5.7 EXAMPLES OF LINK-STATE PROTOCOLS

The following sections provide descriptions of several link-state routing protocols. The environment that each protocol was designed to handle is first described briefly. Some of the unique link-state features of each protocol are then detailed. An attempt has been made to keep these features arranged into the categories explained above: (1) describing the routing domain via LSAs, (2) flooding, (3) routing calculations, and (4) area routing.

The link-state routing protocols below were selected to cover a broad range of routing environments. Notice, however, that a number of link-state protocols have been omitted (e.g., IBM's APPN[8]).

5.7.1 The ARPANET's Routing Protocol

The first link-state protocol was developed by Bolt Beranek and Newman for use in the ARPANET.[11,12,22] The ARPANET, a packet-switching network performing routing at level 2 (data-link layer) of the OSI reference model, provided functionality similar to that of an X.25 PDN. Its packet switches were called *IMPs* (interface message processors) or *PSNs* (packet switching nodes). An application was addressed by the switch and port connecting the application to the network. At its zenith, the ARPANET consisted of several hundred IMPs, all interconnected via synchronous serial lines.

The ARPANET link-state protocol calculated least-delay paths, and employed hop-by-hop routing. The protocol was extensively monitored throughout its development and deployment. Its control traffic was found to consume less than 1 percent of link bandwidth and its routing calculations less than 2 percent of switch CPU resources, but still responded to network changes within 100 milliseconds.

In this protocol, each switch originated a single LSA listing all the switch's neighbors, together with the packet delay imposed by the serial lines connecting to said neighbors. This delay was calculated as a 10-second average, taking into account queuing, transmission, and propagation delays, as well as any delay incurred by link-layer retransmissions due to lossy serial lines. Changes in the delay could cause updated LSAs to be flooded, leading to a protocol that actually detected and routed around congested links. In fact, of the protocols described in detail in this chapter, the ARPANET routing protocol is the only one that dynamically responds to congestion. (Dynamically routing around congestion can be tricky—one must be careful to avoid introducing excessive route oscillations. References 9 and 10 propose modifications to the ARPANET routing protocol's link cost to reduce route oscillation.) A threshold that decreased with time was imposed; only delay changes exceeding the threshold would cause LSA updates. Thus, large delay changes were flooded quickly (within 10 seconds), and when the threshold fell to zero (after 60 seconds) LSAs were refreshed even if unchanged.

On average, LSAs in this protocol were short, averaging 176 bits in length. Thus the flooding of routing updates interfered very little with application traffic.

The flooding algorithm used in the ARPANET had several interesting properties. The time to bring a link from inoperative to fully operational state was constrained to take at least 60 seconds. During this time, flooding was performed over the link, but the link was not reported in LSAs. Bounding the bring-up time from below by the LSA-refresh interval accomplished three things. First, it ensured that upon power-up, switches would receive a full link-state database before forwarding application traffic. It also ensured that the switch's previously originated LSA would time out before the switch's new LSA was originated. Finally, if the network partitioned, the wait imposed on link bring-up guaranteed that both sides of the partition would have synchronized databases by the time the partition was fully healed. Based on suggestions made in reference 20, this waiting period has been replaced by an explicit exchange of link-state databases during link initialization in the newer link-state protocols such as OSPF and IS-IS. Removing the waiting period has allowed the time between LSA refreshes to be considerably lengthened in these protocols, substantially reducing the bandwidth consumed by the routing protocol's control traffic.

In a circular space of size N, an LSA having a sequence number of X is considered to be more recent than an LSA having a sequence number of Y when either $0 < (X - Y) < S$ or $0 < (N - S) < (Y - X)$. In a circular-sequence space, an LSA having a sequence number of X is considered to be more recent than an LSA having a sequence number of Y when $0 < (X - Y) < S$, where S is a positive integer defining the window of acceptability. The ARPANET's window of acceptability was fully half the circular sequence space. Such an arrangement can have three sequence numbers X, Y, and Z such that X is more recent than Y, which is more recent than Z, which in turn is more recent than X! It is then necessary to ensure that these three sequence numbers do not exist simultaneously in the routing domain, or confusion will arise about which is more recent. The ARPANET attempted to ensure this by limiting the rate at which new LSA instances could be generated; this limitation, combined with the aging out of all LSA instances in 60 seconds, meant that all possible sequence numbers for a given LSA would at any time exist in the same half of the circular space. However, reference 23 documents an actual occurrence in the ARPANET of three sequence numbers having the above anomalous property, because of switch-hardware errors. The three LSA instances were continually flooded and reflooded, stopping only when the entire ARPANET was powered off. As a result, reference 20 suggested several modifications to the flooding algorithm, covered above in Section 5.6. Modern link-state algorithms such as OSPF and IS-IS have adopted large linear-sequence spaces for LSAs instead of the ARPANET's original circular configuration.

The ARPANET's routing calculation used the Dijkstra algorithm. An incremental version of the Dijkstra was designed, however, so that when the cost of any link was changed, only part of the tree of shortest paths was recalculated, reducing computation time considerably.

An area-routing scheme for the ARPANET was designed in reference 25, but never implemented. This area scheme was interesting in that the areas were self-configuring after the interarea links were specified, and in that the area definitions responded quickly and naturally to partitions and partition recovery.

5.7.2 OSPF

The *open shortest path first* (OSPF) protocol is a TCP/IP routing protocol. In TCP/IP, the switches perform routing at level 3 of the OSI reference model, and are called *routers*. The locations of TCP/IP applications are indicated by their *IP addresses*. It is the job of an IP routing protocol to determine whether an IP address is reachable, and, if so, the best path to that address. OSPF handles routing inside a single autonomous system. In TCP/IP, an autonomous system is a collection of routers under a single administrative control and running a common routing protocol. Such routing protocols are classified as *interior gateway protocols* (IGPs). OSPF is documented in reference 16, and is the recommended IGP for use in the TCP/IP Internet.

OSPF has five types of LSAs. All LSAs are kept small, describing only a small portion of the routing domain. The average OSPF LSA is around 40 bytes. Keeping the LSAs small means that changes to the routing domain can be flooded quickly to all routers, enabling fast calculation of new routes. The LSA types are: 1 for router-LSAs, 2 for network-LSAs, 3 and 4 for summary-link-LSAs, and 5 for external-link-LSAs. Each router in an OSPF routing domain originates a *router-LSA* that lists the router's operational interfaces, their cost, the network or router that the interfaces connect to, and the range of IP addresses directly accessible via the interfaces. The *network-LSA* performs the abstraction function explained in Section 5.2.1, listing all the routers connected to a network. *Summary-link-LSAs* advertise IP addresses between areas, and *external-link-LSAs* import routing information from other autonomous systems.

OSPF allows routers to calculate separate routes for each separate IP type of service (TOS; low delay and high bandwidth are two examples). For this reason, all OSPF LSAs that include costs can actually carry separate costs for each value of IP TOS.

Because OSPF wants to keep the LSAs small, new functionality is added to OSPF by adding new LSA types rather than appending information to existing LSAs. For example, a multicast-routing capability has been added to OSPF by adding a type 6 LSA (see Section 5.7.5).

In OSPF, when a link comes up an explicit synchronization procedure called *database exchange* is performed to ensure that both ends have identical link-state databases before the link is advertised in LSAs, hence before application data can flow over the link. This precaution minimizes any transient loops that can occur during synchronization.

To minimize the flooding on LANs, OSPF elects a *designated router* for each LAN and synchronizes all other routers on the LAN with the designated router (see Section 5.3). Flooding between the designated router and any other router on the LAN proceeds exactly as if the two routers were connected by a point-to-point link. To ease the transition to a new designated router when the current designated router fails (which requires all routers to resynchronize with a new router), OSPF essentially prequalifies the next designated router by electing a *backup designated router*. Additionally, because a change in designated router causes disruption in the network (e.g., all routers attached to the LAN have to reoriginate their LSAs), OSPF introduces hysteresis into the designated router election so that, in time, the most stable router will become designated router and will stay designated router. Finally, finding that all this flooding support is not really specific to LANs, OSPF performs exactly the same algorithms over other network types that support the attachment of multiple routers, such as X.25 PDNs.

OSPF uses the standard Dijkstra algorithm for its base routing calculation. However, the processing of leaf segments of the routing domain, including all summary-link-LSAs and external-link-LSAs, is separated from the Dijkstra calculation and handled in an $O(n)$ manner (instead of $O(n \times \log(n))$, see Section 5.4). When an updated OSPF LSA is received, the LSA's type provides a hint of which routing calculation needs to be performed. Updated summary-link-LSAs and external-link-LSAs can be handled by a simple incremental calculation resembling that used by Bellman-Ford algorithms (e.g., TCP/IP's RIP protocol[6]).

An autonomous system running OSPF can be split into areas. A special area must be defined, called the backbone area, which is responsible for distributing routing information between the other areas. The backbone area must be contiguous, and all other areas must attach directly to the backbone area. The backbone area need not be physically contiguous, however, and indeed there are no physical restrictions on OSPF area configuration. No matter what the area configuration, OSPF *virtual links* can be configured to establish or restore the connectivity and ubiquity to the backbone area.

Interarea routing in OSPF strongly resembles a Bellman-Ford calculation. The rules on area connectivity avoid the problems inherent in some Bellman-Ford algorithms (e.g., "counting to infinity") by restricting the interarea topology to a simple hub-and-spoke configuration.

There is no facility for repairing partitions of nonbackbone areas. A partitioned nonbackbone area will automatically become several separate areas. Routing failure can occur, though, if summarization has been configured at area boundaries and a summarized address range becomes split across multiple-area components.

5.7.3 IS-IS

IS-IS is the Intra-Domain routing algorithm used at level 3 in OSI connectionless networks. In these networks, switches are called *intermediate systems* (or ISes, hence the name IS-IS). Applications reside in *end systems,* which are addressed by their *network system attachment points* (NSAPs). OSI routes to each individual end system, instead of routing to network segments as in protocol stacks such as TCP/IP. It is the job of the IS-IS protocol to determine whether a given NSAP is reachable, and if so, the path to reach it. The IS-IS protocol is documented in reference 7.

In IS-IS, the LSAs are called *LSPs* (link-state protocol data units). Each intermediate system originates a single LSP. An LSP is also originated on behalf of each LAN segment (see Section 5.3). In IS-IS, a LAN segment is called a *pseudonode;* the LSP representing a LAN is called a *pseudonode LSP.* IS-IS LSPs can get quite large, because all information originated by and associated with a particular intermediate system or pseudonode is contained in a single LSP. Because the size of an LSP is also bounded above, however, by the smallest network segment MTU, a way is provided to fragment LSPs into as many as 255 pieces.

Typically, the LSP generated by an intermediate system includes a list of all the intermediate system's neighboring ISes and pseudonodes, together with their associated cost. A LAN's pseudonode LSP contains a list of all intermediate systems and end systems (and hence NSAPs) directly attached to the LAN.

All data contained in LSPs are explicitly typed and variable-length encoded. To extend the protocol, information is added to the end of an existing LSP. A separate cost can be included in LSPs for each of the three OSI quality-of-service (QOS) classes: transit delay, expense, and residual-error probability. As a result a datagram's path can vary based on the datagram's QOS classification.

In IS-IS, flooding reliability over point-to-point circuits proceeds as in other link-state algorithms, using explicit acknowledgments and retransmissions. However, flooding reliability over LANs is accomplished differently. A *designated intermediate system* is elected from all the intermediate systems attached to the LAN. The designated intermediate system then periodically broadcasts (every 10 seconds) a collection of *complete sequence number PDUs* (CSNPs) describing the entire link-state database. An intermediate system finding that one of its LSPs is out of date will request the newer LSP instance. An intermediate system finding that it has a newer LSP instance than that advertised in the designated intermediate system's CSNPs will reflood the newer LSP. CSNPs are also used to establish database synchronization over a newly established point-to-point link. Unlike some other link-state algorithms, however, application traffic is allowed to flow over the link before synchronization is achieved.

In IS-IS, the routing calculation has complexity $O(n)$ instead of $O(n \times \log(n))$ (see Section 5.4), because the candidate set is maintained as a table hashed according to path length rather than as a heap sorted according to path length. To make this implementation practical, link costs are limited to the range of 1 to 63 and total path cost in an IS-IS domain is limited to 1023.

IS-IS domains are typically split into areas. The area configuration has two levels. Level 2 routing comprises the top level. A single *level 2 subdomain* must be physically connected, with each level 1 area directly connected to the level 2 subdomain. A level 1 area's address is part of each of the area's end systems' NSAP addresses. A partition of a level 1 area can be detected and repaired. After repair, application traffic is encapsulated when forwarded from one area component to another. An intermediate system can belong to at most one level 1 area, and may or may not belong to the level 2 subdomain. Often Intermediate Systems on a LAN participate in both level 2 and level 1 routing, in which case two copies of the link-state algorithm (flooding, LSP generation, etc.) are actually executing on the LAN at once.

5.7.4 IDPR

IDPR (inter-domain policy routing) is a TCP/IP routing protocol providing policy routing among *administrative domains* (ADs). An administrative domain is defined to be a collection of contiguous network segments, routers, links, and hosts governed by a single administrative authority who, among other things, specifies service restrictions for transit traffic and defines service requirements for locally generated traffic.

IDPR enables applications to request sophisticated services for their network traffic. For example, an application can request that it wants a minimum-delay path that has at least bandwidth of X bits per second and costs no more than Y. In addition, it allows each AD to specify which types of traffic it will and will not carry. For example, an AD can specify that it will not carry commercial traffic, or that it will do so only during off-peak hours.

IDPR routes to ADs. The first IDPR router to receive an IP datagram discovers the AD containing the datagram's destination IP address using a *mapping server* (e.g., a TCP/IP domain name server[13]). Based on the service requirements specified by the application, an appropriate path is then constructed. This path is explicitly installed in all IDPR routers along the path. Subsequent application traffic flowing to the destination is encapsulated in an IDPR-specific header containing the path identifier.

This source-specific rather than hop-by-hop routing eases some of the usual requirements on link-state protocols (see Section 5.4). IDPR routers do not need to have synchronized link-state databases. IDPR also does not need a routing calculation that, like the standard Dijkstra algorithm, produces consistent routes at each router. In fact, different ADs may even use different route-computation algorithms.

Each LSA in IDPR describes a particular administrative domain. These LSAs come in two flavors: configuration and dynamic. *Configuration LSAs,* sent infrequently, contain the list of services offered by the AD (e.g., charge per byte, average bandwidth available), the restrictions that the AD imposes on forwarded traffic (e.g., no commercial traffic), and a list of all possible adjacent ADs. *Dynamic LSAs,* sent in response to network changes such as link outages, describe the AD's current set of adjacent ADs, together with the set of services (a subset of those configured) currently in effect.

Flooding in IDPR proceeds like other link-state protocols. Because IDPR does not require completely synchronized databases, though, the ability to restrict delivery of LSAs to a subset of ADs is included.

Route calculation is the most computationally intensive part of IDPR. An application may request to minimize delay and monetary cost, while maintaining a minimum bandwidth for its traffic. Trying to calculate such a route—optimizing a set of requested services while also respecting bounds on other service parameters—is an NP-complete problem. For this reason, IDPR separates the job of route calculation into separate *route servers,* and all but the most common routes are calculated in an on-demand fashion. Because not all ADs are required to use the same routing calculation, an AD may opt to perform simpler route calculations while settling for less optimal routes for its application traffic.

The ability to group ADs into *super domains* is provided. This is a way of reducing the size of the IDPR link-state database.

5.7.5 MOSPF

The multicast extensions to OSPF (MOSPF[17]) enable the routing of *IP multicast datagrams*. IP multicast datagrams are identified as those addressed to IP class D addresses, also called *multicast groups*. When a single IP multicast datagram is sent, it is the job of a multicast routing protocol such as MOSPF to efficiently deliver copies of the datagram to all group members, regardless of how the members are distributed throughout the routing domain. See reference 3, upon which MOSPF is based, for a good description of multicast routing. Multicasting can be very effective for applications such as voice and video conferencing, distributed simulations, and distributed databases.

To prevent unwanted datagram replication, MOSPF forwards multicast datagrams based on both their source and destination addresses. This method contrasts with most unicast routing algorithms, which look only at destination addresses. The path calculated by MOSPF between a multicast datagram's source and any group member is always lowest in cost. To forward a copy to multiple group members, MOSPF must sometimes replicate a datagram, but this replication is postponed as long as possible to conserve network bandwidth.

A router running MOSPF makes use of the *Internet Group Membership Protocol* (IGMP[2]) to keep track of group membership on its attached LANs. It then originates a type 6 OSPF LSA, the *group-membership-LSA,* to inform all other MOSPF routers of the group member's location. MOSPF and regular OSPF (i.e, non-MOSPF) routers can be mixed in an OSPF routing domain, cooperating in the forwarding of IP unicast datagrams. Group-membership-LSAs are not flooded to non-MOSPF routers, however, following the OSPF philosophy that routers should not have to deal with LSAs whose contents they do not understand.

Like the OSPF unicast calculation, the MOSPF multicast routing calculation uses the Dijkstra algorithm. In MOSPF, however, the root of the shortest-path tree is the multicast datagram's source instead of the calculating router. The MOSPF router prunes all tree branches that do not contain group members; in this way, multicast datagrams are never forwarded further than they need to be. A MOSPF router can run many routing calculations, potentially one for each datagram source and destination combination. For this reason, a calculation is run only when a matching datagram has actually been received. This "on-demand" calculation distributes the calculation load over time.

Tiebreakers are imposed on MOSPF's Dijkstra calculation to ensure that all MOSPF routers calculate exactly the same datagram path, which is a requirement for successful multicast forwarding. MOSPF's routing calculation also avoids all non-MOSPF routers, allowing a mixture of MOSPF and non-MOSPF routers to be deployed.

When the source of a multicast datagram is external to an area, or external to the autonomous system, the precise neighborhood of the source is unknown. This lack makes formation of a normal shortest-path tree rooted at the source impossible. Instead, OSPF summary-link-LSAs and external-link-LSAs are used to approximate the source's immediate neighborhood. Because the cost of these links is specified in the reverse direction, toward rather than away from the source, the routing calculations in these cases use reverse costs throughout.

5.8 SUMMARY

At the core of all link-state routing protocols is a distributed and replicated database that represents a dynamic map of the network: the available switches, network segments, and their active interconnections. This database is kept in each switch, and database synchronization among switches is maintained through a reliable flooding algorithm. From the database, each switch independently calculates the paths to network destinations.

Link-state routing has become popular recently—link-state routing protocols can be found in all major protocol stacks, performing varied functions, ranging from standard hop-by-hop destination routing to policy and multicast routing.

REFERENCES

1   K. Bharath-Kumar and J. Jaffe, "Routing to Multiple Destinations in Computer Networks," *IEEE Transactions on Communications,* Vol. COM-31, No. 3, March 1983.

2   S. Deering, "Host Extensions for IP Multicasting," *Internet Request for Comments 1112,* May 1988.

3   S. Deering, "Multicast Routing in Internetworks and Extended LANs," *SIGCOMM Summer 1988 Proceedings,* August 1988.

4   S. Deering, *Multicast Routing in a Datagram Internetwork,* Stanford Technical Report STAN-CS-92-1415, Department of Computer Science, Stanford University, December 1991.

5   P. Green, R. Chappuis, J. Fisher, P. Frosch, and C. Wood, "A Perspective on Advanced Peer to Peer Networking," *IBM Systems Journal,* Vol. 26, No. 4, 1987, pp. 414–428.

6   C. Hedrick, "Routing Information Protocol," *Internet Request for Comments 1058,* June 1988.

7   ISO/IEC, *ISO/IEC 10589: Information Processing Systems—Data Communications—Intermediate System to Intermediate System Intra-Domain Routing Protocol,* 1992.

8   S. Joyce and J. Walker, "Advanced Peer-to-Peer Networking (APPN): An Overview," *IBM Personal Systems Technical Solutions, No. G325-5014-00,* January 1992, pp. 67–72.

9   A. Khanna, "Short-Term Modifications to Routing and Congestion Control," *BBN Report 6714,* Bolt Beranek and Newman, February 1988.

10 A. Khanna and J. Zinky, "The Revised ARPANET Routing Metric," *Proceedings of the 1989 ACM SIGCOMM,* Austin, September 1989.

11 J. McQuillan, I. Richer, and E. Rosen, "ARPANET Routing Algorithm Improvements," *BBN Technical Report 3803,* Bolt Beranek and Newman, April 1978.

12 J. McQuillan, I. Richer, and E. Rosen, "The New Routing Algorithm for the ARPANET," *IEEE Transactions on Communications,* Vol. COM-28, No. 5, May 1980.

13 P. Mockapetris, "Domain Names—Implementation and Specification," *Internet Request for Comments 1035,* November 1987.

14 J. Moy, ed., "OSPF Protocol Analysis," *Internet Request for Comments 1245,* July 1991.

15 J. Moy, "Experience with OSPF," *Internet Request for Comments 1246,* July 1991.

16 J. Moy, "OSPF Version 2," *Internet Request for Comments 1583,* March 1994.

17 J. Moy, "Multicast Extensions to OSPF," *Internet Request for Comments 1584,* March 1994.

18 J. Moy, "MOSPF: Analysis and Experience," *Internet Request for Comments 1585,* March 1994.

19 Novell, Inc., *NetWare Link Services Protocol (NLSP) Specification,* 1993.

20 R. Perlman, "Fault-Tolerant Broadcast of Routing Information," *Computer Networks,* December 1983.

21 J. Postel, "Internet Protocol," *Internet Request for Comments 791,* September 1981.

22 E. Rosen, "The Updating Protocol of ARPANET's New Routing Algorithm," *Computer Networks 4,* 1980, pp. 11–19.

23 E. Rosen, "Vulnerabilities of Network Control Protocols: An Example," *Computer Communication Review,* July 1981.

24 R. Sedgewick, *Algorithms,* Reading: Addison-Wesley, August 1984.

25 J. Seeger and A. Khanna, "Reducing Routing Overhead in a Growing DDN," *MILCOMM 86,* 1986.

26 W. Simpson, "The Point-to-Point Protocol (PPP)," *Internet Request for Comments 1548,* December 1993.

27 M. Steenstrup, "IDPR as a Proposed Standard," *Internet Request for Comments 1477,* July 1993.

28 M. Steenstrup, "An Architecture for Inter-Domain Policy Routing," *Internet Request for Comments 1478,* June 1993.

29 M. Steenstrup, "Inter-Domain Policy Routing Protocol Specification: Version 1," *Internet Request for Comments 1479,* July 1993.

CHAPTER 6   ❖   ❖   ❖   ❖

AppleTalk Routing

ALAN B. OPPENHEIMER AND FIDELIA KUANG

CONTENTS

Unlike other chapters in the book, this one covers a set of routing mechanisms designed specifically for a commercial product, namely the AppleTalk (inter)networking system, primarily used to interconnect Macintosh computers and peripherals. The design and evolution of AppleTalk has been driven by customer requirements, especially ease of use and interoperability with other internetworking systems. Shaped by these requirements, AppleTalk has unique features that enable it to configure, organize, and route traffic through a network, requiring virtually no human intervention. This chapter describes the protocols that constitute AppleTalk and offers insight into the development of routing systems for specific commercial purposes.

6.1 INTRODUCTION

The AppleTalk[1] network system was designed from day one with the user as its primary focus. Although AppleTalk was always intended to be a full-fledged, general-purpose networking system, its linkage with the Macintosh computer provided its developers with additional, unique requirements. Unlike other network systems being designed at the time, the principal design element in AppleTalk was (and continues to be) ease of use.

Just as the Macintosh was designed in a world where command lines and magic incantations were the norm, the networking world in which AppleTalk was designed was no less user-hostile. Networks of the day included such standard elements as terminators (little resistors that had to be put on the end of network segments), hard-coded unique addresses that users had to type in to identify network nodes, and static routing tables. As developers of a network to be used with "the computer for the rest of us," the AppleTalk development team was burdened with figuring out how to develop the network for the rest of us.

As the team set out to define the first *plug-and-play* network system, it tried to avoid compromising the functionality or the future of the network in any way. The concept of dynamic node addressing, for instance, was coupled with such standard local-area networking concepts as network numbers and sockets.[6] And when it was determined that a dynamic naming system was needed to simplify the location of network services, that system was designed to work, not just in a local environment, but across a full AppleTalk internet. (In this chapter, unless otherwise specified, *internet* always refers to an *AppleTalk internet*.)

The first AppleTalk system, AppleTalk Phase 1, was in many ways too successful. Primarily because of the phenomenon that the Macintosh created, the uses to which AppleTalk was put quickly exceeded those of its design center. AppleTalk internets were anticipated, but the size of those internets was not. The need to support various data links was anticipated, but the degree to which AppleTalk would be used with other protocols on those data links was not. And so, just like the Macintosh, Apple-Talk was forced to evolve.

AppleTalk Phase 2 was introduced in 1989. Its primary focus was enabling the creation of large AppleTalk internets, and better interaction with other protocols. Because the Macintosh and its associated network products such as the LaserWriter printer had succeeded so well, the limitations under which Phase 2 was designed were even more severe than those imposed on Phase 1. Not only did the developers have to continue and extend the plug-and-play simplicity of AppleTalk Phase 1, but they had to do so in a backward-compatible manner, at least for the end nodes. With an installed base of more than a million nodes at the time, such nodes had to be upgradable only as necessary. It was required, however, that all the routers on an internet be upgraded before users could take advantage of many of the Phase 2 features, and even this limited requirement slowed the adoption of Phase 2 in many of the larger sites.

AppleTalk Phase 2 addressed most of the then-current issues around local-area networking. Much larger AppleTalk internets could be built, and they were. Customers for the first time also could successfully build large, wide-area AppleTalk internets. AppleTalk customers' desire to build large, efficient, multiprotocol WANs, however, exposed yet another set of issues that needed to be dealt with. These included the need to provide a much more efficient routing protocol on WAN links and to tunnel AppleTalk through other protocol systems, specifically TCP/IP.[5] Many customers also expressed a desire for interorganizational connectivity such as that provided by the (TCP/IP) Internet.

Having learned a lesson from the resistance to upgrading all routers in Phase 2, instead of creating a Phase 3, Apple introduced, early in 1993, a series of backward-compatible enhancements to AppleTalk routing referred to collectively as the AppleTalk Update-based Routing Protocol, or AURP. AURP provided a number of enhancements to AppleTalk routing, especially in WAN environments, and required no changes to currently installed Phase 2 routers.

6.2 APPLETALK INTERNETWORKING BASICS

An AppleTalk internet includes the basic pieces found in most network systems: nodes, networks, network numbers, and routers. AppleTalk, as originally designed in Phase 1, defined an 8-bit node ID and a 16-bit network number. When it became clear that 254 nodes on one network would be insufficient, for compatibility reasons, Phase 2 had to utilize these same 24 bits in a manner that would circumvent the 254-node limitation. Thus, like IP and subnets,[5] AppleTalk Phase 2 introduced *network-number ranges.* An AppleTalk network (other than one using the LocalTalk data link,[1] which continues to use a single network number) is now identified by a range of network numbers. For each network number in the range, 253-node IDs are available. By configuring network-number ranges, an administrator can thus specify the maximum number of nodes on an AppleTalk network.

Fundamental to AppleTalk's ease of use, and a key aspect of any plug-and-play network, is a system for *dynamic node address assignment.* Nodes dynamically choose their network-number/node-ID combination (referred to as the node's address) with help from the routers on their network. Apple developed and patented a set of techniques whereby a node dynamically acquires a unique address on a particular LAN, in the absence of any routers (AppleTalk LANs are fully functional even when no routers are present—AppleTalk has always avoided requiring any centrally administered entity). When routers are present, this dynamic address-acquisition technique is extended to choose an internet-wide unique address.

Nodes first choose a LAN-wide unique tentative node address using a special reserved range of network numbers that are never propagated off the LAN. Nodes then use this tentative node address to talk to a router and determine the range of network numbers that is valid for their network. Finally the nodes dynamically choose a unique node address within this range.

Equally important to AppleTalk's ease of use is its *dynamic naming service.* To simplify the user's experience in browsing and selecting internet services, AppleTalk introduced the concept of *zones.* A zone is a logical group of nodes on an internet. Like area codes, zones subdivide the internet into more human-manageable regions. Zones are assigned human-readable zone names, and naming services are always performed within a particular zone. In Phase 1, each AppleTalk network was assigned, through configuration in the routers, a single zone name. In Phase 2, each AppleTalk network (other than LocalTalk networks, which continue to have only one zone name) is now assigned a zone list of up to 255 zone names. Zone names are not necessarily related in any way to physical locality, and the same zone name can be used on any number of networks—nodes with the same zone name on all such networks are grouped into the same zone (like an area code that was used in different states).

As part of their dynamic address assignment, nodes select their zone name from the list of zones available on their network. To handle the case where a node cannot or does not choose a specific zone from the list, one of the zone names in the list is designated the *default zone* for that network. All nodes that do not otherwise choose a specific zone name are placed in the default zone for their network.

Each zone on a non-LocalTalk network has an associated *zone-multicast address.* Once a node has chosen its zone, it registers to receive packets sent to the specific zone-multicast address associated with that zone. Zone-multicast addresses are used to significantly reduce the overhead associated with dynamic naming. As will be described, routers ensure that name lookups are sent only to the appropriate zone-multicast address.

6.3 APPLETALK PROTOCOL SUMMARY

Figure 6.1 details the current AppleTalk protocol stack. The shaded protocols are discussed in this chapter. AppleTalk's data-link–independent network-layer protocol is the Datagram Delivery Protocol (DDP). DDP provides simple datagram service between two sockets on an internet. The Routing Table Maintenance Protocol (RTMP) is built on DDP and is responsible for propagating routing information on LANs throughout the internet. AppleTalk Update-based Routing Protocol (AURP) is responsible for equivalent functionality on WAN links. The Name Binding Protocol (NBP) is responsible for the dynamic binding of user-visible names to network-layer addresses and is one of the principal contributors to AppleTalk's ease of use. NBP includes the concept of zones to greatly simplify service location for the user. Zone information is maintained in routers using the Zone Information Protocol (ZIP).

Because a network system is needed that is essentially as easy to use as the Macintosh itself, AppleTalk routing protocols have had to provide richer functionality than that in most present network systems. Plug-and-play networking does not come free. In addition to the standard features of propagating routing information and forwarding data packets, AppleTalk routing includes the ability to propagate the zone information needed for NBP, and to route the name-binding requests themselves. Finally, with the addition of AURP, AppleTalk provides the ability to build interorganizational internets without the need for any sort of centralized administration. Each piece of AppleTalk routing is discussed in turn.

Application			File Servers		Printers	
Presentation			AFP		Postscript	
Session	ADSP	ZIP	ASP		PAP	
Transport	SNMP	RTMP	AEP	ATP	NBP	AURP
Network			DDP			UDP/IP
Data Link	TLAP	ELAP		LLAP	ARAP	Point-to-Point
Physical	Token Ring	Ethernet		LocalTalk	Modem Link	

Figure 6.1   AppleTalk protocols mapped into ISO seven-layer model

6.4 PROPAGATING ROUTING INFORMATION
ON LANS—RTMP

The Routing-Table Maintenance Protocol (RTMP) is used by AppleTalk routers to propagate network-reachability information. It is a classic distance-vector routing algorithm, much like the Routing Information Protocol (RIP,[5] see also Chapter 3 of this volume) and includes *split horizon* to minimize the data sent in the routers' periodic multicasts. These multicasts are sent once every ten seconds. This rate supports the system's plug-and-play simplicity. AppleTalk networks (especially LocalTalk networks) tend to go up and down more often than those of most other network systems. AppleTalk routers multicast their routing information at a rate which generally results in alternate routes being adopted without tearing down of higher-level connections, and which also causes routes to new networks to be available quickly. Alternate route adoption is also aided by a technique referred to as *notify neighbor,* whereby routers indicate networks that have been aged out with a special tuple in their RTMP packets.

One of the most difficult aspects of setting up routers in an AppleTalk internet is configuring the routers with network-number ranges and zone information. To simplify configuration and minimize errors, the *seed router* was developed. A seed router is responsible for supplying (or *seeding*) the network-number range and zone list for a network. Only one router on any network need be a seed router. All others can be *nonseed,* meaning that they need not be configured with network information, and can thus be plug-and-play. More than one router on a network can be a seed router for redundancy, as long as all seed routers on the network are configured with the same seed information. Nonseed routers learn their network's number range by listening in on RTMP packets sent from seed routers. RTMP also provides the ability for both routers and end nodes to query for network information.

In addition to propagating routing information between routers, RTMP provides end nodes with just enough information to allow these nodes to communicate on an internet without configuration of any sort. Specifically, end nodes implement a small subsection of RTMP referred to as the *RTMP stub.* The RTMP stub is responsible for maintaining a node's network-number information, and for providing DDP with information needed to make forwarding decisions. Details of the RTMP stub's operation are provided in the section on AppleTalk data-packet forwarding.

6.5 PROPAGATING ZONE INFORMATION—ZIP

The Zone Information Protocol (ZIP) is used by AppleTalk routers to propagate zone-to-network mapping information. ZIP is also used by end nodes, both as part of their dynamic node-address acquisition, and for enumerating the zones available on the internet.

The principal function of ZIP is to propagate the zone information associated with each network in an AppleTalk internet. ZIP works in concert with RTMP to perform this function. When an AppleTalk router obtains, through RTMP, the network-number range of a new network, the router uses ZIP to obtain the associated zone list of that network. The router first examines RTMP's routing database to determine the next router in the path to the new network. It then sends a ZIP query packet to that router, requesting the zone list for the network. If the receiving router has the full zone list, it sends the list in a series of ZIP reply packets. Otherwise it ignores the request (in this case the receiving router itself is still querying for the information).

A router's ZIP implementation periodically retransmits, to the next router in the path, requests for the zone information associated with any networks for which it does not have a complete zone list. (The number of zones in the zone list can be determined from any ZIP reply received for the network—each reply includes the total number of zones for the network.) Once a full zone list is received for a network, ZIP is free to propagate that information further by answering other routers' ZIP queries. Through ZIP, zone lists propagate outward from the associated network itself. Eventually, on a stable internet, every router will have the complete network-to-zone-list mapping of the internet. Such a list can be somewhat large, but the network operates much more efficiently with each router maintaining a full list (and the size of the list is almost always insignificant compared to the amount of memory used for forwarding buffers and the like).

ZIP monitors RTMP's routing database to determine when a network becomes unreachable. When a network is removed from the routing database, ZIP deletes the corresponding zone information. It does so to enable a network's zone list to be changed. Specifically, a network's zone list is changed by bringing the network down, waiting for its network-number range to be removed from the routing tables of all the routers on the internet (at which time the previously associated zone information is also deleted), and then bringing the network back up with a new zone list, which is then propagated throughout the internet by ZIP.

ZIP also plays a key role in a node's dynamic address acquisiton. As part of this process, a node must select a node address including a network-number part that is within the network-number range of the node's network. The node must also select a zone name that is in the zone list for that network. Additionally, the node must be given the zone-multicast address associated with the chosen zone.

End nodes utilize the ZIP GetNetInfo command at startup time to determine information about their local environment. A ZIP GetNetInfo request is broadcast on the node's network and responded to by routers on that network. If the end node was previously active on the network, the GetNetInfo request contains information that the end node has saved from the last time it was active. Specifically, it contains the network number and zone name the node was using at that time. The routers, upon receiving the request, verify whether the information is still valid. If it is valid, they inform the end node with a GetNetInfo reply, and the node is able to continue the startup. If not, the reply contains the network-number range for the network, and also the name of the network's default zone (which the device can use until another zone is selected). The GetNetInfo reply also contains the node's zone-multicast address. The node registers on the multicast address so that it will receive zone-wide NBP lookups sent to the zone-multicast address.

Routers independently calculate zone-multicast addresses using the algorithm specified by AppleTalk Phase 2. A zone-multicast address depends on the characters in the zone name and the specific data link on which the multicast packets will be sent (that is, zone-multicast addresses are different on Ethernet and token ring). The ZIP implementation in a router first converts the zone name to all uppercase characters. Then it hashes the string into a two-byte number using the same algorithm that DDP uses for performing checksum calculations.[1] Using the resulting two-byte hash value as an index, ZIP determines the corresponding zone-multicast address from the table of multicast addresses associated with the underlying data link.

Just as end nodes utilize a subset of RTMP to find out information about their internet environment, they also utilize a subset of ZIP for this purpose. Specifically, ZIP provides three functions that enable an end node to determine zone information for its local and global environment. These functions are implemented in simple request-and-response transactions, and utilize the AppleTalk Transaction Protocol (ATP) for this purpose. ATP is a transaction protocol that provides guaranteed delivery. ZIP requests are sent by an end node to any router on the node's local network. The three functions provided by ZIP for use by end nodes are:

- *GetZoneList*   Returns a list of all zones in the internet

- *GetLocalZones*   Returns a list of all zones on the sender's network

- *GetMyZone*   Returns sender's zone name (used only on LocalTalk networks)

The responses for both the GetZoneList and the GetLocalZones requests list zones for the internet or for the sender's network respectively. Because the list of zones may not fit in one response packet, the end node may have to send multiple requests to the same router to obtain the whole list. Each request specifies a starting index for the zones to be returned in the response.

When an end node on a network chooses a new zone name (a rare event), it can obtain the list of zones for its network through the GetLocalZones request. After choosing a new zone name, the node must also configure itself to accept packets sent to the new zone's multicast address, which it can obtain with a ZIPGetNetInfo request.

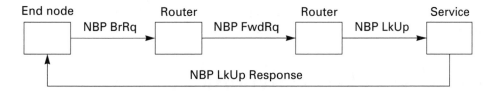

Figure 6.2 NBP packet forwarding

6.6 NBP PACKET FORWARDING

A router on an AppleTalk internet performs an important function in AppleTalk's dynamic name binding (Figure 6.2). The Name-Binding Protocol (NBP) enables the binding of network addresses to entity names. Name binding is an integral component of AppleTalk's service-location mechanism and of the ease with which it can be used. Because nodes obtain their network addresses dynamically, the network address of a service may change from time to time. The entity's user-visible name, however, changes infrequently. AppleTalk users generally locate services by name rather than network address.

An entity name consists of three identifiers: the object's name, the service type, and the name of the zone in which the service resides. An end node locates network services by performing a lookup on the service's object name and type in a specified zone. Wild cards are allowed in the name and type fields. The service or services that match the request respond to the requesting node. Through this exchange, the end node determines the network address of the service or services it specified by name. Routers on an internet facilitate the procedure by propagating the lookup request through the internet to all networks in the specified zone.

In an internet environment, an end node sends an NBP Broadcast-Request (BrRq) packet with the specified name, type, and zone to a router on its network. The NBP implementation in the router is responsible for propagating the node's request through the internet by converting the broadcast-request packet to Forward-Request (FwdRq) packets. The router sends one Forward-Request packet to a router on each network that has the specified zone in its zone list, utilizing the network-to-zone mapping maintained by ZIP.

When a router receives a Forward-Request packet, it is responsible for multicasting the request to all nodes in the specified zone on the destination network. It converts the Forward-Request packet to a Lookup (LkUp) packet. The router uses a zone-specific multicast rather than broadcast so that the packet interrupts only nodes on the network that are in the destination zone. To send a zone-specific multicast, the router addresses the lookup packet to the zone-multicast address corresponding to the destination-zone name. Nodes with a service matching the request respond to the original requesting node with the service's network address and completely specified service name. Notice that the BrRq, FwdRq, and LkUp packets carry the address of the original requesting node, which makes this direct responding possible.

6.7   APPLETALK DATA-PACKET FORWARDING

Both end nodes and routers have *data-packet forwarding* capability, end nodes to a limited extent and routers to a great extent. When an end node's DDP implementation sends a packet out on the network, the data-link-independent network-layer implementation in the end node looks at the destination-network number of the packet. If the destination network is one that is directly connected to the node, the data-link layer sends the packet directly to the specified destination node. Otherwise, the data-link layer sends the packet to an internet router on the local network.

To enable this packet-forwarding capability, an end node keeps track of two pieces of information: the network-number range of its local network and the network address of an internet router on the local network. A node obtains this information through its RTMP stub, which listens to the RTMP packets sent by routers on its network. The node may send data packets to any of the routers on its network. Because the router picked may not be along the shortest path to the destination, however, it is possible for a data packet to travel an extra hop before reaching its destination.

To optimize the router selection, a node may implement the optional *best-router* algorithm, which enables the node to pick the best router for the destination of a data packet. A DDP implementation using the best-router algorithm looks at packets that come in from other, nonlocal networks and caches the source network number and the source data-link address, which indicate the address of the best router for that network number. The route through the best router should be the shortest route, by number of hops. When a node determines it needs to send a packet to a router for forwarding, the DDP implementation tries to find the destination network in its best router cache. If it succeeds, it sends the packet to the corresponding best router. Otherwise, it sends the packet to any known router.

Routers handle the bulk of data-packet forwarding in AppleTalk internets. A router manages any number of logical ports, which correspond to the different paths a packet may take. A router forwards packets through one of its ports from a source node or a previous router to the next router, or from a source node or a previous router to the destination node. The router keeps track of all reachable networks by listening to RTMP packets sent by other routers. The router stores information about each reachable network and the corresponding next-router address in internal routing tables. When the router receives a packet to be forwarded, it looks at the packet's DDP destination-network number. If the router can locate a routing-table entry corresponding to the destination network, it proceeds to forward the packet.

The routing-table entry contains information such as the network range, the network's distance in hops, the address of the next router, and the forwarding port. If the network's distance is zero, the destination network is directly connected to another port of the router. In that case, the router sends the packet to the destination node through the forwarding port specified in the routing-table entry. If the network's distance is greater than zero, the router ensures that the packet's hop count is less than the maximum, 15, before forwarding the packet. To forward the packet, the router increments the packet's hop count and sends the packet to the next router specified in the routing-table entry through the corresponding forwarding port.

6.8 APPLETALK UPDATE-BASED ROUTING PROTOCOL (AURP)

The AppleTalk Update-based Routing Protocol (AURP)[2] is more than just a routing protocol. It encompasses a number of techniques for enhancing AppleTalk routing, especially in WAN environments. These techniques are completely compatible with Phase 2. The main techniques are the update-based propagation of distance-vector routing information and the tunneling of AppleTalk in other protocol systems such as TCP/IP. These core techniques feature little or no routing traffic on a stable internet, as well as scaling from point-to-point modem links to large, wide-area internets. They also provide a specification of AppleTalk tunneling over IP with the same functionality as AppleTalk's LAN routing protocols, RTMP and ZIP. Other techniques defined in AURP include network-number remapping, clustering, hop-count reduction, and two security techniques: device hiding and network hiding.

Tunneling AppleTalk in other protocol systems enables an AppleTalk internet to span much wider areas. A *tunnel* is thus a virtual data link between two or more segments of an AppleTalk internet. (AURP supports the concept of multipoint tunnels.) An AppleTalk router that connects a local AppleTalk internet to a tunnel is referred to as an exterior router.

An exterior router continues to speak RTMP and ZIP on AppleTalk networks while speaking AURP across a tunnel (Figure 6.3). AURP remains compatible with Phase 2 by providing all the functionality of RTMP and ZIP on the tunnel. Exterior routers use AURP to exchange across the tunnel the same network information and zone information that RTMP and ZIP provide on AppleTalk networks. Exterior routers can use this information exchange to maintain the same routing tables and zone tables used by RTMP and ZIP. As a result, nodes on AppleTalk internets connected by a tunnel perceive no difference between AURP exterior routers and ordinary Phase 2 routers.

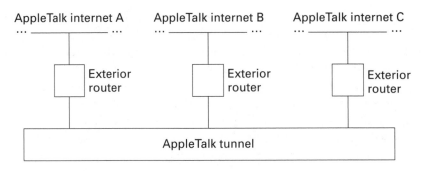

Figure 6.3   AppleTalk tunnel

6.8.1   Update-Based Routing—The Core of AURP

Because AURP is *update* based, exterior routers generally send routing packets only if the network topology changes. In contrast, RTMP routers send periodic multicasts regardless of any network changes. For exterior routers to maintain a view of the internet that is consistent with RTMP routers, the exterior routers depend on reliable connections among themselves. To simplify router discovery, an exterior router is generally configured with an address of at least one other known exterior router. Router discovery is thus static rather than dynamic.

After establishing a connection with another exterior router, the exterior routers initially exchange complete routing information for each router's local internet. As in RTMP and ZIP, the routing information includes both network ranges and zone lists. Once the initial exchange is complete, the routers have successfully established a tunnel connecting their AppleTalk internets. Because the routers maintain a reliable connection, they depend on each other to send reliable updates containing topology changes. The minimal interval between sending of updates is a parameter that can be adjusted for a network's characteristics. If a router has no update information to send at an update interval, it does not send routing packets. As a result, stable internets have essentially no AURP routing traffic, compared to the periodic traffic of RTMP.

During the update interval, the exterior router buffers pending update events. Possible events include:

- Addition or removal of a network from the routing table

- A change in the routing path so that the router accesses the network through its local internet rather than the tunnel, or vice versa, through the tunnel rather than locally

- A change in distance to a network

At the end of the interval, an exterior router sends a routing-update packet if at least one change in routing information occurs during the update interval. An update packet may carry different types of update information for different network ranges, but it may include only one update event for a given network range. If multiple events occur for a given network during the interval, the router combines those events into one resulting event. For example, if a network is deleted from the routing table and then added back in, the resulting event is a distance-change event because the distance to the network may have changed. Buffering of events allows the router to smooth out fluctuations in the internet.

6.8.2 IP Tunneling in AURP

Because TCP/IP networks are prevalent, a goal for AURP was to specify a standard way of tunneling AppleTalk through TCP/IP, to take advantage of the infrastructure of TCP/IP installations. As a result, in addition to specifications for point-to-point tunneling, AURP specifies a method for multipoint IP tunneling using *user datagram protocol* (UDP)[5] packets. A datagram-oriented protocol, UDP provides a simple best-effort transport mechanism for AURP.

Exterior routers that connect AppleTalk internets through an IP tunnel act as routers on an AppleTalk internet and as hosts on the TCP/IP internet. The exterior routers use IP only for tunneling, that is, for propagating AppleTalk routing information and for forwarding AppleTalk data packets. AURP defines a simple transaction protocol on top of UDP to ensure reliable delivery of routing information. The routing protocol defines transactions for establishing a connection between exterior routers, for exchanging routing information, and for maintaining both the connection and the routing information. For data forwarding, an exterior router encapsulates AppleTalk data in UDP datagrams and sends the resulting packets across the TCP/IP internet to the next exterior router. The destination exterior router decapsulates the AppleTalk data and then forwards the AppleTalk packets to the destination Apple-Talk network.

The AURP packet format includes the network system's headers (IP and UDP) followed by an AURP domain header followed by either AppleTalk data or AURP routing data. The current version of AURP specifies that a domain represents the exterior router's local AppleTalk internet. The domain header includes the destination- and source-domain identifiers and the packet type (data or routing). A domain identifier uniquely specifies an AppleTalk domain. Exterior routers currently use domain identifiers based on IP addresses. Because the exterior router can derive its domain identifier from its IP address, it is not necessary to configure the domain identifier. Notice that UDP port 387 is reserved for use by AURP.

6.8.3   Network-Number Remapping with AURP

By allowing disparate AppleTalk internets to connect through a tunnel, AURP enables connectivity between organizations' internets that are likely to be administered independently. As a result, conflicting AppleTalk network numbers may exist. AURP specifies a technique for resolving network-number conflicts—*network-number remapping*.

A network administrator for an organization is aware of the network ranges used locally, but not necessarily those used by other administrators on the same tunnel. When configuring a port on an exterior router that supports remapping, the administrator can specify a range of network numbers that is not used locally. By reserving this range for network-number remapping, the exterior router can map the network numbers of networks imported over the tunnel into network numbers in the remapping range. The router represents these imported networks to the local internet as networks with ranges in the remapping range.

An exterior router internally keeps track of network-number mappings by keeping a table of the domain identifiers and the remote-network numbers from each domain. Together the domain identifier and the remote-network number make up a unique identifier for the imported network. Each unique identifier corresponds to a network number in the remap range, which the router uses to represent the network locally. The exterior router uses the unique identifier in incoming packets to identify the corresponding local-network number and conversely, the local-network number in outgoing packets to identify the corresponding unique identifier.

To achieve network-number remapping transparently, the exterior router is responsible not only for representing the imported networks in the remap range locally, but also for ensuring that AppleTalk data packets between the local networks and the remote remapped networks contain correctly mapped addresses. The remapping exterior router maps the network numbers in incoming packets into the remap range. Similarly, it maps network numbers in outgoing packets back to the actual network numbers. Specifically, the exterior router remaps network numbers in the DDP source-address field of incoming packets, the DDP destination-address field of outgoing packets, the NBP entity-address field in AppleTalk NBP packets, and the routing-data field in AURP routing-information packets.

Remapping of network numbers is possible because of AppleTalk's dynamic addressing capability. Remapping would not be practical to implement if exterior routers had to remap network numbers carried in the data portion of AppleTalk packets. However, because network addresses are dynamic, the data portion of a packet generally carries NBP entity names instead of network numbers. Dynamic addressing, developed to make AppleTalk easier to use, thus makes possible network-number remapping, which, in turn, further enhances AppleTalk's ease of use.

Because network-number remapping allows networks to be represented by different network numbers, some problems arise when routing loops are present across a tunnel. A routing loop is present when more than one path exists between two exterior routers. One path is across the tunnel and another path may be through the local internets of the routers. After a remapping router maps an imported network into its local-remap range, the routing information for the remapped network propagates throughout the local internet. If a redundant path (a path other than the tunnel) exists, it is possible for that routing information to reach the exterior router that originally exported the network. Because the network number is remapped, the routing information appears to be new information to the exporting exterior router, which then exports the routing information across the tunnel. The original remapping router cannot determine that this new network number actually represents the same network that was previously remapped. The remapped network number appears to represent a new network, which is referred to as a *shadow network*. Because of the loop, each shadow network can be repeatedly remapped until the distance to the last shadow network reaches the hop-count limit.

To avoid infinite remapping loops, the exterior router should implement at a minimum the loop-detection techniques specified by AURP. Loop detection is essentially a two-step process: looking for loop indicative information and then verifying the presence of a loop. If a loop is verified, the exterior router is responsible for eliminating the loop by disconnecting from the tunnel and thus eliminating the path through the tunnel.

Loop-indicative information seems to refer to a network across a tunnel, but could in fact refer to a network in the local internet. Specifically, loop-indicative information is a network range of exactly the same size as a network directly connected to a port of the exterior router, and a corresponding zone list that is exactly the same as the zone list for the local network. If these two parameters—the network-range size and the zone list—match those of the directly connected network, it is possible that the local-network range was remapped and exported back to the router through a loop.

After detecting loop-indicative information, an exterior router verifies the existence of a loop by sending out a Loop-Probe packet, which carries unique information about the sending router so that the router recognizes the packet if it receives it. The exterior router sets the destination address of the packet to be the suspected shadow address of the port for the directly connected network. For example, if the port for the directly connected network is at network 100, node ID 128, and the remapping router remaps the network number to 1000, the destination-network address of the packet will be network 1000, node 128. The exterior router sends the packet through the tunnel to the router that provided the loop-indicative information. If a loop is present, the exterior router that sent the Loop-Probe packet receives the packet through its local internet. After verifying the unique packet data, the exterior router determines the existence of a loop and eliminates the loop. If a loop is not present, the exterior router does not receive its Loop-Probe packet. The exterior router should send a Loop-Probe packet at least four times with retransmission time-outs no less than two seconds. If it does not receive its Loop-Probe packet after four attempts, it determines that a loop does not exist.

6.8.4 Clustering in AURP

AURP specifies a *clustering* technique that allows exterior routers to represent multiple networks accessible through the tunnel as a single network range within its local internet. Because a router generally tracks each existing network range in its internal-routing tables and sends information about each range in its RTMP routing packets, clustering reduces the size of routing tables and reduces routing traffic within a local AppleTalk internet. Remapping networks into a sequential range of network numbers enables an exterior router to represent a series of networks as one network. For example, if an exterior router is remapping networks into a range 1000–1500, such that there is a network 1000–1005, 1006, and 1007–1010, it can represent those networks as a clustered network with a range of 1000–1010. The zone list for the resulting cluster includes all the zones associated with any of the individual networks. Because a zone list for a network may never exceed 255 zones, a cluster may never have more than 255 zones in its zone list.

Just as in remapping, the exterior router is responsible for ensuring that packets between the local networks and the remote clustered networks contain correctly mapped addresses. The exterior router has the additional responsibility of monitoring NBP Forward-Request packets to be sent across the tunnel. From the DDP destination-network number in a Forward-Request packet, the exterior router determines the corresponding cluster. Rather than sending the packet to every network in the cluster, the router sends the packet only to networks whose corresponding zone list includes the zone name present in the Forward-Request packet. Because the router must determine the destination networks corresponding to the specified zone, it must maintain a list of the actual networks and a mapping of those networks to their corresponding zone lists.

6.8.5 Hop-Count Reduction with AURP

Normally, every router increments a packet's hop count when forwarding a packet. To prevent a packet from looping continuously, a forwarding router discards the packet when the hop count reaches the limit of 15. The AppleTalk hop-count limit constrains the diameter of an AppleTalk internet to 15 hops. (In AppleTalk's original design center, a maximum of 15 hops was sufficiently high for an AppleTalk internet.) When a tunnel connects AppleTalk internets, the diameter of the resulting internet may exceed 15 hops. To maintain full connectivity between the two segments of the internet, an exterior router may implement the AURP technique for hop-count reduction.

To allow a DDP packet to go beyond the hop-count limit, an exterior router may reduce the hop-count value in a packet received through the tunnel before forwarding the packet to the local internet. The exterior router reduces the hop count only by the amount necessary to allow the packet to reach its destination. Because the exterior router knows the distance to the destination network, it can calculate the maximum adjusted hop-count value. If, for example, the packet will reach its destination without hop-count reduction, the router just forwards the packet. If the packet's hop count plus the distance to the destination exceeds the limit of 15, the router reduces the hop count to a value calculated by subtracting the distance in hops to the destination network from 15. The adjusted hop-count value allows the packet to traverse the local internet and reach its destination.

In addition to reducing the hop count of DDP packets, a hop-count-reducing router is responsible for representing, within its local internet, reachable distances to the networks accessible through the tunnel. AURP specifies that the exterior router represent all networks through the tunnel as one hop away. Other routers on the local internet then perceive those networks to be reachable and maintain full connectivity.

With hop-count reduction, loops in an internet topology allow an errant packet to potentially circulate forever, for the hop count may never reach the limit. As a result, usage of hop-count reduction is recommended only in topologies without loops. Because AURP's loop-detection technique ensures there are no loops in a remapping environment, an exterior router performs hop-count reduction only when remapping is active and thus there are no loops.

6.8.6 Security through AURP

AURP specifies two types of basic security: device hiding and network hiding. Both types allow a network administrator to determine which services or networks should be visible to which portions of the internet. These hiding functionalities are particularly useful in wide-area environments in which different organizations connect their internets.

A network administrator can configure any AppleTalk Phase 2 router that supports device hiding to hide a particular device. The router keeps the specified device in its local internet from being visible to end nodes on the internet by filtering out NBP Lookup-Reply packets from that device. If nodes cannot receive the device's NBP replies, they cannot locate the service. That is, they cannot learn the device's name and they cannot associate its name with a network address. As a result, device hiding makes it difficult for nodes to access the hidden device. It does not, however, provide true device security because it does not limit direct network access to the device. A node can still send packets to a hidden device's dynamic network address, if known. Thus, device hiding provides a simple security technique that prevents locating services through NBP.

With network hiding, a network administrator can configure a tunneling port to hide routing information for networks being imported across a tunnel or to hide routing information being exported across a tunnel. By limiting imported routing information to information about specific networks, an exterior router reduces routing information that is maintained and propagated by routers on its local internet. Because the networks are not available to nodes on the local internet, neither are the corresponding zones and devices on the networks visible. Similarly, by exporting no information about hidden networks, an exterior router prevents other exterior routers from learning about the existence of those networks. Whether limiting imported or exported routing information, network hiding provides a technique for security across tunnels at the network level. By reducing the number of accessible networks, network hiding also reduces network traffic across the tunnel as well as in the local internets.

Network hiding prevents nodes on networks across the tunnel from accessing any devices on the hidden networks. Conversely, it prevents nodes on the hidden networks from accessing any devices across the tunnel (nodes cannot respond to packets from a hidden and therefore unknown network).

By employing network hiding, a network administrator can set up an internet area known as a *free-trade zone*, an area of the internet accessible by two other parts of the internet that cannot access each other. For example, two organizations may want to share information, but they may not wish to have direct connectivity. A free-trade zone allows both organizations to access a common area and to keep their internets isolated otherwise. A router that is creating a free-trade zone through network hiding exports only networks that are in the free-trade zone. Each organization can see the free-trade networks, but not the networks from the other organization.

6.9 ALTERNATIVE APPLETALK ROUTING METHODS

Besides AppleTalk routing through RTMP, ZIP, and AURP, other mechanisms can extend the user's reach with AppleTalk connectivity. Some of these methods require encapsulation of other protocols, such as TCP/IP, within AppleTalk or, conversely, AppleTalk within other protocols. Two such methods of providing gateways between DDP and IP, MacIP and IPTalk,[4] are described below. Another method, used in Apple Remote Access, allows remote nodes to access an AppleTalk internet over a point-to-point link.

6.9.1 Gateways between DDP and IP (MacIP and IPTalk)

Gateways are devices that translate between sets of protocols, such as AppleTalk and TCP/IP. Because TCP/IP connectivity is a basic requirement in the university environment, early university Macintosh users spearheaded work to allow integration of the Macintosh in their TCP/IP internets. Macintosh computers communicated using AppleTalk, and so the goal was to create a gateway (and client software) that would allow Macintosh computers to communicate through TCP/IP. One such gateway was initially developed at Stanford University. The client software encapsulated IP datagrams in AppleTalk DDP packets, which were then sent to a gateway. The gateway decapsulated the packets and forwarded them to the TCP/IP internet. The Stanford work also specified the inverse: encapsulation of AppleTalk DDP data in IP (UDP) packets. A networking company called Kinetics used the Stanford technology in a gateway product. Kinetics called the gateway a Kinetics IP, or KIP,[4] gateway. Today, KIP continues to be one of the primary implementations for providing a gateway between DDP and IP. The Columbia AppleTalk Package (CAP)[4] is another primary implementation for encapsulating DDP in UDP. The two types of encapsulation, IP in DDP (referred to as MacIP or DDP/IP) and DDP in UDP (referred to as IPTalk), provide distinct ways of integrating AppleTalk nodes in an IP environment.

MacIP allows AppleTalk nodes without direct IP connectivity to have access to a TCP/IP internet nevertheless. The MacIP gateway, both an AppleTalk node and an IP host, has a configured-client range of IP addresses and can assign one of its IP addresses dynamically to an AppleTalk node. The gateway maintains a mapping between DDP node addresses and their assigned IP addresses. IP hosts on the TCP/IP internet perceive the AppleTalk nodes to be ordinary IP hosts. The MacIP gateway creates the perception by acting as a proxy for the AppleTalk nodes. When the MacIP gateway receives an Address Resolution Protocol (ARP)[5] packet for an IP address assigned to a MacIP client, it answers the request with its own physical address. This action is called *proxy ARPing*. Packets destined for the MacIP client will thus be physically addressed to the MacIP gateway, which forwards the packets to the correct AppleTalk node.

ARP functionality is performed on the AppleTalk internet through NBP. Each MacIP client registers with an NBP name containing its own IP address and responds to NBP Lookups for its IP address. When a MacIP client wishes to send a packet to another IP host, it tries to locate the IP host by issuing an NBP Lookup for the IP address. If the Lookup is for another MacIP client managed by the MacIP gateway, the specified client responds directly to the Lookup. Otherwise, the MacIP gateway acts as a proxy for the other IP hosts. When the gateway receives NBP Lookups for any IP addresses that are outside its client range, it responds to the Lookup with its AppleTalk address. When the requesting MacIP client receives the Lookup response, it learns the destination AppleTalk address for the IP packet (encapsulated in DDP) that it is sending. The gateway's NBP proxying ensures that the MacIP clients send the gateway any IP packets destined for the TCP/IP internet.

To communicate with services on a TCP/IP internet, an AppleTalk node sends IP data encapsulated in DDP to a MacIP gateway. The gateway strips off the DDP headers and then sends the packet through the TCP/IP internet. For packets going from TCP/IP to AppleTalk, the gateway encapsulates the IP data in DDP, addresses the packet to the AppleTalk node corresponding to the IP destination address, and sends the packet out. By handling dynamic IP address assignment, address resolution, and packet encapsulation, MacIP enables AppleTalk nodes to fully participate on a TCP/IP internet.

IPTalk allows AppleTalk nodes to communicate by way of an existing TCP/IP internet. Instead of tunneling through the IP internet with point-to-point connections as in AURP, IPTalk treats the IP internet as a virtual AppleTalk network. The IP network on which an IPTalk host resides has an assigned AppleTalk network number. The IPTalk host is a node on this AppleTalk network. Less dynamic than AppleTalk, IPTalk relies upon static, central administration of routes within the TCP/IP internet. IPTalk employs its own protocol to distribute routing information. Rather than using update-based propagation of routing information as in AURP, IPTalk relies initially on configured routing information and thereafter on periodic (once-a-minute) updates. IPTalk hosts rely on the IPTalk version of ZIP query and reply packets to obtain zone information.

An IPTalk gateway maintains a mapping between the IPTalk hosts' AppleTalk addresses and their corresponding IP addresses. The gateway also maintains IP routes (routes to access other IPTalk hosts or gateways) in addition to any local AppleTalk routes. It establishes IP routes both statically (at configuration time) and dynamically (from routing information learned from other gateways). To communicate to a node on the other side of a TCP/IP internet, an end node on an AppleTalk network sends an AppleTalk packet to an IPTalk gateway. The gateway then encapsulates the packet in UDP and sends the packet to the IPTalk host or gateway corresponding to the destination DDP network. The destination gateway, in turn, decapsulates the packet and sends it on to the destination DDP network. By using the TCP/IP internet as a virtual AppleTalk network, IPTalk thus enables AppleTalk nodes to send and receive packets across a TCP/IP internet.

6.9.2 Apple Remote Access

Apple Remote Access (ARA)[3] is a product developed by Apple Computer that allows remote users to dial into an AppleTalk internet (Figure 6.4). Through protocols specially designed to handle remote access via dial-up lines and routing techniques such as remapping and network hiding, ARA enables users to access remote Apple-Talk network resources with virtually the same ease as accessing local resources.

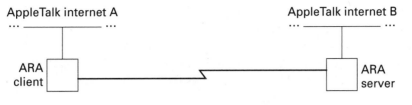

Figure 6.4   Apple Remote Access

When an ARA client connects to an ARA server, the client is able to participate on the server's network in addition to its own local network. ARA does not provide true routing or bridging between the two internets. Instead, the client maintains a unique vantage point. The other nodes on its local internet cannot see the nodes on the remote internet, and similarly the remote nodes cannot see the local nodes. In contrast, the client is able to see both internets and all the nodes on both networks can see the client. The client becomes a virtual node on the remote network in addition to being a node on the local network.

   In the initial exchange of information, the server sends the client the list of zones accessible to the client in the remote internet (possibly filtering certain zones based on the client's authorization rights). The client's own zone name depends on the situation. If the client was already in a zone on its local internet, it maintains that zone name. Otherwise, it joins the zone of the remote network. In either case, remote nodes perceive the client to be in the server's zone, given that it is a virtual node on the server's network.

   In the initial exchange the server also sends the network number and node ID that the client should use when sending AppleTalk packets. ARA resolves any network-number conflicts between the client and the server's network by remapping the two network numbers. ARA provides only remapping between the client and server networks. ARA eliminates other conflicts by hiding from the client any other remote-network numbers that conflict with those in the client's local internet. As a result, the services on the conflicting remote networks are not available to the client. (The client must disconnect from its local network to access those services.) ARA's method of resolving network conflicts places priority on the consistency of the client's internet.

   Because the client clearly must send all packets destined for the remote internet to the server, which in turn forwards the packets, the client has no need for any RTMP routing information. As a result, the ARA server filters RTMP packets and does not forward them to the client. In addition, ARA compensates for the relatively slow link speed of dial-up lines by requiring a reliable connection and by using a technique called *smart buffering*. Smart buffering is a method for reducing line traffic by using tokens. Because retransmission of data can unnecessarily consume bandwidth over a reliable link, ARA does not send duplicate packets or even duplicate parts of packets.

Instead, an ARA client sends tokens to represent the retransmitted, duplicate information, substantially reducing the amount of data sent.

ARA handles NBP similarly to routers. When the client needs to look up a network service, it sends an NBP *Broadcast-Request* (BrRq) packet, regardless of whether a router exists. When the ARA server receives the NBP BrRq packet, it treats it much as a router would. It determines whether to forward the lookup to a router or whether to send it out on its local network.

Thus, through a combination of routing and forwarding techniques, an ARA server creates a virtual node on its network for every connected ARA client. Without providing full routing or bridging, the ARA server provides connectivity between remote nodes and the server's AppleTalk internet. The remote node, the ARA client, thus gains full access to the server's internet while maintaining access to its own local internet.

6.10 SUMMARY

The AppleTalk suite of protocols supports routing in large data networks and has been designed for "plug-and-play" operation. AppleTalk not only provides dynamic routing for data messages but also dynamic name and address assignment for end nodes. With AppleTalk, network connection of an end node such as a computer or peripheral device requires almost no preconfiguration. Moreover, communication with that end node may begin almost immediately after it is connected to the Apple-Talk network. AppleTalk includes protocols for binding end-node names and addresses, distributing network reachability and naming information among routers, and forwarding data messages between end nodes. It also includes protocols to support communication in multiprotocol internetworks. Specifically, AppleTalk employs tunneling for connecting noncontiguous AppleTalk networks, gateways for communicating between AppleTalk and TCP/IP networks, and remote access facilities for connecting users to distant AppleTalk networks over point-to-point links. Its ease of use combined with its ability to function in multiprotocol environments has made AppleTalk one of the most popular routing systems for corporate and academic internetworks.

REFERENCES

1   G. Sidhu, R. Andrews, and A. Oppenheimer, *Inside AppleTalk,* 2nd ed.,
    Apple Computer, Inc., Reading: Addison-Wesley, May 1990.

2 *AppleTalk Update-Based Routing Protocol: Enhanced AppleTalk Routing,* Apple Computer, Inc. Available through APDA, Apple Computer, Inc. Also available as *Internet Request for Comments 1504,* through the Internet Engineering Task Force (IETF).

3 "AppleTalk Remote Access Protocol Version 1.0," Apple Computer, Inc. Available in the *AppleTalk Remote Access Developer's Toolkit v. 1.0,* through APDA, Apple Computer, Inc.

4 P. Budne, "KIP AppleTalk/IP Gateway Functionality," Information Internet Draft, Shiva Corporation. Available through the Internet Engineering Task Force (IETF).

5 D. Comer, *Internetworking with TCP/IP,* 2nd ed., Vol. I, Englewood Cliffs: Prentice Hall, 1991.

6 A. Tanenbaum, *Computer Networks,* Englewood Cliffs: Prentice Hall, 1981.

PART III   ❖ ❖ ❖ ❖

HIGH-SPEED
NETWORKS

Users of communications networks are coming to expect these networks to accommodate widely varied applications with heterogeneous service requirements. Multimedia applications require simultaneous communication of different types of traffic, including voice, data, and video. Each of these traffic types has different bandwidth requirements and tolerances for network-introduced delay, errors, and loss. For a given type of traffic (e.g., video), the required transmission rate depends upon the information encoding scheme used. Furthermore, over the duration of a single traffic session, the transmission rate may fluctuate because the application (e.g., interactive database query/response) generates traffic bursts. Applications also vary according to their traffic delivery patterns. In particular, distributed applications (e.g., videoconferencing) may require multipoint as well as point-to-point peer communication.

Today, users customarily obtain different services through different networks (e.g., telephone networks, data networks, and cable television networks) tailored to specific uses. In the long term, however, this approach is impractical for the following reasons. First, managing multiple parallel networks is complicated and expensive. Second, supporting multimedia applications involves tightly coordinated, simultaneous use of multiple networks. Third, providing new services requires building new networks.

High-speed networks are a highly flexible and cost-effective alternative, offering diverse communication services to large numbers of users within a single network. The development of high-speed networks, fueled by demands for heterogeneous services, has been made possible by recent advances in high-speed transmission and switching technology. These include fiber optics, digital devices, and switching architectures based on interconnection networks of simple switching nodes with minimal buffering capabilities. An excellent treatment of high-speed switch architectures and their performance can be found in suggested reading 1.

As providers of services that have traditionally been offered only in circuit-switched networks or only in packet-switched networks, high-speed networks have fostered a synergy between circuit switching and packet switching. The most promising switching techniques proposed for high-speed networks have been hybrids of circuit switching and packet switching. Many of these hybrids are capable of eliminating delay variance and guaranteeing bandwidth (as in circuit switching) and are also capable of using resources efficiently and accommodating variable-rate traffic (as in packet switching).

Some of these hybrids combine features of circuit switching and packet switching within a new switching technique. *Burst switching*[5,6] allocates network resources to traffic sessions, but only when the users need to send traffic. Thus, it promotes resource sharing among multiple bursty traffic sessions. *Fast packet switching*[7] reduces packet handling delay, using short (fixed- or variable-length) packets. Each packet carries forwarding information designed to minimize packet processing time at a switch. Combined burst/fast-packet switching approaches[8] have also been proposed.

Another hybrid is the integrated circuit–packet switch, which maintains the distinction between circuit switching and packet switching but integrates the two techniques in a single network. Integrated networks use time-division multiplexing to combine circuit-switched and packet-switched traffic, which is transmitted in slotted frames. In most variants, circuit-switched traffic takes precedence over packet-switched traffic. Each frame includes a portion containing circuit-switched traffic followed by a portion containing packet-switched traffic. Some variants of this approach allow variable-length frames and a moving boundary between the circuit-switched and packet-switched portions.[9]

In high-speed networks, the main routing problems involve selecting feasible routes and forwarding traffic so as to reduce loss under load. Accurate models of user traffic and link loading as well as efficient multiobjective, multiconstraint route generation algorithms are required to obtain feasible routes that satisfy the diverse service requirements of the applications. Traffic scheduling and diverting techniques are required to minimize traffic loss in the presence of heavily loaded switches. (During output contention within a switch, buffering traffic or recirculating traffic through the interconnection network further helps reduce loss.)

The switch interconnection networks themselves also present interesting routing problems. These are not covered in detail in this section but are briefly described below. High-speed switches must deal with internal contention for paths through the interconnection network, which can impose traffic delay or result in traffic loss. Internal blocking can be eliminated by an interconnection network with dedicated paths between all input/output pairs of the switch. This approach is impractical, however, for switches connecting large numbers of inputs and outputs. A more economical alternative is the *sort-banyan* interconnection network. This is a combination of a banyan network (which is internally nonblocking under certain conditions on traffic output ordering) with a sorting network (which ensures that traffic is presented to the banyan network in a nonblocking output ordering).

To further reduce the delay through their interconnection networks, some high-speed switches make use of fast forwarding techniques originally developed for packet-switched networks. These include source-specified forwarding (referred to as *self routing* in the interconnection network context) and virtual cut-through, both of which are described in the packet-switching section of this book. Moreover, to improve the performance of multipoint communication within the larger network, some high-speed switches have incorporated multicast capabilities into their interconnection networks.

The three chapters contained within this section—"Routing in Optical Networks" by J. Bannister, M. Gerla, and M. Kovacevic, "Routing in the plaNET Network" by I. Cidon and Roch Guérin, and "Deflection Routing" by F. Borgonovo—reflect the great variety in today's high-speed networking technologies and associated routing strategies. High-speed networking is a young and rapidly growing field, and thus one can look forward to many exciting advances in the future.

SELECTED SUGGESTIONS FOR FURTHER READING

1   J. Y. Hui, *Switching and Traffic Theory for Integrated Broadband Networks,* Boston: Kluwer Academic Publishers, 1990.

2   M. Schwartz, *Telecommunication Networks: Protocols, Modeling and Analysis,* Reading: Addison-Wesley, 1987.

3   C. Partridge, *Gigabit Networking,* Reading: Addison-Wesley, 1994.

4   *IEEE Communications,* Vol. 31, No. 2, February 1993.

5   S. R. Amstutz, "Burst Switching—An Introduction," *IEEE Communications,* November 1983, pp. 36–42.

6   B. N. W. Ma and J. W. Mark, "Performance Analysis of Burst Switching for Integrated Voice/Data Services," *IEEE Transactions on Communications,* Vol. 36, No. 3, March 1988, pp. 282–297.

7   J. S. Turner, "New Directions in Communications (or Which Way to the Information Age?)," *IEEE Communications,* Vol. 24, No. 10, October 1986, pp. 8–15.

8   H. Suzuki and F. A. Tobagi, "Fast Bandwidth Reservation Scheme with Multi-Link and Multi-Path Routing in ATM Networks," *Proceedings of the INFOCOM '92,* Florence, May 1992, pp. 2233–2240.

9   B. Maglaris and M. Schwartz, "Performance Evaluation of a Variable Frame Multiplexer for Integrated Switched Networks," *IEEE Transactions on Communications,* Vol. Com-29, No. 6, June 1981, pp. 800–807.

CHAPTER 7   ❖ ❖ ❖ ❖

Routing in Optical Networks

JOSEPH BANNISTER, MARIO GERLA,
AND MILAN KOVAČEVIĆ

CONTENTS

Networks with optical components hold great promise for supporting real-time high-resolution multimedia applications, because these networks are capable of transmitting data at much higher rates and more reliably than their conventional electronic counterparts. Already, optical transmission links have replaced copper wire in many networks. Truly optical networks, namely those with optical-transmission, switching, and even packet-processing capabilities, are only in the early stages of development, however. Optical networking technology is capable of supporting both circuit switching and packet switching, hence existing routing techniques may be successfully applied to certain types of optical networks. Nevertheless, new routing schemes are necessary for some optical networks, to take advantage of new features (e.g., wavelength division multiplexing) and to address new problems (e.g., the difficulty of buffering) inherent in optical information transfer. This chapter comprehensively catalogs the various routing algorithms that have been proposed for optical networks, covering single-hop, multihop, and hybrid optical networks as well as photonic networks.

7.1 INTRODUCTION

Optical communication networks carry messages that are encoded as lightwave signals—electromagnetic radiation in the visible and near-visible spectrum. The ability to transmit lightwave signals over silica-based optical-fiber waveguides at very high data rates and with superior reliability has accelerated the development of optical networks. Optical networking embraces systems that range from simple fiber-upgrade networks, replacing electrical transmission lines with optical-fiber links, to recently proposed all-optical networks, in which message transmission and processing are entirely in the optical domain.

Because the technologies that underlie optical networking are evolving rapidly, optical networks are appearing in greatly diverse forms, both implemented and proposed (see, e.g., reference 22). An advance in technology will almost always be accompanied by novel network architectures that take advantage of it. The rich possibilities in optical networking explain why many unique routing strategies have been born and nurtured in the context of optical networking.

Optical networks share with conventional electronic networks the fundamental goal of efficiently delivering integrated traffic (e.g., video, voice, and data) under varied unpredictable conditions (e.g., failures, congestion, and malicious misuse). Thus, we need packet-switching, datagram services, and circuit-switching—which is technically a misnomer in optical networks, because electrical circuits are not required—connection-oriented services. Packet-switched traffic can tolerate the network layer nondeterministic delay, out-of-sequence delivery, and packet loss. The traffic class either does not require guaranteed end-to-end delivery or else relies on upper-layer protocols to provide guaranteed end-to-end delivery. The so-called real-time traffic class, however, demands deterministic delay and in-order delivery of information; it may also require that specified error rates not be exceeded and that the virtual circuit provide a given throughput.

But profound differences distinguish optical from conventional electronic networks. The single-mode optical fiber—the primary medium for transmitting lightwave signals—can effectively guide light with wavelengths in the 0.8-, 1.3-, and 1.5-μm windows, which correspond to regions for which light sources and detectors are readily obtained. These windows represent a combined bandwidth of about 75 THz. The staggering bandwidth inherent in the optical network dwarfs by orders of magnitude the bandwidth provided by electronic transmission systems. Thus, the engineering tradeoffs in optical networking are radically different from those in conventional electronic networking. This complete reordering of the design space significantly affects the routing schemes to be used. Amid this relative abundance of bandwidth, one might even argue that bandwidth can be wasted with little adverse consequence. Our goal in this chapter is to gain insight into the interplay between optical-networking technologies and routing.

Our scope in this chapter is wide-, metropolitan-, and local-area optical networks. Although optical networks for computer interconnection (e.g., optical backplanes) are assuming prominence, they are not included in this survey because routing is not a significant problem in these networks.

In summary, optical networks present unique, challenging routing problems, and several novel solutions have been proposed. In this chapter we classify optical networks and describe how messages are routed in each of these network classes. We begin by surveying the technologies upon which optical networks are based. We then present a taxonomy of optical networks, classifying networks according to the way messages are routed. Routing procedures for each of the network classes are discussed in detail.

7.2 OPTICAL NETWORKS: SURVEYING THE TECHNOLOGY

In this section we review the foundations of optical networking. Lightwave, photonic, and optical-waveguide technologies have made great strides, and these trends will certainly continue. Therefore, to understand routing in optical networks, the reader should have a working knowledge of the technological underpinnings of this family of networks. We first describe the devices that have become part of the repertory of the optical-network architect.

Figure 7.1   Four-port fused biconical-taper coupler

A range of unique optical devices has been investigated for use in communication networks, and we review the characteristics of and basic functions performed by these devices. New componentry is being developed steadily; here is a partial sampling of what is available today and will be available tomorrow.

- *Optical Fibers   Optical-fiber waveguides* consist of a central cylinder—or core—of low-loss material such as silica glass, surrounded by an outer cladding of slightly lower refractive index. Single-mode optical fibers, which have cores about 10 μm in diameter, transmit only one mode of light, thereby eliminating the gradual spreading of pulse energy that limits speed and distance of transmission in multimode fibers. Such single-mode fibers exhibit attenuation loss as low as 0.16 dB/km. Although free from modal dispersion, single-mode optical fibers are subject to the effects of chromatic dispersion, in which different wavelengths propagate through the fiber at different speeds so that signals temporally spread out. Partial compensation for these effects can be achieved by techniques for manufacturing dispersion-shifted and -flattened fibers, which allow improved operation in the 1.3- and 1.5-μm windows. Because of their small physical dimension (cladding diameters of about 100 μm), a great many fibers can be packaged in a cable. Cables containing hundreds of fibers have been manufactured.

- *Optical Couplers   A* ubiquitous device in optical networks, the *optical coupler* is used to split power from an incoming optical fiber to its outgoing optical fibers. Furthermore, it can also merge lightwave signals from two incoming fibers into an outgoing fiber. The coupler's splitting and merging characteristics are determined at the time of manufacture and cannot be altered. Pairs of single-mode optical fibers are coupled by the fused biconical-taper process,[70] as shown in Figure 7.1. The geometry of the taper can be adjusted to produce the desired coupling ratio. Four-port couplers can be interconnected to create generalized star couplers of *n* inputs and outputs, or star couplers with up to 128 ports can be fabricated as integrated devices.[31] Being a completely passive device that requires no power supply, the coupler is extremely reliable and inexpensive. Its excess loss is very low.

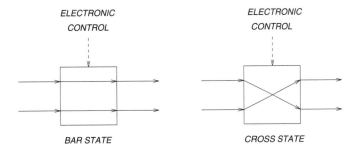

Figure 7.2   2 × 2 optical space switch

- *Optical Space Switches*   The *optical space switch*—the 2 × 2 version of which is illustrated in Figure 7.2—implements, in response to a control signal, any permutation of input ports to output ports. The devices are usually constructed by diffusing titanium into a lithium-niobate substrate (Ti:LiNbO$_3$),[71] but they can also be made of semiconductor compounds.[59] Capable of fast switching, these devices are found in many optical networks. These switches generally have high insertion loss (4 to 5 dB). More general $n \times n$ switches can also be manufactured.[40]

- *Linear Divider–Combiners*   A lithium-niobate device, the *linear divider– combiner* (LDC) is a generalization of the optical space switch that can be configured to provide arbitrary power coupling among inputs and outputs. The LDC is a device of n inputs and outputs that passes lightwave signals according to a user-specified optical-power transfer matrix a_{ij}, where entry a_{ij} indicates the fraction of power sent from input i to output j. Figure 7.3 illustrates the dividing and combining of optical signals. Coefficient δ_{ij} represents the portion of optical power from input port i distributed to output port j, and coefficient σ_{ij} represents the portion of optical power from input port i that is directed to output port j. Clearly $a_{ij} = \delta_{ij} \, \sigma_{ij}$. As a generalized coupler, the LDC can simultaneously divide and combine lightwave signals in accordance with the wishes of the device's owner. A wavelength-selective LDC is one in which specific wavelengths have distinct transfer matrices. This device allows different dividing and combining coefficients to be applied to different wavelengths simultaneously, so that different wavelengths that enter the LDC through the same input can have different power distributions to the outputs.

- *Wavelength-Division Multiplexers and Demultiplexers*   The multiplexing and demultiplexing of wavelengths is made possible by diffraction gratings that can spatially separate wavelengths from each other.[41] The demultiplexer takes an inbound composite lightwave signal and passes each constituent signal to a different outbound port. Conversely, the multiplexer combines individual signals

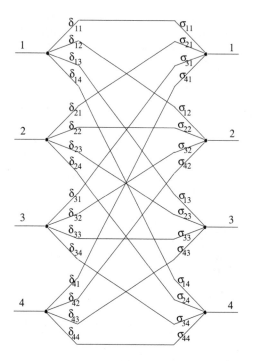

Figure 7.3   4 × 4 linear divider–combiner

from the inbound ports and merges them into the single outbound port. In Figure 7.4 we show the functions of an *n*-port wavelength multiplexer and demultiplexer.

- *Wavelength Routers*   A component that sends an input signal to a particular output on the basis of the signal's wavelength is a *wavelength router*. The wavelength router is a generalization of the wavelength-division demultiplexer. In fact, the wavelength router can be implemented as a network of demultiplexers.[41] Normal wavelength routers merely pass a wavelength from an input port to

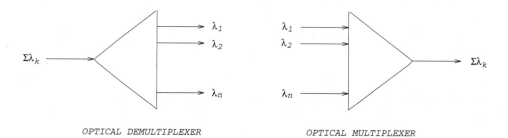

Figure 7.4   Wavelength-division multiplexer and demultiplexer

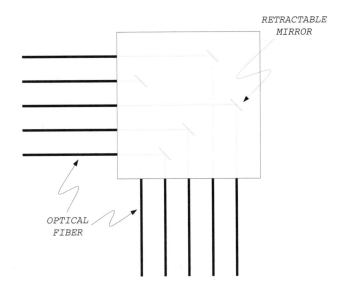

Figure 7.5 *n* × *n* optomechanical crossbar

an output port. *Converting* wavelength routers not only route the incoming wavelength but also translate it to a new wavelength, thereby improving the utilization of wavelengths by reducing wavelength conflicts.

- *Optomechanical Switches*   The *optomechanical switch* functions like the space switch discussed above, except that lightwave signals are switched by mechanical means. These devices, which are slow but inexpensive, are typically mirror-, prism-, or solenoid-based designs. A mirror-based optomechanical crossbar is shown in Figure 7.5.

- *Acoustooptical Tunable Filters*   The *acoustooptical tunable filter* (AOTF) permits selection of one or more wavelengths from an aggregate signal that consists of many wavelengths. Soundwaves traveling through an optical material interact with lightwaves through the photoelastic effect, inducing destructive interference that changes the properties of the incident lightwave. These devices have a wide tuning range, but their tuning times are relatively long (on the order of several µs). The AOTF with multiwavelength selectivity is shown in Figure 7.6.

- *Optical Amplifiers*   Although understanding routing in optical networks does not necessarily require familiarity with optical-amplification technology, development of the *erbium-doped fiber amplifier* (EDFA) has greatly accelerated the growth of optical networking.[73] Capable of amplifying wideband lightwave signals in the 1.5-µm wavelength window, the EDFA boosts power of an incoming signal without the need for signal regeneration. Other rare-earth–doped fiber

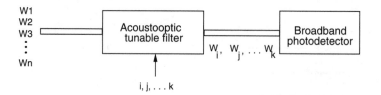

Figure 7.6   Acoustooptical tunable filter with multiwavelength selectivity

amplifiers, such as praseodymium- or neodymium-doped fluoride-fiber amplifiers, can be similarly constructed to amplify lightwave signals in the 1.3-μm window.

7.3 OPTICAL NETWORKS: A ROUTING-BASED TAXONOMY

Although other taxonomies of optical networks have been proposed,[41,60,61] we present a taxonomy that is based on how the network routes messages from sources to destinations. Such a taxonomy provides the most natural framework within which to discuss routing.

Our taxonomy classifies an optical network as a member of one of these five categories:

- Optical-Link Networks

- Single-Hop Optical Networks

- Multihop Optical Networks

- Hybrid Optical Networks

- Photonic Networks

Each network category is determined by the way in which a message is routed through the network. In *optical-link networks,* electronic links are replaced by optical fibers to achieve higher data-rates and lower error rates. Thus, routing is accomplished analogously to routing in conventional electronic networks such as the Internet, System Network Architecture, and DECnet. *Single-hop networks* route messages from a source to a destination in one hop, that is, no in-band processing of the message takes place at intermediate points. However, some networks use out-of-band signaling to establish and release physical paths from a source to a destination. The routing procedure in a single-hop network must therefore select a physical route that connects the source and destination without intervention by electronic switches. *Multihop optical networks* allow the message to be processed at intermediate points, delivering it after several electrooptical conversions have been made. Routing in multihop optical networks is focused on the problem of determining the best sequence of electronic switches by which to relay a message from its source to its destination. *Hybrid optical networks* combine single- and multihop techniques. The hybrid network consists of single- and multihop subnetworks that must incorporate the routing procedures of their respective type of network. *Photonic networks* are all-optical networks that can process information in a message photonically. Each category is discussed here in greater detail, with emphasis on routing.

7.4   OPTICAL-LINK NETWORKS

An optical-link network uses optical fiber instead of metallic wire. These networks consist of electronic switches connected in a mesh topology by point-to-point optical links. This approach guarantees higher transmission rates and lower error rates than nonoptical systems but does not take advantage of the unique properties of optical technology. The advantages of an optical-link network over a conventional electronic-link network are the higher bandwidth and lower error rates that optical-fiber transmission provides. On the other hand, optical links are more expensive than electronic links, and it is more difficult to implement electronic switches that match the speeds of optical links.

Examples of optical-link networks include the *Broadband Integrated Services Digital Network* (B-ISDN), which uses *asynchronous transfer mode* (ATM) cell switching, and the gigabit testbed networks,[38] which are sponsored by the U.S. government to promote the so-called information superhighway.

The main challenge in designing a routing scheme for these networks is high speed, which requires that the packet-by-packet processing overhead be kept as low as possible. Typical solutions include source routing, virtual-circuit routing, and cut-through switching to minimize packet buffering. Such solutions are described in detail in Chapters 2 and 8.

Routing in optical-link networks is fundamentally the same as in conventional electronic networks. Surveys of routing in packet-switching networks can be found in references 34 and 69 as well as in the chapters in Part II of this volume. For these reasons we do not cover routing in optical-link networks in this chapter.

7.5   SINGLE-HOP OPTICAL NETWORKS

In a single-hop optical network a message moves from the source to a destination in one hop without conversion from the optical domain and without having in-band control information processed. The defining schema for the single-hop optical

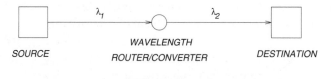

- MESSAGE ENTIRELY IN OPTICAL DOMAIN
- NO PROCESSING OF IN-BAND CONTROL INFORMATION
- OPTIONAL WAVELENGTH ROUTING/CONVERSION

Figure 7.7   Single-hop optical network

network is shown in Figure 7.7. Notice that wavelength routing and conversion are permitted. The message travels through the network in one hop, and routing is essentially done by finding a channel from the source to the destination, given that several channels are provided. In single-channel, single-hop networks routing trivially reduces to the multiaccess problem.

Many single-hop optical networks consist of stations attached to an *optical star coupler,* which broadcasts any signal sent to it to all stations of the network, as shown in Figure 7.8. Examples include LAMBDANET[36] and Rainbow.[30] In LAMBDA-NET, which is intended to provide connectivity among telecommunication central

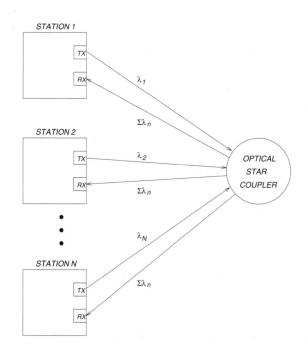

Figure 7.8   Broadcast-and-select star network

offices, each station has a unique-wavelength transmitter by which it transmits time-division–multiplexed messages. The station has a grating demultiplexer that feeds into a bank of receivers. Each receiver selects a wavelength and a time slot from which the message is to be extracted. Thus, tunability is not required, but each station must possess a full complement of receivers. Stations also have a common-wavelength transmitter, which is used for signaling and call management. Access to the common wavelength is governed by *time-division multiplexing* (TDM). A station in the Rainbow network transmits on a unique wavelength. Each station has a slowly tunable filter that can pick out the proper wavelength for the receiver. Rainbow is primarily for circuit switching, and does not operate efficiently as a packet-switching network. The star-based networks do not support a large population of stations, because star couplers are port limited, and stations cannot easily achieve the wavelength agility needed to communicate with all other stations.

Quadro[24] is another single-hop network based on *wavelength-division multiplexing* (WDM) in a star topology. It circumvents many issues of transmitter–receiver coordination by allowing a receiver to get multiple simultaneous transmissions. Quadro stations have one fixed-wavelength transmitter and one tunable receiver equipped with a series of optical delay-line stages that are used like reception buffers. If two stations transmit simultaneously to the same destination, the destination can route the two modulated wavelengths through the delay lines, picking off the first wavelength before the signals enter the first stage of the delay line and then picking off the second when the signals exit from the stage. This routing can be done repeatedly, if necessary, but the signals are forever lost once they exit the final stage. A reservation protocol is used to notify the receiver of planned transmissions.

TreeNet,[35] on the other hand, is a single-hop network that uses the tree topology for signal distribution. The tree is constructed of optical fiber joined by fused biconical-taper couplers at the interior nodes. Stations are located only at the leaves of the tree. Whereas the star-based single-hop networks have a centrally located star coupler, TreeNet geographically distributes coupling devices to achieve greater fault tolerance and scalability. The tree forms a broadcast medium upon which a multichannel access protocol is used, given stations with tunable transceivers. Providing amplification at the root allows for a station population of several hundred to be supported. TreeNet is depicted in Figure 7.9.

Single-hop networks that use wavelength-routing devices have also been proposed. In reference 15, networks are based on *periodic Latin routers,* which are static wavelength routers that route groups of wavelengths from inputs to outputs in a manner suggested by the familiar Latin square (a two-dimensional matrix in which no entries are repeated in any row or any column). The physical realization of the periodic Latin router is a *Mach–Zehnder interferometer,* a device that sends periodically spaced wavelengths of light to alternating output ports. Single-hop networks can be devised from periodic Latin routers. Stations must be able to tune over the range of wavelengths,

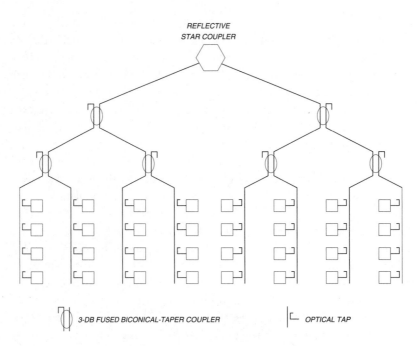

Figure 7.9   32-station TreeNet physical layout

and a wavelength-assignment protocol is used in establishing virtual circuits from a source to a destination. Multicasting cannot be performed at the physical level.

Marsan et al.[58] studied routing in wavelength-routing networks with structured topologies and no wavelength conversion. Wavelength routers are arranged in bidirectional toroidal,[65] shuffle-based,[1] or de Bruijn topologies,[28] and multifiber links are provided between the routers. The routers are configured to realize a fixed algorithm that guarantees shortest paths. The near-optimal wavelength-allocation strategy can in some cases be shown to require the fewest wavelengths possible.

The network of reference 57 also is based on wavelength routers, but these routers can convert a signal from one wavelength to another while routing it. Unlike the Latin-router approach, these routers are configured during network operation, as through an out-of-band control network. Such a feature allows better link utilization by reducing call blocking in the network. The network uses *centralized dynamic routing*, in which call requests are processed by a route server that keeps track of the total resource usage in the network and provides to the caller the best route for the call. This procedure supports circuit switching exclusively. Physical-level multicasting is possible in this type of network, but the setup of multicast calls complicates routing.

The linear lightwave network (LLN)[68] is also a single-hop network. The LLN uses LDCs as nodes in a mesh topology. User stations are attached to the LDCs, which are programmed to create broadcast media among sets of stations, as shown in

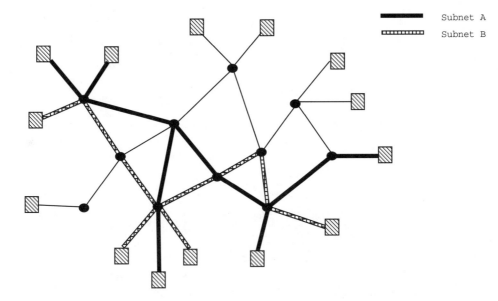

Figure 7.10   Linear lightwave network overlaid with two subnets

Figure 7.10. The LLN architecture was extended in reference 67 to include wavelength-selective LDCs. This enhancement permits even greater flexibility in defining subnetworks—that is, a subnetwork is defined by a set of LCDs and a waveband of several contiguous wavelengths. The LLN changes and maintains its subnetworks by an out-of-band control network that allows a controller to configure the LDCs.

Single-hop networks can establish a dedicated optical path between source and destination, and so they support circuit-switched connections very well. Multicast transmission is also achievable in principle, but for optical networks that use wavelength tuning, it could be difficult to prearrange for all members of a multicast group to simultaneously tune to the wavelength of the multicasting station.

In single-hop networks that provide broadcast media, such as stars and trees, routing is straightforward. When the broadcast medium supports a multichannel access scheme, receiver–transmitter coordination is the main problem. However, not all single-hop networks employ full broadcast media. Such single-hop networks can use different physical paths to deliver messages from a source to a destination. The routing problem in these networks is how to determine and manage the physical path to be used.

Passive optical networks (PONs) route signals over physical paths that remain fixed for a long time. These networks include broadcast-star networks, such as LAMBDA-NET and Rainbow, as well as broadcast-tree networks, such as TreeNet. These networks establish a single-hop route from a source to a destination merely by assigning the right wavelength for the job. For instance, a source in the Rainbow network

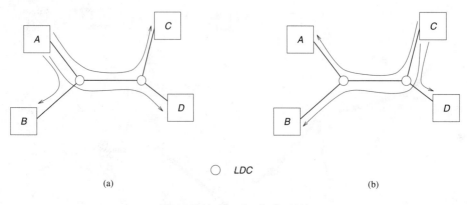

○ *LDC*

(a)   (b)

Figure 7.11   Routing in the LLN

delivers its message to a destination by transmitting the message on its fixed wave-length during a specific time slot. The destination tunes its receiver to the source's wavelength during the specified time slot. These networks are consequently restricted to circuit-switched operation, in which a wavelength (and possibly a time slot) is dedicated to a given connection. In general, multicast routing is not possible in these PONs.

We recall that the internal nodes of a PON consist only of switches, couplers, wavelength filters, and possibly, optical amplifiers. Functionally, in a node, an incoming wavelength can be split and distributed, in different power ratios, to different output ports. No header processing or packet storing and forwarding of any sort is performed. Thus, routing in a PON is essentially circuit switching and consists of establishing paths (between source–destination pairs) or broadcast trees (between subsets of stations) within a physical topology. This topology is generally a mesh, but can also be a tree, as we shall see.

The fiber layout in a PON may also include multifiber links. That is, a link is implemented with a fiber ribbon, or a bundle containing dozens, or even hundreds of fibers. This feature clearly introduces a large number of alternate-path options, which can be selected using space-division multiplexing. In this way the multifiber-cable technique can effectively complement WDM, compensating for the scarcity of wavelengths (a few dozen) available in a single fiber with today's technology.

Let us start with the broadcast-tree routing problem. For simplicity, we assume single-fiber, single-wavelength links, though the results can easily be generalized to more complex cases. In a PON mesh we have two basic alternatives for broadcast-tree routing: shortest-path routing and *rooted routing*.

The LLN can establish subnetworks, as in the basic LLN[68] and LLN with wave-band reuse.[67] In the original LLN proposal the routing of optical signals in a subnetwork is performed with shortest-path routing, as illustrated in Figure 7.11. If *A* transmits, then the routing pattern in Figure 7.11(a) is followed. If *C* transmits, then the pattern shown in Figure 7.11(b) is followed. In general a separate broadcast tree is associated with each source; the tree consists of all stations that can "hear" the source. LDCs are configured to support such distinct broadcast trees. Although it appears natural, this routing approach has serious limitations if the subnetwork resources are shared using time-division or time- and wavelength-division multiaccess (TDMA and T/WDMA) schemes. The problem lies in the difficulties of coordinating and synchronizing transmissions.[68] The synchronization problem is difficult because in the LLN there is no single point of synchronization (as there is in a broadcast-star topology), so that transmissions must be synchronized for not just one (central) node, but several nodes. Furthermore, these synchronization requirements may conflict, making it impossible to achieve the optimal utilization of a shared channel.[48]

In reference 48 the synchronization problem is solved with rooted routing, in which a tree is constructed for each source as a broadcast tree to all destinations (see Figure 7.10). But here all trees share the same root (and, in fact, are overlapped for most of the way).[48] The main advantage of rooted routing is that the root represents a single synchronization point for all transmissions. Using this common reference, it becomes much easier to coordinate the transmissions from all sources, in a TDMA or T/WDMA scheme, as is done in a star network. There is slight degradation in propagation delay and power attenuation with respect to shortest-path routing, but it was shown that this degradation becomes negligible as network size grows.[48,51] Finally, a problem to be addressed in rooted routing is the choice of the root node. Clearly, the root node must be chosen so that the longest path from station to root is minimized, in order to minimize attenuation. This criterion is dictated by the fact that in a PON we wish to avoid, if possible, or minimize attenuation. The actual selection of the root, following the attenuation criterion, can be accomplished with a center-of-mass algorithm on the mesh.[51]

Bala et al.[23] proposed a different approach for using the LLN. Instead of setting up static subnetworks (i.e., using static routing), an optical path is established dynamically for a circuit-switched connection between a pair of stations by configuring the LDCs over an out-of-band control network. In this work only non–wavelength-selective LDCs are used, and different signals (wavelengths) are allowed to share the same fiber. Because the LDCs are not wavelength-selective, signals combined on one optical fiber cannot be separated within the LLN (this is the *inseparability property*). This condition can lead to the situation where the same signal is split into multiple paths in the network and then recombined on a link. A special constraint on establishing connections has to be imposed to prevent such a situation, which would create the undesirable multipath interference of signals. Algorithms for dynamic routing in the LLN are proposed in reference 23. In reference 19, dynamic routing algorithms for multicast connections are also proposed.

The *wavelength-selective transmission network*, described in references 42 and 43, uses static wavelength routing to distribute signals among stations. In this network wavelength routers are arranged in a star, bus, or ring topology so as to exploit spatial reuse of wavelengths. A multitransmitter source station sends messages to a multireceiver destination over a prespecified wavelength.

The *single-hop interconnection* (SHI) is a static PON that provides a communication path between each pair of attached stations. Reference 17 shows how to cable together stations and schedule their message exchanges in a power-efficient manner (which is essential in PONs). This PON uses optical star couplers and multiple transceivers per station. When a source station wishes to transmit its message to a destination station, it selects a fixed-wavelength transmitter to launch the message over a particular path and a time slot during which to launch the message. Birk[18] presents a three-stage layout of stars and cables and a transmission schedule that permits the SHI to accommodate $\log_2 N$ concurrent message exchanges per time slot. Because the physical topology is static, the network routes messages merely by choosing which transmitter to use. Multicasting cannot be accomplished in a single-hop manner.

Routing in single-hop networks uses diverse techniques. These networks are usually PONs, which require no in-band control information to configure. The network is almost always static or pseudostatic, with reconfigurations or retunings occurring infrequently. If single-hop paths are fixed, then a source station initiates a call by consulting its own directory. If the paths can change, then a source must consult a well-known route server, which provides to it the method for accessing its route. Because single-hop networks resort primarily to circuit switching for message exchange, their routing techniques are sometimes similar to multiaccess methods in multichannel local area networks.

7.6 MULTIHOP OPTICAL NETWORKS

A *multihop optical network* carries a message from the source to a destination through intermediate electronic switches. Multihop optical networks are distinguished from optical-link networks by the former's use of multiple wavelengths. A multihop optical network is typically embedded within a PON, in which WDM is employed to distribute signals among stations. This system more effectively exploits the properties of lightwave systems, which can multiplex many high-speed channels in one single-mode optical fiber. The quintessential multihop optical network is illustrated in Figure 7.12.

The multihop optical network is characterized by having a *physical topology*, which consists of the actual links and stations of the network, and a *virtual topology*, which is the logical interconnection of stations. Physical and virtual topologies are independent of one another.

The prototype for the multihop optical network is *ShuffleNet*.[1] ShuffleNet is a multichannel network with a PON physical topology and a recirculating–perfect-shuffle virtual topology. Each station has p transmitters and p receivers

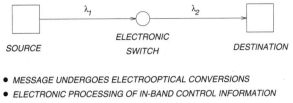

- MESSAGE UNDERGOES ELECTROOPTICAL CONVERSIONS
- ELECTRONIC PROCESSING OF IN-BAND CONTROL INFORMATION
- MESSAGE USES MULTIPLE WAVELENGTHS

Figure 7.12 Multihop optical network

(commonly $p = 2$) that are tuned to realize the ShuffleNet interconnection graph. The (p,k) ShuffleNet graph is constructed from kp^k stations arranged as k stages of p^k stations each; the stations of a stage are connected to the stations of the following stage in a perfect p-shuffle. ShuffleNet can be embedded in any PON, including the linear bus, central star, and tree. In Figure 7.13 we show an eight-station (binary) ShuffleNet virtual topology embedded in a star physical topology. Each WDM

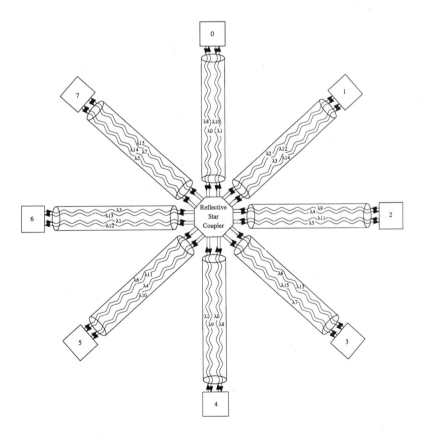

Figure 7.13 ShuffleNet virtual topology embedded in a star physical topology

channel is allocated to a single transmitter and a single receiver, for a total of pN channels, where N is the station population. The stations function as routing nodes, performing electrooptical conversion, buffering, and switching of packets.

There are many variations on the ShuffleNet theme. The virtual topology of a multihop optical network can be changed by retuning transceivers (either at network installation time, or when the network is operational, if stations have tunable transceivers). The *wavelength-division optical network* (WON)[11] is a generalization of ShuffleNet that provides stations with slowly tunable transceivers that can be used to redefine the virtual topology whenever performance must be improved or connectivity reestablished. The *shared-channel* multihop network[2] allows multiple stations to be allocated to a single WDM channel (and requires a contention-resolution algorithm for the shared channel), giving relief from the requirement for the high degree of WDM used in the *dedicated-channel* ShuffleNet. Radio frequency subcarrier multiplexing is also used to modulate wavelengths and provide a multichannel multihop network.[37,66]

A hallmark of multihop optical networks is their use of both a physical and a virtual topology, which are essentially independent of each other. The physical topology is usually a PON, such as the broadcast-and-select star, bus, or tree, and the virtual topology can take the form of any p-regular directed graph (i.e., a graph in which all nodes have p incoming and p outgoing arcs). The recirculating perfect shuffle,[1] de Bruijn graph,[28] hypercube,[63] and torus[65] are all popular virtual topologies because of their low hop counts under uniform traffic. Generalized virtual topologies with useful mathematical properties have been extensively studied.[16] In particular, these structured topologies have properties that are very beneficial in routing. It is also possible to embed a "customized" virtual topology that has been determined by specialized optimization routines, as in references 7 and 54.

Multihop networks support packet-switching, datagram services well. However, it is difficult to guarantee bandwidth or achieve deterministic delay when packets must traverse multiple hops and compete with other packets for resources. Broadcast and multicast transmission is also problematic, unless channel sharing is used.

At first glance the problem of routing in multihop optical networks may seem no different from routing in optical-link networks, because these networks are essentially store-and-forward routing nodes interconnected by logical channels or physical links. However, another type of routing problem arises in the multihop optical network. Routing in these networks is of a packet-switching nature, but the novelty is that the routing problem is tightly coupled with the virtual-topology design problem. On further examination other differences also become apparent: channels are not duplex, because the underlying directed graph of the virtual topology associates an explicit direction with each channel, and the effect of a failure in one part of the physical topology can be wide-ranging, affecting a set of virtual channels, in stark contrast to a simple link failure in the optical-link networks.

Basic ShuffleNet uses simple store-and-forward routing with shortest paths.[1] The path taken from a given source to a given destination is fixed. This idea was pursued further, and in reference 44 a fixed-path routing algorithm perfectly balances the traffic load on all links of a shared-channel ShuffleNet with single-transceiver stations when the offered traffic is uniform. At each hop this algorithm examines a single bit of the (binary ShuffleNet) destination address, using its value to decide whether or not the message is to be repeated. Because the routing rule for repeating the packet is "isotropic," in the sense that the destinations of repeated packets look the same regardless of which station is making the routing decision, the number of packets repeated per unit of time is the same on all links—that is, the link loadings are perfectly balanced. Although the same algorithm can be used in the dedicated-channel ShuffleNet, balanced link loading cannot be guaranteed. In practice, however, the link loading is acceptably well balanced when the algorithm is used in the dedicated-channel ShuffleNet under uniform traffic.

Structured virtual topologies like ShuffleNet have the advantage of being dense, in the sense that the number of nodes N corresponding to a given diameter D (i.e., the maximum length of shortest paths between all pairs of nodes) in a degree-p digraph (i.e., a directed graph in which each node has p incoming and p outgoing arcs) approaches the so-called *Moore bound*:

$$N \approx \frac{p^{D+1} - 1}{p - 1}$$

Dense virtual topologies—those in which the number of nodes approaches the Moore bound for a given diameter—are desirable for routing, because the shortest path from one node to another varies roughly as the inverse of the graph's density. Thus, dense virtual topologies tend to have low delay under light uniform traffic, if shortest-path routing is used. In reference 66 the de Bruijn graph and ShuffleNet are compared. Being denser than ShuffleNet, the de Bruijn graph achieves lower delay under light traffic than ShuffleNet, but ShuffleNet more evenly distributes traffic over its channels, providing higher throughput than the de Bruijn graph. In reference 16 the *GEMNET* and *MRNET* virtual topologies, high-density generalizations of ShuffleNet and the de Bruijn graph, were shown to provide lower delay and higher maximum throughput, compared to ShuffleNet and the de Bruijn graph, when a specialized shortest-path routing algorithm is used.

In reference 5 the balanced-routing algorithm proposed in reference 44 is used on dedicated-channel ShuffleNet and shown to provide significantly higher network throughput than routing over arbitrarily chosen shortest paths. The results of this comparison are shown in the graph of Figure 7.14. Although both algorithms achieve indistinguishable delay under light-to-moderate uniform traffic, the balanced-routing algorithm pushes about twice as much traffic through the network, because it more effectively avoids bottlenecks on channels.

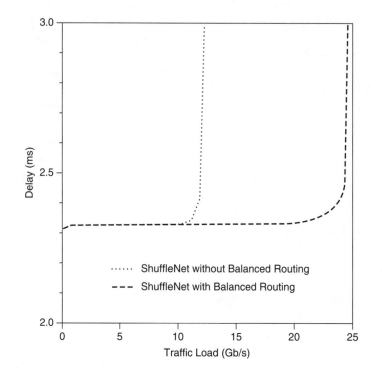

Figure 7.14   Effect of different routing protocols on the performance of a 64-station ShuffleNet under uniform traffic

Despite the attractiveness of structured virtual topologies like ShuffleNet and the de Bruijn graph, it is unrealistic to expect the virtual topology to be static. For example, in a 2048-station ShuffleNet, if each station has an availability of 0.999, then all stations will be simultaneously operational less than 13 percent of the time. Reliance on a topology that exists so infrequently is not practical. Furthermore, structured virtual topologies can lack the modularity required to accommodate a continually growing population of stations, because their "numerology" requires specific configurations of stations. Therefore, other solutions to routing and virtual-topology design have been proposed.

In references 5, 6, 7, and 12, the problems of routing and virtual-topology design in the multihop WON are studied. Simulated-annealing[50] and genetic algorithms[45] are used to optimize virtual topologies for both delay and throughput. Such an algorithm would be periodically executed in a network-management center in response to long-term changes in the traffic pattern. Sample results, obtained in reference 5 by applying simulated annealing to a 64-station network, are shown for uniform traffic in Figure 7.15 and for nonuniform traffic in Figure 7.16. The nonuniform traffic matrix used in this example was generated by considering the entries of the matrix to be independent Bernoulli random variables. The networks consist of stations

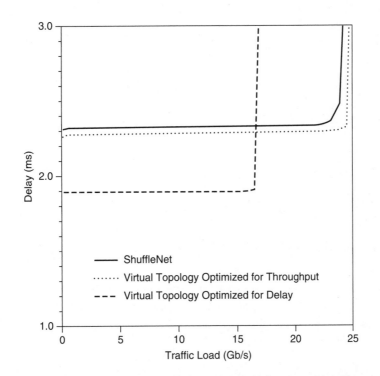

Figure 7.15 Comparison of delay in ShuffleNet and optimized WONs with uniform traffic

randomly scattered over a geographical region with a 50-km radius. All routes are shortest paths, and there is no bifurcation of traffic along multiple paths. These algorithms were applied to dedicated- and shared-channel WONs of up to 196 stations, and substantial improvements in both delay and maximum throughput were demonstrated when the optimized networks were compared to ShuffleNet.

Multipath shortest-path routing in ShuffleNet and other virtual topologies is studied in references 54 and 55. The routing in these studies is bifurcated though not adaptive. The objective is to minimize the maximally utilized link (the so-called minimax criterion) and thereby to provide lower packet delay or call-blocking probability. The routing and virtual-topology design problem is in two components, the connectivity problem and the routing problem. The connectivity problem is an integer linear-programming problem that seeks to maximize the traffic carried over single hops; the constraints of integrality are relaxed, and the simplex algorithm is applied. Once the network's virtual topology has been established, routing can be cast as a multicommodity-flow problem, as originally done in reference 32. Because the minimax objective function can be linearized, the routing problem can also be expressed as a linear program. The full algorithm first solves the connectivity and routing problems, followed by an improvement phase in which the virtual topology is perturbed until an improved solution is found. In accordance with the work of Bannister et al.[5,7]

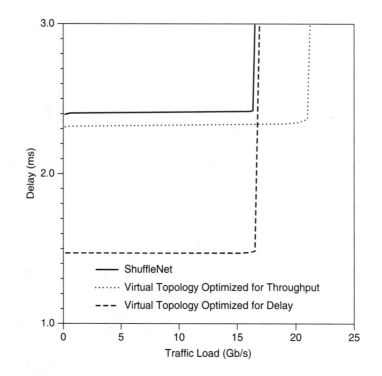

Figure 7.16   Comparison of delay in ShuffleNet and optimized WONs with nonuniform traffic

the heuristic approach was found to produce significant gains over ShuffleNet for networks of up to 81 stations.

Source routing, or the source's explicit specification within the packet header of the route to be taken, is a simple way to route packets in the WON.[8] No routing tables are needed, and switching is simplified by the requirement that only the relevant field (usually the leading field) of the addressing header be processed. The WON must use a discovery protocol to find the shortest path between a source and a destination. The routes between all station pairs can be maintained by a route server, and stations can request routes as needed. Frequently used routes are then cached for future use. In references 8 and 9 the combination of source routing and *detour routing* is studied. Detour routing sends a message over an alternate link when the message arrives at a switch to find its primary link busy; the message is then returned to the switch in as few hops as possible. Having returned to the switch, it can reattempt to make progress toward its destination. Detour routing is easily combined with source routing: when a message is detoured by a switch, the switch need only insert the sequence of hops that will return it to the switch. This mechanism can be readily implemented in hardware, requiring neither routing tables nor rapid-lookup capabilities. This work introduced procedures for constructing virtual topologies that accommodate detour routing by providing very short return paths at every station. The construction of similar networks, called "go-back" networks, is examined in reference 20.

In a WON it is reasonable to assume that components (e.g., lasers and filters) tune over only a fraction of the system bandwidth. Extending their earlier work, Labourdette and Acampora considered the problem of virtual-topology design and routing in the context of limited transceiver tunability.[53] The procedure used to solve this problem is the same as that used in reference 54, but the results are quite different. When transceivers have a severely limited tuning range, the heuristically determined topology and routing policy often perform worse than ShuffleNet with a standard routing policy. Only as the tuning range is broadened does the heuristic solution outperform ShuffleNet.

Another extension, reported in reference 56, was to consider how to redefine the virtual topology and reroute messages without bringing down the entire network. To this end several algorithms are evaluated to see how many incremental retunings each requires to transition from the original to a new virtual topology. Essentially, the algorithms produce retuning schedules whose lengths grow linearly with the number of stations. As the network is reconfigured, the routing procedure must take into account the newly created paths, thus establishing new routing-table entries to mirror the new topology.

In reference 52, Karol and Shaikh study an adaptive-routing algorithm that takes advantage of ShuffleNet's cylindrical topology and its many alternate shortest paths. Their algorithm always routes messages with alternate shortest paths over the least-congested link. When a message has only one preferred link leading out of a switch, it is "bumped" to the least-utilized link according to a "shortest-queue + bias" criterion.[33] The special properties of the ShuffleNet topology make it easy to determine in hardware whether or not a message has alternate paths from a switch to its destination. This adaptive-routing scheme exhibits significant performance improvement over the balanced-routing ShuffleNet algorithm, especially in reducing the variance of output-buffer queue lengths. In reference 46, adaptive routing in ShuffleNet is also studied, emphasizing its performance under nonuniform traffic loading.

Several open problems remain in multihop networks. Not much work has been done on circuit switching in multihop optical networks. The work of reference 25 proposes a TDM solution that is similar to ATM cell relay. Similarly, the problem of providing multicasting has not been extensively explored. Network-layer multicasting, such as that proposed in reference 29, could be used in this context. *Convergence routing,* proposed originally to support traffic integration and multicasting in *MetaNet,*[62] can be applied to multihop optical networks as well. The MetaNet protocols are based on the distribution of a global clock, which imposes a time-slot structure on each link so that real-time and non–real-time traffic can be separated into two distinct streams. MetaNet embeds within its physical topology an Eulerian circuit, which visits every station at least once and is called the *virtual ring.* Such a circuit is guaranteed to exist in a regular virtual topology. The channels that participate in the virtual ring are called *ring links,* and all other channels are called *thread links.* The real-time traffic is sent along fixed paths in the network. The default route for non–real-time traffic is the shortest segment of the virtual ring, but shortcuts may be taken in two cases if they will not interfere with real-time traffic: (1) if there is a thread link between stations on the ring that shortens the path, or (2) if the message can eliminate hops on the ring by exiting the station through an output link other than the next hop on the ring. To multicast a message, the source transmits it on the virtual ring, so that each recipient can copy and forward it as it passes, and the source can remove it when it has made a complete tour of the ring.

Multihop optical networks have much in common with conventional packet-switching networks. Consequently their routing algorithms are often similar. A principal differentiator is that multihop optical networks can rearrange their virtual topologies. Many routing functions are thus subsumed under topology management, such as congestion avoidance, error recovery, and performance optimization. Yet multihop optical networks face the same difficulties as conventional packet-switching networks in providing circuit-switching and multicast services.

7.7 HYBRID OPTICAL NETWORKS

Single-hop networks support the transfer of real-time, delay-sensitive traffic (e.g., voice and video) very well, though they are inefficient for packet switching, especially of bursty, non–real-time traffic. Multihop packet-switching networks, on the other hand, are well suited to transporting bursty traffic but cannot easily provide the guarantee of bounded delays and dedicated bandwidth required by real-time traffic. One solution to this dilemma is to combine a single- and a multihop network into one hybrid network.

In this context the *hybrid optical network* is both a single-hop and a multihop network. The concept of the hybrid network, which has both a single-hop and a multihop subnetwork, is illustrated in Figure 7.17. Given that single-hop networks support circuit switching well and multihop networks support packet switching well, the principal advantage of the hybrid optical network is that it handles integrated traffic well. Moreover, the circuit-switching service of the single-hop subnetwork relies on out-of-band signaling and control to manage (e.g., to establish and tear down) its circuits. Given this need for an out-of-band signaling network and because network-management functions can tolerate variations in delay, a multihop packet-switching subnetwork can meet the requirements for both the out-of-band control network and the non–real-time transport network.

The hybrid optical networks combine the routing techniques of single- and multihop networks to provide both circuit- and packet-switching services.* The multihop subnetwork provides the means for exchanging messages that are not time-constrained.

---

* The many examples of hybrid optical networks include *MONET,*[39] *HONET,*[47] the *multifiber tree network,*[14] *Lightnet,*[27] *STARNET,*[74] and the *time and wavelength division multiaccess (T/WDMA) network.*[49]

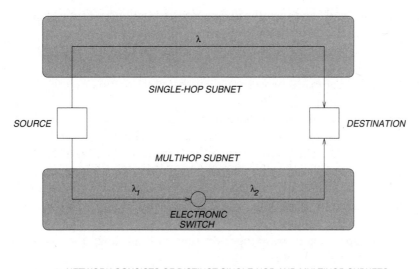

- NETWORK CONSISTS OF DISTINCT SINGLE-HOP AND MULTIHOP SUBNETS
- MESSAGE CAN USE EITHER SUBNET

Figure 7.17   Hybrid optical network

This category includes bursty traffic that can tolerate best-effort delivery service, network-management traffic, and out-of-band signaling to manage connections in the single-hop subnetwork. However, some networks, such as those presented in references 21 and 26, use multihop transport to alleviate the problem of blocking when no single-hop path can be found from a source to a destination; in such cases the network attempts to establish a multihop path.

In references 21 and 26 a hybrid optical network is proposed that uses *lightpaths*— or single-hop paths between two stations—to communicate. Circuit-switched traffic requires a lightpath from source to destination, but packet-switched traffic can employ the concatenation of several lightpaths (with switching at intermediate nodes). The network of reference 26 (known as *Lightnet*) is based on an optical space switch connected to wavelength multiplexers and demultiplexers, but the network of reference 21 uses AOTFs to implement WDM cross-connects. By configuring the switching nodes, a variety of virtual topologies can be embedded within the physical network. Two approaches to routing can be taken in networks of the Lightnet type: (1) establish lightpaths on demand, or (2) establish a virtual topology and use multihop routing. In fact, both options can be combined to produce a true hybrid network with subnetworks for circuit and packet switching. This approach establishes a multihop topology that uses a fraction of the available wavelengths of the network, reserving the remaining wavelengths for dynamic circuit switching. How to embed virtual topologies is addressed in reference 27, where the use of toroidal[65] and hypercube[63] topologies is emphasized. The physical topology is first mapped into a "linear" version of the network, and then the linearly ordered stations are connected by available wavelengths to form the desired virtual topology. The procedure is able to embed specific topologies without having to use more than a bounded number of wavelengths. Given a set of free wavelengths and a "linearized" network, a principal problem is to find lightpaths between stations that wish to initiate a call. Centralized and distributed heuristic algorithms for establishing lightpaths (which was shown to be a computationally intractable problem) were analyzed in reference 26. The heuristics are essentially greedy best-fit algorithms that seek to use the most utilized wavelength for a lightpath. The performance of both the centralized and the distributed algorithms is comparable, with the centralized algorithm performing somewhat better than the distributed algorithm. Simulating several networks confirmed that the lightpath-establishment algorithms would perform just slightly better were wavelength conversion permitted.

Combining space- and wavelength-division multiplexing, the *multifiber tree network*[13] routes signals between nodes on a per-call basis. The single-hop subnetwork may be viewed as a *cable plant* composed of a collection of *fiber plants*. Each fiber plant is a fully broadcast medium that can be selected by a subset of the network's stations. Restricting the number of stations that can select a fiber plant is dictated by the desire not to dissipate too much optical power. Furthermore, each fiber plant hosts a few on-demand WDM channels that can be tuned to. In this case, we may assume that the physical topology is a tree, which is actually the overlay of B single-fiber trees (i.e., B is the number of fibers in a multifiber bundle).[14] As the tree grows large, the number of levels in the tree also grows, and so too does the attenuation (assuming that all paths are routed through the root). The question is whether one can contain attenuation, and thus avoid costly optical amplification, by subdividing the station population into groups and by interconnecting these groups with smaller trees (i.e., lower attenuation). Clearly, we also want to maintain full interconnectivity—that is, we want to make it possible for all stations to communicate with one another. Thus, the station groupings must be overlapped, and enough groupings must be available for every station pair to be in at least one group (see Figure 7.18).

Subtree construction is thus a joint routing and partitioning problem, which is related to an old problem in combinatorial design, known as the *set-covering problem*, which is very difficult to solve exactly. A simple, intuitive—though nonoptimal—solution is presented and analyzed extensively in reference 14. This solution approach is similar in spirit to that used to lay out the SHI, in that common mathematical principles are used by both. The subtrees are "routed" by properly setting switches, and by utilizing binary couplers and reflective stars in the internal nodes of the multifiber plant. In a case study reported in reference 14, more than 2000 stations are interconnected by an unamplified, 256-fiber cable plant.

Setting up circuit-switched connections in the multifiber tree network is assisted by a centralized station that keeps track of the usage of WDM channels on the fiber plants of the single-hop subnetwork. Alternatively, given a small database of which

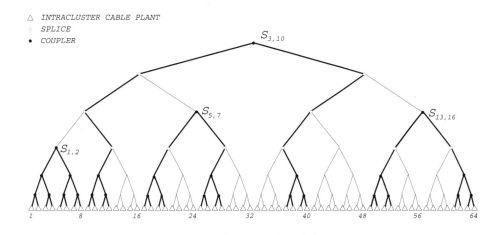

△ INTRACLUSTER CABLE PLANT
○ SPLICE
● COUPLER

Figure 7.18 Embedding fiber plants within a cable plant

stations can access which fiber plants, a source station can search for a free WDM channel in a fiber plant to which it shares access with its destination station and inform the destination of its discovery by means of the multihop subnetwork.

The *multilevel optical network* (MONET),[39] the *hybrid optical network* (HONET),[47] and the *time- and wavelength-division multiaccess* (T/WDMA) *network*[49] use connection-management protocols that are similar to those of the multifiber tree network, but they employ different kinds of single-hop subnetworks. Here we discuss only the T/WDMA single-hop network, which uses a broadcast medium to carry a modest number of WDM channels. The WDM channels are divided into frames, which are further divided into subframes, which are further divided into slots. Stations have a single fixed-wavelength transmitter and two or more receivers that are tunable over the entire range of WDM channels. The receivers are based on AOTFs, which have tuning times of one subframe and can be commanded to pass several wavelengths at once. Two or more receivers are pipelined by alternately tuning one while the other is receiving information. In this way a station has at least one receiver tuned to a subframe at all times. A calling station requests (over the multihop subnetwork) a virtual circuit that consists of one or more slots per frame, in accordance with its bandwidth requirement. A call manager is responsible for keeping track of all calls in progress and allocating new slots to calls in such a way that no conflicts arise. Conflicts within a subframe arise when either no free slots are available in the subframe or when the called station's receiver is already tuned during that subframe. The call-blocking probability is analyzed in reference 49, and it was found that, paradoxically, when the number of WDM channels increases beyond a specific point, the performance begins to drop. It does so because receivers have to tune more frequently to access a set of transmitters on widely dispersed channels. For instance, for one WDM channel, the number of calls is limited by the number of slots in a frame; but, for one

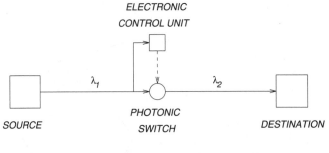

- MESSAGE UNDERGOES NO ELECTROOPTICAL CONVERSIONS
- IN-BAND CONTROL INFORMATION MAY BE PROCESSED ELECTRONICALLY OR PHOTONICALLY

Figure 7.19   Photonic network

transmitter per WDM channel, the number of calls is limited because a receiver can tune to only one transmitter's channel in any subframe.

Single-hop networks provide good circuit-switching service but poor packet-switching service, but the opposite is true of multihop networks. One solution is to combine in one network single-hop and multihop subnetworks. As single-hop optical networks grow to support larger populations, it becomes less reasonable to rely on static or "hard-wired" solutions for message routing. Therefore, hybrid optical networks, which provide a sophisticated subnetwork to control routing devices and request routing information (as well as to transport datagrams), are a realistic choice for integrating traffic. Numerous architectures for hybrid networks have been proposed and analyzed.

7.8   PHOTONIC NETWORKS

Photonic networks are the most advanced high-speed networks of those considered here. A message in a photonic network remains in the optical domain from its source to its destination, but—in contrast to single-hop optical networks—in-band control information is processed by intermediate switching centers. Two types of photonic networks are possible. In the first type, known as an *almost–all-optical network,* although the message is never converted from the optical domain, in-band control information (in the form of packet headers) is siphoned off the message path and converted to the electrical domain at each routing node. This header information is then used by the routing node to control switching of the packet, as shown in Figure 7.19. In a *truly all-optical network,* however, any processing of the message is entirely photonic, and the electronic control unit of Figure 7.19 is not present. Such

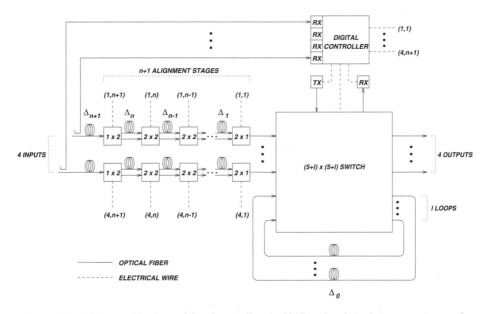

Figure 7.20 Station architecture of the almost–all-optical bidirectional Manhattan street network

an approach is taken in references 10 and 64, where self-routing optical switches are proposed.

If each station has the same number of input ports from the network as output ports to the network, and fixed-length packets arrive at the station during a time slot, then *deflection routing* can be used. When all packets have arrived at the beginning of a time slot, the station, having determined the preferred output port of all stations, may misroute—or deflect—some packets to alternate output ports if there are competing preferences for an output port. Thus, all packets are forwarded during the time slot, and no packet buffers are required. As an extension of basic deflection routing, a few packet buffers can be used, so that deflections occur only when a packet cannot be buffered.

Deflection routing is attractive in photonic networks because a deflection-routing switching node does not require packet buffers. Given that fast optical storage has been difficult to achieve, the utility of deflection routing in all-optical networks is immediately apparent. For a detailed discussion of deflection routing, the reader is directed to Chapter 9 in this volume.

The study of deflection routing in all-optical networks has begun only recently. Almost–all-optical networks that use deflection routing are studied in references 3 and 4. Photonic switching nodes, such as the one shown in Figure 7.20, are connected in a bidirectional Manhattan street topology, and packets are deflection routed. It is found that unslotted deflection routing, in which packet arrivals are not synchronized with each other, causes serious performance problems, including

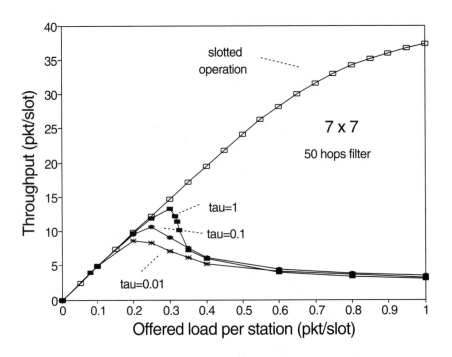

Figure 7.21   Maximum throughput versus offered load for different link propagation times τ (tau)

congestion and throughput collapse, unless specific measures are taken to combat them. In Figure 7.21, taken from reference 4, the throughput of a deflection-routing 7 × 7 bidirectional Manhattan street network versus uniform offered load is shown for both the slotted and unslotted modes of operation with a 50-hop packet filter, which removes undelivered packets that have made more than 50 hops. We see that, although the slotted network performs well in all traffic regimes, the unslotted network suffers a drop in performance after a given load is reached. Furthermore, throughput is sensitive even to the propagation delay τ on a link. However, it is found that the choice of the switch-access policy could substantially improve performance.

It was also found in reference 4 that unless the packet headers contain a time-to-live field, which governs the maximum number of hops that a packet can take before it is removed from the network, the throughput in the unslotted network tends asymptotically to zero. This need for a time-to-live field that is decremented on every hop poses daunting challenges to photonic implementation. Writing a field of a packet without converting it to the electrical domain is difficult, and solutions to this problem are still being sought. One possibility is to mark packets with a time stamp that is compared to a coarse-resolution global clock at each hop; if the packet is

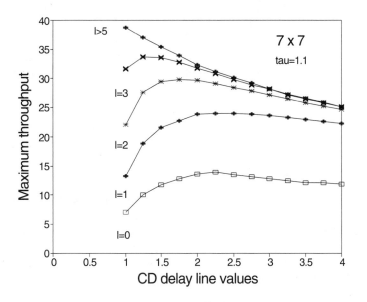

Figure 7.22 **Maximum throughput versus offered load for different numbers *l* of delay loops**

found to exceed the maximum permitted age, then it is discarded. This step further improves the throughput of the all-optical bidirectional Manhattan street network.

Using optical-packet buffers in the photonic network is limited because random-access optical memories do not exist. Moreover, fiber delay loops must be used sparingly, because each delay stage can introduce a nonnegligible optical-power loss. Figure 7.20 indicates that fiber delay loops can be used to recirculate packets temporarily rather than deflect them. Providing a limited number of fiber delay loops can increase the network throughput significantly, as shown in Figure 7.22, which plots throughput versus uniform offered load for different numbers *l* of fiber delay loops in a deflection-routing 7 × 7 bidirectional Manhattan street network. When switch-access, time-to-live, and fiber-delay-loop mechanisms are introduced, the performance of unslotted-deflection routing can surpass that of slotted deflection routing.[4]

Route-division multiple access (RDMA)[72] is a novel way to provide different levels of service to users in a class of networks called *Isochronets*. In RDMA a root station is allocated a time band during which all other stations have the opportunity to send messages to it. During the root station's time band, a transmitting source station has exclusive use of the routing tree for the destination (i.e., the tree of shortest paths from each source station to the root station). This arrangement greatly reduces contention among the transmitting stations. Also, several stations can be allocated overlapped time bands, if their routing trees have disjoint links, because traffic in different routing trees would not interfere with each other. In a photonic network

RDMA can be used to route traffic by allocating to each station a time band during which all-optical paths have been set up for the duration of the band.

Three RDMA techniques are employed to resolve contention within the same routing tree. RDMA– discards one packet when two packets contend for a resource, allowing the other packet to proceed unmolested. RDMA+ buffers one packet when two packets contend for a resource and sends the buffered packet after the first one has gone. When two packets contend for a resource, RDMA++ stores one packet for later transmission in the next time band. A special band-allocation protocol determines the band to be used by a specific routing tree so that it does not intersect with any other routing tree that uses the same time band. A simple band-allocation strategy and a synchronization protocol are presented in reference 72 and their performance is compared to pure circuit and packet switching. These protocols work on a routing-tree basis and proceed in a breadth-first manner to allocate and synchronize time bands. Once all time bands have been allocated, each station holds packets for a given destination until the destination's time band. The direction of a time band can also be reversed so that the root uses the routing tree to multicast to a subset of stations. Simulating a small network with uniform traffic showed that Isochronets achieve lower delay than circuit- and packet-switching networks.

Photonic networks are the most technologically advanced of the optical networks. They can achieve very high data rates because they avoid intermediate electrooptical conversions, which tend to cause bottlenecks in the data path. Because photonic technology has no viable counterpart to the electronic random-access memory, optical packet buffers are usually implemented as fiber delay lines. Such an approach, however, can provide only limited capability to buffer packets. Therefore, deflection routing, which does not even require—but can benefit from—packet buffers, is the solution for most of these networks. The problems of implementing all-optical deflection-routing networks are many and are just beginning to be solved.

7.9 CONCLUSION

Optical networks pose novel, challenging problems both in circuit (or signal) routing and in packet routing. They cause difficulty because (1) optical nets operate at much higher data rates than conventional nets, (2) optical nets introduce a dimension in trunk-facility multiplexing besides space and time, namely wavelength-division multiplexing, and (3) optical nets attempt to remove the electronic bottleneck by establishing, whenever possible, end-to-end optical paths. In this chapter we propose a taxonomy of optical networks, and a corresponding classification of routing problems and solutions. First, we present in the single-hop optical networks the signal routing problems associated with the static and dynamic embedding of paths and trees in a physical topology. New challenges here are problems in attenuation, global time synchronization, and resolving wavelength conflicts. Next, we introduce the problem of routing in multihop optical networks. The most innovative aspect of routing in a multihop context is the interplay between packet routing at the switches and virtual-topology reconfiguration. Third, we introduce hybrids of single- and multihop optical networks, where both single-hop (i.e., circuit-switched) and multihop packet-switched routes are supported, and are used to provide integrated transport of different types of traffic. Finally, we examine the class of photonically (as opposed to electronically) packet-switching networks. The main challenge here is to develop a routing algorithm (implemented in electronic or even all-optical logic) that can operate rapidly enough to permit transferring data on an optical, multihop path, without intermediate electronic buffering. The absence of random-access optical memories for packet buffering profoundly influences the routing algorithms used in photonic networks.

Optical network architectures and protocols are undergoing continuing evolution, driven by advances in technology as well as by new user applications. Routing will undoubtedly be important in this evolution. The most radical routing innovations are expected in photonic packet switching.

REFERENCES

1 A. S. Acampora, "A Multichannel Multihop Local Lightwave Network," *Proceedings of the GLOBECOM '87,* Tokyo, November 1987, pp. 37.5.1–37.5.9.

2 A. S. Acampora, M. J. Karol, and M. G. Hluchyj, "Terabit Lightwave Networks: The Multihop Approach," *AT&T Technical Journal,* Vol. 66, No. 6, November/December 1987, pp. 21–34.

3 F. Borgonovo, L. Fratta, and J. A. Bannister, "Problems of Unslotted Deflection Routing in All-Optical Networks," *Proceedings of the IC^{3}N '93,* San Diego, June 1993, pp. 439–444.

4 F. Borgonovo, L. Fratta, and J. A. Bannister, "Unslotted Deflection Routing in All-Optical Networks," *Proceedings of the IEEE GLOBE-COM '93,* Vol. 1, Houston, November 1993, pp. 119–125.

5 J. A. Bannister, L. Fratta, and M. Gerla, "Optimal Topologies for the Wavelength-Division Optical Network," *Proceedings of the EFOC/LAN '90,* Munich, June 1990, pp. 53–57.

6 J. A. Bannister, L. Fratta, and M. Gerla, "Designing Metropolitan Area Networks for High-Performance Applications," *Computer Networks and ISDN Systems,* Vol. 20, Nos. 1–5, December 1990, pp. 223–230.

7   J. A. Bannister, L. Fratta, and M. Gerla, "Topological Design of the Wavelength-Division Optical Network," *Proceedings of the IEEE INFO-COM '90,* Vol. 3, San Francisco, June 1990, pp. 1005–1013.

8   J. A. Bannister, L. Fratta, and M. Gerla, "Detour Routing in High-Speed Multichannel Networks," in Marjory J. Johnson, ed., *Protocols for High-Speed Networks, II: Proceedings of the IFIP WG 6.1/WG 6.4 Second International Workshop on Protocols for High-Speed Networks,* Amsterdam: Elsevier Science Publishers, 1991, pp. 75–90.

9   J. A. Bannister, L. Fratta, and M. Gerla, "Routing in Large Metropolitan Area Networks Based on Wavelength-Division Multiplexing Technology," in Guy Pujolle, ed., *High-Capacity Local and Metropolitan Area Networks,* Berlin: Springer-Verlag, 1991, pp. 181–197.

10 A. Bononi, F. Forghieri, and P. R. Prucnal, "Analysis of One-Buffer Deflection Routing in Ultra-Fast Optical Mesh Networks," *Proceedings of IEEE INFOCOM '93,* Vol. 1, San Francisco, April 1993, pp. 303–311.

11 J. A. Bannister and M. Gerla, "Design of the Wavelength-Division Optical Network," *Technical Report CSD-890022,* Los Angeles: UCLA Computer Science Department, May 1989.

12 J. A. Bannister and M. Gerla, "Design of the Wavelength-Division Optical Network," *Proceedings of the IEEE ICC '90,* Atlanta, April 1990, pp. 962–967.

13 J. A. Bannister, M. Gerla, and M. Kovacevic, "An All-Optical Multifiber Network," *Proceedings of the INFOCOM '93,* Vol. 1, San Francisco, April 1993, pp. 282–292.

14 J. A. Bannister, M. Gerla, and M. Kovacevic, "An All-Optical Multifiber Tree Network," *Journal of Lightwave Technology,* Vol. 11, Nos. 5/6, May/June 1993, pp. 997–1008. Special issue on broadband optical networks.

15 R. A. Barry and P. A. Humblet, "Bounds on the Number of Wavelengths Needed in WDM Networks," *Digest of the IEEE LEOS Summer Topical Meeting on Optical Multiple Access Networks,* Santa Barbara, August 1992, pp. 21–22.

16 S. Banerjee, J. Iness, and B. Mukherjee, "New Modular Architectures for Regular Multihop Lightwave Networks," *Technical Digest of OFC '93,* San Jose, February 1993, pp. 147–148.

17 Y. Birk, "Fiber-Optic Bus-Oriented Single-Hop Interconnections among Multi-Transceiver Stations," *Journal of Lightwave Technology,* Vol. 9, No. 12, December 1991, pp. 1657–1664.

18 Y. Birk, "Power-Efficient Layout of a Fiber-Optic Multistar That Permits $\log_2 n$ Concurrent Baseband Transmissions among n Stations," *Journal of Lightwave Technology*, Vol. 11, Nos. 5/6, May/June 1993, pp. 908–913.

19 K. Bala, K. Petropoulos, and T. E. Stern, "Multicasting in a Linear Lightwave Network," *Proceedings of the IEEE INFOCOM '93*, Vol. 3, San Francisco, April 1993, pp. 1350–1358.

20 J. T. Brassil, "Deflection Routing in Certain Regular Networks," Ph.D. thesis, San Diego: Electrical Engineering Department, University of California, 1991.

21 C. A. Bracket, "Scalability and Modularity in Multiwavelength Optical Networks," *Digest of the IEEE LEOS Summer Topical Meeting on Optical Multiple Access Networks,* Santa Barbara, August 1992, pp. 35–36.

22 M. J. Karol, G. Hill, C. Lin, and K. Nosu, eds., *Journal of Lightwave Technology,* Vol. 11, Nos. 5/6, May/June 1993. Special issues on broad-band optical networks.

23 K. Bala, T. E. Stern, and K. Bala, "Algorithms for Routing in a Linear Lightwave Network," *Proceedings of IEEE INFOCOM '91,* Vol. 1, Bal Harbour, FL, April 1991, pp. 1–9.

24 I. Chlamtac and A. Fumagalli, "QUADRO-Star: High Performance Optical WDM Star Networks," *Proceedings of the IEEE GLOBECOM '91,* Phoenix, December 1991, pp. 1224–1229.

25 I. Chlamtac, A. Ganz, and G. Karmi, "Circuit Switching in Multi-Hop Lightwave Networks," *Proceedings of the ACM SIGCOMM '88 Symposium,* Stanford, August 1988, pp. 188–199.

26 I. Chlamtac, A. Ganz, and G. Karmi, "Lightpath Communications: A Novel Approach to High Bandwidth Optical WANs," *IEEE Transactions on Communications,* Vol. 40, No. 7, July 1992, pp. 1171–1182.

27 I. Chlamtac, A. Ganz, and G. Karmi, "Lightnets: Topologies for High-Speed Optical Networks," *Journal of Lightwave Technology,* Vol. 11, Nos. 5/6, May/June 1993, pp. 951–961.

28 N. G. de Bruijn, "A Combinatorial Problem. Koninklijke Nederlandsche Akademie van Wetenschappen te Amsterdam," *Proceedings of the Section of Sciences,* Vol. 49, No. 7, 1946, pp. 758–764.

29 S. E. Deering, "Multicast Routing in Internetworks and Extended LANs," *Proceedings of the ACM SIGCOMM '88 Symposium,* Stanford, August 1988, pp. 55–63.

30 N. R. Dono, P. E. Green Jr., K. Liu, R. Ramaswami, and F. F.-K. Tong, "A Wavelength Division Multiple Access Network for Computer Communication," *IEEE Journal on Selected Areas in Communications,* Vol. 8, No. 6, August 1990, pp. 983–994.

31 C. Dragone, "Efficient N × N Star Couplers Using Fourier Optics," *Journal of Lightwave Technology,* Vol. 7, No. 3, March 1989, pp. 479–489.

32 L. Fratta, M. Gerla, and L. Kleinrock, "The Flow Deviation Method—An Approach to Store-and-Forward Communication Network Design," *Networks,* Vol. 3, 1973, pp. 97–133.

33 G. L. Fultz and L. Kleinrock, "Adaptive Routing Techniques for Store-and-Forward Computer Communication Networks," *Proceedings of the IEEE ICC '71,* Montreal, June 1971.

34 M. Gerla, "Routing and Flow Control," in Franklin F. Kuo, ed., *Protocols and Techniques for Data Communication Networks,* Englewood Cliffs: Prentice Hall, 1981, pp. 122–174.

35 M. Gerla and L. Fratta, "Tree Structured Fiber Optic MANs," *IEEE Journal on Selected Areas in Communications,* Vol. SAC-6, No. 6, July 1988, pp. 934–943.

36 M. S. Goodman, J. L. Gimlett, H. Kobrinski, M. P. Vecchi, and R. M. Bulley, "The LAMBDANET Multiwavelength Network: Architecture, Applications, and Demonstrations," *IEEE Journal on Selected Areas in Communications,* Vol. 8, No. 6, August 1990, pp. 995–1004.

37 R. Gidron, "TeraNet: A Multi-Gigabits Per Second ATM Network," *Computer Communications,* Vol. 15, No. 3, April 1992, pp. 143–152.

38 "Gigabit Network Testbeds," *IEEE Computer,* Vol. 23, No. 9, September 1990, pp. 77–80.

39 M. Gerla, M. Kovacevic, and J. Bannister, "Multilevel Optical Networks," *Proceedings of the IEEE ICC '92,* Vol. 3, Chicago, June 1992, pp. 1168–1172.

40 P. Granestrand et al., "Strictly Nonblocking 8 × 8 Integrated Optical Switch Matrix," *Electronics Letters,* Vol. 22, No. 15, July 1986, pp. 816–818.

41 P. E. Green Jr, *Fiber Optic Networks,* Englewood Cliffs: Prentice Hall, 1993.

42 G. R. Hill, "A Wavelength Routing Approach to Optical Communication Networks," *Proceedings of the IEEE INFOCOM '88,* New Orleans, March 1988, pp. 354–362.

43 G. R. Hill, "Wavelength Domain Optical Network Techniques," *Proceedings of the IEEE,* Vol. 77, No. 1, January 1989, pp. 121–132.

44 M. G. Hluchyj and M. J. Karol, "ShuffleNet: An Application of Generalized Perfect Shuffles to Multihop Lightwave Networks," *Journal of Lightwave Technology,* Vol. 9, No. 10, October 1991, pp. 1386–1387.

45 J. H. Holland, *Adaptation in Natural and Artificial Systems,* Ann Arbor: University of Michigan Press, 1975.

46 M. Kadoch and A. K. Elhakeem, "Adaptive Routing for Lightwave ShuffleNet Under Unbalanced Loads," *Proceedings of the IEEE GLOBECOM '91,* Phoenix, December 1991, pp. 52.7.1–52.7.6.

47 M. Kovacevic and M. Gerla, "HONET—A New Hybrid Optical Network Architecture," *Proceedings of the First International Conference on Computer Communications and Networks,* San Diego, June 1992, pp. 92–96.

48 M. Kovacevic and M. Gerla, "Rooted Routing in Linear Lightwave Networks," *Proceedings of the IEEE INFOCOM '92,* Florence, May 1992, pp. 39–48.

49 M. Kovacevic, M. Gerla, and J. Bannister, "Time and Wavelength Division Multiaccess with Acoustooptic Tunable Filters," *Fiber and Integrated Optics,* Vol. 12, No. 2, 1993, pp. 113–132.

50 S. Kirkpatrick, C. D. Gelatt Jr., and M. P. Vecchi, "Optimization by Simulated Annealing," *Science,* Vol. 220, No. 4598, May 1983, pp. 671–680.

51 M. Kovacevic, "HONET: An Integrated Services Wavelength Division Optical Network," *Technical Report CSD-93028,* Los Angeles: Computer Science Department, UCLA, August 1993.

52 M. J. Karol and S. Z. Shaikh, "A Simple Adaptive Routing Scheme for Congestion Control in ShuffleNet Multihop Lightwave Networks," *IEEE Journal on Selected Areas in Communications,* Vol. 8, No. 6, September 1991, pp. 1040–1051.

53 J-F. P. Labourdette and A. S. Acampora, "Partially Reconfigurable Multihop Lightwave Networks," *Proceedings of the GLOBECOM '90,* San Diego, December 1990.

54 J-F. P. Labourdette and A. S. Acampora, "Wavelength Agility in Multihop Lightwave Networks," *Proceedings of the IEEE INFOCOM '90,* Vol. 3, San Francisco, June 1990, pp. 1022–1029.

55 Jean-François P. Labourdette and Anthony S. Acampora, "Logically Rearrangeable Multihop Lightwave Networks," *IEEE Transactions on Communications,* Vol. 29, No. 8, August 1991, pp. 1223–1230.

56 J-F. P. Labourdette, "Rearrangeability Techniques for Multihop Lightwave Networks and Application to Distributed ATM Switching Systems," *Technical Report CU/CTR/TR 244-91-25,* New York: Department of Electrical Engineering, Columbia University, 1991.

57 K-C. Lee and V. O. K. Li, "Routing and Switching in a Wavelength Convertible Optical Network," *Proceedings of the IEEE INFOCOM '93,* Vol. 2, San Francisco, April 1993, pp. 578–585.

58 M. Ajmone Marsan, A. Bianco, E. Leonardi, and F. Neri, "Topologies for Wavelength-Routing All-Optical Networks," *IEEE/ACM Transactions on Networking,* Vol. 1, No. 5, October 1993, pp. 534–546.

59 J. E. Midwinter and Y. L. Guo, *Optoelectronis and Lightwave Technology,* Chichester, England: John Wiley & Sons, 1992.

60 B. Mukherjee, "Architectures and Protocols for WDM-Based Local Lightwave Networks—Part I: Single-Hop Systems," *IEEE Network,* Vol. 6, No. 3, May 1992, pp. 12–27.

61 B. Mukherjee, "WDM-Based Local Lightwave Networks—Part II: Multihop Systems," *IEEE Network,* Vol. 6, No. 4, July 1992, pp. 20–32.

62 Y. Ofek and M. Yung, "The Integrated MetaNet Architecture: A Switch-Based Multimedia LAN for Parallel Computing and Real-Time Traffic," *Proceedings of the IEEE INFOCOM '94,* Toronto, June 1994.

63 M. C. Pease III, "The Indirect Binary *n*-Cube Microprocessor Array," *IEEE Transactions on Computers,* Vol. C-26, No. 5, May 1977, pp. 458–473.

64 P. R. Prucnal, "Optically Processed Self-Routing, Synchronization, and Contention Resolution for 1-D and 2-D Photonic Switching Architectures," *IEEE Journal of Quantum Electronics,* Vol. 29, No. 2, February 1993, pp. 600–612.

65 T. G. Robertazzi, "Toroidal Networks," *IEEE Communications Magazine,* Vol. 26, No. 6, June 1988, pp. 45–50.

66 K. Sivarajan and R. Ramaswami, "Multihop Lightwave Networks Based on de Bruijn Graphs," *Proceedings of the IEEE INFOCOM '91,* Vol. 3, Bal Harbour, FL, April 1991, pp. 1001–1011.

67 T. E. Stern, "Linear Lightwave Networks: How Far Can They Go?" *Proceedings of the IEEE GLOBECOM '90,* San Diego, December 1990, pp. 1866–1872.

68 T. E. Stern, "A Linear Lightwave MAN Architecture," in Guy Pujolle, ed., *High-Capacity Local and Metropolitan Area Networks,* Berlin: Springer-Verlag, 1991, pp. 161–179.

69 C. A. Sunshine, ed., *Computer Network Architectures and Protocols,* Part IV: Network Layer, New York: Plenum Press, 1989.

70 V. J. Tekippe, "Passive Fiber-Optic Components Made by the Fused Biconical Taper Process," *Fiber and Integrated Optics,* Vol. 9, No. 2, 1990, pp. 97–123.

71 L. Thylén, "Integrated Optics in $LiNbO_3$: Recent Developments in Devices for Telecommunications," *Journal of Lightwave Technology,* Vol. 6, No. 6, June 1988, pp. 847–861.

72 Y. Yemini and D. Florissi, "Isochronets: A High-Speed Network Switching Architecture," *Proceedings of the IEEE INFOCOM '93,* Vol. 2, San Francisco, April 1993, pp. 740–747.

73 J. L. Zyskind, C. R. Giles, J. R. Simpson, and D. J. DiGiovanni, "Erbium-Doped Fiber Amplifiers and the Next Generation of Lightwave Systems," *AT&T Technical Journal,* Vol. 71, No. 1, January/February 1992, pp. 53–62.

74 P. T. Poggiolini and L. G. Kazovsky, "STARNET: An Integrated Services Broadband Optical Network with Physical Star Topology," *SPIE Proceedings on Advanced Fiber Communications Technology,* Vol. 1579, 1991, pp. 14–29.

CHAPTER 8

Routing in the plaNET Network

ISRAEL CIDON AND ROCH GUÉRIN

CONTENTS

Routing algorithms for packet-switched networks were originally designed to provide efficient best-effort data transport between a source and destination. These conventional routing algorithms are, however, inadequate for supporting distributed real-time applications (e.g., desktop videoconferencing) that require specific service guarantees as well as point-to-multipoint communication. This chapter describes plaNET, an experimental gigabit-speed packet-switched network together with its sophisticated routing strategies, which offers an integrated solution to the problem of providing service for widely varied traffic types. The plaNET route selection process involves several steps, including characterizing session traffic parameters and bandwidth requirements, assessing the session's potential effect on network links, and selecting routes that provide the services required by users yet minimally affect the rest of the network. In addition, plaNET provides several native packet-forwarding modes that enable efficient handling of connection-oriented as well as connectionless traffic for point-to-point and point-to-multipoint communication.

8.1 INTRODUCTION

In this chapter we describe the various techniques and components that are instrumental in supporting the plaNET routing functions. plaNET is a fast–packet-switched network[1] capable of carrying a variety of traffic types and offering a range of service levels. Routing is probably the most important component of the network operation, for it is involved in nearly all phases of data transfer. Routing can be looked at from two related perspectives, which are representative of two time scales in the network.

At the lowest time scale, that of steady-state packet transmissions, routing consists of the actual forwarding of packets toward their intended destination(s). In the plaNET network as in most fast–packet-switched networks, the path to be followed by any packet is selected at the time the packet is injected into the network. In other words, contrary to the approach followed in traditional packet-switched networks like the Internet,[2] the packet-level routing function in plaNET requires only minimal processing at intermediate nodes. Each packet includes specific information identifying the link(s) on which it should be forwarded next. This labeling limits the adaptability of packet routing, but is imposed by the speed at which routing decisions have to be performed and the requirement for bandwidth guarantees (and hence reservations). Such guarantees, which apply mainly to real-time connections, are hard to enforce in a datagram-routing environment. The need to preserve some flexibility at the packet-routing level has, however, been recognized in the plaNET network. This awareness has resulted in the introduction of several *routing modes,* which offer a number of approaches for the routing of packets at intermediate nodes. In Section 8.2, the characteristics and operation of these different routing modes are described, and examples are provided that illustrate the benefits afforded by their availability.

Routing can also be viewed at the coarser time scale of calls rather than packets. There, it consists of the set of decisions involved in identifying the path that should be assigned to a new call request. The criterion involved in such a selection is typically some form of optimizing usage of network resources. This is the perspective that has traditionally been of interest in the context of circuit-switched networks. Because fast–packet-switched networks bear similarities to both packet- and circuit-switched networks, the issue of call routing is also of great significance in that environment. In Section 8.3, the different aspects of call routing in the plaNET network are reviewed. First, we address the problem of how to characterize call requests by identifying which information is to be provided by a new call, and how it is to be interpreted by the network. Next, we describe how this information is used in determining the path for a new call, together with the network-optimization criteria that are applied.

After reviewing the two major aspects of routing in the plaNET network, we briefly identify the different components and systems that are used to implement the plaNET routing functions. The description again distinguishes between components that are relevant to packet- and call-level routing. Specifically, we explain how plaNET switches and the associated buffer structure operate in their role in routing individual packets. Conversely, the plaNET call-routing algorithms require specific information to properly route calls, and we next describe the mechanisms used to distribute and update that information. Thus we complete our exposition of the plaNET routing functions and the components used to support them.

8.2 PACKET-LEVEL ROUTING

At the lowest level of the routing infrastructure are the methods and mechanisms by which individual packets are forwarded at each node. Here we assume that setup operations or table-recording information that might be needed prior to the handling of individual packets are already in effect. The plaNET network offers a rich set of routing options that have been carefully selected to compromise between, on the one hand, extended functionality and streamlining of common routing applications, and on the other hand, maintaining utilization efficiency and retaining low-cost hardware implementation. The implementation implications of the extended routing capabilities are in fact quite small, as demonstrated by implementation of the Gigabit plaNET switch.[1] The various routing modes are implemented via straightforward RAM lookup tables and pipelined header processors that were incorporated in a single-chip programmable-logic device. The implementation cost is low and the support for multiple routing modes results in no performance reductions. In reference 3, we outline the advantages of this approach and argue that the advantages heavily outweigh the cost. As a result, the transport architecture for plaNET is a heterogeneous one, providing support for various transfer (or routing) modes such as ATM, source routing, multicast, and various priority and loss-sensitivity classes.

8.2.1   Routing Modes and Routing Options

We now briefly describe the routing modes available in plaNET and the rationales behind them. As explained above, all routing modes are natively supported in the plaNET hardware, which is detailed in reference 1. This availability ensures that plaNET users can select any of the routing modes best suited to their own requirements, without sacrificing performance or ability to fully utilize the network.

In addition to the routing modes that dictate the actual routes of the packets, plaNET supports several *routing options* that can be used in similar ways by all packet routing modes (excluding the fixed-size cell mode). The routing options provide additional functions that assist in effectively using the various routing modes. The routing options are:

- The *COPY* option   The packet carries a copy identity at a fixed location in its routing header (the all-zero value means no copy at all). When the message is switched within a node, a copy of the message may be delivered to one or more of the switch ports programmed to accept such a copy. We illustrate the exact use of the copy option by the different routing modes.

- The *reverse-path accumulation* option   A single bit, again at a fixed position in the routing header, can trigger accumulation of routing information (link labels) identifying the path along which the message traveled. Recipients of the message then have all the necessary routing information to reply to the origin of the message.

From an architectural point of view, routing options are orthogonal to the routing modes and should be usable by any one of them. In practice, some deviation from this concept was implemented because of the need for native support of ATM.[4–6] ATM is a fixed packet-size international standard that does not support such routing options and also leaves little optional space in its headers. Because of the growing importance of this standard, it was decided to support its exact cell structure, forgoing, therefore, the ability to exercise these additional functions.

Description of the Routing Modes

The four basic routing modes in plaNET are the source routing mode, the label-swapping routing mode, the cell or ATM routing mode, and the multicast routing mode. A short field at the beginning of each packet identifies the routing mode used (see Figure 8.1 for the plaNET packet format). All modes except the cell mode allow

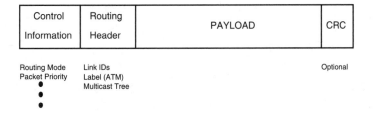

Figure 8.1   plaNET packet format

for variable packet sizes. A fifth routing mode, a remote access to a multicast tree, is a sequential combination of the source routing and the multicast modes.

The source routing mode (also called *automatic network routing* or ANR) is a routing mode whereby the packet carries all the necessary routing information required for reaching its destination. Therefore, the origin is responsible for providing in the header of the packet the complete path information between the source and the destination. This information consists of a sequence of ANR labels, each label corresponding to a *local* link identifier that uniquely identifies the desired outgoing link within a particular node. (Thus, labels are unique only within a nodal domain and the same label can be used by any other node.) The ANR labels are stripped as the packet progresses on the path, exposing at a fixed header location the label to be used by the next node (see Figure 8.2). For architectural flexibility, ANR labels can be either one or two bytes in length, and this choice is local to each node rather than network wide; that is, nodes with different label sizes coexist within a network. In fact, longer ANR labels are also possible but do not seem necessary given the current node sizes.

The source routing mode has a number of advantages. It eliminates the need for maintaining connection tables at intermediate nodes. Because it requires no prior setup, it is suitable for connectionless services. It can also support connection-oriented services, for it provides a fixed path that can be fully selected and defined by the source.

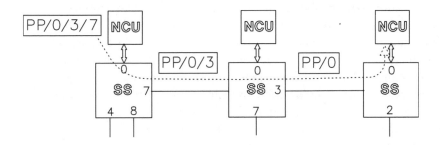

Figure 8.2   Example of ANR routing

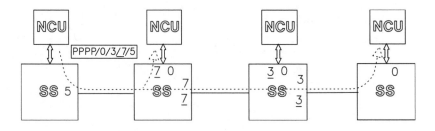

Figure 8.3   Example of ANR routing with selective COPY option

With the help of optional bits in the packet header the source-routing mode can also support all previously described routing options. The COPY option permits "copies" of a packet to be delivered *selectively* at intermediate nodes on its path to entities identified by the previously described copy ID. The selective copy is accomplished by including a copy bit (in addition to the copy ID) at a fixed location in each ANR label. The copy bit enables or disables the copy function at the node that uses the ANR label just being exposed (see Figure 8.3). The copy is performed "on the fly" without slowing the packet flow. The reverse-path accumulation option is also simple and is triggered by the setting of a bit (again at a fixed location) in the routing header. Assuming that this bit has been set, the incoming link upon receipt of a packet will insert its own ANR label at the head of the current reverse-path field (which starts after the end of the forward ANR label sequence). At any intermediate node (and not only the final destination), the information thus far accumulated describes the complete path (or ANR label sequence) back to the origin. Insertion of the ANR label of the incoming link is carried out in the link adapters by pipelined header-processing hardware, without slowing the progress of the packet.

As discussed in reference 3, the flexibility available from the source routing mode is key to transparent support of a number of applications, and to more efficient implementation of network-control functions and services, such as fast setup and nondisruptive path switching. In particular, the combined use of the ANR routing mode, COPY function, and reverse-path accumulation simplifies the negotiations needed to establish connections across the network.

The second routing mode available in plaNET is a label-swapping routing mode similar to the ones used in many other networks, such as ATM[5] and frame relay.[7] In this mode, routing information is carried in a fixed-size field or label, which at each node (link) uniquely identifies the connection and the desired local outgoing link. The swapping of this label from node to node ensures that the assigned value will remain local to that node (or link), and eliminates the need for a unique, network-wide identifier for each connection. The label routing mode can also support the COPY and reverse-path accumulation options. Reverse-path accumulation is again triggered by the setting of the appropriate bit in the routing header. The ANR labels of incoming links will be accumulated after the label-swapping field as the packet traverses each node on its path. The COPY function option is also available and performed as determined by the content of the COPY ID field. Notice that because this routing mode uses a single connection identifier (label) instead of successive link identifiers (ANR labels), the COPY function is disabled or enabled for the entire path and cannot be set selectively for each node.

The third routing mode is, in fact, a special case of label swapping restricted to fixed 53-byte packets with 5-byte network headers. This is the cell mode, which is designed to carry ATM information without needing additional overhead. Support for ATM is provided by performing a very simple and restricted bit shuffling of the ATM header at the input-link interface so that it appears within the plaNET switch as a plaNET label-swapping routing-mode packet. The switching hardware deals with the packet in its plaNET format and the output-link interface performs the reverse transformation to reconvert the packet to the standard ATM format. The cell-routing mode allows plaNET to transport ATM cells as efficiently as any "native" ATM network, that is, without additional overhead beyond the regular 5-byte header. The exact mapping performed from/to an ATM cell to/from a plaNET packet is outlined in reference 8. As mentioned earlier, because of the restrictions imposed by the ATM header format, this routing mode cannot use the COPY and reverse-path accumulation options.

The advantage of a label-swapping mode (ATM or not) compared to source routing is the use of a fixed size and relatively short routing header. Therefore, it may be more efficient in bandwidth utilization over long paths and for small packets. A label that uniquely identifies a connection within a node (link) may also be useful in providing various levels of quality of service (QOS) in the network—that is, apply different buffering and scheduling policies as a function of a connection's identity. On the other hand, the need for a connection identifier also translates to additional costs and limitations for the label-swapping routing mode. In particular, it requires tables in each node or link, which store for any assigned incoming label the value of the corresponding outgoing label. The tables grow with the number of connections supported, and, more importantly, require additional mechanisms to update and maintain them. The need to initialize table entries also imposes constraints on the establishment of connections—that is, the flow of packets cannot start before all labels have been assigned. For these reasons, label swapping is not an attractive routing mode alternative for quickly setting up new connections. The approach taken in plaNET is to support the label-swapping mode for applications that may require it, but take advantage of the benefits available from the ANR routing mode for most network-control flows, such as connection setup.

The ANR routing mode is mainly intended for point-to-point applications even though it offers limited multicast capability through the COPY option. The limitations come from both the few copy identities available and the fact that copies of the packets can be delivered to (a subset of) nodes only on a linear path described by a sequence of ANR labels (see reference 9 for the design of good linear multicast

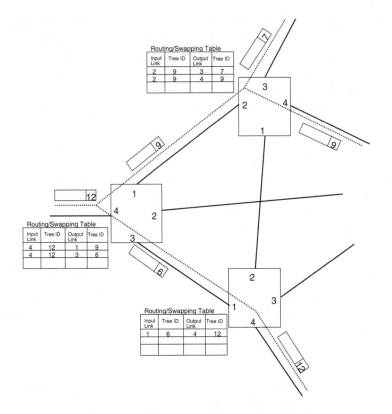

Figure 8.4   Multicast tree with swapping of labels

paths). Multicast is, however, a highly desirable routing mode required by a fast growing number of applications, and its native support may substantially increase network efficiency and utilization. Efficient distribution of multicast messages is generally achieved with a tree structure connecting the multicast origins and destinations (multiple trees can also be used, for example, a tree for each origin). Because many multicast applications and groups can coexist in the network, a multicast routing mode should be able to support simultaneously a large number of such multicast trees.

The main purpose of the fourth plaNET routing mode, the TREE routing mode, is to provide native multicast capability. The TREE routing mode is based on a packet format similar to that of the label-swapping mode with a fixed-size routing field, which at each node uniquely identifies the links that are "branches" on the multicast tree. This label is either unique network wide, or as shown in Figure 8.4, is optionally swapped independently before the packet is forwarded on the output links (branches). The use of a global tree ID simplifies tree establishment for some network-wide applications and is useful in implementing important network-control functions—for example, all network-control points are linked together through a unique, well-known spanning tree for specific network-wide tasks.[10–15] On the other hand, as for the label-swapping routing mode, the ability to swap IDs lowers the probability of label contention and simplifies assignment of new tree IDs.[16] The mechanism of the TREE routing mode is quite simple. When a TREE packet is received over an input link, it is locally *multicast to all links* that are branches of the tree identified by this tree ID. The input link over which the packet was received is an exception to this rule, for the packet has already traveled on it. It should therefore not be sent back by that link even if the link belongs to the tree, for this routing would create loops and packet multiplication in the network. The optional tree-label swapping is performed at each output port before forwarding the packet on the link. As with the label-routing mode, the COPY and reverse-path accumulation options are also available in the TREE routing mode. Notice that the reverse-path accumulation option will cause each packet to carry the exact path description from any point in the tree back to the origin. This choice is very useful, for responses to a multicast message are often of the point-to-point type—that is, a direct response to a global query.

The fifth routing mode of plaNET is a sequential combination of the ANR and the TREE routing modes. It is *remote access to TREE.* This feature allows a remote station that is not member of a multicast tree, and even remote from that tree, to multicast messages to all stations on that tree. It does so by combining the ANR and TREE routing modes. The ANR routing mode is first used to deliver the packet from the remote station to one of the nodes on the tree. Here, the TREE routing mode takes over and ensures delivery of the packet to all the stations on the tree. Notice that the first application of the TREE routing mode at the point of conversion from the ANR to the TREE routing mode may be slightly different from the mechanism described above because the multicast packet should be forwarded over *all* branches of the tree, possibly including the link over which the packet was just received.

Specifically, remote access to a tree takes place as follows: First, the packet is treated as an ANR packet and forwarded along the path described by the ANR labels. Once the ANR header has been consumed, the routing mode is changed from ANR to an intermediate mode named TREE'. This routing mode remains in effect only for a single hop and is identical to the TREE routing mode except that the incoming TREE' packet is forwarded on all branches of the tree identified by the carried tree ID. The routing mode is then changed to the normal TREE multicast mode and the packet is treated accordingly. The information needed to enable a node to access a remote tree—that is, a path to one of the nodes on the tree—is made available through the plaNET Directory Services.[1] The COPY and reverse-path accumulation options can also be used with the remote access to TREE routing mode. Notice that the availability of reverse-path accumulation is particularly important because the source of the message is not even a member of the multicast group.

8.2.2 Routing Mode Motivations and Scenarios

We next give two examples of network-control applications illustrating how the various intermediate routing mechanisms supported in plaNET facilitate their operation. In particular, the availability of several native routing modes and options implemented by the network hardware results in enhanced speed of operation, simplified actions, and increased efficiency. Numerous similar examples can be found in reference 11. It is also easy to realize that not only network control functions but also many user applications such as video teleconferencing, distributed database management, distributed computing, and so on, can take advantage of the different plaNET routing modes and options.

8.2.2.1 The Call Setup Example

The first example is the connection-setup mechanism. Connection setup is the testing and modifying of state information on available bandwidth and label tables at intermediate nodes on a connection's path before user data can be transferred. For example, in the plaNET network call setup is required with all routing modes, including source routing, for all data transports requesting service guarantees, to ensure that the bandwidth requested by a connection is available and secured on the selected path.[15] Additional actions such as setup and exchange of label information are also required by some routing modes. In plaNET, connection setup involves a setup message sent along the selected path, and carrying information specifying the resources, such as buffer, bandwidth, routing mode, and class of service requested by the connection. The setup is considered complete only when all requested resources have been secured and new resource states at intermediate nodes, if any, have been modified accordingly. This condition requires that all intermediate nodes on the connection's path have received and processed the setup message, and that the origin has received confirmation that this distributed processing is completed.

In high-speed networks, it is desirable to complete the setup phase as rapidly as possible to improve resource utilization—that is, to minimize time during which resources are allocated but unused and to minimize the connection-setup delay to applications. This speed requires timely delivery of the setup message to all intermediate nodes on the path, and fast notification of the origin after the necessary processing is completed. The COPY function of the ANR routing mode is used to expedite the connection-setup phase. The origin node in effect broadcasts the setup packet to all nodes on the connection's path by using the source-routing mode with a routing header consisting of the string of link labels corresponding to the selected path, and with the COPY option enabled for each intermediate node. The COPY ID used identifies the nodal bandwidth-management entity as the address destination of the message copy. The reverse-path accumulation option is also enabled, so that intermediate nodes can readily reply to the connection's origin once they have completed their processing of the connection request.

Using the approach just described, the setup packet is delivered to the destination node without being slowed by any processing at intermediate nodes. At the same time, the COPY function ensures that as the packet traverses intermediate nodes, the switching hardware copies the setup packet to its local bandwidth-management entity.[1] Using this facility, all intermediate nodes receive, process, and reply (using the reverse-path ANR label sequence) to the setup message nearly in parallel. As soon as the origin has received positive replies from all nodes on the path,* transmission can start. This procedure provides for a total setup delay that is generally close to the lowest possible value achievable (one round-trip packet delay + twice the processing time).

Notice that in the plaNET network, the setup mechanism above is also used to establish label-swapping (including ATM) connections, for it provides the most effective solution. For such label-based connections, an additional step may take place between neighboring nodes (as identified from the forward and reverse ANR field), to allow for the exchange of new labels when necessary. Because this negotiation is local to neighbor nodes, its effect on the setup delay is minimal.

In comparison, if the source routing mode and its COPY function were not available, the setup message would either have to be forwarded hop by hop from the origin to the destination nodes, or multiple copies of the messages would have to be sent to each node on the path. The first approach would result in a significantly higher setup delay (that is, processing delays are concatenated), and the second would, in addition to requiring more messages, impose the existence of control channels (routes) between the origin node and all nodes on the path. This step may not be practical in reasonably large networks. Notice that the importance of rapidly reserving, releasing, or simply adjusting the resources assigned to a connection on its path has been recognized by the ATM community, as indicated in recent proposals for *fast-reservation* protocols[17–19] in ATM networks, which allow rapid updates of connection-state information, such as bandwidth. However, because the ATM network layer supports only a single label-based routing mode, these protocols are applicable only to established connections, and therefore cannot be extended to improving connection-setup speed.

Another flavor of connection setup is a TREE or multicast connection setup. Although the issue of multicast groups and their management is a complex one, discussed extensively in reference 20, we illustrate a simple client/server example of a multicast tree setup where a single server wishes to broadcast and receive information to and from a known group of clients. To set up the connection, a "best" spanning tree is computed at the source. Then the setup of the tree needs to be performed. This setup requires that all nodes (both branch and leaf nodes) in the tree be informed of the new tree ID and the corresponding local connectivity (branches on

---

* After a timeout, the source resends the setup message, using the selective COPY option, to nodes from which it failed to receive a reply.

which to forward packets). To save on communications and number of messages involved, the setup is done with a linear path that traverses the entire tree (touches all the nodes in the tree). Determining the most "efficient" linear path is a problem of independent interest, and we shall not dwell on it further in this chapter but refer the interested reader to reference 9 for discussions on this topic. As with regular point-to-point connections, the ANR routing mode is used to send the setup message on this traversal linear path. Because this traversal crosses links (and nodes) more than once, the selective-copy feature is used to ensure that the message is received only once at its first passage. Confirmation messages are sent back to the origin, again using the route gathered by the reverse-path accumulation option.

8.2.2.2 *The Directory Querying Example*

The second example elaborates on the use of the multicast routing modes (TREE and remote access to TREE) and how their combination with some of the other plaNET routing options can facilitate common network control and user-application processes. Our example is a distributed directory maintained by a group of nodes we denote as agents. Agents can be distributed database servers (say a distributed phone number directory in which each node is responsible for a range of numbers) or access agents to services (say each node provides specific application programs or is a gateway for reaching LAN users). We assume that all agents are preconnected through a multicast TREE connection. Users, however, are not necessarily directly connected to the tree. Now assume that a user wants to set up a connection to an agent that is associated with a piece of information or a resource. In the plaNET network, all the user needs to know is an ANR path to one of the agents, which then serves as its access point to the distributed directory. The user sends its query about the requested resource, using the remote access to TREE routing mode. The user also sets the reverse-path accumulation bit in the routing header. As described earlier, after the sequence of ANR labels appended to the query message has been exhausted, the routing mode is changed to multicast and the message is forwarded to all the agents on the directory tree. If the message reaches an agent that owns the requested resource, the agent replies using a point-to-point connection based on the path accumulated in the reverse-path field of the query message. The agent also sets the reverse-path accumulation bit in its reply. Therefore, upon receipt of the reply, the user receives not only a confirmation to its request, but also the complete path to reach the desired resource.

A similar procedure is used in the plaNET system for implementing a "Transparent Bridging" function.[3]

8.3 CALL-LEVEL ROUTING

In the plaNET network, several steps are involved in determining the route that is to be assigned to an incoming call request. The first step is to accurately determine the nature of the call request. The plaNET network supports several types of connections, which correspond to different levels of service provided by the network. These differences in level of service impose differing constraints on the route to be assigned to the call, and therefore influence computation of the route. The second step assumes that the connection has been properly characterized, and proceeds with the actual computation of a path between the origin(s) and destination(s) of the call. This computation takes into account both the service requirements of the connection and its "cost" to the network. The goal is to minimize this cost while meeting the required level of service. The route computation is performed by the plaNET network node that is adjacent to the source of the call. The node uses a local replica of a routing database that includes the network topology, link capacities and utilizations, and additional link and nodal characteristics. The update and maintenance of the routing database are described in a subsequent section. The last step in routing a new connection consists of actually establishing the route and securing the necessary resources. These are achieved through a setup that must complete before data are allowed to flow over the new route. In the rest of this section we provide additional details and motivations for the first two of the three steps above. The interested reader is directed to reference 15 for more on the third step.

8.3.1 Call Characterization

plaNET offers two major types of connections: connections with and without QOS guarantees. Additional subclasses are supported within each of these two classes, but this broad partitioning provides the right framework for routing. Where service quality need not be guaranteed, as in nonreserved connections,[15] no explicit call characterization is needed except for the intended destination(s) and an indication of the routing mode (see Section 8.2.1) to be used. Traffic from such connections will be delivered on a best-effort basis, as is typical in most of today's data networks, such as TCP/IP.[2] The routing algorithm used for such connections is therefore quite similar to that of traditional networks. Because of this similarity, the algorithm is only briefly reviewed in the next section, and we concentrate instead on the routing of connections with specific QOS requirements.

Connections that require QOS guarantees must first be properly characterized by the network, so that it can decide on the appropriate amount of resources (bandwidth) to allocate. Once this amount has been determined, it is used as an input to the route-computation algorithm, because it affects which network links are capable of accommodating the new connection. The rest of this section is devoted to describing how the network characterizes connections and translates this information into resources to be allocated.

8.3.1.1 Call Metric

The first step consists of defining a connection's representation that properly describes its characteristics, particularly those that significantly affect network performance. For this purpose we define a quantity named *call metric,* which models a source using a simple two-state (ON-OFF) representation. This description captures the basic nature of data generation associated with a connection. A source is either idle, generating no data, or active and transmitting data at its peak rate. This two-state representation is quite flexible and general. For example, it includes constant bit-rate connections as a limiting case, and accounts for some of the key dynamics of data generation. Based on this two-state representation, the call metric $\mathbf{c}$ associated with a connection is defined as a vector:

$$\mathbf{c} = (R_{\text{peak}}, \rho, b) \tag{1}$$

with three components: the peak rate, the utilization, and the mean burst period. From these three components we can determine the amount of bandwidth that should be allocated to a connection.[21]

The peak rate R_{peak} indicates how fast a source is capable of generating data when it is active. Typically, the higher the peak rate of a source, the more resources it requires from the network to be guaranteed a given level of service (even assuming a fixed average rate). The utilization ρ gives the fraction of time the source is active and generating data. Together with the peak rate, it determines both the mean and the variance of the bit rate generated by the source. The amount of resources required by the connection is again an increasing function of this quantity. Finally, the mean burst period b indicates how much data the source generates whenever it enters an active period. The greater this quantity, the more bandwidth or buffering needs to be allocated to the connection.

The call metric definition of equation 1 represents a tradeoff between complexity and accuracy. On one hand, most users can be expected to have at most rudimentary knowledge of the characteristics of the traffic generated by their application. In the past, connections required either no information on the bit rate, or specification of only a constant bit rate (circuit-switched connections). It is unlikely, therefore, that users will initially be able to provide much detail on the traffic patterns they generate. On the other hand, allocating minimally sufficient resources to a connection does require accurate knowledge of the traffic it generates. For example, two connections with identical mean and peak rates but different burst durations can require significantly different amounts of bandwidth from the network.[21] It is therefore not only desirable but also necessary for efficient use of network resources that users provide as much information as possible on their traffic characteristics.

The call metric vector **c** above includes information that is relatively easy to obtain (peak and mean rates can be readily determined or measured), and can be used to provide a reasonably accurate estimate of the bandwidth requirements of a connection.[21] As mentioned above, this representation is an attempt to balance the availability of connection information and the accuracy of the bandwidth estimates it allows. Accuracy can be improved with an *equivalent* call metric of the simple form above, but incorporating the effect of traffic characteristics such as high-order moments and correlation. This equivalent call metric can be obtained either with standard moment-matching techniques as in Section V.A of reference 21, or with some simple traffic monitoring techniques as in references 22 and 23. Where monitoring is used, a call is typically assigned an "initial" call metric that is subsequently refined as monitoring information becomes available.

We now briefly review the monitoring approach because it allows us to both account for the influence of complex source behaviors and compensate for the lack of readily available user traffic characteristics. The main characteristic of this monitoring is that it does not attempt to estimate the statistics of the traffic associated with a given connection. Rather, it focuses directly on the only quantity of real interest to the network, namely the influence of the connection's traffic on the network resources. In particular, we do not wish to differentiate connections with drastically different traffic patterns but nearly identical effect on network resources.

Estimating a connection's effect on network resources is achieved by monitoring its network-access queue, and particularly the probability that this queue exceeds a specific level (see references 22 and 23 for more motivations and details). From that information it is possible to determine an equivalent burst duration for the original traffic source, which can then be used to construct an "equivalent" call metric of the form given in equation 1. In essence, the average burst duration is changed from its true value, so that the modified call metric corresponds to a source with resource requirements similar to those of the actual connection. It can be shown[22,23] that this equivalent call metric yields the appropriate bandwidth allocation for the connection (see next section). In addition to accounting for the effect of complex traffic patterns, this on-line monitoring allows us to help the user determine its traffic characteristics. This monitoring is carried out as part of the standard plaNET rate-control component, and therefore does not add to the connection-processing load. Furthermore, it gives us the ability to adjust resource allocation in response to significant changes in user traffic.[15,22]

8.3.1.2 *Bandwidth Allocation*

Once the call metric of a new request is known, it must be translated into the amount of bandwidth that the network needs to set aside for it. In the rest of this section we outline a generic approach, used in the plaNET network, to determine how much bandwidth to allocate to a connection based on its call metric and service requirements. The required amount is somewhere between the mean and peak rates of the connection. Allocating only the mean rate is typically insufficient to meet a desired level of service, and though peak allocation provides adequate performance guarantees, it is usually wasteful of network resources. The goal is therefore to provide a simple method for determining the "right" level of allocation.

The approach is based on the combination of two approximations. The first one considers a connection in isolation and determines its bandwidth requirements as a function of its traffic parameters. The second focuses on the interaction of connections within the network, and explains the effect of statistical multiplexing on bandwidth requirements. As shown in reference 21, these two approximations yield reasonably accurate bandwidth estimates over different ranges of connection characteristics. Together, therefore, they give adequate and computationally efficient estimates for the bandwidth requirements of connections and the associated link loads. The main computational cost is in computing for each new connection the expression given in equation 2, which is dominated by the evaluation of the square root term.

Recalling the results of reference 21, the equivalent bandwidth $\hat{c}$ required by an individual connection with call metric vector $\mathbf{c} = (R_{peak}, \rho, b)$, can be estimated using a simple fluid-flow model and is given by:

$$\hat{c} \approx \frac{\alpha b (1-\rho) R_{peak} - x + \sqrt{[\alpha b (1-\rho) R_{peak} - x]^2 + 4x\alpha b\rho (1-\rho) R_{peak}}}{2\alpha b (1-\rho)} \quad (2)$$

where x represents the available buffer space, and $\alpha = \ln(1/\varepsilon)$ with ε the desired loss probability (QOS) in the network. In other words, equation 2 gives us the amount of bandwidth needed by a new connection with call metric $\mathbf{c}$, given that it requires a packet-loss probability below ε and that the network can provide a buffer of size x. Equation 2 can be extended to multiple connections, for it can be shown[21] that the total amount of bandwidth $\hat{C}_{(F)}$ needed by N connections with individual equivalent bandwidths $\hat{c}_i$, $1 \le i \le N$, can be approximated by:

$$\hat{C}_{(F)} = \sum_{i=1}^{N} \hat{c}_i \quad (3)$$

The quantities $\hat{c}_i$ can be viewed as the circuit rates required if the network were to dedicate bandwidth to individual connections. The packet-switched nature of the network typically implies sharing of resources and, therefore, no real dedication of bandwidth to individual connections. The estimates above for the bandwidth requirements of individual connections are nevertheless useful in characterizing the effect of different connections on the network. This relation, however, also means that equation 3 may overestimate the necessary amount of bandwidth, when connections' statistics offer the potential for significant sharing of network resources. Another approximation is then needed to better determine the (statistical-multiplexing) gain available from this sharing.

To obtain such an approximation, we focus on the stationary distribution of the aggregate bit rate of multiple connections (see reference 21 for motivations). Based on this estimate, we then allocate only enough bandwidth to ensure that the aggregate bit rate remains below this allocated value with sufficiently large probability. This provision essentially amounts to requiring that the probability of "overload" be kept below a desired level. There are many possible approaches for approximating the distribution of the aggregate bit rate of multiplexed connections, but a simple and effective one is to rely on a Gaussian distribution.[21] The availability of standard expressions for the tail probabilities of Gaussian distributions then provides us with the tools needed to estimate the amount of bandwidth that needs to be allocated.

In particular, the bandwidth $\hat{C}_{(S)}$ required by N connections multiplexed on the same link can be approximated by:

$$\hat{C}_{(S)} \approx m + \alpha'\sigma \quad \text{with} \quad \alpha' = \sqrt{-2\ln(\varepsilon) - \ln(2\pi)} \tag{4}$$

where m is the mean aggregate bit rate

$$m = \sum_{i=1}^{N} m_i$$

and σ is the standard deviation of the aggregate bit rate

$$\sigma^2 = \sum_{i=1}^{N} \sigma_i^2$$

of the N connections. Equation 4 states that the aggregate bit rate exceeds the value $\hat{C}_{(S)}$ only with probability ε, under the assumption that its distribution is well approximated by a Gaussian distribution. Allocating this amount of bandwidth should therefore ensure a packet loss probability below ε. This approach provides a reasonably accurate bandwidth-allocation rule, when there is significant statistical sharing of network resources. As with equation 3, however, it can also overestimate the required amount of bandwidth for certain types of connections.

Fortunately, the two approximations above are inaccurate over different ranges of connection characteristics.[21] It is therefore possible to combine them to obtain a simple and yet reasonably accurate expression for the amount $\hat{C}$ of link bandwidth that the network should allocate to ensure the desired level of service to connections. For N connections sharing the same network link, this expression is of the form:

$$\hat{C} = \min\left[m + \alpha'\sigma, \sum_{i=1}^{N} \hat{c}_i \right] \tag{5}$$

where the quantities $\hat{c}_i$ are computed from equation 2, and m and σ stand again for the mean and standard deviation of the aggregate bit rate.

Based on this bandwidth allocation and computation procedure, we are now in a position to compare the loading level of links in the network. Specifically, for each link the network maintains a link-metric vector from which the loading of that link can be readily obtained. For the kth link, this vector is of the form:

$$\mathbf{L}_k = \left[m = \sum_{i=1}^{N} m_i, \sigma^2 = \sum_{i=1}^{N} \sigma_i^2, \hat{C}_{(F)} = \sum_{i=1}^{N} \hat{c}_i \right] \tag{6}$$

where N is the number of connections currently multiplexed on link k, m and σ^2 are the mean and variance of the aggregate bit rate, and $\hat{C}_{(F)}$ is the sum of the N individual equivalent bandwidths as given in equation 2.

The procedure for distributing and updating link-metric vectors is covered later in this chapter, but it can be seen that based on this information the loading on network links is readily obtained using equation 5. This ability to determine link loads is critical in properly selecting paths through the network for new incoming connection requests. In the next section, we describe the approach taken in the plaNET network for computing such paths.

8.3.2 Computing Paths

In this section we concentrate on the procedure used to compute the path that the network will assign to a new connection request with given characteristics (call metric). The focus is on computing paths for connections with specific QOS requirements, but connections without such requirements are briefly considered. As discussed above, the provision of QOS guarantees implies allocation of some network resources to each new connection that is to be routed. In this environment, the goal of the routing- or path-computation algorithm is to generate a path with enough resources available to accommodate the new connection, at the same time trying to optimize some long-term network-revenue function, such as overall utilization.

This technique is somewhat different from the traditional objectives of data networks, which usually try to minimize quantities such as the average delay. (See, for example, reference 24 for a review of such criteria and related algorithms.) Instead, the perspective is closer to that of circuit-switched networks, where the goal is typically to maximize some measure of network performance such as the number of calls carried. (See, for example, reference 25 for an introduction to these techniques.) This similarity to circuit-switched networks reflects the guaranteed QOS requirements of connections, because the need to dedicate enough bandwidth to each connection is akin to the allocation of a "circuit" (see earlier comment).

There are, however, significant differences between the environment considered here and that of a circuit-switched network. The heterogeneity of connection requests introduces different constraints, and particularly as seen in equation 5, can result in a connection being assigned different amounts of bandwidth on different links depending on the respective traffic mix on the links. Similarly, though delay may not be a primary consideration given the high speed of the links, the packet-switched network nevertheless makes it a significant factor. Specifically, connection requests may often specify, in addition to their call metric, a maximum acceptable delay through the network. It is then necessary for the routing algorithm to take this additional constraint into account.

From the discussion above, it is clear that the routing algorithm faces a rather complex optimization task. Even in the simpler environment of a circuit-switched network with homogeneous- and fixed-bandwidth calls, determining "optimal" paths that maximize network throughput is difficult. Most existing proposals[25–30] rely on some form of approximations or heuristics. Because of this inherent complexity, which is further complicated in the plaNET environment by the combination of both loss and delay constraints, we rely on a simple heuristic that reflects these requirements. We now describe and motivate this simple heuristic.

Routing Algorithm

The plaNET routing algorithm is an attempt to both balance the load in the network and favor short (fewer links) paths, while also controlling when and how calls can be routed over costlier (longer) paths.

Balancing the load in the network is intuitively desirable to avoid early link saturation, which may result in more connections routed over longer, and therefore costlier, alternate paths. This rule is similar to the one that, in circuit-switched networks, favors links with the largest number of idle trunks.[31,32] Another advantage of load balancing is that in a packet-switched network it also tends to minimize the end-to-end delay. Notice that in plaNET, link load is defined as the ratio of the allocated bandwidth $\hat{C}$ computed from the link-metric vector (see equation 5 and equation 6) and the total link bandwidth C.

A potential drawback of load balancing in networks carrying connections with heterogeneous bandwidth requirements is the well-known "packing" problem, also known as "bandwidth fragmentation." To illustrate this problem, consider two identical paths (of unit capacity) that are available from a given source to a given destination. Also assume that the traffic intensity between them (composed of many small calls) is currently 0.8. A load-balancing scheme will allocate traffic to create an equal loading of 0.4 on each of the paths. Now assume that a single large call arrives with bandwidth requirements of 0.8. Neither of the links then has enough residual capacity to carry this new call. If all the traffic had originally been routed on only one of the two links, however, the call could have been accepted. This packing problem usually arises when call-bandwidth requirements are of the same magnitude as the link capacity (or residual capacity, i.e., loaded networks). This is not a typical scenario in plaNET, where link capacities are on the order of Gigabits/sec. A possible solution to the packing problem is to allow rearrangements of already routed connections to make better use of the fragmented available capacity. Another possible solution is to allow connections to be split across multiple paths. Such an approach, however, requires resequencing at the destination, which may not be practical in high-speed networks. These topics are beyond the scope of this chapter.

The motivation for favoring short paths is that it helps minimize the amount of network resources allocated to a connection, so that more connections can be routed, thereby improving network throughput. This strategy is again inspired by heuristics used in circuit-switched networks, where direct paths are typically favored.[28] Notice, however, that even in circuit-switched networks this technique does not always yield optimal routes,[33] because of the influence of the underlying network topology.[31] This simple rule has, however, generally been found to generate "reasonable" paths, and is applied in the plaNET network. Notice, though, that it often conflicts with the previous load-balancing criterion (a heavily loaded two-hop path is selected over a lightly loaded three-hop one). The plaNET routing algorithm is an attempt to reconcile these two potentially contradictory criteria.

Before formulating the details of this algorithm, we describe one last important issue dealing with the problem of call admission. Call admission deals with the decision of whether or not to accept certain feasible paths. The issue here is that the resources on a path assigned to a given connection may later be put to better use and allow the network to carry *several* connections, which would otherwise have been rejected. Hence, it is preferable to block that first connection even though it could have been accepted. Several approaches have been proposed, again in the context of circuit-switched networks, to deal with this problem. For example, the shadow cost[29,34] or state-dependent[27,33] approaches attempt to forecast the influence on the network revenue of accepting a new connection on a given path. Connections are accepted only if they are expected to positively affect the network revenue. Though these methods are quite powerful, they are not easily extended to the plaNET environment because of both the heterogeneity and variability of connections, and the less-structured topology of the network, which need not be fully connected.

In addition to the network throughput aspect, fairness may also lead to the rejection of some connections even when a feasible path has been identified. For example, in the simple case of three nodes, A, B, C, in tandem, traffic from B and destined to C should not be allowed to shut off all traffic from A to C even though it requires fewer resources (one versus two links). This problem does not usually arise in circuit-switched networks where direct paths are again most often available.[26,28,35,36] In packet-switched networks such as plaNET, this difficulty need not always arise and special attention is required to avoid potential problems, such as starving some nodes.

The plaNET routing algorithm addresses these issues by introducing a concept similar to that of trunk reservation in circuit-switched networks.[31,32,37,38] The goal is again to avoid both instability and unfairness as the network load increases. This balance is achieved by preventing the use of longer *alternate* paths, when link loads exceed certain levels. The motivation is to ensure that excess traffic is carried only when there are enough idle resources, so that it does not affect regular traffic. The approach relies on the use of primary and secondary paths associated with each origin and destination pair (OD pair) in the network.

For a given OD pair, primary paths are those of minimum length (fewest links). Links that belong to the primary paths of an OD pair are identified as primary links for that pair, and all others are deemed secondary links. Notice that not all links on a secondary path are necessarily secondary links; some may also belong to primary paths for the same OD pair. Associated with each link are primary- and secondary-load thresholds, which are used to determine the acceptability of a path. A primary path is accepted if the loads on all its (primary) links are below the levels corresponding to primary-load thresholds. A secondary path is accepted if the load levels on all its primary links are below their primary-load thresholds, *and* the load levels on all its secondary links (there must be at least one, otherwise the path would not be secondary) are below their secondary-load thresholds. Primary- and secondary-load thresholds are typically set to 100 percent and 95 percent of the maximum reservable link capacity, and have been found effective in maintaining throughput while preserving fairness at high network loads.[39] We now at last proceed with the details of the plaNET routing algorithm.

The routing algorithm is a modified shortest-path algorithm, where path length is a function of both hop count and individual link lengths. The length of a link is defined as an increasing function of its load in order to promote load balancing. In particular, link k between nodes i and j is characterized by three values: its total bandwidth C_k, the allocated bandwidth before adding the new connection $\hat{C}_k^{(1)}$, and the allocated bandwidth after adding the new connection $\hat{C}_k^{(2)}$. The distance between nodes i and j when using link k, i.e., the length d_k of link k, is then assumed to be given by this expression:

$$d_k = \frac{C_k}{\left(C_k - \hat{C}_k^{(1)}\right)\left(C_k - \hat{C}_k^{(2)}\right)} \qquad (7)$$

Notice that this distance function, although characteristic of a "delay-type" criterion, has the general effect of making highly congested links less desirable.

The length l_P of a path P is then defined by the pair (n_P, d_P), where n_P is the number of links/hops in P and d_P is the sum of the individual lengths of links in P. Path P_1 is said to be shorter than path P_2, $(l_{P_1} < l_{P_2})$, if the following relation holds:

$$l_{P_1} < l_{P_2} \Leftrightarrow \begin{cases} n_{P_1} < n_{P_2} \\ \text{or } n_{P_1} = n_{P_2} \text{ and } d_{P_1} < d_{P_2} \end{cases} \qquad (8)$$

The plaNET routing algorithm is based on the distance function above, but includes two modifications when compared to a traditional shortest-path algorithm.

The first difference is relatively minor and comes from the need to distinguish between primary and secondary links. Thus, when computing a path for a given OD pair, it is necessary to check links as they are being considered, to ensure that their current loading does not exceed the appropriate (primary or secondary) load threshold. Such a checking can easily be integrated in the standard path-length computations. Notice that we assume here the *a priori* knowledge of which links are primary and secondary for a given OD pair. This information is typically either obtained off-line or computed on the fly using a simplified version of the routing algorithm itself. We shall not further discuss this issue here.

The second difference from traditional shortest-path algorithms is more significant and is introduced by including a maximum path-length constraint $l_P(2) \leq P_T$. Specifically, connections are allowed to specify a maximum path length (delay) they are willing to tolerate. Such a constraint is useful, for example, to let connections avoid paths that include too many low-speed links. This constraint substantially complicates path computation, for the algorithm must now ensure that the selected path has a total length below this value. The increase in complexity comes from its influencing the additivity of the path-length function. This increase requires that intermediate steps of the algorithm store, not only the current minimum-hop feasible paths to intermediate nodes, but also feasible paths with higher hop count and shorter length.

The final algorithm incorporating the two modifications above is inspired by the Bellman-Ford shortest-path algorithm.[24] Computations progress by increasing hop count to account for the first component of the path-length function specified in equation 8. For each increase in hop count, that is, from $h - 1$ to h, the algorithm obtains minimum-length paths of exactly h hops between the connection's origin and all nodes. This progression ensures that at each step, the algorithm produces paths with minimal total link length (second component of equation 8). The algorithm terminates either when the maximum possible number of hops is reached without finding a feasible path, or at the first hop-count value for which a path is found to the connection's destination with a total length below the maximum-length threshold P_T.

The computational complexity of the algorithm is similar to that of the standard Bellman-Ford shortest-path algorithm, but it allows us to achieve paths that satisfy maximum-length constraints. In conclusion, the algorithm generates a path with minimum length according to equation 8, and satisfying a maximum-length constraint. From experimental results,[39] the algorithm has been found useful in satisfying worst-case delay requirements of connections, while allowing high network utilization and protecting nodes from excess traffic originating at other nodes.

In concluding this section, we briefly mention the routing algorithm used to determine paths for connections without QOS guarantees. Because no explicit allocation of network resources is performed for these connections, the use of a network-based optimization criterion is not as meaningful in selecting their paths. Instead, the goal is to optimize some expected measure of the performance, specifically the average end-to-end delay, provided them by the network. To achieve this goal, the network maintains for each link a running estimate of its average (true) utilization, which is then used to determine the "best" possible paths for connections without QOS requirements. The average utilization induced on a link by connections with QOS guarantees is often lower than the amount of allocated bandwidth, for this quantity typically exceeds the sum of the average rates (see equation 5). Nonreserved connections attempt to take advantage of this difference, and the goal of their routing algorithm is to best exploit unused capacity wherever available.

The routing algorithm for connections without QOS guarantees is then a standard shortest-path algorithm, based essentially on the distance function given in equations 7 and 8. The only modification is to equation 7, where for link k the quantities $\hat{C}_k^{(1)}$ and $\hat{C}_k^{(2)}$ are both taken as equal to the estimated average utilization on that link. The algorithm therefore selects paths with minimum hop count and links as lightly loaded as possible, to provide for the lowest possible end-to-end delay at the time of the connection request. Notice, however, that because new connections with QOS guarantees may be added on initially lightly loaded links, it may occasionally be necessary to reroute connections without QOS guarantees. The plaNET network supports this feature, while ensuring that the lower-priority traffic from these connections cannot affect connections with QOS guarantees (see next section). Rerouting can be triggered either by the network or by the connection itself, upon detecting a significant reduction in the throughput achievable on its current path. There, the routing algorithm will again be invoked to determine a better path through the network given the current link loads.

8.4   NETWORK INFRASTRUCTURE

In this section we briefly review two network components that are instrumental in implementing the routing functions of the plaNET network. The description of these two components mirrors the partition of this chapter into *packet-level* and *call-level* routing functions. First, we outline the structure of the plaNET switching system and buffers, which enable provision of the previously described rich set of routing modes and support for several classes of service. Next, we describe how the information (topology, link loads, etc.), needed by the routing algorithms is maintained and distributed in the plaNET network.

8.4.1   Switching and Buffering

A key aspect of the plaNET switch, common to all fast-packet switches, is that *all* intermediate packet-handling functions are performed on the fly by dedicated hardware, with no software involvement. This tactic enables routing of packets at a speed consistent with that of network links and independent of packet sizes (switching throughput is in bits/sec and not packets/sec). As described in reference 1, the plaNET switch is an output-queuing switch capable of handling packets of variable size. It consists of a common high-speed backplane to which link adapters are attached, as shown in Figure 8.5. All packets are routed through the backplane and can therefore be delivered (routed) to any desired subset of adapters for transmission on the corresponding links. All the packet-handling functions needed by the different routing modes and the provision of a number of control functions are performed in the adapters.

Details on the switch implementation are not our topic in this chapter and can be found in reference 1. A simple algorithm is used, however, to arbitrate between contending packets requesting access to the common backplane. The algorithm essentially implements a gated round-robin policy that guarantees a bounded-switch access delay to all packets. Thus, minimal queuing takes place in the input side of the switch adapters. Most of the necessary buffering is then on the output, where packets may have to wait for transmission on the link after being routed through the backplane.

The output buffers, therefore, play a critical role in enforcing the different QOS guarantees that the network offers. As mentioned in the preceding section, it is particularly important that connections without QOS "contracts" be prevented from affecting connections that have been guaranteed a certain level of service. This precaution is particularly important because the routing algorithm used for the former connections may result in temporarily overloading links. In plaNET, enforcement of different QOS guarantees is achieved through a buffering structure that implements different levels of delay and loss priorities. The current implementation supports

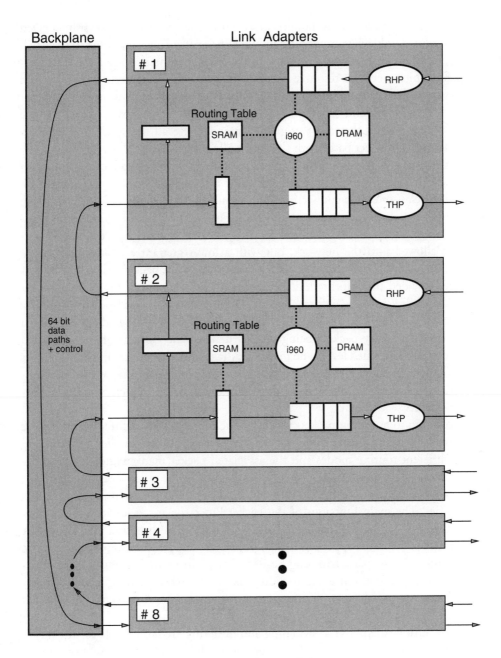

Figure 8.5   plaNET switch

three delay classes, each able to provide two levels of loss probabilities. Extensions to more flexible scheduling and buffering policies are being considered, and may be added in the future as permitted by implementation constraints.

Delay classes correspond to nonpreemptive priorities, so that packets from a given class are routed only when no packets of higher priority are waiting. This strategy will ensure, for example, that connections without QOS guarantees do not affect connections for which network resources have been reserved. This tactic works because packets from the latter can be transmitted only when nothing else is present. In other words, the buffering and scheduling rules successfully make these connections use idle resources only as they were originally intended. Recall that their routing algorithm attempts to select paths with the "most idle" links.

Ensuring that packets for which network resources have been allocated cannot be influenced by unexpected or unreserved traffic also applies within the context of a given delay class or even a connection. This is one of the purposes behind supporting different loss probabilities within a delay class. For example, a connection routed on a given path may generate more traffic than it has been allocated. Such traffic will typically be allowed into the network, but with a lower guarantee of loss probability. Conversely, a connection can itself elect to send some of its packets using a lower loss priority, provided the information they contain is indeed of less value. Support for such a capability requires enforcement of different packet-discard policies within a delay class. In plaNET, this is achieved through a threshold-based policy, which results in low-priority packets being discarded when the content of the associated buffer exceeds a specified level. The main advantage of such a policy, in addition to its simple implementation, is that it allows the network to guarantee a set level of performance to high-priority packets, irrespective of the type and intensity of the low-priority traffic.[40]

In addition to buffering packets waiting to be routed or transmitted on a link, the other main function performed in the adapters is, as mentioned earlier, the handling of the different routing modes and the associated packet manipulations. This function is under the responsibility of the Packet Processor. The reader is again referred to reference 1 for details on this component, but we briefly review its packet-routing capabilities. The main functions of the Packet Processor are to identify the routing mode used by each packet, make the associated routing information available to the switch, and perform the appropriate manipulations (stripping or swapping of routing information) on the packet-routing headers. For performance purposes, these functions are again carried out using dedicated hardware, which can be made relatively simple because of the significant processing similarities between the different modes.[1,3]

In conclusion, the plaNET switching and buffering are responsible for the physical routing of packets, and the enforcement of the different classes of services offered by the network. For performance purposes, these functions are provided by dedicated hardware, which is nevertheless capable of significant flexibility—that is, multiple routing modes and service classes. The ability to support different levels of physical packet routing translates into differences in the algorithms used to compute routes through the network. In particular, different algorithms are used for connections with and without QOS guarantees (see Section 8.3.2). As technology improves and switches start offering more flexible service policies in support of a wider range of QOS classes, the challenge will be to account for these new capabilities in the routing algorithms themselves. This is an area where much research remains to be done.

8.4.2 Routing Database Update and Maintenance

In this section we briefly explain how a replica of the network topology including various link metrics (utilization and other important features) is maintained at each network node. This replica is used to compute paths for calls that originate within the domain of this network node.

Each network node is responsible for determining the bandwidth utilization of its outgoing or adjacent links, for determining when to inform remote nodes of changes in the utilization of its links, and for distributing this information to remote nodes. Distributing link-load information is called a *utilization update*. A similar task is the *topology update,* where information about changes in link status is distributed. The status of a link as stored in the routing topology database and distributed in topology and utilization update messages identifies if the link is active or not. It also includes an indication of whether the link is part of the hardware-based control-spanning tree mentioned earlier, as well as measures of its reliability, security, and so on.

For both utilization and topology updates, it is possible to rely on a conventional flooding-based broadcast algorithm, such as the one used in ARPANET[41] and APPN.[42] However, the flooding algorithm has some deficiencies that make it suboptimal for our purpose. First, it delivers a copy of every message over every link (which can be translated to $O(|E|)$ overhead per topology item change, where E denotes the set of network links). Thus, each node has to process a large amount of redundant packets, but it is clearly sufficient for a node to receive only one copy of each message. This requirement considerably limits the effective size of the distributed database and the rate at which database changes can be processed. Second, this algorithm does not take advantage of the availability of hardware-based multicast and relies on software-based hop-by-hop forwarding. The propagation of the update messages hop by hop through the software layers makes the algorithm too slow to operate in a rapidly changing traffic environment.

The method used in plaNET relies on the hardware-based TREE-multicast routing mode, which delivers messages directly from the source to all potential recipients with no software involvement in the transfer. Moreover, only one copy of each message is delivered to the endpoints. Hence, the processing cost is only $O(|V|)$ and the delay is only a function of the hardware switching and the propagation delays in the network. The tree used for topology and utilization updates is a spanning tree that connects all network nodes into one multicast group.

Topology updates are triggered whenever a node senses the failure or recovery of one of its adjacent links. Utilization updates are triggered whenever the node senses that the utilization of an adjacent link has changed substantially since the time of the previous update. Utilization updates are also sent periodically (as described below) to guarantee reliability. Although the cumulative load induced on the network links by such updates is kept minimal (see below), a small portion of link bandwidth is always kept available to carry this traffic. This provision is achieved by constraining the reserved bandwidth on any link to be smaller than about 90 percent of the available bandwidth.

The multicast messages as defined above have no built-in error-recovery mechanism. There is some finite (very small) probability that a multicast message sent on the tree will not arrive at some of its destinations. In both the topology and the utilization-update tasks, we make use of a "backup" periodic multicast (on the spanning tree) of utilization updates to achieve reliability. This approach is suitable for such update tasks because it is important only that nodes receive the most recent link information (previous updates become obsolete once a new one is received). Because a link-utilization message is also implicitly a link topology message, the periodic multicast of utilization messages can also provide reliable topology updates. (Notice that we assume here that some form of "garbage-collection" algorithm removes from the topology database the entries associated with failed links whose update message was not received.) The periodic multicast used to achieve reliability is implemented by having each node maintain a timeout timer and perform an automatic multicast when this timer expires. The timer is reset every time a utilization update is sent, so that this automatic multicast is triggered only if no such multicast has occurred for a complete timeout period. Notice that we expect utilization updates to be rather frequent, and therefore do not expect this periodic mechanism to be triggered very often.

We would like to use a hardware-based multicast tree for the topology-update protocol, and so we need a mechanism that allows, even in the face of failures and recoveries, network nodes to correctly and consistently label those of their adjacent links which belong to the multicast tree. Because all nodes maintain a local network-topology database, it appears that they could all compute a tree according to some consistent procedure, such as a minimum-spanning tree, and thereby know how to label their adjacent links (as either belonging to the tree or not). In a dynamically changing network, however, this simple approach can result in transient loops in the tree because of temporary and improper labeling of some links. This effect will then cause looping of messages, which will generate excessive traffic in the network. To remedy this problem, we introduce a tree-maintenance algorithm that, though relying on the topology information available at each node, also imposes careful coordination between nodes to prevent transient loops from occurring.

The protocol used at each node to correctly disseminate and process topology (and utilization) updates, therefore, consists of two modules (see Figure 8.6). The first

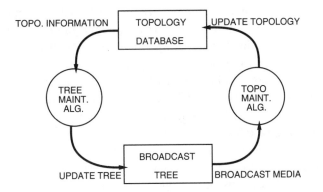

Figure 8.6 Relations of topology update and tree-maintenance routines

module executes a topology-maintenance algorithm, which, upon detecting a local topology (or utilization) change, is responsible for broadcasting over the current multicast-spanning tree an update notifying other nodes of this change. The second module is responsible for maintaining the spanning tree, using its knowledge of the current network topology and information it receives from updates. For example, when the tree becomes disconnected because of a link or node failure, the replicated topology database available in the node is used to locate edges that will reconnect the tree. The details of the topology and tree-maintenance algorithms and their coordination are provided in reference 43.

It is, however, worth mentioning that the tree maintenance algorithm is in fact not restricted to "patching" broken components of the spanning tree. It also monitors constantly whether the links currently used by the spanning tree are the best possible ones. If a significantly better link is identified (or has recently come up), a planned "breakage" of the corresponding inferior link is performed by its adjacent node, so that the "patch" applied by the tree-maintenance algorithm upon detecting this breakage results in a better link being used in rejoining the tree. Notice that because reliability is a major component in the link metric determining the goodness of a link for use in the multicast spanning tree, an unstable link that tends to fail and recover frequently will be judged a poor tree-link candidate. This awareness ensures that the planned breakages and patching above will not cause instability in the tree structure itself.

Finally, a somewhat similar tree-maintenance protocol appears in reference 44. This protocol, however, cannot make use of a hardware-based multicast, because it assumes reliable delivery of messages (which our basic multicast does not provide). Also, the protocol of reference 44 is more complex than required because it does not permit use of sequence numbers (used in the plaNET protocol). Even if sequence numbers are theoretically undesirable because they can lead to unbounded message lengths, 64 bits of sequence numbering have been found more than sufficient for all practical purposes. More important, using sequence numbers greatly simplifies the tree-maintenance and topology and utilization update protocols, as well as the data structures used in the topology database itself.

The last component of the plaNET update protocol is the mechanism used to decide if and when a change in link utilization is significant enough to warrant an update. We now proceed to describe this mechanism.

Perfect knowledge of load information on all network links (within the limitations of delay in propagation of information) requires triggering of updates after any adding or removing of connections on any link. Such an approach would clearly induce a heavy update-processing load on nodes. The goal of the utilization-update mechanism is therefore to provide reasonably accurate information on link loads while limiting the number of updates.

The need for accurate load information is especially high at high loads, where inaccuracies are magnified in link-length computations (see equation 7). At high loads, however, utilization is likely to change frequently because of the many connections coming and going. This condition points to a potential problem if updates are event driven because too many updates may then be generated. A periodic update policy therefore appears preferable for controlling the rate of updates. This approach, however, has its own limitations, as in large changes in utilization of a link, when it delays availability of important information until the scheduled time of the next update.

To reconcile the need for rapid availability of important information with the need to limit the rate of updates, plaNET uses a hybrid policy combining event-driven and periodic-update strategies. Each network node maintains current link-metric vectors (utilization measures) for all the links it owns. It also remembers the utilization value reported in the last update sent for any of its links. The algorithm used to decide when and if to send updates is based on a monitoring interval of duration T_u and two constants, δ and Δ, which are defined as fractions of the link bandwidth, where $\Delta > \delta$. A typical value for δ may be around 1 percent of link capacity, and Δ is usually set at about 10 percent of link capacity. The idea behind the algorithm is to monitor changes in link utilization, compare the new value to the last broadcasted one, and trigger an update depending on the magnitude of the change. If the change is below δ the node will not trigger any special update and will rely solely on the periodic update performed for error recovery. If the change is between δ and Δ, the node increases the rate of the periodic update by scheduling the next update to happen within the next T_u period. Finally, if the change exceeds the larger value Δ, the node immediately triggers an (event-driven) update. This update will ensure that information about large changes is rapidly disseminated, and will limit the steady-state number of updates being generated.

8.5 CONCLUSIONS AND FUTURE WORK

In this chapter we describe the routing components and mechanisms of the Gigabit plaNET architecture. At the lowest level of individual packet routing, an efficient hardware-based routing mechanism supports a rich set of routing modes and options. Such a mechanism is required on the one hand to deliver high switching throughput, and on the other hand to offer a high degree of flexibility and low latency to typical network-control functions and common applications.

At the higher level of call routing, a complete control framework is presented that takes into account the heterogeneous user population with its different and at times conflicting requirements. Specifically, plaNET uses a metric-based methodology to represent the influence of individual calls on the network and to describe the load situation of the network links. These metrics are then translated into the amount of resources required and already reserved. They also provide the necessary inputs to the route-computation procedure in selecting "good" paths through the network. In particular, the goals of the route-computation algorithm are two. It attempts to maximize the network utilization by employing shortest-path routing and load balancing. It also enforces quality of service by rejecting calls that would overload network links or adversely affect other calls.

Much work remains to be done to adequately solve the many new problems that arise in high-speed integrated networks. We have pointed to the problem of "packing" or bandwidth fragmentation that can occur when routing calls with different bandwidth requirements. Rerouting of calls is required to efficiently solve this problem, and appropriate algorithms must be found. Similarly, rerouting is also needed to maintain connections despite topological changes (link failures). Such a service is commonly referred to as "nondisruptive route switching." A common methodology and framework are currently being developed for these two problems.

Many other "routing" problems need further study. Computing efficient (optimal) trees to support multicast sessions with bandwidth guarantees, or algorithms for effective call preemption in networks that support multiple call classes, are two of the many examples that are currently being worked on as extensions to the plaNET architecture.

8.6 ACKNOWLEDGMENTS

The authors acknowledge the many people who contributed to different aspects of the work described in this chapter, and in particular H. Ahmadi, J. S.-C. Chen, P. Chimento, C.-S. Chow, J. Derby, J. Drake, I. Gopal, P. M. Gopal, L. Gün, J. Janniello, M. Kaplan, S. Kutten, M. Naghshineh, K. Potter, K. Sohraby, M. Sidi, and T. Tedijanto.

REFERENCES

1   I. Cidon, I. Gopal, P. M. Gopal, R. Guérin, J. Janniello, and M. Kaplan, "The plaNET/ORBIT High Speed Network," *Journal of High Speed Networks,* Vol. 2, No. 3, September 1993, pp. 1–38.

2   D. E. Comer, *Internetworking with TCP/IP,* 2nd ed., Vol. I, *Principles, Protocols, and Architecture,* Englewood Cliffs: Prentice Hall, 1991.

3   I. Gopal and R. Guérin, "Network Transparency: The plaNET Approach," *Proceedings of the INFOCOM '92,* Florence, May 1992, pp. 590–601.

4   *International Journal of Digital & Analog Cabled Systems,* Vol. 1, No. 4, 1988. Special Issue on Asynchronous Transfer Mode.

5   "Draft—General B-ISDN Aspects," *CCITT Study Group XVIII, Report R 34,* June 1990.

6   J.-Y. Le Boudec, "The Asynchronous Transfer Mode: A Tutorial," *Computer Networks and ISDN Systems,* Vol. 24, No. 4, May 1992, pp. 279–309.

7   "Framework for Providing Additional Packet Mode Bearer Services," *CCITT Subworking Party XVIII/1-2,* CCITT Recommendation, No. I.122, 1988.

8   I. Gopal, R. Guérin, J. Janniello, and V. Theoharakis, "ATM Support in a Transparent Network," *IEEE Networks Magazine,* Vol. 6, No. 6, November 1992, pp. 62–68. (See also *Proceedings of the GLOBECOM '92.*)

9   C. T. Chou and I. Gopal, "Linear Broadcast Routing," *Journal of Algorithms,* Vol. 10, 1989, pp. 490–517.

10 I. Cidon, I. S. Gopal, and S. Kutten, "New Models and Algorithms for Future Networks," *Proceedings of the Seventh Annual ACM Symposium on Principles of Distributed Computing,* Toronto, August 1988, pp. 75–89.

11 B. Awerbuch, I. Cidon, I. Gopal, M. Kaplan, and S. Kutten, "Distributed Control for PARIS," *Proceedings of the Ninth Annual ACM Symposium on Principles of Distributed Computing,* 1990, pp. 145–160.

12 I. Cidon, I. Gopal, and A. Segall, "Connection Establishment in High-Speed Networks," *IEEE/ACM Transactions on Networking,* Vol. 1, No. 4, August 1993, pp. 469–481. (See also *Proceedings of the SIG-COMM '90.*)

13 I. Cidon, I. Gopal, and S. Kutten, "Optimal Computation of Global Sensitive Functions in Fast Networks," in J. Van Leeuwen and N. Santoro, eds., *Distributed Algorithms, Proceedings of the Fourth International Workshop on Distributed Algorithms,* Bari, Berlin: Springer-Verlag, September 1990, pp. 185–191.

14 A. S. Gopal, I. S. Gopal, and S. Kutten, "Broadcast in Fast Networks," *Proceedings of the INFOCOM '90,* San Francisco, June 1990.

15 I. Cidon, I. Gopal, and R. Guérin, "Bandwidth Management and Congestion Control in plaNET," *IEEE Communications Magazine,* Vol. 29, No. 10, October 1991, pp. 54–63.

16 A. Segall, T. P. Barzilai, and Y. Ofek, "Reliable Multiuser Tree Setup with Local Identifiers," *IEEE Journal on Selected Areas in Communications,* Vol. 9, No. 9, December 1991, pp. 1427–1439.

17 P. E. Boyer, "A Congestion Control for the ATM," *Proceedings of the Seventh ITC Seminar,* Morristown, NJ, October 1990.

18 P. E. Boyer, J.-R. Louvion, and D. P. Tranchier, "Intelligent Multiplexing in ATM Based Networks," *Proceedings of the IEEE MULTIMEDIA '90,* Bordeaux, November 1990.

19 P. E. Boyer and D. P. Tranchier, "A Reservation Principle with Applications to the ATM Traffic Control," *Computer Networks and ISDN Systems,* Vol. 24, 1992, pp. 321–334.

20 D. C. Verma and P. M. Gopal, "Routing Reserved Bandwidth Multi-Point Connections," *Proceedings of the SIGCOMM '93,* San Francisco, September 1993, pp. 96–105.

21 R. Guérin, H. Ahmadi, and M. Naghshineh, "Equivalent Capacity and Its Application to Bandwidth Allocation in High-Speed Networks," *IEEE Journal of Selected Areas in Communications,* Vol. SAC-9, No. 7, September 1991, pp. 968–981.

22 R. Guérin and L. Gün, "A Unified Approach to Bandwidth Allocation and Access Control in Fast Packet-Switched Networks," *Proceedings of the INFOCOM '92,* Florence, May 1992, pp. 1–12.

23 L. Gün, "An Approximation Method for Capturing Complex Behavior in High Speed Networks," *Performance Evaluation,* Vol. 19, No. 1, January 1994, pp. 5–23.

24 D. Bertsekas and R. Gallager, *Data Networks,* 2nd ed., Englewood Cliffs: Prentice Hall, 1992.

25 A. Girard, *Routing and Dimensioning in Circuit-Switched Networks,* Reading: Addison-Wesley, 1990.

26 G. R. Ash, R. H. Caldwell, and R. P. Murray, "Design and Optimiza-tion of Networks with Dynamic Routing," *Bell Systems Technical Journal (B.S.T.J.)*, Vol. 60, No. 8, October 1981, pp. 1787–1820.

27 T. J. Ott and K. R. Krishnan, "State Dependent Routing of Telephone Traffic and the Use of Separable Routing Schemes," in M. Akiyama, ed., *Proceedings of the Eleventh International Teletraffic Congress,* Kyoto, Amsterdam: Elsevier Science Publishers B.V. (North-Holland), September 1985, pp. 5.1A-5.1–5.1A-5.6.

28 R. J. Gibbens, F. P. Kelly, and P. B. Key, "Dynamic Alternative Routing Modelling and Behaviour," in M. Bonatti, ed., *Proceedings of the Twelfth International Teletraffic Congress,* Torino, Amsterdam: Elsevier Science Publishers B.V. (North-Holland), June 1988, pp. 1019–1025.

29 F. P. Kelly, "Routing in Circuit-Switched Networks: Optimization, Shadow Prices and Decentralization," *Advances in Applied Probability,* Vol. 20, 1988, pp. 112–144.

30 D. Mitra, R. J. Gibbens, and B. D. Huang, "Analysis and Optimal Design of Aggregated Least Busy-Alternative Routing on Symmetric Loss Networks with Trunk Reservation," in A. Jensen and V. B. Iversen, eds., *Proceedings of the Thirteenth International Teletraffic Congress,* Copenhagen, Amsterdam: Elsevier Science Publishers B.V. (North-Holland), June 1991, pp. 477–482.

31 G. R. Ash, "Use of a Trunk Status Map for Real-Time DNHR," in M. Akiyama, ed., *Proceedings of the eleventh International Teletraffic Congress,* Kyoto, Amsterdam: Elsevier Science Publishers B.V. (North-Holland), September 1985, pp. 4.4A-4.1–4.4A-4.7.

32 E. W. M. Wong and T.-S. Yum, "Maximum Free Circuit Routing in Circuit-Switched Networks," *Proceedings of the INFOCOM '90,* San Francisco, June 1990, pp. 934–937.

33 K. R. Krishnan and T. J. Ott, "Forward Routing: A New State Dependent Routing Scheme," in M. Bonatti, ed., *Proceedings of the Twelfth International Teletraffic Congress,* Turin, Amsterdam: Elsevier Science Publishers B.V. (North-Holland), June 1988, pp. 1026–1032.

34 F. P. Kelly, "Fixed Point Models of Loss Networks," *Journal of the Australian Mathematics Society, Series B,* Vol. 31, Part 2, 1989, pp. 204–218.

35 A. Girard and Y. Cote, "Sequential Routing Optimization for Circuit-Switched Networks," *IEEE Transactions on Communications,* Vol. COM-32, No. 12, December 1984, pp. 1234–1242.

36   P. B. Key, "Implied Cost Methodology and Software Tools for a Fully Connected Network with DAR and Trunk Reservation," *British Tele-communications Technology,* Vol. 6, No. 3, July 1988, pp. 52–65.

37   J. M. Akinpelu, "The Overload Performance of Engineered Networks with Nonhierarchical and Hierarchical Routing," *Bell Systems Technical Journal (B.S.T.J.),* Vol. 63, No. 7, 1984, pp. 1261–1281.

38   R. S. Krupp, "Stabilization of Alternate Routing Networks," *Proceedings of the ICC '82,* Philadelphia, June 1982, pp. 31.2.1–31.2.5.

39   H. Ahmadi, J. S.-C. Chen, and R. Guérin, "Dynamic Routing and Call Control in High-Speed Integrated Networks," *Proceedings of the Workshop on Systems Engineering and Traffic Engineering, Thirteenth International Teletraffic Congress,* Copenhagen, 1991, pp. 397–403.

40   I. Cidon, R. Guérin, and A. Khamisy, "Protective Buffer Management Policies," *Proceedings of the INFOCOM '93,* San Francisco, March 1993, pp. 1051–1058.

41   J. M. McQuillan, I. Richer, and E. C. Rosen, "The New Routing Algorithm for the ARPANET," *IEEE Transactions on Communications,* Vol. COM-28, No. 5, May 1980, pp. 711–719.

42   A. E. Baratz, J. P. Gray, P. E. Green, Jr., J. M. Jaffe, and D. P. Podzefsky, "SNA Networks of Small Systems," *IEEE Journal on Selected Areas in Communications,* Vol. SAC-3, No. 3, May 1985, pp. 416–426.

43   I. Cidon, I. Gopal, M. Kaplan, and S. Kutten, "A Distributed Control Architecture of High-Speed Networks," *IEEE Transactions on Communications,* 1994, in press.

44   B. Awerbuch, I. Cidon, and S. Kutten, "Communication-Optimal Maintenance of Replicated Information," *Proceedings of the Annual Symposium on Foundations of Computer Science,* Vol. 2, 1990, pp. 492–502.

CHAPTER 9 ❖ ❖ ❖ ❖

_____

Deflection Routing

FLAMINIO BORGONOVO

CONTENTS

Deflection routing, the diversion of packets away from their preferred outgoing links when these links are busy, was first proposed in the early 1960s and later applied to packet switching among the components of a distributed computer. In the late 1980s, deflection routing reemerged as a promising technique for achieving high throughput in packet-switched networks with regular mesh topologies and limited buffering capabilities. Most recently, multihop all-optical networks have stimulated renewed interest in deflection routing research. This chapter examines deflection routing in depth, providing comparative performance analyses of different deflection algorithms on a variety of topologies, both static and dynamic, and covering topics such as congestion, fairness, slotted and unslotted operation, and buffering.

9.1   A DESIGN PHILOSOPHY

In packet-switching systems, deflections are said to occur whenever packets are diverted from their most convenient path to their destination. In traditional networks only one path at a time, between source and destination, is selected as the most convenient, and deflections are always exceptional, unwanted events that are often avoided by dropping packets. Such architectural choices have been dictated by the technology available a few decades ago, which was dominated by the high cost, low speed, and low noise immunity of the transmission links of that time.

The high cost of links has led to network designs based on loose-mesh topologies, where the traffic is routed over relatively few highly utilized channels. High link utilization is attained by queuing packets at nodes and by operating sophisticated routing algorithms that, on account of the low ratio of the propagation delay to the transmission delay, can use information gathered throughout the network. For example, when a queue in a node becomes too long, the routing algorithm operating in neighbor nodes may decide to drop that node from the list of available paths. Besides the task of running routing algorithms, nodes manage queues, and process, collect, and send all data necessary for routing and congestion-control procedures. Because all these functions demand resources, they may form a serious bottleneck if a high link rate is considered.

In metropolitan areas, which are expected to be crowded with a high density of users and very high speed transmission links, new problems arise that the design criteria of classical packet-switching networks cannot resolve. The link speed will be at the technological edge, thus exacerbating the nodal bottleneck problem. Moreover, at those speeds the packet transmission time can be very short compared to the propagation time, and several packets can be in flight between nodes. The time scale of

traffic fluctuation is thus noticeably shortened, and the influence on routing efficiency of the real-time gathering of traffic information is greatly reduced if not absent
(deeper insights on the subject can be found, for example, in reference 50). In this
context *deflection networks* (DNs) introduce a design philosophy that proves crucial
in attaining simple and very effective communication architectures. In DNs the use
of multiple paths and deflections, if convenient paths are not available, is included in
the network's normal operation. Thus, routing is extremely simplified and queues are
no longer needed. Throughput efficiency is guaranteed by highly connected mesh
topologies, which present small penalties upon deflection while providing flexible
and fail-safe service.

The advantages of multiple paths and deflections can be understood by comparing
the two situations encountered by a car that must cross, in one case, a wide country
and, in the other case, a metropolitan area. In the former case, classic shortest-path
techniques are vital for the economy of travel. In the latter case, a flexible strategy
that attempts different routes, depending on local conditions, can give better results.
Short detours and deflections are effectively undertaken to avoid congested paths,
and in this way the point-to-point capacity is substantially increased.

The DN design philosophy provides further benefits that go well beyond those
already mentioned. It allows one to extend to metropolitan and wide-area networks
many positive features of LANs, such as fairness in network access and simplicity of
congestion control. In WANs, congestion occurs when the network accepts more
traffic than it can handle. This overloading can happen because the congestion-prone
resources, such as queuing buffers and processing power at nodes, are not under the
direct and immediate control of the network-admission entities, which are located at
the network's edge. Thus, nodes must exchange control information that may itself
be subject to the network problems encountered by ordinary traffic. Fairness, that is,
the guarantee that no user can prevail in accessing congested resources, is hard to
achieve in classical networks. The reasons are manifold, starting from the multiplicity
of resources to be arbitrated and ending with the very same reasons that entangle
congestion control. These problems, of some relevance in existing networks, worsen
when speed scaling of classical architectures is attempted.

Congestion control and fairness are much simpler to attain in LANs because there
are no congestion-prone or allocable resources other than the transmission resource
itself, which, furthermore, is under direct control of the *medium access control* (MAC)
protocol. Thus, fairness and congestion control are reduced to a correct MAC design.
DN operation also can be almost completely controlled by MAC, making its trans-
portation service very similar, but for one characteristic, to that of LANs. The difference, a relevant one indeed, is that DNs cannot guarantee the delivery sequence. In
fact, DN packets directed to the same destination can take different paths and over-
take each other, so that the delivery order does not necessarily match the transmission
order. Though this problem is also encountered in networks that use dynamic routing, in DNs it is aggravated by the use of an intrinsically bifurcated routing technique

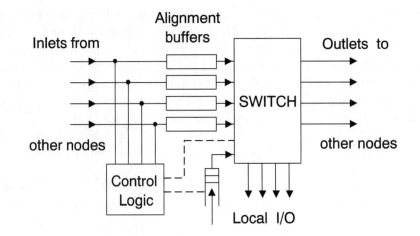

Figure 9.1   Architectural scheme of a DN node of degree 4

in conjunction with a very high transmission speed. As a consequence, the technique can become impracticable if the correct sequence cannot be reestablished by network-edge routines either because of the amount of buffers and processing power needed or because of the delay incurred.

DN principles were first theorized by Baran in reference 1, where the term *hot-potato* routing was coined. Because of the reasons given above, however, the proposal was too advanced for the technology available at the time. It took about two decades before Baran's ideas were reconsidered. Early descriptions of deflection routing as applied to multiprocessor interconnection networks appeared in references 2 and 3. Maxemchuck, in references 4 and 5, introduced LAN and MAN topologies that could benefit from deflections and gave the basic node architecture, and in reference 15 the backward-learning technique, a way to have the network learn about topology changes, has been proven to integrate deflection routing optimally.

9.2   NODE ARCHITECTURE

DNs are based on nodes that are able to switch packets among a few high-speed links, whose basic architecture for four links is represented in Figure 9.1. The node is composed of (1) a receiving section that is in charge of receiving the packets from adjacent nodes and reading their headers; (2) alignment buffers that temporarily hold packets for synchronized operation; and (3) the switching and transmission section, which routes packets in the buffers toward the node's outlets. The local input-output section and the routing logic complete the design. The node's operation obeys these principles:

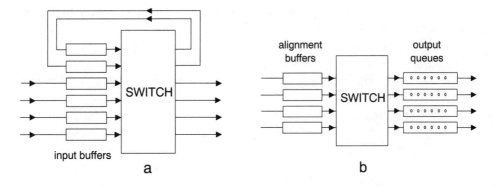

Figure 9.2 Node of degree 4: (a) input queuing with two additional buffers, (b) output queuing

- All links have the same transmission speed.

- The number of input links equals the number of output links.

- Packets have a fixed length.

- Switching and transmission are slotted and locally synchronized; that is, packets are forwarded at synchronized instants that occur every T seconds (time slots), where T is the packet transmission time.

- Received packets are temporarily stored in alignment buffers. At each time slot, all the packets present in the alignment buffers are forwarded to the output links through the switching matrix.

- A packet in the input queue enters the network if an empty slot is available—that is, if either a slot has been received empty or a packet is being extracted.

As a result of the rules above, no packets can be stored at nodes for an entire time slot or multiples. The network's operation is much the same as that of slotted rings. A constant number of packet slots is kept recirculating within the network. Packet slots are captured and occupied by packets entering the network and are evacuated as packets reach their destinations. Packet slots are the only network resource administered by the network access and routing protocols. The routing protocol, if possible, forwards packets to optimal outlets; but because it must forward all packets in any case, it may happen that some packets are forced toward nonoptimal outlets, in which case we say that they are *deflected*.

Deflections may force packets to take longer paths, which wastes transmission resources. To reduce the occurrence of deflections, the basic architecture can be enhanced by extra packet storage to be added before or after the switching section, implementing configurations called *input queuing* and *output queuing*, respectively (here, *input* and *output* refer to the switch, not to the network). In the first case (Figure 9.2a), the node must forward d packets chosen among $d + b$ packets, where d

denotes the number of links and b the number of additional input buffers. In the second case (Figure 9.2b), a separate queue of length b is provided at each output link and packets can be routed simultaneously to the same queue. In both cases, however, the network operation remains substantially the same as in the no-buffer case, because deflections are still allowed to prevent queue overflows when nodal buffers fill up.

Notice that buffers may seem useless because, when filled up, they cannot prevent packet deflections. Nevertheless, they help to reduce the deflection probability. In fact, with input queuing the choice of the d packets to be forwarded increases with b, which increases the number of favorable routing possibilities. With output queuing, room is always available at some output queues, so that there is always the chance that packets are more conveniently queued than deflected.

To understand why output queues cannot all be full at the same time, consider that the number of packets globally queued at a node increases only if at least one queue is empty, otherwise the number of packets that leave the node is d, which is never smaller than the number of arrivals. In the worst case only one queue is empty and, once the others have become full, the fraction of global storage occupied is $(d - 1)/d$ and can be increased no further, because deflections are enforced to prevent overflow. In any case, buffering at nodes increases nodal and routing complexity and its convenience must be carefully evaluated. As for the choice between input and output queuing, the latter appears simplest and is usually the one analyzed. However, if nodes are implemented using optical technology, input queuing appears to be the only possible solution, because input buffers can be implemented by using one-slot delay lines, but output queuing is not feasible with today's technology.

Minor architectural differences may arise in the access and extraction mechanisms. One is the maximum number of packets that can be inserted and extracted in a time slot. Although a maximum of d packets/slot could be inserted at each node, the value of one packet/slot is a peak value well beyond the average nodal throughput for sufficiently large networks. The ability to extract up to d packets/slot is critical, however, for throughput performance. Otherwise, some packets could be deflected into the network and waste considerable resources. Other differences may regard possible throttling mechanisms inserted to avoid network congestion.

The routing logic is driven by the header content of packets in the receiving section and in the local queue. In the simplest cases, a few arithmetic operations are sufficient to determine the configuration of the switch. In more sophisticated cases, the routing configuration can be obtained from additional information stored in lookup tables. In any case, all these operations must be performed within one time slot and therefore may form the network bottleneck.

Under normal conditions all packets reach their destinations. It is still possible, however, that some packets recirculate endlessly because of link or node failures or header corruption. To prevent this possibility, the packet's header includes a *time-to-live* (TTL) field, which is initially set to a fixed value by the originating node and is decremented at each succeeding node through which the packet passes. When the TTL field falls to 0, the decrementing node removes the packet from the network (i.e., the packet is discarded).

9.3 TOPOLOGIES

The choice of topology plays a determining role in DNs, because not all topologies can exploit effectively the possibilities offered by deflection routing. As a rule, topologies should implement a dense-mesh network with several paths (a few of them almost equivalent in length) between source and destination. They should also provide efficient connections among nodes, so that the average path length is as close as possible to the minimum. Unfortunately, these general goals are in conflict once the maximum degree of nodes has been fixed.

Some topology characteristics are dictated by the environment for which the topology is designed. For example, in multiprocessor systems, regular structures are suggested by the interchangeable roles of processing nodes. Moreover, regular topologies, such as shuffle-exchange networks[4,12,20,40] allow simple and fast methods to execute addressing mechanisms, which reduce the node complexity. In these systems planar-connection constraints are either absent or more easily violated. Links are inexpensive and the connection degree of nodes can grow, as in hypercube networks,[19,36] to simplify the entire network operation. In local and metropolitan environments, networks must be able to expand flexibly, according to needs, and without redirecting network connections or affecting network operation.[4] Moreover, links are an expensive resource, which is better administered by using clever routing schemes than by increasing the connectivity. For these reasons a node connectivity beyond four is never considered. Link and physical constraints could also limit the choice of topologies should an unfavorable location of nodes occur. Within the limits imposed by the scenario, an attractive solution is represented by the one indicated in reference 10 that allows a variety of virtual topologies to be mapped into a simple physical topology.

The efficiency that a topology presents in exploiting the bandwidth depends on the traffic matrix, which determines the fraction of throughput to be allocated to each source–destination pair. It can be expressed by the *capacity C,* defined as the maximum steady-state throughput that the network can provide under the assumed traffic matrix. The capacity of networks having equal transmission-rate links can be bounded above by

$$C \leq \frac{l}{L_0} \tag{1}$$

where the capacity is expressed in packets/slot (i.e., packets per packet-transmission time) units, the link-transmission rate is assumed to be 1 packet/slot (otherwise the bound must be multiplied by the effective rate), l is the global number of links in the network, and L_0 is the source–destination distance in hops, that is, the shortest-path distance averaged over all source–destination pairs.

In equation 1 the equality sign holds for symmetric networks, in which all paths have the same topological properties, under a uniform-traffic matrix. In these networks the load distributes evenly among links, in such a way that all links have the same utilization factor ρ. The capacity is thus reached when ρ equals one and all packets are on their shortest paths (this condition is possible if unlimited queuing resources are provided at nodes). In this case, the throughput, that is, the right-hand side of equation 1, is obtained by Little's result, observing that l is the number of packets in the network (i.e., the number of packets to be routed at nodes at each routing step), and L_0 represents the crossing delay measured in routing steps. In the general case, links are unevenly loaded, and, as long as packets travel on their shortest paths to destinations, the link utilization can hardly reach one on all links. The throughput can perhaps be increased by rerouting some traffic to non–shortest-path routes; perhaps, in this way, $\rho = 1$ can be reached on all links. In any case, the number of packets to be routed cannot exceed l and the average distance traveled cannot be less than L_0, so that the capacity cannot exceed l/L_0.

A lower bound to the average distance of any two-connected topology with M nodes and a uniform-traffic matrix has been derived in reference 5 as

$$L_0 \geq \frac{(\lceil \log_2 (M+1) \rceil - 1)\,(M+1) + 2 - 2^{\lceil \log_2 (M+1) \rceil}}{M-1} \tag{2}$$

where $\lceil x \rceil$ is the smallest integer $\geq x$. This result, together with equation 1, provides an upper bound to the uniform capacity of two-connected networks.

Among the proposed regular two-connected topologies, the *Manhattan street network* (MSN) is by far the best known. Introduced for the first time in reference 4, it is based, as the name implies, on a grid of one-way *streets* and *avenues* that alternate in opposite directions (Figure 9.3), with nodes being placed at the intersections of streets and avenues. Streets and avenues are wrapped around to form a variety of orthogonal loops, giving rise to a complete isotropic structure in which all nodes have the same view of the remaining part of the network. The resulting grid can be imagined as lying on the surface of a torus, and hence is also known as a *toroidal network*.

The MSN provides a variety of paths for any source–destination pair. It can be implemented for any number of nodes, because it does not need to have nodes at every intersection of street and avenue, and allows modular growth by adding streets and avenues as needs require and without affecting the network's operation. It is particularly suited for deflection routing because often both outlets present the same

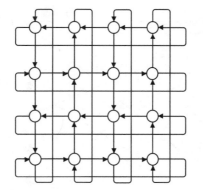

Figure 9.3   4 × 4 Manhattan street network

distance to the destination; consequently, when a deflection occurs, the path to the destination is increased by at most four links. Moreover, simple addressing schemes have been proposed that eliminate the need for routing tables to find the best route, even if the topology is incomplete.

The first proposal, called the *integer addressing scheme,* numbers rows and columns sequentially, starting from zero. If the numbers of rows and columns are known, and the node address is determined by the row-column pair, each node has complete knowledge of the location of nodes on the topology and, hence, of optimal paths. The best route can be obtained by means of simple arithmetic operations, as shown in reference 8. When the network expands, however, with new rows and columns that can be placed anywhere, the addressing scheme above can no longer be applied, because the numbering scheme changes and node operation must be updated.

In reference 8 other schemes have been analyzed that provide almost the same performance as the preceding one without affecting the routing routines when the network changes. One is the *fractional-addressing scheme,* in which two columns are assigned the addresses 0 and 1 (the same applies to rows). Any column added between 0 and 1 is assigned a fractional value between the values of the adjacent columns. For any column added between 1 and 0 the same procedure is followed, but 0 is treated as 2—that is, fractional addresses x are in the range $1 < x < 2$. Assuming $(0 - 0)$ as destination node, routing is performed by pushing packets either toward a reduction of x if $x < 1$, or toward an increase of x if $x > 1$ (a similar procedure applies to y). As a consequence, packets follow the shortest path if the column $x = 1$ and the row $y = 1$ represent the edges of the network. Otherwise an error occurs, which reduces if rows and columns are added uniformly. Other errors arise because nodes do not know the labels of neighbor nodes, or the directions of destination rows and columns. This ignorance, of no consequence in a bidirectional topology, affects optimal choices in the destination's proximity.

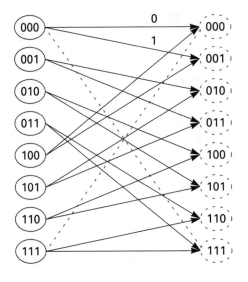

Figure 9.4   8-node shuffle exchange network

A simple approximation to the capacity of an $N \times N$ MSN can be found in this way. If links could be traversed in both ways (bidirectional topology), then the average distance would be about $N/2$. In an MSN, about half the nodes can be reached in the same number of hops as in the bidirectional topology. The remaining nodes can be reached in about $N/2 + 2$ hops because their neighbors can be reached in the same number of hops as in the bidirectional topology and the last hop, being in the opposite direction, must be replaced by a turnaround that takes three hops. We thus have

$$L_{0-\text{MSN}} \cong \frac{N}{2} + 1$$

and, from equation 1, we get

$$C_{\text{MSN}} \cong \frac{4N^2}{N+2} \tag{3}$$

This approximation becomes more precise as N increases and the error vanishes as $N \to \infty$.

Other popular topologies are those derived from shuffle topologies of multistage switches. The *shuffle exchange network* (SXN) is the first example of such networks.[4] It is defined for a number of nodes M that is constrained to be a power of two. Nodes are connected as shown in Figure 9.4, following a regular pattern typical of shuffle networks and that provides a straightforward way to implement shortest-path routing. In fact, if nodes are numbered consecutively in binary representation, as shown in the figure, the next node on the shortest path is simply determined by deleting those high-order bits of the destination address which match low-order bits of the node address. The highest-order remaining bit gives the output link to the shortest path. Notice that in two cases a link connects a node to itself. These two links are of no use and can be replaced by other connections, as shown by the dotted links in Figure 9.4.

As a nice property, a SXN presents the minimum network's diameter, which is $\log_2 M$. Furthermore, the average distance is very close to the bound given by equation 2. However, there are several problems with SXN structures. One is that they have almost no nodes in which both paths have the same distance to the destination and when a packet is deflected from the shortest path it is sent the maximum distance from the destination. Thus, there are no valid routing alternatives, which makes the network vulnerable to congestion and failures. Another problem is that the number of nodes is constrained to be an integer power of two and no way exists to add nodes or even to increase the size from 2^i to 2^{i+1} without changing a great number of connections. Finally, implementing a SXN topology over nodes dispersed on a geographical area requires a connection pattern that hardly matches the natural connection layout, and this might limit the applicability of the SXN topology to small areas.

Other shuffle structures can be obtained by arranging nodes in different cascaded columns and connecting the last column back to the first, thus creating a logical topology that is wrapped around a cylinder. This network, first considered in reference 10, is called the *recirculating shuffle network* (RSN). Its number of nodes is constrained to be $M = kd^k$, where k is the number of cascaded stages. The average distance with $d = 2$ has been shown to be

$$L_{0-\text{RSN}} = (3k(k-1)2^{k-1} + 2k) / (k2^k)$$

which is very close to the bound given by equation 2. The other properties of the RSN are much the same as those of the SXN.

Turning to four-connected networks, a toroidal topology with full-duplex links is considered in reference 7. This topology is referred to here as the *bidirectional Manhattan street network* (BMSN). Compared to the MSN, the switching function of the BMSN is more complicated, but is still sufficiently simple to allow fast routing algorithms. Bidirectionality accentuates the advantages already present in the MSN: the number of paths to the destination is increased; the cost of deflections is reduced to two additional hops for each deflection (instead of four for the MSN); and, of course, the network capacity is doubled, because it uses double transmission resources. The average distance in an $N \times N$ topology is $L_{0-\text{BMSN}} \cong N/2$, and the capacity is

$$C_{\text{BMSN}} \cong 8N \tag{4}$$

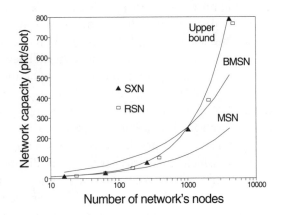

Figure 9.5   Capacities of MSN, SXN, RSN, BMSN, and the upper bound for two-connected topologies versus the number of nodes

The use of bidirectional links presents other advantages that are particularly appealing for MANs. First, the equality between input and output capacity at nodes can be maintained in all working conditions, especially in link or node failures. In fact, even if a link fails in one direction only, the balance can be immediately and locally reestablished by stopping transmission in the opposite direction. On the contrary, in networks that use unidirectional links the rebalancing procedure requires removal of an entire loop that comprises the failed link—that is, at least four links in the MSN.

Second, traffic locality is better exploited when full-duplex links connect different user communities and a great amount of traffic is exchanged within each community. Further advantages result from the possible implementation of nonregular topologies. The symmetry gained with full-duplex links allows a broad class of topologies to be used. Moreover, if the topology changes, full-duplex links allow one to keep track of those changes by the backward-learning technique, which provides estimates of distances by observing the distance traveled in the opposite direction. This technique is discussed in detail in Section 9.7 of this chapter.

Figure 9.5 shows the capacities of the topologies cited in this section versus the number of nodes. The upper bound on the capacity of two-connected networks is also shown.

Other topological structures proposed for DN can be found in references 17 and 18. Interesting properties of toroidal networks are discussed in reference 11, and a method for designing optimal virtual topologies is described in reference 25.

9.4 DEFLECTION-ROUTING ALGORITHMS

Deflection-routing algorithms are distributed procedures, independently operated at each node, which provide the mapping of any input packet configuration into an output configuration χ in such a way that all packets are assigned to outlets with at most one packet per outlet. If some queuing is performed, then the routing task increases in complexity, for, if output queuing is used, more than one packet can be routed to the same queue, but if input queuing is used, the packets to be forwarded have to be selected from among those queued. In what follows we explain how different deflection-routing schemes operate with respect to the no-queuing case; extensions to algorithms that make use of queues are in most cases straightforward. We also assume that local input/output operations are performed before and independently of routing.

Deflection-routing algorithms can be seen as composed of two parts. The first part determines, for each packet, a *preference vector* $\mathbf{v} = (v(1), \ldots, v(d))$, whose components $v(k)$ represent the rates of preference that a packet has with respect to outlet k. The second part, common to all algorithms, selects the switching configuration χ, which maximizes the sum of preferences—that is, the sum

$$B(\chi) = \sum_i v_i(u_i(\chi)) \tag{5}$$

over all packets $i = 1, 2, \ldots, d$ present in the node, where $u_i(\chi)$ is the output selected for packet i under the switching configuration χ. If more than one switching configuration maximizes the function above, then a random choice is enforced. This second part routes packets to their most preferred outlets, whenever possible; otherwise contentions are solved by deflecting some packets.

The first part represents the routing strategy, and is largely responsible for achieving good performance. Preferences may be calculated once in a while and stored in routing tables. Alternatively, if the procedure is fast enough, it may be performed at each routing step. The second part must be performed at each routing step and may be simplified, thus leading to suboptimal outlet assignments, if its execution is a bottleneck.

For example, in an MSN the *random rule* (RR), studied in reference 43, is obtained by assigning preference 1 to the shortest-path (s-p) outlets and 0 to the others. This operation can be quickly performed by one of the simple algorithms cited in Section 9.3. In this example, the second part of the algorithm maximizes the number of packets that are routed to their shortest path. The *straight-through* rule, also studied in reference 43, can be obtained as the preceding one was by changing to a value greater than 1, such as 2, the preference for the s-p outlet, if it is the unique s-p outlet and lies on the same row or column as the inlet. Notice that ties cannot happen here because in case of a conflict only one packet has preference 2 to the s-p outlet. A third routing algorithm often considered, the *closer* algorithm, gives priority in case of conflict to the packet closest to the destination.[20,29,43] This rule can be implemented as in the RR by adding, to the preference for a unique s-p outlet, a term inversely proportional to the distance to the destination.

In a BMSN things are a little more complicated, since there are 24 possible switching configurations. In many cases, several of these configurations are equivalent with respect to the number of shortest-path outlets assigned, but differently affect network performance. This difference brings attention to the performance measures to be used for classifying routing algorithms in DNs. In fact, it turns out that the major performance measure is different from that used in WANs.

Wide-area networks are operated, because of congestion problems, far from capacity and the main performance measure used there is the average end-to-end packet delay. Deflection networks do not suffer from the congestion problem and are conveniently operated at full link utilization. In these conditions, deflections waste transmission capacity and reduce the network throughput. Thus, deflection-routing algorithms are more usefully compared by the maximum throughput they can provide.

As mentioned in the preceding section, the maximum throughput changes with the network's topology and the traffic matrix considered, so that comparisons can be performed only within a reference scenario. Regular topologies and a uniform traffic matrix can well represent a candidate scenario for DNs, for the reasons exposed in Section 9.3. Moreover, in regular networks, the relative performance of routing algorithms is hardly affected by changes in the network's size, because topological properties are preserved.

Assuming the scenario indicated above, the link-utilization factor ρ is the same for all links in the network. With 1-packet/slot link capacities, the network throughput (pkts/slot) can be expressed as:

$$S(\rho) = \frac{dM\rho}{L(\rho)} \tag{6}$$

where M is the number of nodes and L is the average source–destination path length. Relation 6 comes from Little's result by observing that $dM\rho$ is the average number of packets present at nodes at every routing step. Neither assumptions about routing nor about node architecture are used. Thus, the throughput expression 6 is quite general and, in particular, is also valid for the store-and-forward technique with shortest-path routing. In this case, we have $L = L_0$, and the throughput is better expressed as

$$S_0(\rho) = \frac{dM\rho}{L_0} \tag{7}$$

In particular, $S_0(1)$ coincides with the network capacity C.

Analytical evaluations of L, and thus of S, have appeared in the literature, most dealing with two-connected regular networks under uniform traffic and RR routing.[14,20,31,37,43] Other analytical models have been introduced for multiconnected hypercube networks[19,36] and multidimensional regular mesh networks.[27,35] Nonuniform traffic is considered in references 17 and 32, and models for nonuniform traffic and general topologies are given in references 25, 34, and 41. Also, a model capable of predicting performance under many routing strategies exists.[48] These models have not, however, been able to describe directly the interdependence of performance and routing strategies, so that the problem of finding the optimal strategy—the one providing the maximum throughput—has not yet been solved. Thus, only heuristic preference assignments have been tried, in the attempt to reduce the deflection probability.

Among the mechanisms analyzed for a BMSN, the one called *minimum distance* (MD) is discussed in references 9 and 16. It assumes as preference of a packet i for outlet u the negative of the shortest-path distance to the destination through outlet u —*that is*, we have $v_i(u) = -d_i(u)$. Thus, maximizing expression 5 requires minimizing the global distance (hence the name):

$$\sum_i d_i(u_i(\chi)) = \sum_i d_{\min, i} + \sum_i c(u_i(\chi)) \qquad (8)$$

At the right-hand side of expression 8, the global distance is expressed as the sum of two terms. The first, in which $d_{\min, i} = \min_u d_i(u)$, represents the global minimum distance and is not a function of the switching configuration. The second is the global distance increase due to deflections caused by the chosen configuration χ. In a BMSN all deflections from the shortest path cause a path increase of two hops (except in a particular case that occurs when N is odd), so that minimizing

$$\sum_i c(u_i(\chi))$$

minimizes the number of deflections, which is exactly what the RR algorithm of the MSN does.

It soon becomes evident that assigning equal preferences to all the shortest-path outlets in a node—if more than one exists—does not provide the best performance. For example, in MSN, the *closer* algorithm presents a higher throughput than the RR.[29,48] To avoid confusion, notice that the *closer* algorithm does not minimize the global distance. Instead, it minimizes the distance to the destination of the packet assigned to the shortest-path outlet in case of conflicts. An algorithm for bidirectional-link networks, which corresponds to *closer*, is investigated in reference 16. It has been called *minimum weights* (MW) because the expression to be minimized is changed, with respect to MD, into

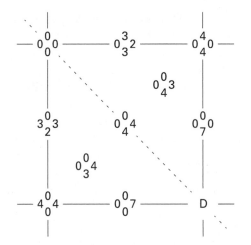

Figure 9.6   Optimal-preference assignment in a BMSN for packets directed to node D

$$\sum_i d_i(u_i(\chi))\,(H - d_{\min,\,i}) \tag{9}$$

where H is a constant greater than the network's diameter. In equation 9, the distance weighting factors $(H - d_{\min,i})$ increase the preference for the switching configurations, among those which satisfy the MD criterion, which give priority to packets closest to their destinations. This criterion will be shown to be always superior to MD, even in nonregular topologies such as those considered in Section 9.7. The rationale underlying the technique is that routing should forward packets in such a way that future contentions are minimized. The packets closest to destinations are more likely to be exposed to future conflicts, because their choices reduce as they proceed, and hence are favored.

The only knowledge required by MW is the distance to all possible destinations. However, routing mechanisms that have knowledge of the complete topology provide still better performance because they can identify routes toward nodes expected to minimize conflicts. For example, in toroidal or square-grid networks a good heuristic principle for minimizing future conflicts is the one implemented in *diagonal routing* (DR).[17,28] This algorithm routes packets preferably toward nodes that are as close as possible to the diagonal route to the destination, because these nodes present, on the average, the highest number of shortest-path outlets. In a BMSN the optimal-preference assignment, with the constraint of a three-bit representation, has been experimentally found[28] to be the one schematically depicted in Figure 9.6. In this figure the topology is represented by the network's edges, that is, the two loops of the grid that intersect at the destination node D, and the two loops at the maximum distance from D. The ideal line connecting the nodes along the diagonal to D is also

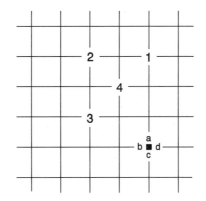

Figure 9.7 Destinations of packets 1, 2, 3, 4, to be routed at the node represented by the filled square, in a 6 × 6 BMSN

drawn. The groups of four digits also shown represent the preferences that packets directed to D present at different nodes with respect to the four outlets.

As an example of the operation of the three algorithms so far presented, consider a 6×6 BMSN and the node represented in Figure 9.7 by a filled square. Labels *a, b, c,* and *d* represent the node outlets, and the nodes labeled 1, 2, 3, and 4 represent the destinations of four packets in transit at the considered node. Table 9.1 lists the outlet assignments that maximize the number (three in this case) of s-p outlets (MD criterion). In correspondence, the global-preference values for the three algorithms MD, MW, and DR are reported. Out of 24 possible switching configurations, 10 satisfy the MD criterion, 2 satisfy the MW, and only one satisfies the DR criterion.

Table 9.1 Some outlet assignments and the corresponding global-preference value for the example shown in Figure 9.7

Outlet assignment for packets				Global preferences $B(\chi)$ for		
1	2	3	4	MD	MW	DR
d	c	b	a	−16	−38	11
d	c	a	b	−16	−38	9
c	d	b	a	−16	−34	12
c	d	a	b	−16	−34	10
c	a	b	d	−16	−38	11
c	a	d	b	−16	−38	10
c	b	d	a	−16	−38	10
c	b	a	d	−16	−38	9
a	c	b	d	−16	−38	11
a	c	d	b	−16	−38	10

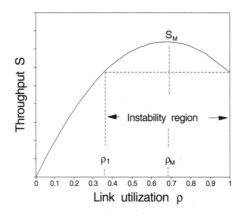

Figure 9.8   Example of a throughput curve $S(\rho)$ that represents congestion

Other routing policies have been proposed, particularly to reduce the spread in the distribution of the network crossing delay. They will be discussed in Section 9.6.

9.5   CONGESTION

The curve represented by equation 6 entirely describes the effect of the topology and the routing rules and determines the maximum throughput S_M that can be carried by the network. In some cases it happens that S_M is reached at a value $\rho_M < 1$, as exemplified in Figure 9.8. This phenomenon, called *congestion,* is often encountered in communication networks.[49] In DN, however, it originates from different causes and deserves some explanation.

Congestion in a DN is a combined effect of routing algorithm and topology. It occurs when, under some deflection strategy, topologies are such that an increase in link utilization causes an increase in deflections and finally an increase in the path length L, which offsets the increase of ρ in equation 6. The most prominent effect of congestion is that, if no control procedures are provided, *the network cannot operate with a steady-state throughput in the range $S(1) < S \le S_M$.* Hence this region is often referred to as the *instability region.* The instability appears for two reasons. The first is that a local input queue is always used to match access requests to access opportunities. The second is that uncontrolled networks accept load up to the saturation condition, that is, $\rho = 1$. The uncontrolled access is of no consequence if the network does not present congestion. On the contrary, it has beneficial effects on the queuing delay because it drains local queues at the maximum rate.

If congestion is present and queues are used, the instability phenomenon appears. In fact, suppose the system could operate in steady state with utilization ρ_0 in the region $\rho_M \leq \rho_0 < 1$, exemplified by Figure 9.8. A small increase of ρ from this point leads to a decrease in the network throughput and to an unbalanced operation of local queues, still filled at rate $S(\rho_0)$. Eventually, all local queues fill up and the network is driven steadily into saturation. Though the argument above does not strictly apply in the region $\rho_1 < \rho < \rho_M$, statistical fluctuations sooner or later drive the system to the scenario depicted above, ending eventually in saturation.

The instability problem is often encountered in communication systems, and simulations confirm the behavior depicted above. However, a formal proof can be obtained only for simpler systems, such those discussed in reference 49. Another case in which congestion occurs is the ALOHA random-access technique, in which the saturated throughput $S(1)$ tends to zero as the population to be served increases.[50]

Once detected, congestion can be dealt with by control procedures that limit network utilization so that throughput close to the maximum can be achieved. The problem arises, however, of detecting possible congestion or determining the maximum throughput when the network cannot operate in the instability region for a prolonged time. A possible solution, and one frequently reported in the literature, is to use the so-called *pure-loss traffic* model, in which no input queue is present and packets that cannot enter the network immediately upon arrival are discarded. With this model, the instability due to the queuing effect is avoided and ρ can be set to any value by properly setting the frequency λ of the offered packets (or equivalently, setting the probability of packet arrivals per slot). Furthermore, because there is a strict increasing relationship $\lambda(\rho)$, all the useful information on $S(\rho)$ appears also on curve $S(\lambda)$. All this explains why such a curve is so popular in dealing with congestion-prone systems.

Notice that a question arises about the relevance of the curve of equation 6 obtained under the pure-loss traffic model, for this model can hardly represent the access process under normal operation. In fact, queues and different insertion mechanisms can influence the second-order statistic of link load and produce slightly different deflection probabilities, which lead to different maximum throughputs S_M. This influence, however, vanishes as $\rho \rightarrow 1$; it becomes less and less appreciable as the network connectivity increases because of the consequent mixing of packets that occur on the path from the source to the destination, as it is indirectly proven in the several analytic models that have been developed.[14,20,31,37,43] All these models assume that *packets are received at a node according to d independent Bernoulli processes of mean* ρ, which implies that the statistical effect of packets entering the node is not taken into account, for packets are necessarily transmitted according to the same process as that by which they are received. These models can be quite accurate in predicting throughput, which shows the limited relevance of the input-traffic model. And so it has become usual for people investigating the field to neglect this residual influence and to regard as maximal throughput the one obtained under the pure-loss model.

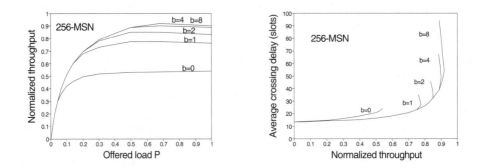

Figure 9.9   Normalized throughput and average network-crossing delay of a square MSN
with 256 nodes for different numbers *b* of output buffers

9.6   PERFORMANCE OF ROUTING ALGORITHMS ON REGULAR TOPOLOGIES

In this section we discuss the performance of the MSN, BMSN, and SXN with respect to the throughput they offer under uniform traffic. The data reported have all been obtained by simulation and are taken from references 13, 16, 28, and 29.

Figure 9.9 shows the normalized throughput (or *efficiency*) S/C of a square MSN having 256 nodes, when output queues of length *b* are used. The throughput is plotted versus the network-offered load, modeled as pure-loss traffic that fills empty slots with the probability indicated on the abscissa. The routing algorithm is RR, that is, shortest-path with random selection on contention. The average network-crossing delay versus the normalized throughput is also reported. The crossing delay accounts for the alignment, transmission, propagation, and queuing delays at nodes. The alignment delay has been assumed to equal half the transmission time, and the propagation delay has been disregarded. Such a choice enhances the effect of queues and allows us to understand better the network's behavior. One should consider, however, that the effect of queuing delays is reduced as the transmission speed or the link-propagation delays are increased. In reference 23, similar results are also available for networks with 1024 and 4096 nodes.

Figure 9.9 shows that the MSN with no output queuing does not present congestion, so that its maximum throughput is obtained in saturation ($\rho = 1$). The efficiency is almost 0.55 and the increased delay with throughput is due only to deflections. As we consider output buffering, the throughput increases with a gain that is relevant for the first buffer but becomes marginal as more buffers are added. Furthermore, a small amount of congestion appears, as confirmed by the backward bend of the delay curve. Notice that adding more than two buffers increases the throughput only scarcely, but increases the queuing delay, which is maximum at satu-

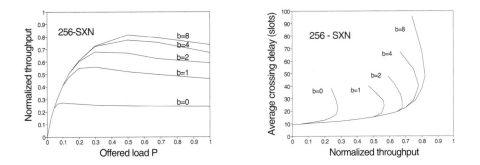

Figure 9.10 **Normalized throughput and average network-crossing delay of an SXN with 256 nodes for different numbers *b* of output buffers**

ration. Also notice the difference in the delay behavior as *b* changes. For *b* = 0 the curve is almost flat, but for *b* = 8 it presents a steep increase as the throughput approaches its maximum value. The latter behavior shows that the maximum throughput is practically reached for a moderate value of link utilization ρ. From this point, a further increase in the offered load increases ρ but does not increase the throughput because the gain in ρ is offset by the increase in path length, as a result of the increase in queue length and in the consequent number of deflections. Thus, even if the network barely suffers from throughput congestion, a large number of output buffers causes *delay congestion,* and it is therefore advisable to introduce some control on the link load to control the delay. In the no-buffer case, on the contrary, the flatness of the delay curve shows that the maximum throughput is obtained at $\rho \cong 1$ so that a load control is not needed.

The SXN presents a different behavior, as shown in Figure 9.10, which refers to the same case study as Figure 9.9. The throughput presents a marked congestion that worsens as the size of the network increases. The maximum efficiency in the no-buffer case is about 0.28, but a noticeable gain is achieved by adding output buffers. In this case a congestion-control mechanism is mandatory, as can also be inferred by the pronounced backward bend presented by the delay curves.

Figure 9.11 shows the performance of a 10×10 BMSN under the MW algorithm. The BMSN appears to be more efficient than the MSN because of its higher degree of connectivity, which reduces the effect of deflections. Output queuing is not decisive in providing good performance, which makes this network particularly suited to operation without buffers. Furthermore, no congestion is observed, even with output queuing.

The maximum efficiencies of the MSN, SXN, and BMSN without queuing are summarized in Figure 9.12 as a function of network size. The BMSN's performance is shown in the three cases corresponding to three routing algorithms, namely MD,

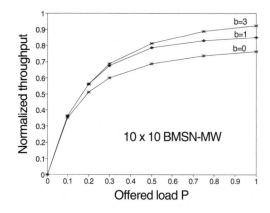

Figure 9.11   Normalized throughput of a BMSN with 100 nodes versus the packet-generation probability *P* and for different number of output buffers

MW, and DR, discussed in the preceding section. Other BMSN algorithms that make use of reduced information and simpler routines are discussed in Section 9.4. MSN and SXN performance is relative to RR routing only, because the gain achieved with more efficient routing techniques, such as diagonal routing, is barely noticeable. From this figure we learn that toroidal networks are intrinsically better suited to exploiting the potential of deflection routing than the SXN. In fact, the SXN becomes less and less efficient as the number of nodes increases, but it is proven in reference 43 that for the MSN the maximum efficiency tends to one as $M \to \infty$. The

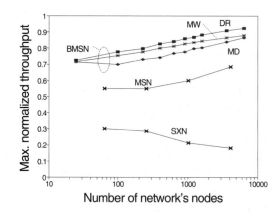

Figure 9.12   Maximum normalized throughput of MSN, BMSN, and SXN versus the number of nodes in the no-buffer case

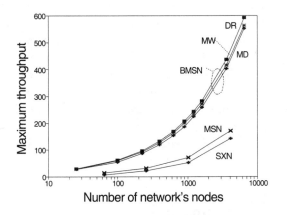

Figure 9.13 Maximum throughputs of the MSN, BMSN, and SXN versus the number of nodes in the no-buffer case

situation improves when output buffers are used, and in all cases we obtain efficiency one when the number of buffers is unlimited. The maximum throughputs for the cases shown in Figure 9.12 are shown in Figure 9.13. Other interesting results about the performance of shufflelike topologies are given in reference 20.

The distribution of the delay, defined as the number of hops needed to reach the destination, is considered in reference 29. Here the authors have studied the ability of several routing strategies to reduce the maximum delay incurred by packets in a 64-node MSN. Their main results are shown in Figure 9.14, where the performance of

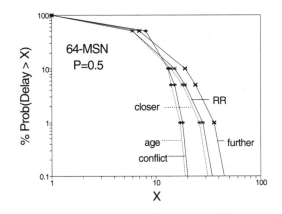

Figure 9.14 Complementary distribution function of the delay in crossing the network under several algorithms in a 64-node MSN with packet-arrival probability $P = 0.5$

five algorithms is compared for an assumed packet-arrival probability of $P = 0.5$. RR is the standard algorithm that, when a conflict occurs, chooses either configuration randomly. In *age* and *conflict* algorithms the priority is given to the packet with the highest hop count and deflection count, respectively. In *closer* and *farther* algorithms the priority is given to the packet that is, respectively, closest to the destination or farthest from it. The age algorithm is the most effective in reducing the delay spread, but it also offers the minimum average delay, and hence the maximum throughput, among the reported algorithms. Other results for BMSN and multidimensional regular-mesh networks can be found in references 19, 21, 27, 35, 36, and 48.

9.7 DEFLECTION ROUTING ON TIME-VARYING TOPOLOGIES

An intrinsic feature of the deflection mechanism is its ability to try alternate paths even if these paths are not preferred. If we add a means for estimating continuously the goodness of the newly attempted paths, we obtain a routing mechanism capable of adapting dynamically to topology changes and of providing graceful throughput degradation after failure.

In this section we report some results presented in references 15 and 33, which refer to the simulated performance of a 10×10 BMSN with heavy link failures under MD and MW routing algorithms, no buffers, and a uniform traffic matrix. The distances needed by the algorithms are continuously estimated, and the corresponding preferences are stored in lookup tables to be read by the routing algorithm. The distance estimates are obtained by the backward-learning technique,[1] which consists of estimating the distance d_{ki} from node k to node i by observing the distance d'_{ik} traveled by packets originating at node i as they come in to node k. This procedure is consistent with the topologies assumed, for the use of full-duplex links implies that $d_{ki} = d_{ik}$. Moreover, deflections can at most increase the observed distance d'_{ik}, so that, in steady state, the distance estimate is simply the smallest value observed. If the topology changes, the estimation process must forget the old estimates. Baran[1] suggested an exponentially decreasing memory of the old estimate, but the method that has provided the best results[15] is different and operates as follows.

Let P_x be a packet incoming through inlet x, and V_x and D_x the source node and the distance traveled, as obtained from the source address and hop count, respectively, which are contained in the packet's header. To obtain the estimate $\hat{d}(V_x, x)$ of the distance $d(V_x, x)$ to node V_j through outlet j, the algorithm uses a support estimate $\hat{s}(V_x, x)$ and a source counter $c(V_x)$. The estimate $\hat{d}$ is replaced by D_x each

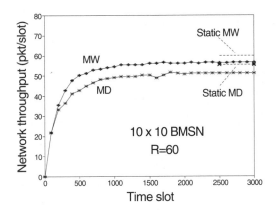

Figure 9.15 Throughput transients of a 10×10 BMSN with MD and MW routing algorithms and backward learning, when starting the network at full load with empty routing tables

time D_x is found to be lower than $\hat{d}$. The same procedure is applied to $\hat{s}$. When a fixed number of observations R, called the *estimate reset period*, is measured by the counter c, the support estimate $\hat{s}$ is transferred to the estimate $\hat{d}$ and then set to infinity.

By using the support estimate the procedure can forget old estimates completely and can follow an increase of the true distance within at most a $2R$ period. The estimation parameters should be set in such a way that, in steady state, the support estimate approaches closely the true distance, so that the estimate will oscillate like a sawtooth pattern of period R—the longer period R is, the smaller and closer to the true value is the oscillation. Also, having the reset period based on a fixed number of observations, rather than on a fixed time interval, ensures the same degree of accuracy for all the estimated values in the tables of all nodes, regardless of the intensity of the traffic used for the different estimates.

Figure 9.15 shows the convergence of the throughput of MD and MW algorithms to their steady-state value starting from a condition in which no estimates are available. The throughput is averaged over 100 slots and several simulation runs. At time $t = 0$ the network is driven into saturation starting from the no-load condition in which all routing table entries have the same value (infinite distance). In this case the algorithm starts operating with purely random routing choices. The values of throughputs when distances are known exactly (static values) are also reported. The throughput of both algorithms approaches its steady-state value very quickly. Successively, it proceeds in its convergence, but at a slower pace, until it stabilizes within

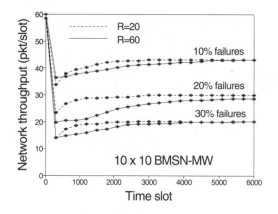

Figure 9.16   Throughput transients of a 10 × 10 BMSN with MW algorithm and backward learning, in the presence of different percentages of failed links

about 1 percent of the static value. The error arises because of the error in the distance estimates. A high value of R reduces the error but also diminishes the speed of convergence to the new steady-state values, as clearly appears in the next figure.

Figure 9.16 shows the transient behavior of the MW throughput, for two values of the reset period R, when several links are removed at one time to simulate massively concurrent failures. Links are removed at time $t = 0$, when the network operates at full throughput in saturation. The results have been averaged over several runs and over three failed topologies, obtained by removing at random a fraction of links equal to 0.1, 0.2, and 0.3, respectively, with the constraint that the resulting topologies be connected. The results show that the network can recover very quickly (in less than 5 ms if a 1-Gbit/s speed and 1000-bit time slots are assumed) with both values of R. However, the smaller value promotes faster convergence (the behavior beyond slot 6000, not reported in the figure, shows that the curves cross each other, leading to higher steady-state throughput for the case $R = 60$, as expected).

The convergence toward an asymptotic positive throughput is not a guaranteed result, because the network collapse immediately following a massive failure can lead to congestion in which throughput drops to zero and never recovers. In fact, packets could wander a long time in trying new paths and thus affect routing tables, so that a stable equilibrium point might never be reached. This risk is much reduced (we cannot say that it is completely avoided) by the packet-filtering mechanism, based on the TTL field, cited in Section 9.2. This mechanism proved necessary to ensure network recovery in the 30 percent failure case, where the maximum TTL value has been set to 30. The ability of this technique to exploit efficiently the paths to the destination even in the worst case is further demonstrated by Table 9.2, which presents capacity

C, together with throughputs S_b obtained with different numbers of output buffers b, for the two networks shown in Figure 9.17. These networks have the same capacity, evaluated as

$$C = \min_{T_{ij}} C_{ij} \frac{M(M-1)}{M_i M_j}$$

(10)

where T_{ij} is a cut that splits the network into two disjoint parts i and j, each having M_i and M_j nodes with $M = M_i + M_j$ and C_{ij} is the capacity of the cut. The minimum is computed over all possible cuts T_{ij}.

Table 9.2

Network	C	S_0	S_1	S_5	S_{10}
a	14.286	12.8	13.4	14.1	14.28
b	14.286	13.6	13.9	14.2	14.28

Unfortunately, results are not available on transients when one or more output buffers are used. However, the queuing of packets at nodes is hardly expected to improve transient performance, because it increases the overall network memory—which is harder to modify as changes occur. Queues increase the number of packets carrying wrong distance information, cause delay in propagating the new information, and eventually increase the risk of network collapse. Moreover, with output queuing, all packets in a queue are lost if the corresponding link fails. All these reasons indicate that use of buffers should be avoided.

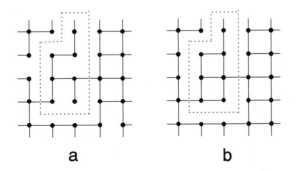

a   b

Figure 9.17   Different networks derived from a 5 × 5 BMSN whose capacities and throughputs are shown in Table 9.2

The uniform-traffic matrix assumed in all simulations guarantees that, in any topology condition in which all nodes are connected, all nodes have the same saturation throughput. In fact, each packet entering the network is uniformly directed to any other node and will provide an empty slot upon exit. When failures occur and the capacity between some pairs of nodes is reduced, the packets exchanged between these nodes find their path with increased difficulty. Thus, they accumulate within the network and diminish the throughput available to other nodes. Moreover, if failures disconnect some nodes, the same mechanism reduces the throughput to zero, except for the small throughput fraction allowed by packets extracted by the filtering mechanism.

The situation described is highly undesirable, but it cannot be ascribed to the DN architecture. In fact, it arises because of the mismatch between the topology and the offered traffic matrix. To avoid such circumstances, provision should be made to discover such a mismatch, such as disconnected nodes, and reduce the traffic between affected nodes. The problem can be solved in DNs by letting in a small fraction of artificial and uniformly distributed background traffic. The received background traffic can be measured to evaluate available capacities between nodes and the result can be sent to higher-level protocols to determine connection parameters and enforce flow control. Furthermore, the background traffic can ensure proper working of the backward-learning technique when some traffic relations are idle.

All the results and considerations above show that deflection routing and backward learning can be integrated with great advantage in throughput flexibility and optimality. Different procedures to propagate the information about topology changes could also be used, perhaps more effectively. Those indicated are the simplest, however, because they do not require coordination among nodes.

9.8 LIVE LOCK, FAIRNESS, AND SOURCE LOCKOUT

In reference 23 it is shown that, under some traffic circumstances, deterministic rules (such as the straight-through rule in the MSN) can lead to a *live-lock* situation in which packets never reach their destinations. Also, one may expect that, because of a network's complexity, a variety of uncontrollable and undesired load patterns can arise if random decisions are completely eliminated. Moreover, deterministic rules could prevent exploration of new paths should the topology change. In fact, the principles that underlie deflection networks suggest that a certain amount of randomness be included in the routing mechanism, so that the advantages of random walk and deterministic routing can be merged (as in the random walk under a "gravitational" field as modeled by physicists). Unfortunately, the correct combination of the two components—that is, the one that optimally combines the flexibility of randomness with the efficiency of determinism—has not been subjected to thorough investigation, even though in reference 23 it is proved that RR routing can avoid live locks in the MSN.

Live lock is not the only way a station is prevented from communicating with other stations. In fact, because a packet can enter the network only if an empty slot is available, it may happen that some station is locked out—it never sees empty slots—because of the activity of other stations. This condition is particularly evident in two-connected networks,[23] but it can also occur in a BMSN. More generally, the basic access mechanism described in Section 9.2 cannot guarantee access fairness, because it cannot control the average rate at which empty slots arrive.

In references 24, 26, and 33, a mechanism is proposed, called the *priority access mechanism* (PAM), by which a station can "piggyback" requests for empty slots to packets in transit. In response, it receives some packets (called token packets) that, upon extraction, provide the required empty slots. The requests are satisfied by other nodes and are arbitrated in a distributed way by a priority mechanism that is based on the priority levels represented by the age of packets waiting for access in local queues. Requests and priorities are propagated by using additional fields in the packet's header, namely the *request address,* the *request priority,* the *token flag,* and the *token priority.* Briefly, the mechanism is based on these main points:

- A station that has a packet waiting in the local queue and no chance to transmit it tries to fill the request fields of packets in transit with its own address and priority, the latter representing the age of the packet in the queue. It can overwrite fields already written by other stations if the written request priority is lower than its own.

- A station that has a packet waiting in the local queue can use—that is, extract and access—any token it sees whose priority is lower than its own.

- A station that at the same time observes both a free slot and a request on a packet in transit whose priority is higher than its own creates a token packet (token flag on). It fills the token destination address and the token priority with the request address and the request priority respectively, and clears the original request.

The points above do not completely describe the algorithm, because many mixed situations not addressed above are possible, together with different uses of the information available. Rather, they must be regarded as principles that, if observed in their main lines, can overcome all the problems treated in this section. Specifically, they can guarantee that:

1 *No station can be locked out*   Otherwise: (a) it reaches the highest priority in
   the network; (b) it can overwrite any request field; (c) the packet carrying the
   request will eventually reach the destination and provide an empty slot that is
   immediately replaced by a token; (d) the token cannot be captured by other stations because of point (a), and the requesting station eventually receives the
   token and gets access to the network.

2 *Fairness is enforced*   In fact, stations that without PAM would not receive
   their fair share of empty slots, suffer higher delays and present higher priorities
   than other stations. As a consequence, PAM delivers to them a higher share of
   tokens. Also, these stations cannot capture more than their fair share, for otherwise the mechanism would give an advantage to the other stations that get less.

The implementation of PAM could appear in contrast with the overall DN philosophy, which requires simple and fast procedures. However, the mechanism can be
implemented at different complexity levels, depending on the required performance
and the speed and the processing power available at nodes. For example, priority arbitration can be operated for local packets only; alternatively, in more sophisticated
mechanisms, all the requests, tokens, and local packets present at a node could be
concurrently arbitrated (e.g., a request of node A and a token directed to node B of
lower priority could be interchanged upon meeting at node C).

Tuning parameters also are available, such as the number of queue positions Z in
the local queue (the aging zone) that undergo the increase in priority with time, and
the aging period H (slots), i.e., the number of slots after which the priority of waiting
packets is increased by one. In reference 33 the performance of PAM is investigated
for the case in which priority arbitration operates on the priorities of all packets both
present and in transit at a node. The results are reported in Figures 9.18 and 9.19.
The first shows the maximum nodal throughputs of two classes of stations in a 5×5
BMSN-MW with no output buffers and $H = 1$, versus the aging zone size Z. The
traffic matrix is such that all stations have a backlog of packets directed only to odd-
numbered nodes. As a result, when $Z = 0$, and thus the mechanism is not in operation, only odd-numbered nodes can send traffic because they are the only nodes that
receive packets and see empty slots. As PAM is enforced, even-numbered nodes can
have access to the network, and when PAM is properly set ($Z = 8$) the network
becomes completely fair. We thus observe that complete fairness requires that priority
levels be applied to a sufficient number of packets in the local queue. Notice that the
sum of the two throughputs decreases as Z is increased, showing the penalty caused
by tokens—which use network capacity but do not carry useful information.

Figure 9.19 shows the effect of the tuning parameter H. The results refer to the
same network as before except for the traffic matrix, which is now uniform. It shows
the delays, as a function of the throughput, suffered in local buffers in the two cases
$H = 1$ and $H = 10$. The curve with $H = 10$ is practically the same as the one we
obtain without PAM. In fact, due to the particular traffic matrix, the network is

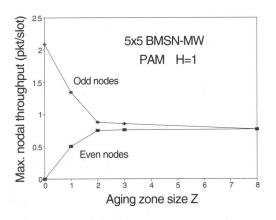

Figure 9.18 Maximum nodal throughput of even- and odd-numbered nodes of a 5×5 BMSN with MW and PAM versus size Z of the aging zone, when all nodes send traffic to the odd-numbered ones

completely fair even without PAM, and all local queues suffer the same delay. With PAM and $H = 10$, that is, a priority increase every 10 slots, requests are sent, but have no practical effect, for almost all packets in the network have the same (the lowest) priority (in fact the average delay is well below 10), and tokens are created only when local queues are empty. As H decreases, the statistical fluctuations in local delays make the mechanism operate and tokens are created even when packets are present in

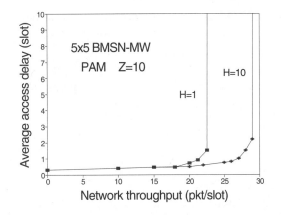

Figure 9.19 Average delay suffered by packets in the local queue versus the throughput in the two cases $H = 1$ and $H = 10$, in a 5×5 BMSN with MW under uniform-traffic matrix

local queues. When $H = 1$, many packets are transmitted on token returns. Tokens increase the use of the network and cause a reduction in the maximum throughput.

When the network is not intrinsically fair, as happens with the traffic matrix considered in Figure 9.18, the PAM mechanism enforces fairness even with high values of H but, in this case, the overall access delay increases because the mechanism takes longer to operate. As a final remark, notice that the flatness of the delay curve for $H = 1$ in Figure 9.19 clears the suspicion that PAM could noticeably affect the access delay.

The mechanism presented so far is quite general and can also be used in other kinds of networks. It can also use access classes of different (fixed) priority. In fact, a hierarchy of classes can be implemented by letting the more significant digits of the priority field indicate the class priority, and the less significant digits denote the age priority. Using these classes, a variety of end-to-end network services can be built, including the bandwidth-guaranteed service described in references 24, 26, and 33.

9.9   RESEQUENCING

In deflection networks successive packets in a message can follow different paths and arrive out of sequence, even when using the best routing mechanism available. Thus, reassembly buffers must be maintained at the receiver to reestablish the correct packet-delivery sequence. However, reassembly buffers are of finite size and it may happen that some arriving packets find the buffer full and are discarded. Thus, a problem arises: how to properly set the network-control parameters that can influence the packet-overflow probability P_{ov}.

In the following we report the main results obtained in references 23 and 30 for the MSN. The network parameters are the link transmission rate r (pkt/s), the link-propagation delay a (slots) assumed equal for all links, and the mean m_h and standard deviation σ_h of the network-crossing delay, expressed in number of hops. The control parameters are the reassembly buffer length K and the source-transmission rate s (pkt/s), which, of course, cannot be larger than the maximum nodal throughput. It has been found that $P_{ov}(\psi)$ is a decreasing function of

$$\psi = \frac{K}{\sigma_h a s} \qquad (11)$$

but it does not depend on m_h or r.

Notice that, for a given routing algorithm and K, P_{ov} depends solely on the statistics of the packet-interarrival time. From basic queuing theory, we know that P_{ov} is an increasing function of the mean, m_I, and the standard deviation, σ_I, of the interarrival time. If packets are transmitted at constant rate s, we have $m_I = 1/s$ and σ_I is an increasing function of $\sigma_h a$, which explains the inverse dependence of equation 11 on σ_h, a and s. Thus, it should be possible to match any desired overflow probability, for reasonable values of a, by properly setting the ratio K/s. Unfortunately, a general approach in deriving P_{ov} is complicated by the fact that σ_h depends on several unknown and variable factors such as the traffic distribution and intensity; it even changes with the considered source-destination pairs. In reference 30 some practical evaluations have been performed for a 16×16 MSN using a particular traffic model. The results show that a number of buffers between 10 and 20 should provide a sufficiently low P_{ov}.

The dependence on a in equation 11 shows that increasing the link lengths has a negative effect on P_{ov}. Hence, a topology and a parameter setting good for a LAN can be unsuitable for a *wide-area network* (WAN), for which it might even be impossible to get a satisfactory P_{ov}. However, things can turn out quite differently if the geographical span is increased by adding nodes and links rather than increasing the link length: in other words, switching nodes can be inserted into long-distance connections with the sole purpose of reducing the effects of deflections, much as indicated in reference 22. As an example, suppose that nodes and links are added uniformly. In this case, only the change in deviation σ_h affects equation 11. To estimate how σ_h is affected in bidirectional networks, let p denote the average deflection probability. A deflection causes an increase in the path length of two hops (in fact, a packet can always return through the same link to which it was deflected) and thus we have

$$\frac{L - L_0}{L} = 2p \tag{12}$$

In a network with high efficiency, as is the BMSN, p is small so that for large L_0 we can use the approximation

$$\frac{L - L_0}{L} \cong \frac{L - L_0}{L_0} \tag{13}$$

If we also consider that the independence of deflection probabilities over different hops has often been assumed with success in the mathematical models already cited in this chapter, then the increment $L - L_0$ can be approximated by a random variable having binomial distribution. This approximation implies that σ_h increases as the square root of L_0, which is more favorable than the linear increase of a in equation 11. Furthermore, p decreases as the number of nodes M increases. This can be seen from equation 12, because the ratio $L_0/L = S/C$ was shown, in Section 9.6, to be an increasing function of the number of nodes M. In conclusion, the law by which σ_h increases with L_0 should be even more favorable than the square root law. Unfortunately, details on this topic are not available, and additional investigations are needed before DNs can also be proved suitable for WANs.

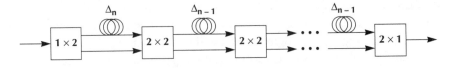

Figure 9.20   Example of an alignment stage

9.10   UNSLOTTED OPERATION

The problem of the unslotted operation of DNs arises when considering an optical implementation of deflection-network nodes.[44,45,47] In Section 9.2 we saw that slotted operation requires buffers in which packets can be aligned to time-slot boundaries. Unfortunately, optical buffers do not exist. However, it is possible to conceive alignment stages that use all optical components.[42,47] Those stages are composed of a cascade of $n + 1$, 2×2 optical switches, as exemplified in Figure 9.20, and n fiber loops that introduce the delays $\Delta_i = 2^{-i}$ (slots) ($i = 1, \ldots, n$). By appropriately setting the switches, the alignment stage can delay an incoming packet of any value equal to $i2^{-n}$, with $0 \leq i \leq 2^n - 1$. These stages can be used to enforce slotted operation if the ratio between the slot length and the packet's transmission time is $2^n / (2^n - 1)$, which reduces the throughput of a factor $(2^n - 1)/2^n$ compared to perfect slotting. The problems posed by the implementation of such stages, namely attenuation and complexity, add to those posed by the switching fabric, so that a quite limited value of n, such as $n = 1$ or $n = 2$, appears appropriate.[40]

With unslotted operation, packet alignment is not required by definition. Packets arrive asynchronously and routing is performed as soon as a packet is available from the receiver. As a consequence, the routing choice must be taken among outlets that happen to be free. The operation is greatly simplified compared to the slotted case, but the restriction on routing choices affects the throughput performance. As a further attractive feature, unslotted operation allows transmission of variable-length packets, a possibility that also proves attractive for use with electronic components.

A major problem that unslotted operation apparently poses is that it can cause complete congestion with zero throughput at $\rho = 1$. In fact, at full load, the route that a packet follows is constrained by the paths taken by packets already in transit. Because at $\rho = 1$ packets succeed each other on a link with no intervening free space, all packets coming from the same link are forced on the same path and, this situation being repeated at each node, fixed routing patterns tend to occur. All paths will eventually close back onto themselves in cycles and, at the end of a transient phase, the entire network will be filled with endlessly recirculating packets that produce no throughput. Thus, it is mandatory to verify if, and to what extent, unslotted operation allows steady-state conditions with nonzero throughput.

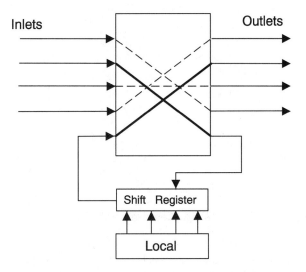

Figure 9.21 **Register insertion (RI) technique in a node with four links and one local insertion**

Here, a second architectural difference, with respect to the slotted case, appears in the access mechanism. In slotted networks, packets can be inserted starting at slot boundaries, because if a slot is empty at the slot boundary it will be empty until the next boundary. This condition is not ensured with unslotted operation; thus, some storage must be provided to accommodate incoming packets that would otherwise conflict with the packet being inserted. There are many ways, compatible with an optical implementation, to provide the required storage,[47] and one of them is described later in this section. Here, we present the *register insertion* (RI) technique, already proposed in the past for LANs. This technique uses temporary elastic storage and its optical implementation poses the problems already cited at the beginning of this section. Here, though, the RI technique is considered a performance-analysis tool, because it is the only technique that allows nodes to load the network up to $\rho = 1$.

The RI technique can be envisioned in the way schematically illustrated in Figure 9.21. Whenever the register is empty and a packet is present at the head of the local queue, the packet is transferred into the register, the register length is set equal to the packet length, and transmission is started as soon as an outlet is free. The length of the register is reduced as the transmission proceeds and the register empties. If, during the packet insertion, a packet from an inlet cannot find an outlet free (it is easily seen that at most one packet at a time can be in such a situation), the latter is routed into the register, where it follows the packet being transmitted with no intervening free space. The procedure goes on as long as the register is busy with packets. When the register empties the insertion cycle is completed and a new insertion can take place.

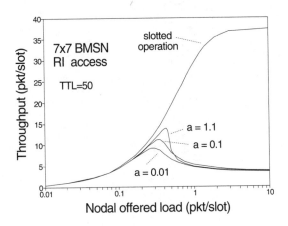

Figure 9.22   Throughput of a 7 × 7 BMSN versus the nodal-offered load for the RI insertion technique and different values of the link-propagation delay *a*

Figure 9.22 shows the simulated performance of a 7 × 7 BMSN, whose links are of equal length, denoted *a* (slots), under the RI access technique and uniform traffic (though slotting is no longer enforced, the term *slot* is retained to denote the packet-transmission time). The routing technique used is the one that chooses uniformly among shortest-path outlets as a first choice and among the others as a second choice. The network throughput is plotted versus the intensity λ of the nodal-offered load, which has been assumed to be a Poisson stream under the pure-loss model, and for different values of *a*. The network behavior does not change if *a* is increased beyond 1.1, and so other curves in this range are omitted. For comparison, the throughput of the same network under slotted operation is also reported. From these curves we see that unslotted operation significantly diminishes the throughput of the network, heavy congestion occurs, and performance is very sensitive to the link-propagation delay *a* for *a* < 1. At high load values the curves level off to a constant value because the TTL mechanism extracts almost all the packets and some of the new packets inserted can reach their destination. Total congestion with zero throughput has been observed only with saturating load and input queues, and the TTL mechanism disabled.

The exposed results are reassuring because, in spite of the congestion they reveal, they confirm that steady-state operation with positive throughput is possible. Then, it is also possible, by using some load-stabilizing mechanism, to have the network operated at maximum throughput. It turns out that simple modifications in the node architecture (see Figure 9.23) can eliminate all the drawbacks mentioned, stabilize the network, and improve the throughput.

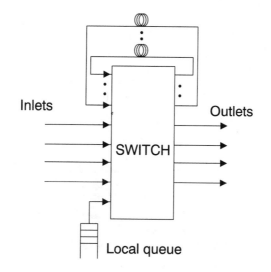

Figure 9.23 Modified switching architecture

The changes introduced are such that they can easily be implemented in optics. First, some delay loops are added across the switch to delay, possibly, by a packet-transmission time, the packets that cannot be routed to the preferred outlets (hence the name *recirculating loop-b* (RL-*b*), where *b* refers to the number of loops). Second, packets can be inserted only if at least one delay loop is free. In this case, packets are transmitted directly on the preferred outlet, if available, and the free loop is used to store an incoming packet that cannot find an outlet free. Otherwise, packets are directly inserted into the free loop.

The use of delay loops decreases the deflection probability—that is, increases the network throughput for a given ρ, and pushes toward higher values the value of ρ at which maximum throughput is achieved. Fortunately, the free-loop constraint on the insertion mechanism prevents link load ρ from reaching 100 percent. Better than that, it even prevents link load ρ from going into the region in which throughput decreases, so that stable operation at maximum throughput is achieved. These results are proved by Figure 9.24, which shows the throughputs obtained under the same conditions as in Figure 9.22 but with the RL-*b* technique and different values of *b*. Here the RL-0 curve refers to the case in which just one loop is present, and this technique is used only for inserting packets—it corresponds to the RI technique, where the variable delay is replaced by a fixed one. Further results show that this technique can reach, for $b \rightarrow \infty$, the network capacity—as happens with the slotted technique. Readers interested in additional details such as the effects of different access techniques, network size, and comparisons with the slotted case, are referred to the cited literature.

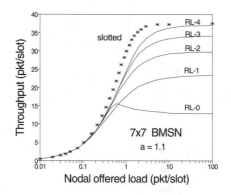

Figure 9.24   Throughput of a 7 × 7 BMSN versus the nodal-offered load for the RL-*b* insertion technique and different number of loops *b*

9.11 EXPERIMENTAL WORK

A few experimental implementations of DNs have been announced, almost all using optical technology. Unfortunately, for some of them, details on implementation are not available at the time of this writing.

At the University of Colorado at Boulder, an optical DN is being planned as a photonic interconnect for multicomputer parallel processing. The idea is to use the *wavelength division multiplexing* technique to achieve a data parallelism of 64 channels. This transmission technique, in a 2048-node *recirculating shuffle network* with a synchronous bit clock at 0.3 GHz, will provide a peak access rate of 38 Gb/s and an aggregate throughput of a few Terabits per second. A 2 × 2 self-routing photonic switch, which uses reduced-transmission parallelism and reduced clock speed, is demonstrated in reference 39.

The operation of a bidirectional DN with four nodes used as a transparent backbone for LAN interconnections is demonstrated in reference 51. This experimental work was funded by the Italian National Research Council and aimed at verifying the capability of backbone networks built with off-the-shelf components, providing an aggregate throughput of tenths of Gb/s. A description of the network implementation can be found in reference 38. Briefly, nodes connect four bidirectional optical links, each operating at 100 Mb/s, and can implement any topology, which also is allowed to vary in time as described in Section 9.7. An *application specific integrated circuit* (ASIC) chip (1.2 μm technology, CMOS, 8 × 8-mm die size) implements I/O and switching functions, and a 25-MHz microcomputer executes the addressing function, processes the header information of packets in transit, and updates the routing tables. In its final configuration the network will consist of 16 nodes, deliver an aggregate throughput of about 2 Gb/s, and serve as a testbed for routing techniques and new services, such as the circuit service described in reference 33. It has been verified that the same architecture can be adapted to work at a link speed of 600 Mb/s, thus providing a peak nodal throughput of 2.5 Gb/s. A second-generation node working at this speed and including the PAM mechanism described in Section 9.8 is currently being planned.

9.12   CONCLUSIONS

In this chapter, we present the guidelines for a network architecture capable of supporting high-speed traffic among a multiplicity of users densely distributed in a metropolitan area, or even a region. These guidelines arise from complete adherence to the deflection routing principle, which uses deflections to control storage resources at nodes and to avoid congestion. The architecture is based on highly meshed topologies in which simple and memoryless nodes forward packets according to simple and loose routing rules. By these rules, the packets of a flow exchanged between a pair of nodes cross the network as independent units, possibly following different paths that avoid congested or failed areas. This behavior introduces small irregularities in packet delivery, but real-time performance is statistically guaranteed in very high speed deflection networks because of the very short time scale of the processes involved. Additional features, such as the ability to adapt rapidly to changes in topology, and fair and guaranteed access, can be effectively provided by simple and distributed procedures, together with a range of service priorities.

All the features which deflection networks can provide, and which are discussed in this chapter, make them the unique example that has appeared thus far, which can extend all the attractive features of local area networks, including simplicity and low cost, to future scenarios in data and real-time communications.

REFERENCES

1   P. Baran, "On Distributed Communications Networks," *IEEE Transactions on Communication Systems,* Vol. CS-12, March 1964.

2   D. H. Lawrie and D. A. Padua, "Analysis of Message Switching with Shuffle Exchanges in Multiprocessors," *Proceedings of the Workshop on Interconnection Networks for Parallel and Distributed Processing,* 1980. Reprinted in Wu and Feng, eds., *Interconnection Networks,* Los Alamitos, CA: IEEE Computer Society Press, 1984.

3   B. Smith, "Architecture and Applications of the HEP Multiprocessors Computer System," *Real Time Signal Processing IV, Proceedings of the SPIE,* 1981.

4   N. F. Maxemchuck, "Regular Mesh Topologies in Local and Metropolitan Area Networks," *AT&T Technical Journal,* Vol. 64, No. 7, September 1985.

5   N. F. Maxemchuck, "The MANhattan Street Network," *Proceedings of the IEEE GLOBECOM '85,* New Orleans, December 1985.

6   J. Goodman and A. G. Greenberg, "Sharp Approximate Models of Adaptive Routing in Mesh Networks," in *Teletraffic Analysis and Computer Performance Evaluation,* Amsterdam, North-Holland, June 2–6, 1986.

7   F. Borgonovo and E. Cadorin, "HR^4-NET: A Hierarchical, Random-Routing, Reliable and Reconfigurable Network for Metropolitan Area Networks," *Proceedings of the IEEE INFOCOM '87,* San Francisco, March 1987.

8   N. F. Maxemchuck, "Routing in the Manhattan Street Network," *IEEE Transactions on Communications,* Vol. 35, No. 5, May 1987.

9   F. Borgonovo and E. Cadorin, "Routing in the Bidirectional Manhattan Network," *Proceedings of the Third International Conference on Data Communication Systems and Their Performance,* Rio de Janeiro, June 1987.

10   A. S. Acampora, "A Multichannel Multihop Local Lightwave Network," *Proceedings of the IEEE GLOBECOM '87,* Tokyo, November 1987.

11   T. G. Robertazzi, "Toroidal Networks," *IEEE Communications Magazine,* Vol. 26, No. 6, June 1988.

12   X. N. Tan, K. C. Sevcik, and J. W. Hong, "Optimal Routing in the Shuffle-Exchange Networks for Multiprocessors Systems," *CompEuro 88, Proceedings of the IEEE Euromicro,* Brussels, April 1988.

13   N. F. Maxemchuck, "Comparison of Deflection and Store-and-Forward Techniques in the Manhattan Street and Shuffle-Exchange Networks," *Proceedings of the IEEE INFOCOM '89,* Ottawa, April 1989.

14   E. Ayanoglu, "Signal Flow Graphs for Path Enumeration and Deflection Routing Analysis in Multihop Networks," *Proceedings of the IEEE GLOBECOM '89,* Dallas, November 1989.

15 F. Borgonovo and E. Cadorin, "Packet-Switching Network Architectures for Very-High-Speed Service," *Proceedings of the 1990 International Zurich Seminar on Digital Communications—Electronic Circuits and Systems for Communication,* Zurich: ETH, March 1990.

16 F. Borgonovo and E. Cadorin, "Locally Optimal Deflection Routing in the Bidirectional Manhattan Network," *Proceedings of the IEEE INFOCOM '90,* San Francisco, June 1990.

17 T. D. Todd and A. M. Bignell, "Performance Modeling of the SIGnet MAN Backbone," *Proceedings of the IEEE INFOCOM '90,* San Francisco, June 1990.

18 G. E. Meyers and M. El Zarky, "Routing in TAC—A Triangularly Arranged Network," *Proceedings of the IEEE INFOCOM '90,* San Francisco, June 1990.

19 T. Syzmansky "An Analysis of Hot Potato Routing in a Fiber Optic Packet Switched Hypercube," *Proceedings of the IEEE INFOCOM '90,* San Francisco, June 1990.

20 A. Krishna and B. Hajek, "Performance of Shuffle-Like Switching Networks with Deflection," *Proceedings of the IEEE INFOCOM '90,* San Francisco, June 1990.

21 J. S. K. Wong and Y. Kang, "Distributed and Fail-Safe Routing Algorithms in Toroidal-Based Metropolitan Area Networks," *Computer Networks and ISDN Systems,* Vol. 18, No. 5, June 1990.

22 Z. Haas, "Loop Concatenation and Loop Replication to Improve Blazelan Performance," *IEEE JSAC,* Vol. 8, No. 8, October 1990.

23 N. F. Maxemchuk, "Problems Arising from Deflection Routing: Livelock, Lockout, Congestion and Message Reassembling," *Proceedings of the NATO Advanced Research Workshop,* INRIA, Sophia Antipolis, France, June 1990. Reprinted in G. Pujolle, ed., NATO ASI Series, Vol. 72, Berlin: Springer-Verlag, 1991.

24 F. Borgonovo and L. Fratta, "Fault Tolerance and Circuit Service in Deflection Networks," *Proceedings of the NATO Advanced Research Workshop,* INRIA, Sophia Antipolis, France, June 25–27, 1990. Reprinted in G. Pujolle, ed., NATO ASI Series, Vol. 72, Berlin: Springer-Verlag, 1991.

25 J. Bannister, F. Borgonovo, L. Fratta, and M. Gerla, "A Performance Model of Deflection Routing and Its Application to the Topological Design of Multichannel Networks," *Technical Report CSD-910002,* Los Angeles: UCLA Computer Science Department, January 1991.

26 F. Borgonovo, L. Fratta, and F. Tonelli, "Circuit Service in Deflection Networks," *Proceedings of the IEEE INFOCOM '91,* Bal Harbor, FL, April 1991.

27 C. Fang and T. H. Szymansky, "An Analysis of Deflection Routing in Multidimensional Regular Mesh Networks," *Proceedings of the IEEE INFOCOM '91,* Bal Harbor, FL, April 1991.

28 G. Albertengo, R. Lo Cigno, and G. Panizzardi, "Optimal Routing Algorithms for the Bidirectional Manhattan Street Network," *Proceedings of the ICC '91,* Denver, June 1991.

29 T. Robertazzi and A. A. Lazar, "Deflection Strategies for the Manhattan Street Network," *Proceedings of the ICC '91,* Denver, June 1991.

30 A. K. Choudhury and N. F. Maxemchuck, "Effect of a Finite Reassembly Buffer on the Performance of Deflection Routing," *Proceedings of the ICC '91,* Denver, June 1991.

31 A. K. Choudhury and O. K. Li, "Performance Analysis of Deflection Routing Manhattan Street Network," *Proceedings of the ICC' 91,* Denver, June 1991.

32 J. Brassil and R. Cruz, "Nonuniform Traffic in the Manhattan Street Network," *Proceedings of the ICC '91,* Denver, June 1991.

33 F. Borgonovo and L. Fratta, "Deflection Networks: Architectures for Metropolitan and Wide Area Networks," *Computer Networks and ISDN Systems,* Vol. 24, No. 2, April 1992.

34 J. Bannister, F. Borgonovo, and M. Gerla, "A Procedure to Evaluate the Mean Transport Time in Multibuffer Deflection-Routing Networks with Nonuniform Traffic," *Proceedings of the IEEE INFOCOM '92,* Florence, May 1992.

35 M. Decina, V. Trecordi, and G. Zanolini, "Performance Analysis of Deflection Routing Multichannel-Metropolitan Area Networks," *Proceedings of the IEEE INFOCOM '92,* Florence, May 1992.

36 A. G. Greenberg and B. Hajek, "Deflection Routing in Hypercube Networks," *IEEE Transactions on Communications,* Vol. 40, No. 6, June 1992.

37 A. S. Acampora and S. A. Shah, "Multihop Lightwave Networks: A Comparison of Store-and-Forward and Hot-Potato Routing," *IEEE Transactions on Communications,* Vol. 40, No. 6, June 1992.

38 G. Albertengo, R. Lo Cigno, G. Masera, M. R. Roch, and G. Panizzardi, "D-Net: A Laboratory Prototype of a Deflection Network," *Proceedings of the ICC '92,* Chicago, June 1992.

39 D. J. Blumenthal, K. Y. Chen, J. Ma, R. J. Feuerstein, and J. R. Sauer, "Demonstration of a Deflection Routing 2×2 Photonic Switch for Computers Interconnect," *IEEE Photonic Technology Letters,* Vol. 4, No. 2, 1992.

40 J. R. Sauer, D. J. Blumenthal, and A. Ramanan, "Photonic Interconnects for Gigabit Multicomputer Communications," *IEEE Journal on Lightwave Technology Systems,* August 1992.

41 J. Bannister, F. Borgonovo, L. Fratta, and M. Gerla, "A Versatile Model for Predicting the Performance of Deflection-Routing Networks," *Performance Evaluation,* Vol. 16, Nos. 1–3, November 1992.

42 Z. Haas, "Optical Slot Synchronization Scheme," *Electronic Letters,* Vol. 28, No. 23, November 1992.

43 J. Goodman and A. G. Greenberg, "Sharp Approximate Models of Deflection Routing in Mesh Networks," *IEEE Transactions on Communications,* Vol. 41, No. 1, January 1993.

44 F. Borgonovo, L. Fratta, and J. Bannister, "Problems of Unslotted Deflection Routing in All-Optical Networks," *Proceedings of the ICCCN,* San Diego, June 1993.

45 F. Borgonovo, L. Fratta, and J. Bannister, "Unslotted Deflection Routing in All-Optical Networks," *Proceedings of the IEEE GLOBECOM '93,* Houston, November 1993.

46 M. Decina, V. Trecordi, G. Zanolini, and D. Zucca, "Two Simple Techniques for Broadcasting in Deflection-Routing Multichannel MANs," *Computer Networks and ISDN Systems,* Vol. 26, Nos. 6–8, March 1994.

47 F. Borgonovo, L. Fratta, and J. Bannister, "On the Design of Optical Deflection-Routing Networks," *Proceedings of the IEEE INFOCOM '94,* Toronto, June 1994.

48 G. Bianchi, F. Borgonovo, V. Trecordi, and D. Zucca, "Enhanced Mathematical Models of Regular Deflection Networks," CEFRIEL internal report, August 1993.

49 M. Schwartz, *Telecommunication Networks,* Reading: Addison-Wesley, 1987.

50 D. Bertsekas and R. Gallager, *Data Networks,* Englewood Cliffs: Prentice Hall International, 1987.

51 Consiglio Nazionale delle Ricerche: Reti e Servizi di Telecomunicazioni a Larga Banda, 3d Annual Meeting, Rome, March 3–4, 1993.

PART IV ❖ ❖ ❖ ❖

MOBILE NETWORKS

A mobile network may be broadly defined as any communications network in which at least one of the constituent entities (users, switches, or a combination of both) changes location relative to another. In some mobile networks, users may move among stationary switches, and in others, both users and switches may move around the environment. During movement, communication may continue or may be suspended, depending upon the capabilities of the mobile network and the nature of the communication.

Mobile networking technology has been in existence for more than twenty years, but only in the past decade has it become commercially popular. With computers increasingly portable and networks more accessible, users are coming to demand the same network services from mobile networks as they have been accustomed to obtaining from stationary wireline networks. Like their stationary counterparts, mobile networks have evolved along the parallel tracks of circuit switching and packet switching, with cellular telephony and packet radio as the respective representatives of the two switching technologies. Mobile cellular networks, providing location-independent telephone services to mobile subscribers, are the most prevalent type of mobile networks. Mobile packet-radio networks are favored for tactical military use because they provide robust data communications in highly dynamic network topologies.

Most mobile entities rely on wireless links to communicate with the rest of the network. The quality of a wireless link is less predictable than that of a wireline link and may fluctuate considerably depending upon network conditions. Environmental factors affecting the quality of a wireless link include but are not limited to distance between link endpoints, externally generated noise, interference (both accidental and intentional) among multiple transmissions in a given vicinity, and varied terrain (resulting in multipath propagation and obstructions between endpoints). Although the effects of many of these factors may be mitigated by transmission power adjustments, error correction, data-link control protocols, and channel access procedures, they cannot be eliminated entirely. Hence, mobile networks must accommodate not only moving users and switches but also highly variable links.

Support for mobility is provided primarily by the routing functions. In mobile networks, entity movement combined with fluctuations in link quality imply that user location, network topology, and network link characteristics may change often, hence that the routing functions must cope with frequent changes in user and network state. The mechanisms for determining current user and network state and for adjusting routes according to state changes must be efficient and responsive to enable selection and maintenance of feasible routes in a mobile network. Ideally, two communicating users should be unaware of mobility in each other and in the network switches. The routing functions therefore should not rely on users to supply mobility information and should minimize the number and severity of mobility-induced performance impairments perceived by the users.

The two chapters in this section, "Routing in Cellular Mobile Radio Communications Networks" by J. Ketchum and "Packet-Radio Routing" by G. Lauer, describe the two prevailing mobile networking technologies and their associated routing strategies. Topics not explicitly covered in this section include mobile internetworks and satellite networks. Readers interested in mobile internetworks are encouraged to keep abreast of the standards activity of the Internet Engineering Task Force (IETF), to investigate alternative approaches such as those discussed in section 7 of suggested reading 5, and to compare the emerging IETF standard with the Cellular Digital Packet Data (CDPD) standard discussed in the first chapter in this section. Satellite networks are briefly discussed below.

Traditionally, satellite networks have been employed as backups for terrestrial communications networks. Many satellite networks are composed of satellites placed in geostationary orbits. Each satellite provides extensive ground coverage, except in the polar regions, and hence many users may be reachable via a single satellite hop. Widely separated users may not always be covered by the same satellite, however. In the early satellite networks, such users had to communicate through terrestrial networks or multiple ground-to-satellite hops. Later on, intersatellite links emerged as alternative communications paths. Such links not only increase the survivability and capacity of the network, but also provide lower-delay paths. A number of analytical results[6,7] relate to the performance of packet satellite networks using intersatellite links.

More recently, networks composed of constellations of low-orbit satellites have come to be seen as commercially viable means for providing truly global communications (e.g., the Iridium system[9]). Voice, messaging, and low-rate data are expected to be the services initially provided by these networks. Although they have highly dynamic topologies, satellite constellation networks do not require adaptive topology tracking mechanisms because the satellite switches move in regular, deterministic patterns relative to each other and to the ground. Hence, the network topology at any time is completely predictable.

From the perspective of routing, the network architectures proposed for constellation satellite networks differ in important ways. In some networks, the cell patterns are fixed with respect to the earth,[8] but in others, the cell patterns are fixed relative to the satellites.[9] Some networks use polar orbits,[9] and others use orbits arranged with respect to a regular polyhedron.[10] Cell organization and orbit arrangement influence the practicality and performance of call-handoff mechanisms and intersatellite routing strategies respectively.

The direction of research for routing in mobile networks has been influenced by mobility of network users (e.g., traveling in aircraft as well as terrestrial vehicles and ships), advances in wireless technology (e.g., networks composed of microcells or even picocells), and popularity of distributed, real-time, multimedia applications (e.g., videoconferencing and visualization). Two leading topics of current research are communication with highly mobile entities and providing multiple types of service in mobile networks.[11] These research topics are not addressed in the chapters in this section but are briefly discussed below. Research in these areas is likely to yield novel strategies for routing in mobile networks.

When tracking and adapting to changes in the location of a mobile entity, the routing functions consume network resources in direct proportion to the frequency and speed of the entity's movements. If an entity's movement is extremely rapid, the routing functions may be unable to keep pace, regardless of the number of resources devoted to their execution. For example, a mobile user may be able to change network attachment points in less time than it takes the routing functions to detect and react to the change. This situation occurs when a user is highly mobile relative to its network attachment points, either because the user is moving rapidly or because the distances between its successive network attachment points are short (e.g., a micro-cellular network).

In the presence of highly mobile entities, prediction in addition to observation may be necessary to obtain a reasonable estimate of an entity's current location. Prediction is possible if trajectory information is available *a priori* or through a sequence of previously observed locations of the entity. An alternative approach that may be used when communicating with highly mobile users is to forward traffic to multiple switches in the user's predicted vicinity, thus increasing the chances of reaching the intended user.

Providing multiple types of service (including service guarantees) is a challenging problem and the focus of current research in both stationary and mobile networking. Entity mobility compounds the problem in the following ways. First, some services may not be available between all pairs of locations within the network, and hence it may be impossible to continue to provide a service to a user as it moves around the network. Second, dynamic network topology and wireless links may make it difficult to maintain a specified level of service, even between two fixed locations in the network. A robust but expensive solution to the problem of providing services in mobile networks is to aquire multiple paths and their component resources between each communicating pair of users. When user trajectory information is available and network state changes slowly with respect to user movements, these multiple paths may be used sequentially according to the expected user trajectories. When network state is highly dynamic, these multiple paths are selected to be used simultaneously, increasing the chances of successful communication between users as the network changes.

SELECTED SUGGESTIONS FOR FURTHER READING

1 W. C. Y. Lee, *Mobile Cellular Telecommunications Systems,* New York: McGraw-Hill, 1989.

2 D. Bertsekas and R. Gallager, *Data Networks,* Englewood Cliffs: Prentice Hall, 1991.

3 C. Lynch, *Packet Radio Networks,* New York: Pergamon Press, 1987.

4 "Special Issue on Packet Radio Networks," *Proceedings of the IEEE,* January 1987.

5 Session 7: Designing for Mobility, *Computer Communication Review,* Vol. 21, No. 4, September 1991, pp. 209–245.

6 F. Takahata, "An Optimum Traffic Loading to Intersatellite Links," *IEEE Journal on Selected Areas in Communications,* Vol. SAC-5, No. 4, May 1987, pp. 662–675.

7 A. Ganz and B. Li, "Performance of Packet Networks in Satellite Clusters," *IEEE Journal on Selected Areas in Communications,* Vol. 10, No. 6, August 1992, pp. 1012–1019.

8 R. Binder et al., "Crosslink Architectures for a Multiple Satellite System," *Proceedings of the IEEE,* January 1987, pp. 74–82.

9   J. L. Grubb, "The Traveller's Dream Come True," *IEEE Communications,* Vol. 29, No. 11, November 1991, pp. 48–51.

10 J. Kaniyil et al., "A Global Message Network Employing Low Earth-Orbiting Satellites," *IEEE Journal on Selected Areas in Communications,* Vol. 10, No. 2, February 1992, pp. 418–427.

11 A. Acampora and M. Nagshineh, "Control and Quality-of-Service Provisioning in High-Speed Microcellular Networks," *IEEE Personal Communications,* Second Quarter, 1994, pp. 36–43.

CHAPTER 10

Routing in Cellular Mobile Radio Communications Networks

JOHN W. KETCHUM

CONTENTS

Mobile cellular telephony has gained widespread popularity over the past decade because it offers subscribers location-independent access to a variety of telephone services. In a cellular network, a mobile subscriber indirectly connects to a mobile switching center via a radio base station. Thus, cellular systems not only must manage subscriber mobility (e.g., locate subscribers and maintain calls during movement) but also must solve problems associated with radio links (e.g., achieve high-quality minimally interfering transmissions). This chapter presents the basic concepts of routing in cellular networks, focusing on registration and location of mobile subscribers, call setup, and call handover between radio base stations. It also outlines the emerging standards for cellular systems, including the Cellular Digital Packet Data standard for connectionless data transport in cellular networks.

10.1 INTRODUCTION

Cellular telephone service has become an increasingly important segment of the telecommunications industry as the subscriber base has grown dramatically over the first decade of commercial service. The growth and popularity of cellular service has profoundly influenced the telecommunications industry's image of the role and function of telephone service. When cellular service was first introduced in 1982, and in the decades of its gestation previous to that year, it was viewed simply as an extension of the telephone network to people in moving vehicles. Telephone service was thought of as a location-dependent, point-to-point communication medium—telephone calls were placed to a specific location, rather than a specific person. If the called party did not happen to be at the called location, then the call attempt was unsuccessful.

Particularly with newly available hand-portable subscriber stations, it has become increasingly clear that subscribers find the general concept of mobility to be highly desirable. Furthermore, with the increasing sophistication of the telephone network, introducing mobility into the network will ultimately change the telephone from a location-dependent service to a location-independent service that delivers calls to subscribers regardless of their location.

This new paradigm of "anywhere, any time" telephone service has become known as *personal communication service*—an industry catch phrase intended to evoke the potential of mobile communications. The basis for this potential is a radio connection from a user with a communications terminal that has no fixed or wired connection to the telephone network, but the potential goes far beyond this simple idea, and realizing that potential has broad implications for the structure of the public telephone network. And though supplying a radio connection that provides reliable, high-quality service is an important technical challenge, it is only a beginning. Much

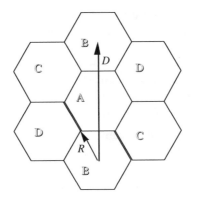

Figure 10.1 Frequency reuse in a cellular system

of the potential of that radio connection lies in the network and its ability to deliver services. The network aspects of cellular mobile telephone service and the related technologies and services included among personal communication services are the subject of this chapter.

Before addressing these issues, however, some background on the radio aspects of cellular technology is needed for understanding the network and routing requirements in cellular communication systems. For this reason, we start with an introduction to the basics of cellular systems.

10.2 CELLULAR SYSTEM BASICS

10.2.1 The Cellular Concept

The cellular concept calls for *frequency reuse*—the ability to use a radio channel at several locations in a geographic area simultaneously. This idea is illustrated in Figure 10.1, which shows a system with seven *cells*—a hexagonal area with an antenna site, or *cell site* at its center. The cell site at the center of each cell provides radio coverage for that cell. Radio service can be provided to each cell, without interference between the cells, if a unique and distinct set of radio frequencies is available for use in each cell. This duplication, however, is generally a very inefficient use of the radio-frequency spectrum; furthermore, the number of users supported cannot readily be increased without a proportional increase in available radio frequency spectrum.

This limitation can be alleviated by applying the *frequency-reuse concept*, according to which a fixed amount of spectrum can be used more efficiently by dividing it into smaller segments and reusing these segments many times throughout a coverage area.

In Figure 10.1, the available spectrum is divided into four reuse groups, labeled A, B, C, and D; frequency sets B, C, and D are used twice, and frequency group A is used once.

Generally, the users of a frequency group in one cell cause interference to users of the same frequency group in another cell. If the cells using a frequency group are spaced far enough apart, though, the levels of interference can be controlled so that they do not degrade service. In Figure 10.1, the distance between cell sites using the same frequency is denoted D, and the range from any cell site to the most distant user in that cell is denoted R. The dependence of received signal strength on distance in cellular systems is conventionally taken to be a power law, that is, $P_r = Kd^{-n}$, where P_r is the received power, K is a constant, d is the distance between the transmitter and receiver, and n is a small positive number. In free-space conditions, with no obstructions between transmitting and receiving antennas, $n = 2$. In cellular systems, however, the subscriber station is typically surrounded by objects and geographic features that block and scatter radiation from the cell-site antenna. As a result, the signal strength decreases much more rapidly as a function of distance than the inverse square law that describes unobstructed paths. Extensive measurements in the mobile radio environment show that in most cases, $3 < n < 4$.

Given this power-law dependence of received signal power on distance, we can derive a simple expression for the ratio of power received from the desired transmitter to the power received from an interfering transmitter using the same frequency:

$$\frac{C}{I} = \left(\frac{D}{R}\right)^n$$

To maintain a high quality connection in any communication system, it is necessary to keep the ratio of desired power to interfering power, or carrier-to-interference ratio, C/I, above some threshold that is determined by the system design. It is clear that the carrier-to-interference ratio depends on the reuse ratio, D/R.

The accuracy of the description above is somewhat limited, primarily because most of the processes involved in determining signal strengths and interference levels are inherently stochastic. The power-law model of propagation loss actually describes the median propagation loss as a function of distance. Furthermore, the location of a subscriber station and the chance of another call being active at the same frequency in a different cell are also random events. As a result the carrier-to-interference ratio is a random variable. In any rigorous analysis of the interference environment in a cellular system, all these factors, and others, must be taken into account. However, these details are beyond the scope of this discussion.

Furthermore, because the interference is controlled by the ratio of two distances, the frequency reuse is scale invariant, if the characteristics of the propagation environment do not change with scale—that is, if n is scale-invariant. Thus, the call-carrying capacity of a system can be controlled by the density of antenna sites in the system. By reducing the spacing of the antenna sites, and keeping the frequency-reuse geometry the same, the overall capacity of the system can be increased. If the spacing is cut in half for antenna sites serving a specific area, for example, the number of antenna sites serving the area will increase by a factor of four. This expansion will increase the call-carrying capacity in that region by a factor of four. This increase in the number of antenna sites to increase system capacity is referred to as *cell splitting*. Although the principle has both technical and economic limits, its application has allowed the cellular service providers in North America and other parts of the world to keep up with very rapid and sustained growth in demand for service.

For a more thorough treatment of the topics touched on here, a classic work, recently reissued, is by Jakes.[6] A more recent and widely available book is that of Lee.[8]

10.2.2 A Note on Terminology

Currently, numerous industry groups in North America and Europe are developing requirements and standards for cellular technology and the related area of *personal communication systems* (PCS). We can hope that all this attention will lead to rapid development of high quality standards and technology to meet the strong demand that is perceived by the industry. An unfortunate side effect of this scrutiny by diverse groups is the proliferation of network reference models and the associated terminology. To establish a common frame of reference, a standards body or industry group needs a reference model that identifies and names network elements and interfaces. More often than not, when such a group starts work it finds current models and terminology lacking in some way, and is thus compelled to develop its own. The result is that numerous reference models are in common use, with an associated confusion of terms and acronyms. In this chapter, we avoid this problem as much as possible by sticking with terminology used by the groups within the Telecommunications Industry Association that are responsible for setting standards for cellular technology in North America.

10.2.3 Frequency Allocations for Cellular Service

In the United States, the FCC originally allocated 40 MHz of spectrum for cellular service in 1982. The FCC at the same time defined license areas, called *Cellular Geographic Serving Areas* (CGSAs), where individual companies are licensed to operate cellular systems. CGSAs typically are made up of either the metropolitan area associated with a medium-to-large city, or a rural area that is not associated with a substantial city.

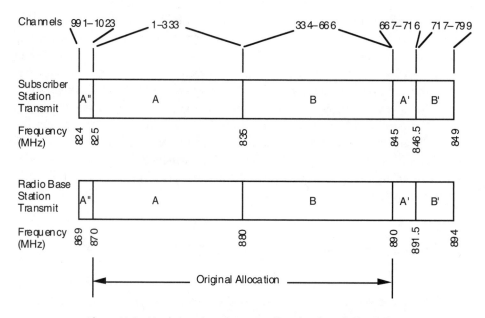

Figure 10.2   North American spectrum allocation for cellular service

The spectrum was divided equally between two system operators that provide service in each CGSA, referred to as the A and B carriers. The A carriers are known as the nonwireline carriers because licenses for operation in the A-designated band are reserved for companies that are not in the business of providing conventional wireline telephone service in the CGSA covered by the license. The B carriers are companies that provide conventional wireline service in the licensed CGSA.

Shortly after the FCC allocated the original 40 MHz and operators began to provide service, it became clear that demand for cellular service was greater than had been anticipated. Although in theory, the operators could keep up with the growing demand by splitting cells, the financial and logistical complications associated with cell splitting led the operators to go back to the FCC and ask for more spectrum. The FCC responded by allocating an additional 10 MHz, again split equally between the A and B carriers. The resulting allocation, and the channel numbers assigned to each carrier, are shown in Figure 10.2. The segments of the second allocation of 10 MHz for use by the A and B carriers are designated A', A'', and B'. The A-designated new spectrum is in two segments, and the B-designated new spectrum is in one segment for reasons of fairness. Because spectrum was not available that could provide a contiguous extension to both the A and B bands, the new spectrum was split in a way that was considered to equally disadvantage the two carriers.

The spectrum is divided into 30-kHz duplex channel pairs, numbered 1–666 for the original allocation, and 667–799 and 991–1023 for the second allocation.

10.2.3.1 New Allocations for PCS

In October 1993, the FCC allocated new spectrum for PCS. Although standards have not been set for this service, there are a number of candidate technologies for standards. All these candidate technologies are either directly derived from technologies that are already in use or under development for cellular systems, or share a heritage and are very similar in many ways to existing cellular technologies. The spectrum allocated by the FCC for licensed operation (similar to current cellular service) is at 1850–1910, and 1930–1990 MHz. A band for unlicensed PCS has also been allocated for applications such as cordless telephones, wireless local-area networks, and wireless PBX. This spectrum is at 1910–1930 MHz.

10.3 NETWORK ARCHITECTURE

Although a number of network architectures have been adopted by standards bodies in Europe and North America, a minimal architecture for providing voice service and connectivity to the *public switched telephone network* (PSTN) consists of at least three functional elements, two internal interfaces, and two external interfaces. These network elements and their associated interfaces are shown in Figure 10.3.

10.3.1 Cellular Network Elements

The *subscriber station* is the terminal unit that performs the function of a conventional telephone. Unlike a conventional telephone, however, the subscriber station includes a full-duplex radio subsystem that provides for a full-duplex voice channel plus the necessary signaling between the subscriber station and the radio base station.

The *radio base station* has the necessary radio, control, and multiplexing functionality to maintain full-duplex radio connections to multiple subscriber stations, set up and tear down connections to subscriber stations, track signal strength and other parameters associated with specific subscriber stations, and provide trunking to the mobile switching center. A single radio base station serves a well-defined geographic area surrounding the base station. The size of the area it serves depends on many factors, but in contemporary cellular systems the area may range from as small as one square mile to as large as 200 square miles.

A *mobile switching center* (MSC) performs the switching function and many control functions for the cellular serving area, which typically consists of tens or hundreds of radio base stations spread over an extended metropolitan or rural area. Unlike a switching end-office in the PSTN, whose primary role in the network is

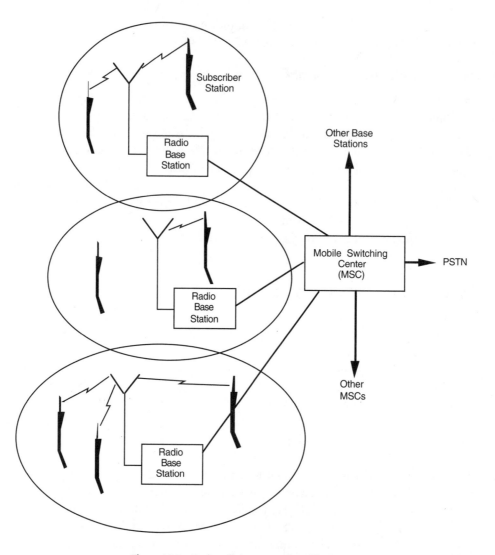

Figure 10.3   Basic cellular network architecture

switching calls, the MSC has a significant processing burden in managing mobility, in addition to its ordinary switching function. At a minimum, the mobility-management function requires the switch to locate subscriber stations to which incoming calls are directed, manage the assignment of radio resources in all of the base stations as calls are originated, and track the motion of subscriber stations as they move between the serving areas of individual radio base stations to ensure continuous and uninterrupted service.

10.3.2 Internal Interfaces

The interface between the subscriber station and the radio base station is also commonly referred to as the *air interface*, because it relies on the radio medium for physical transport. Cellular service in North America currently employs an air interface specification that is commonly referred to as *advanced mobile phone service* (AMPS).[11-14] The specification of the AMPS air interface is embodied in a set of three standards documents that are maintained by the Telecommunications Industry Association (TIA). These documents specify interoperation between the subscriber terminals and the radio base stations, and minimum performance standards for the subscriber stations and the radio base stations. Similar air-interface standards define the air interface for cellular systems in other parts of the world.

Since the introduction of AMPS technology in North America, and its counterparts in the rest of the world, various standards organizations have undertaken to develop and standardize advanced digital technologies for providing cellular service. In Europe, this endeavor has resulted in a specification referred to as GSM,[9] which embodies far more than just the air interface. GSM saw its first commercial deployment in 1992, and continues to be deployed throughout Europe and other parts of the world.

In North America, two competing digital cellular standards have been developed and approved by the TIA. One is referred to as Digital AMPS, or D-AMPS, representing a modest step beyond AMPS technology that employs *time division multiple access* (TDMA)[5,10,15,16,17] for access to the radio channel. The second digital standard, employing *code division multiple access* (CDMA),[4,5,18] is a significant departure from AMPS technology.

The interface between the radio base station and the MSC consists of conventional voice-channel trunking circuits, and a data channel for carrying control and signaling information. In North America, these connections are typically implemented using T1 channels carried on leased lines or line-of-sight microwave circuits. There are no standards governing this interface in North America. As a result, each manufacturer of cellular infrastructure has a proprietary interface specification, and it is not possible to mix and match radio base-station equipment from one manufacturer with switching equipment from another manufacturer.

10.3.3 External Interfaces

MSCs that serve adjacent cellular serving areas need to exchange information in order to allow calls in progress to be handed over from a cell in the serving area associated with one MSC to a cell in the serving area of an adjacent MSC. Voice-channel trunk connections are also necessary between such switches to carry the voice traffic associated with calls handed over in this manner. MSC manufacturers typically define a proprietary interface for MSC-to-MSC interaction, so that a cellular system opera-tor can expand its system by adding switches when the traffic requirements outstrip the capacity of a single switch. In this way the system operates as if it were controlled by one large MSC. Also, if system operators in adjacent cellular serving areas use switches supplied by the same manufacturer, these switches can be interconnected so that service can be supplied to customers in such a way that customers receive seam-less service.

However, when system operators in adjacent serving areas use switches supplied by different manufacturers, it is not possible to rely on proprietary interfaces to govern handover of calls between cells in the two systems. In this case, an industry-standard interface is required if such handover is to occur. In North America, the TIA has developed such a standard for intersystem operation that allows handover to occur between adjacent systems.

Communication between MSCs serving different serving areas is also required to support roaming subscriber stations. *Roaming* occurs when the owner of a subscriber station travels outside of his or her home serving area and requests service. The roam-ing subscriber may want to originate calls, or have incoming calls delivered to his or her subscriber station in the serving area to which he or she has traveled. In this case it is necessary or desirable for the visited-system operator to communicate with the home-system operator to verify the authenticity of the subscriber requesting service, exchange billing information, or make arrangements for forwarding calls. These aspects of the MSC-to-MSC interface are also the subject of standards governing North American operation that have been developed and maintained by the TIA.[19] The GSM specification for European digital cellular systems also deals extensively with roaming operation.

The interface between the MSC and the PSTN is similar to that between a con-ventional *private automatic branch exchange* (PABX) and the PSTN. The MSC is assigned a block of numbers, typically one or more three-digit end-office codes, and calls are delivered to the switch as they would be to a PABX. Cellular service provid-ers are also required to provide equal access to long distance carriers, so that trunks from several long distance providers may also terminate on the MSC.

10.4   AIR INTERFACE FUNCTIONALITY

In this section we describe various basic functions that must be a part of the air interface.

10.4.1 Voice Transmission

Although the need for this function may seem obvious in a voice telephone system, its provision is not always straightforward. Because of the random nature of the radio channel used for the connection, and the random nature of the location and motion of the subscriber station, it is very difficult to maintain uninterrupted, high quality voice service to a mobile user. Users of cellular services are very familiar with the reliability problems, which range from static and interference on the voice channel to calls that are dropped while in progress. It is necessary to provide additional support functionality to minimize these problems, as well as to provide basic functionality required for service delivery.

10.4.2 Color Codes

One source of degraded service in cellular systems is known as *false capture*. This problem arises from the fact that, as described previously, all cellular systems rely to some extent on frequency reuse to provide service to a large number of users in a service area while using a limited set of channels. Thus in any cellular service area as many as five or ten calls may be taking place on one channel simultaneously. A great deal of care is taken in engineering the frequency reuse to ensure that the radio base stations using the same frequency are sufficiently separated so that interference is kept within bounds. However, even with the most conservative engineering, there will be occasions when the signal received at a subscriber station or radio base station from an undesired, interfering source is more powerful than the signal from the desired source. As a result, the receiver may demodulate the undesired signal instead of the desired signal. This is the *false capture* phenomenon.

To prevent false capture, an auxiliary signal component, known as the *color code*, is used. Each frequency-reuse group, which is a set of radio base stations in which no channel is used more than once, is assigned a color code. This code is transmitted by the radio base station and transponded by the subscriber station back to the radio base station. If the radio base station receives the wrong color code, it knows that false capture has occurred either at the subscriber station or the radio base station. At a minimum, the radio base station will mute the voice on the call to prevent parties to the call from hearing the voice signal from another call. If the condition persists, the system can terminate the call. The subscriber station also knows the color code associated with the base station it is attached to, and if it detects the wrong color code, it will mute the voice.

The form of the color code varies from system to system. Analog systems like AMPS use a very simple analog color code in the form of one of three possible tones that are transmitted above the voice band. Digital systems use digital codes that are transmitted as part of the frame structure carrying the voice signal.

10.4.3 Signaling Channels

Various forms of signaling are required in cellular systems for call setup, call control, and mobility management. Some of the signaling for these functions take place on dedicated signaling channels. Other signaling takes place within the structure of a channel that has been assigned to a voice call. The separation of signaling traffic between dedicated signaling channels and voice channels is not unique, and depends on considerations of efficient use of the radio resources and simplicity of equipment design. We define several logical channels, which may or may not be carried on the same physical channel.

10.4.3.1 *System Overhead Message Channel*

There is a certain amount of information that any subscriber station needs to know about a system upon entering the system. This information is broadcast on the *system overhead message channel* from each radio base station. Information provided on this channel includes system identification and parameters that subscriber stations need to know about the system and what services are available from the system.

10.4.3.2 *Paging Channel*

When a call arrives at a cellular system for a subscriber station on that system, the MSC does not necessarily know where the subscriber is, or even if the subscriber station is powered up in the system. The system attempts to locate the subscriber by paging—broadcasting a message that includes the subscriber station's telephone number. The paging channel is the logical channel that carries the paging traffic.

In general, the paging message may be broadcast from every radio base station in the system. Some systems may also employ techniques for reducing the extent of paging required for call delivery. One such technique is registration, in which all subscriber stations periodically contact the nearest radio base station to inform it of their presence. In this case, paging can be restricted to radio base stations in the immediate vicinity of the radio base station with which the mobile most recently registered. The use of registration is determined at least in part by the tradeoff between paging traffic and registration traffic.

10.4.3.3 *Access Channel*

The access channel is used when the subscriber station needs to contact the system, to initiate a call, respond to a page, or initiate some other transaction, such as registration. Typically, many subscriber stations must share one access channel in the service area associated with a radio base station. For this reason, the access channel usually employs some sort of random-access discipline, such as ALOHA,[1] to control access.

10.4.3.4 Call-Control Channel

Various transactions must be supported while a call is in progress to ensure continued service. These transactions take place on the *call-control channel*, which is typically carried on the same physical channel as the voice call. Transactions that occur during a call include

- Power control messages that the radio base station sends to the subscriber station to control the subscriber station transmit power

- Handover messages that command the subscriber station to change channels because the system is changing the channel used by the call either to a different channel in the same radio base station, or to a different channel in a different radio base station

- Measurement-command and information messages that control measurement processes that occur in the subscriber station to gather information about the radio environment, and transmission of the measurement information back to the radio base station

- Other information that may be transmitted between the subscriber station and radio base station during a call, such as information to be displayed on the subscriber station, or messages invoking services like *hook flash* or *dual tone multifrequency* (DTMF) signaling

10.5 CELLULAR SYSTEM STANDARDS

Cellular systems in North America operate in a frequency allocation of 50 MHz at 824–849 MHz and 869–894 MHz, as shown in Figure 10.2. Until very recently, all systems have been based on AMPS technology, in which voice calls are carried on a duplex pair of 30-kHz channels that have a fixed 45-MHz duplexing offset. The high band is used for the forward link (base to subscriber), and the low band is used for the reverse link.

The new North American digital standards operate in the same allocation and must coexist with the preexisting AMPS systems, but deal with channelization somewhat differently. Digital AMPS uses the same carrier spacing as AMPS, but shares each carrier among three or six voice channels using a TDMA scheme. Thus AMPS and D-AMPS channels can be interspersed in the same system so that service can easily be provided to existing AMPS cellular phones and the new dual-mode AMPS/D-AMPS cellular phones.

The CDMA approach is quite different: a channelization of 1.25 MHz is used, but many users can access each 1.25-MHz channel simultaneously without disrupting each other's connection. Systems that deploy CDMA technology will thus have to reserve part of the band for serving existing AMPS mobiles, and clear out other parts of the band in 1.25-MHz segments to provide CDMA operation. The initial loss in AMPS capacity is offset by the high capacity provided by the CDMA access method.

10.5.1 Analog Voice Standards

The AMPS standard is embodied in three documents[12–14] that are maintained by the TIA:

- EIA/TIA 553 (formerly IS-3) Analog Cellular Mobile Station–Base Station Compatibility Standard

- TIA IS-19, Analog Cellular Mobile Station Minimum Performance Specification

- TIA IS-20, Analog Cellular Base Station Minimum Performance Specification

The first of these documents defines the air interface. The other two documents specify minimum performance standards for the subscriber station and the radio base station.

AMPS employs conventional analog FM technology for transmitting voice signals over the air interface. Signaling for call setup and call control is accomplished through a combination of dedicated signaling channels and in-band signaling. The signaling wave form makes use of conventional frequency-shift keying and simple coding techniques to improve the robustness of the transmissions.

The color code in AMPS systems consists of three tones at 5970 Hz, 6000 Hz, and 6030 Hz, known as *supervisory audio tones* (SAT), which are inserted into the voice band signal prior to the frequency modulation. Because the voice signal is band limited to 300–3000 Hz, the SAT tones are outside the audio band and do not interfere with the speech signal.

There is also a signaling tone at 10 kHz that is used to convey some simple acknowledgment information.

Signaling in AMPS is accomplished through a combination of dedicated signaling channels and an in-band signaling technique known as *blank-and-burst*. The system overhead message channel, paging channel, and access channel use the dedicated signaling channels. EIA/TIA 553 specifies that a total of 42 channels out of the 832 channels available must be reserved exclusively for use as signaling channels. These channels are channel 313–333 for the band A licensee, and 334–354 for the band B licensee. There are also provisions for identifying other channels as auxiliary signaling channels, which is accomplished through messages on the system overhead message channel.

Blank-and-burst in-band signaling for the call-control channel is accomplished by briefly muting the audio in the voice channel (for about 600 msec), and transmitting a burst of data. To avoid noticeable disruption of the voice service, use of this technique is limited to messages that are transmitted relatively seldom, such as messages associated with handover and power control. Other message types, such as measurement messages supporting mobile-assisted handover, cannot be carried by blank-and-burst signaling, and thus cannot be accommodated in the AMPS system.

10.5.2 Digital Cellular Standards: TDMA

The TIA has developed a set of standards informally known as D-AMPS, which is intended to provide digital voice services with a significant increase in capacity and functionality. The standard is currently embodied in a set of documents that parallel the AMPS documents in scope and purpose, but provide dual-mode functionality. These documents have the designations IS-54, IS-55, and IS-56,[15-17] with scope analogous to that of EIA/TIA 553, IS-19, and IS-20, respectively. There is also a separate standard for the speech coder, designated IS-85. Because the new digital service must be provided in the same bands as the existing AMPS analog service, and current AMPS customers must continue to be served as long as they have their AMPS subscriber stations, the new standard must be a dual-mode standard. Dual-mode operation is achieved by requiring that all subscriber stations be dual-mode in the sense that they are capable of operating as AMPS subscriber stations or as digital subscriber stations, on command from the system.

TDMA Channel Structure   Digital operation is achieved by transmitting a digital signal at a rate of 48.6 kbps in the same 30-kHz bandwidth used by the AMPS system. This digital stream is divided into six TDMA time slots with a frame duration of 40 msec. In IS-54, two of these time slots are used for each voice channel, for a total of three voice channels. A new half-rate standard, which is under development at this writing, will use all six time slots for separate voice channels by using a lower-rate speech coder. The slot structures for the forward link (radio base station-to-subscriber station) and reverse link are shown in Figures 10.4a and 10.4b, respectively. Each slot has a duration of 324 bits, or 6.667 msec. The duration of each slot component, in bits, is given above the slot.

The dual-mode AMPS/TDMA standard uses the existing AMPS signaling channel, with a slightly enhanced message set to take care of dual-mode operation. This provision is necessary, because cellular service providers must continue to provide service to AMPS-only subscriber stations, and dedicating additional channels for digital-only control channels would waste additional channels that would otherwise be available to carry voice traffic.

In-band signaling traffic is carried on two logical channels that are referred to as the *fast associated control channel* (FACCH) and the *slow associated control channel* (SACCH). The FACCH is created by stealing speech frames, on demand, to carry high-priority signaling information. IS-54 uses an 8-kbps speech coder, which, with error-correcting overhead, requires 13 kbps. Each stolen speech frame represents

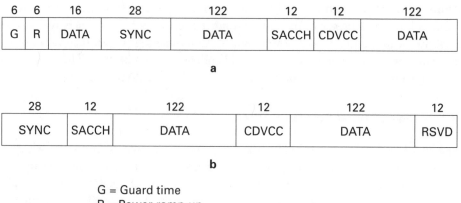

a

b

G = Guard time
R = Power ramp-up
SYNC = Synchronization and training bits
RSVD = Reserved bits, must be set to all 0s
DATA = Speech or FACCH

Figure 10.4   (a) IS-54 reverse-channel time-slot structure, (b) IS-54 forward-channel frame structure

20 msec, or 160 bits of speech data, which is 260 bits of encoded data. For the FACCH, the 260 bits are protected with a rate 1/4 convolutional code, which results in a capacity of 65 information bits per stolen speech frame. This technique differs from the blank-and-burst approach used in AMPS, because it represents a much shorter duration of missing data, and because the speech decoder knows that the speech data are missing and can interpolate data from adjacent frames so that the missing data are not noticeable to the user (as long as speech frames are not stolen too frequently).

The slow associated control channel is created by dedicating 12 bits in each time slot to carrying signaling information, for a total bit rate of 600 bits per second. The SACCH is protected with a rate 1/2 convolutional code, resulting in a protocol information throughput of 300 bits per second.

An important feature of IS-54, which is made possible by the use of the SACCH and FACCH and which is not available in AMPS-only subscriber stations, is known as *mobile assisted handover*. With this technique, the MSC makes use of measurement data provided by the subscriber station to decide when a handover is necessary, and where to make the handover. Because IS-54 uses TDMA, there is at least one time slot during which the subscriber station is neither transmitting nor receiving, and therefore can tune to another channel and measure the received signal strength. The subscriber station can store measurements from twelve channels, other than its assigned traffic channel, specified by the MSC over the SACCH or FACCH, plus the signal strength and bit error rate, on its assigned traffic channel. These values can be reported back to the radio base station and thus onto the MSC, on command. The system thus has a great deal of information about the radio environment as observed by the subscriber station, which can assist in making rapid and high-quality decisions about handover.

IS-54 uses digital color codes instead of the SAT tones used in AMPS. These are known as the *digital verification color codes* (DVCC), or, in their coded form, *coded digital verification color codes* (CDVCC). The color code is an eight-bit value that is transmitted in each time slot, after coding with a (12,8) shortened Hamming code.

10.5.3 Digital Cellular Standards: CDMA

In addition to the TDMA digital cellular standards embodied in the TIA documents IS-54, IS-55, and IS-56, the TIA has undertaken to standardize a dramatically different digital-access technology called *code division multiple access* (CDMA). This standard is to be embodied in an analogous sequence of documents, designated IS-95, IS-96, and IS-97. As of this writing, the initial version of IS-95[18] has been issued. The associated minimum performance requirements documents, IS-96 and IS-97, was to be ready for ballot sometime in 1994. These are dual-mode standards in the same way that IS-54, IS-55, and IS-56 are dual-mode standards, although the manner in which dual-mode operation is achieved is somewhat different.

Instead of dividing up the available frequency and/or time into discrete segments as TDMA and FDMA systems do, CDMA systems operate with numerous users simultaneously occupying the same bandwidth at the same time. Each user in an operating area is assigned a unique digital signature sequence that helps the receivers sort out the intended user's signal from the other signals occupying the same bandwidth. In the system embodied in IS-95, this sequence is augmented by powerful error-correcting codes and a number of other features that help mitigate the effects of the interference that results from this way of sharing spectrum. These features include highly accurate reverse-link power control, speech-activity detection that reduces the speech-coder bit rate during silent intervals, and soft handover, a technique for handing calls from one radio base station to another that is described in a later section.

The IS-95 CDMA system employs a 1.25-MHz channelization. The peak user data rate is 9600 bps; this rate is expanded to approximately 1.25 Mbps through a combination of error-correction coding and other coding techniques that are employed to ensure reliable operation. Users can also operate at lower data rates. The speech coder operates at 1200, 2400, and 4800 bps, as well as at the 9600 bps rate. When the speaker is silent, the speech coder shifts down to a rate of 1200 bps. When the speaker is active, the speech coder normally operates at 9600 bps. The intermediate rates act more or less as transition states between the active and silent states. The result is that, for normal speakers, who are silent more than 50 percent of the time, the average interference that a single user presents to the other users of the same radio base station and the surrounding radio base stations is reduced by at least 50 percent.

In addition to the voice channel, the IS-95 CDMA system provides signaling functions that are analogous to those in the AMPS and IS-54 systems, as well as some specialized functions that are specific to the CDMA system. On the forward link, a *pilot channel* and a *synchronization channel* provide timing and synchronization to the subscriber station. There can also be up to seven paging channels that operate on the forward link at a given radio base station. These paging channels carry both the system overhead message channel and the paging channel information, and operate at a bit rate of either 4800 bps or 9600 bps. On the reverse link, a number of access channels can be supported, running at 4800 bps each. These channels support the access channel functions described previously.

The in-band signaling channels for the call-control channel are carried using a variation on the fast associated control channel concept used in IS-54. Instead of stealing a whole speech frame for signaling traffic, IS-95 uses a dim-and-burst approach that takes advantage of the multirate capabilities of the speech coder. This approach allows for some part or all of a speech frame to be used for sending signaling information. Thus anywhere from 88 to 168 bits of signaling information can be sent in a single 20-msec speech frame.

On the forward link is an additional in-band signaling channel called the *power-control subchannel* that transmits power-control information to the subscriber station at a rate of 800 bits per second. This channel makes it possible for the radio base station to exert quite accurate control of the subscriber station's transmitted power, thus minimizing interference levels in the system, and power consumption in the subscriber station.

10.6 MOBILITY MANAGEMENT IN CELLULAR SYSTEMS

In offering the promise of making telephone service available to subscriber stations independent of their location, cellular systems create a multifaceted problem known as *mobility management*. This scheme covers all aspects of the problem of locating and tracking subscriber stations as they move about in their home service area, or outside where they may be visiting and desire to obtain service.

Before we discuss the various aspects of mobility management in cellular systems, we need a more general network model than that shown in Figure 10.3 because additional network elements are required to manage mobility. The network reference model adopted by the Telecommunications Industry Association is shown in Figure 10.5,[19] with some slight variations in terminology. Also, to understand the operation of mobility, we need to define three parameters that are stored in the subscriber station and give it a unique identity. These are:

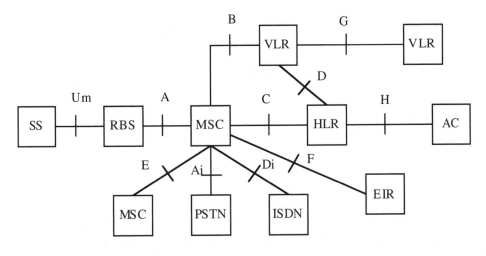

Figure 10.5 TIA cellular-network reference model

- *Home system identity (SID)*   15-bit system identity indicator that is set to the SID of the subscriber station's home system. The FCC has defined a set of *cellular geographic serving areas* (CGSAs), and potentially two cellular systems provide service in each CGSA. Each of these systems has a unique SID. The SID of the system in which the subscriber station subscribes for service is the Home SID.

- *Mobile identification number (MIN)*   10-digit directory number of each subscriber station is encoded into a 34-bit value called the MIN.

- *Electronic serial number (ESN)*   32-bit value that uniquely identifies the subscriber station. This number consists of an 8-bit manufacturer code, an 18-bit serial number, and 6 reserved bits.

The network elements shown in this model are

- *Subscriber station (SS)*

- *Radio base station (RBS)*

- *Mobile switching center (MSC)*

- *Public switched telephone network (PSTN) and integrated services digital network (ISDN)*   These are external networks with which the MSC will be interconnected.

- *Home location register (HLR)*   This is a database containing information about each subscriber that is assigned to serving areas associated with the MSC(s) served by the HLR. Information in the database includes MIN, ESN, current (last reported) location, service profile, and information associated with authentication of users. The HLR may be an integral part of the MSC, or it may be a physically separate entity providing HLR services to one or more MSCs.

- *Visitor location register (VLR)*   This is a database similar to the HLR, except that it holds transient information about active subscribers. This register may consist only of subscriber stations currently visiting the system from other systems, or it may hold information about all subscriber stations that are currently active in the system. Like the HLR, the VLR may be an integral part of the MSC, or it may be a separate entity serving one or more MSCs.

- *Authentication center (AC)*   The procedure for ensuring that subscriber stations requesting service are legitimate subscribers is referred to as *authentication*. The AC manages this procedure, including the exchange of encryption keys. Again, the AC may or may not be an integral part of the MSC.

- *Equipment identity register (EIR)*   This is a database that stores information about the identity of subscriber stations, for authentication and other purposes. The EIR may or may not be an integral part of the MSC.

10.6.1 Paging, Access, and Signaling Channel Selection

When a subscriber station is first powered up, it executes a procedure for determining the radio base station that will provide it the best service, and obtains other information required to operate properly on the system to which the serving radio base station belongs. The subscriber station starts by determining its preferred system status, which is information stored in the subscriber station. The subscriber station then measures the power on the 21 dedicated control channels that belong to its preferred system (313–333 for system A, 334–354 for system B), and chooses the channel with the greatest power. It then attempts to receive a *system parameter overhead* message on this channel. If it cannot successfully receive this message, it tries on the second strongest channel. If it can't receive a system overhead message on either of these channels, it can change serving systems and try again.

Along with the dedicated control channels, there are separate paging and access functions, which may be assigned to the same physical channels as the dedicated control channels, or may be assigned to physically distinct channels. Because all channels, including the control channels, come in duplex pairs, if distinct channels are assigned to the paging function and access function, these are duplex pairs of channels that carry all traffic, on both base-to-subscriber and subscriber-to-base links, associated with the paging and access functions, respectively.

As part of the system parameter overhead message, the subscriber station receives information that allows it to determine what channels to use for paging and for access. The subscriber station must proceed to scan through the set of paging channels and choose the strongest one. This paging channel is then monitored continuously, as long as the subscriber station is otherwise idle.

10.6.2 System Access

Once a subscriber station has powered up and completed any initialization routines, it may try to access the system to make a call attempt, or simply await an incoming call. If the subscriber chooses to initiate a call attempt, or the subscriber station needs to respond to a page, the subscriber station performs the system access function, as follows. First, the subscriber station scans all the access channels and chooses the strongest one. Then it attempts to seize the subscriber-to-base link on the access channel through a random-access procedure. Once the link is seized, the subscriber station transmits its message.

If the system access is for a call origination or a page response, the subscriber station next waits for a subsequent message designating a voice channel, then tunes to the voice channel indicated. The base station powers up the designated voice channel and starts transmitting *supervisory audio tone* (SAT) on the channel at the same time as it transmits the voice-channel designation message. When the subscriber station tunes to the designated voice channel, it starts transponding the SAT. This transmission serves as confirmation to the radio base station that the subscriber station has received its voice-channel designation message and successfully tuned to the designated channel.

Further signaling necessary for call control occurs on the call-control channel that is embedded in the designated voice channel. If the access is a call origination, then the subscriber station goes into conversation mode immediately on tuning to the voice channel. If the access is a page response, then the subscriber station is instructed to alert the user (ring the phone), and wait until the user answers, at which time, the subscriber station goes into conversation mode. The signaling sequence for a system access associated with a call origination is shown in Figure 10.6.

10.6.3 Paging

Paging is the procedure through which a called subscriber station is located by the MSC when a caller dials the directory number of that subscriber station. In its simplest form, paging operates as follows. When a call arrives at the MSC, the MSC sends a page request to all the radio base stations in the cellular serving area. Each of these radio base stations, in turn, broadcasts the page request on its paging channel.

All powered-up subscriber stations that are not occupied by an active call must continuously monitor the paging channel for page messages. When a page message is

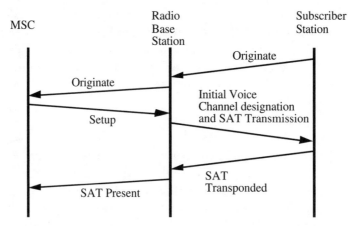

Figure 10.6   Call-origination message sequence

received, the subscriber station attempts to match the MIN (*encoded directory number*) contained in the page message to its programmed MIN. If the MINs don't match, the page message is ignored. If the MINs match, the subscriber station attempts to respond with a page-response message to the radio base station that issued the page message.

When the radio base station receives the page response, it returns a page response to the MSC; when the MSC gets this page response, it issues a setup order to the radio base station that results in a voice-channel designation and SAT tone transmission as in the call-setup sequence originated by the subscriber station. This step is followed by alerting (ringing) and answering if the user is present to respond to the alerting, as shown in Figure 10.8. The subscriber station then goes into conversation mode, and further signaling necessary for call control occurs on the call-control channel that is embedded in the voice channel.

The operation of the page and page-response procedure is shown schematically in Figure 10.7. The signaling sequence for paging is shown in Figure 10.8.

If the mobile is not powered up in the serving area, or for some other reason cannot successfully respond to the page, there will be no response to the page. If, after an appropriate time interval, the MSC does not receive a page response, it responds to the call attempt in some suitable manner. For example, it may use a voice message informing the caller that the subscriber is not responding to the call, or may forward the call to another landline number or voice mailbox.

10.6.4   Registration

For large cellular systems, the capacity of the paging channel eventually becomes an issue, because every incoming call can result in a page message being sent by every radio base station in the system.

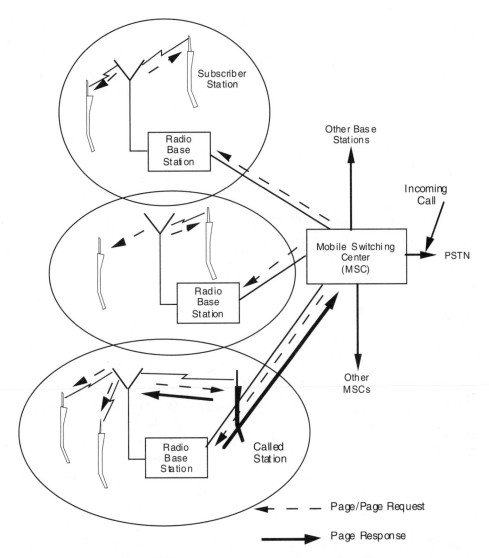

Figure 10.7 Page and page response for incoming call

Consider a cellular system that serves a large metropolitan area, with 300,000 customers. Typical busy-hour traffic levels in such a system may be .025 Erlang per subscriber, resulting in total busy-hour traffic of 7500 Erlangs. Taking the mean holding time (call duration) to be 100 seconds, this traffic results in a total of 270,000 call attempts during the busy hour. If half of these call attempts are incoming calls, the result is 135,000 call attempts that involve a page request, or 37.5 page requests per second. The peak capacity of an AMPS signaling channel, if it is dedicated to broadcasting paging messages only, is fewer than 24 pages per second. Thus, the system load described above clearly outstrips the paging capacity of the system.

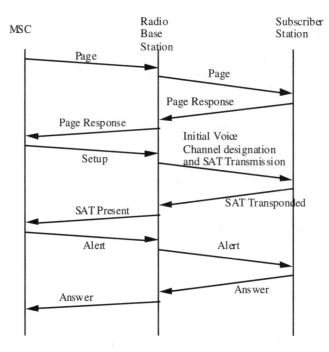

Figure 10.8   Page-message sequence for terminating call on a subscriber station

It is possible that in a large system, the scenario above may exaggerate the paging load, because customer traffic may be only .01 or .015 Erlang per subscriber, and a fraction smaller than half of this traffic may be incoming calls. However, it is clear that paging load can become excessive if all incoming calls result in a page message being broadcast by each cell in the system. In some cases, the system operator has the option of dedicating a set of channels to carry paging traffic only, so that each radio base station has one duplex pair of channels dedicated to page and page-response messages, and a separate set of channels for system access traffic. This arrangement is undesirable, however, because it uses channels that would otherwise be available for voice traffic.

Another way of controlling paging traffic is to require subscriber stations to register their presence with the system. The simplest form of registration consists of requiring the subscriber stations to register their presence with the system when they power up and power down. In this way the MSC knows which subscriber stations are powered up and ready to receive calls, so that it pages only subscriber stations that are present in the system. Furthermore, because the subscriber station sends its registration message to a specific radio base station, the MSC knows where the subscriber station was at power up. If the MSC then sends page requests for that subscriber station only to a group of radio base stations in the area around the radio base station where the subscriber station originally registered, the paging traffic can be cut down considerably. This improvement in paging traffic is offset by a modest amount of extra traffic on the access channels associated with the power-up and power-down registrations. Power-up registration is not a feature of the AMPS standard, and so it is not available for use with the vast majority of AMPS-compatible subscriber stations in existence today. Power-up and power-down registration are features of the IS-54 TDMA and the IS-95 CDMA digital cellular standards.

This simple approach—relying only on power-up and power-down registration— has the disadvantage that if the subscriber station moves a great distance after power up, it may leave the area in which it first registered and thus may not receive page requests. This limitation can be overcome with two-stage paging, where the MSC pages in the area where power-up registration occurred; if there is no response, it will page over a wider area, or over the entire system. However, this procedure increases call-setup time, as well as paging traffic. If a large percentage of customers are highly mobile, then this strategy will not help paging traffic much relative to the simple wide-area paging approach.

The registration process can also be expanded to include periodic registrations by subscriber stations, so that as the subscriber station moves around the system, the MSC can update its knowledge of the position of the subscriber station, and direct page requests accordingly. This method will help limit paging traffic to areas where the subscriber station is likely to be found. However, if the subscriber is not moving, the periodic registrations will provide redundant information to the MSC and unnecessarily load the access channel. The AMPS and TDMA digital cellular standards include features that provide for registration both autonomously and on global command from the system.

10.6.5 Location Areas

A more general form of registration that takes care of tracking highly mobile subscriber stations while limiting access-channel traffic for slowly moving or stationary subscriber stations involves the *location area*. A location area is covered by a group of one or more radio base stations that the system operator identifies as an area where the operator considers all subscriber stations to be in a common paging area.

The operator divides the service area up into a set of nonoverlapping location areas and assigns a number to each location area. Each radio base station includes the number of the location area to which it belongs in the overhead message train that it transmits. When a subscriber powers up, selects the strongest dedicated control channel, and reads the overhead message train, it stores the number of the location area to which the radio base station belongs, and then sends a registration message. Subsequently, when it is in idle mode, it reads the overhead message train on the paging or dedicated control channel to which it is tuned. When it reads a location-area identity that is different from the one that it has stored, it sends another registration message to inform the MSC that it has moved to a new paging area.

In determining appropriate sizes for the location areas, the system operator must consider both reductions in paging traffic that are gained by decreasing the size of the location areas, and reductions in registration traffic that are achieved by increasing the size of the location areas. If each radio base station is a distinct location area, then the MSC needs to send a page request to only one radio base station to complete a call. This act, however, will result in a registration attempt by every subscriber station each time it moves out of the range of a radio base station. At the other extreme, the MSC sends a page request to every radio base station for every incoming call. Between these two extremes is an optimal point that minimizes the load on the paging and access channels. This optimum point will vary according to the size of the system and the mobility profiles exhibited by the subscribers on the system.

10.6.6   Handover

As a subscriber station moves around in a cellular system, the radio base station that provides the best service will change. When the subscriber station is idle and monitoring only paging-channel traffic, as it moves out of range of one radio base station, it will seek out another radio base station that provides the strongest signal, and continue to monitor paging traffic on the paging channel on the new radio base station.

When a call is in progress, however, a more elaborate mechanism is required for changing the radio base station that a subscriber station is communicating with as it moves away from its serving radio base station and the call quality is deteriorated by decreasing signal strength and increasing interference. Changing the radio link from one radio base station to another is called *handover*, or *handoff*. Ideally, the subscriber station will always be communicating with the radio base station that provides the best signal, and handover from one radio base station to another will be accomplished without disrupting the current call. However, many problems are associated with determining which radio base station is the best for providing service at any given time, and with coordinating the handover in a timely fashion and without disrupting the call.

The simplest approach, and the one used in AMPS cellular systems, to decide when it is appropriate to hand over a call, is to monitor average received signal power at the radio base station on which the call is operating, and when it falls below some predetermined threshold, initiate a handover. To perform the handover, the MSC needs to know which base station has the best signal quality for this subscriber station. It sends a measurement request to potential candidate radio base stations, which are the radio base stations that the system operator has previously determined to be neighbors of the radio base station that is currently supporting the call. These radio base stations have dedicated measurement receivers that respond to the measurement request by tuning to the channel that the call in question is using and measuring the average received power on that channel. These measurements are reported back to the MSC, which then decides if any of the radio base stations have sufficiently high

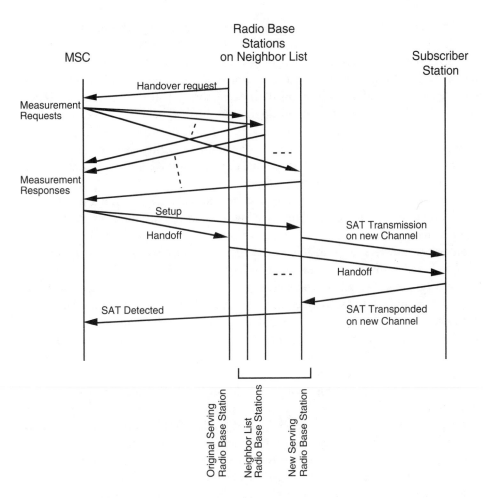

Figure 10.9 Message sequence for subscriber-station handover

received signal strength to support the call, and if so, which one has the highest signal strength. The MSC then checks to see if any channels are available in the chosen radio base station, sets up a circuit to the new radio base station, tells the new radio base station to turn on its transmitter for the channel to which the call is to be handed over, and sends a handover order to the subscriber station. The subscriber station then tunes to the new channel and proceeds to communicate with the new radio base station. The message sequence for this procedure is shown in Figure 10.9.

The disadvantage in this centralized approach to handover is that a significant amount of latency is involved in all steps. It is thus possible for the radio channel to deteriorate significantly before a handover can be arranged and executed. In typical AMPS systems, one measurement receiver in each radio base station is responsible for making all measurements. Sometimes this measurement receiver must measure the power on all the calls that are in progress on its own radio base station, as well as the list of calls that are handover candidates in surrounding cells. As a result, the radio base station may take several seconds to notice that received power on a call has fallen below the handover threshold, and several more seconds for the measurement to be completed by the radio base stations on the neighbor list. If the signal strength deteriorates so that the connection is no longer reliable before a handover can be arranged, it will not be possible to arrange a handover at all. This failure occurs because the message transfer required to inform the subscriber station which channel it is to use on the new radio base station takes place on the connection that is failing. When this happens the call is dropped suddenly.

In many situations a handover latency of five to ten seconds is not a problem. If a subscriber unit is in an automobile traveling in open terrain, for example, where no sudden changes in topography block the signal suddenly, signal strength will decrease more or less slowly and uniformly as the automobile moves away from a radio base station. Usually time is ample to arrange a handover.

Unfortunately, in many circumstances the signal power can decrease very rapidly. A classic example is the subscriber station in an automobile that turns a corner in a high-rise section of a city. Signal strength can change rapidly while the automobile is turning the corner, as the buildings on the corner of the street block the signal. This signal loss can occur in a second or two, which leaves no time for the MSC to detect the problem and arrange for a handover.

Another problem with this approach to handover is that received signal power is not always a good indicator of the quality of the link because cellular systems are designed to operate in interference-limited mode. Calls with sufficient received power levels may still degrade due to interference from calls that are in progress on other radio base stations. For this reason it is highly desirable to have a measure of connection quality that is independent of signal level. This measure is readily available in digital systems, where the receiver can measure the bit-error probability easily, and thus flag deteriorating calls on that basis.

10.6.6.1 *Mobile Assisted Handover*

Some of the problems with the centralized handover strategy used in AMPS systems can be alleviated by *mobile assisted handover*. This help is possible when the subscriber station is capable of making measurements of power on channels other than the one it is operating on. AMPS subscriber stations do not have this ability, for the subscriber-station receiver must be dedicated to receiving the voice channel during a call. TDMA subscriber stations, however, can make use of some of the time that is available during time slots that are not carrying the subscriber station's voice channel to retune to other channels and make power measurements. IS-54 compatible mobiles must be able to do exactly this. IS-54 requires that subscriber stations be capable of making continuing power measurements on up to twelve channels other than the channel assigned to the voice call currently in progress, and also make and store average power measurements and bit error-rate measurements on the channel assigned to the subscriber station's own voice call.

In IS-54 mobile assisted handover, the radio base station sends a neighbor list, which is a list of channels on which the subscriber station must make power measurements, to the subscriber station. The subscriber station then accumulates average power measurements on this list of channels and sends these values, along with the power and bit error rate on the subscriber station's own channel back to the radio base station, on command from the radio base station.

This technique can be used to either replace or supplement the power measurements made at the radio base station. It has the advantage that it uses the subscriber station receiver to accumulate measurements before the information becomes critical, thereby significantly reducing the latency that is encountered in the centralized approach.

In spite of the improvements brought by mobile assisted handover, latency is still involved in the handover execution process, and it is still possible to drop a call when the channel degrades rapidly.

10.6.6.2 Soft Handover

Yet another variation on handover, known as *soft handover*, has been introduced in the CDMA digital cellular standard. The name refers to the fact that subscriber stations that are in transition regions between radio base stations, where the signal from two or more radio base stations may be nearly equal in power (within a factor of ten), may be simultaneously communicating with two or more radio base stations. This technique may also be considered a form of mobile assisted handover, for IS-95 CDMA subscriber stations continuously make power measurements on a list of neighboring radio base stations, and determine whether or not to request soft handover, and which radio base stations to communicate with in soft handover.

Due to properties of the CDMA signaling scheme that are beyond the scope of this discussion, it is possible for a CDMA subscriber station to simultaneously receive signals from two or more radio base stations that are transmitting the same bit stream on the same channel. If the signal power from two or three radio base stations is nearly the same, the subscriber station receiver can combine the received signals in such a way that the bit stream is decoded much more reliably than if only one radio base station were transmitting to the subscriber station. Because more than one radio base station is providing a signal to the subscriber station, if any one of these signals fades significantly, there will still be a relatively high probability of having adequate signal strength from one of the other radio base stations.

On the reverse link, all the radio base stations that are actively supporting a call in soft handover send the bit stream that they receive back to the MSC, along with information about the quality of the received bits. The MSC examines the quality information for all these bit streams, and dynamically chooses the bit stream with the highest quality. Again, if the signal to one of the radio base stations degrades rapidly, the chance is still good that a strong signal will be available at one of the other radio base stations that is supporting the call in soft handover.

As a result of having multiple connections during the handover, the degraded signal quality and frequent dropped calls associated with handover in AMPS systems and IS-54 TDMA systems are dramatically reduced in CDMA systems.

10.6.7   Roaming

So far, we have described techniques for mobility management when the mobility is all within a limited and well-defined geographic service area, which is managed by a single system operator. One of the most powerful features of cellular technology, however, is the potential for delivering service to a subscriber regardless of location. In particular, it is highly desirable to be able to deliver service to a subscriber who is visiting a service area outside of his or her home service area. A subscriber who subscribes for service in Boston, for example, and has a directory number with the Boston area code and Boston exchange, should be able to go to Rapid City, South Dakota, and receive the same service that he or she receives in Boston.

A subscriber unit that is operating outside its home service area is said to be *roaming*. Strictly speaking, a North American subscriber station is said to be roaming when the home SID that is programmed into the subscriber station is different from the SID of the system that is providing service. This condition can happen when the subscriber station is a subscriber on the B system in a given geographic service area and is receiving service from the A system, or vice versa, as well as when the subscriber station is operating outside its home service area. A subscriber station always knows when it is roaming because the SID is always broadcast on the overhead message train, and the subscriber station compares its programmed home SID with the SID that it reads on the overhead message train. Subscriber stations are equipped with an indicator such as a light that is turned on when the subscriber station is roaming.

The easiest form of roaming service to provide is service for calls that are originated by a roaming subscriber station. In this case, when the subscriber station performs a system access to request a call origination, the system will recognize from the subscriber station MIN that is provided in the origination message that the subscriber station is a roaming subscriber, and will also know which system operator is the home service provider for the subscriber station. Based on this information, the MSC will decide how to deal with the roamer's request for service. If the system operator has a billing agreement with the roamer's home service provider, the MSC will probably process the call normally, and the roamer will get billed through an established procedure. If the system operator does not have appropriate arrangements with the roamer's home service provider, the MSC may be rude and simply reject the call by returning a fast busy indication or delivering a recorded message, or it may connect the subscriber station with an operator who will offer to make alternate billing arrangements by taking a credit card number.

It is also highly desirable for the roaming subscriber station to be able to receive incoming calls. This service requires more involved arrangements. The simple approach to the problem does not require much additional infrastructure or arrangements between service providers, other than billing agreements. This approach involves the system operator providing one roaming directory number that can be called by anyone wishing to reach a subscriber station that they believe to be roaming in the system operator's service area. When this number is reached, it will provide a secondary dial tone, at which the subscriber's full directory number can be entered. The MSC will then page the subscriber station and attempt to set the call up. If the targeted subscriber station is powered up, and has its preferred provider status set to that of the system operator doing the paging, it will hear the page and a call will be established.

This kind of roaming arrangement may be convenient for the system operator in amount of effort required to establish the service, but it has a number of drawbacks from the point of view of the customer. The first among these is that the calling party probably does not know the roaming number of the cellular system in which the called party is roaming, even if the caller does know where the called party happens to be at the time the call is placed. A sales representative, for example, may have a territory that spans serving areas operated by several service providers. It may be very inconvenient to keep all potential callers informed of which dialing procedure to use to reach the subscriber at any given time.

This roaming technique can be improved upon by taking advantage of call forwarding features that are available in the standard software feature set that is part of any modern digital switch. When a roaming subscriber decides that he wants calls that are dialed to his home directory number delivered to his subscriber station in the roaming service area, the subscriber dials a special feature code on the subscriber station. The subscriber station treats this as a call origination, and performs a system access, passing the feature code to the MSC as if it were a directory number. When the MSC sees the feature code, along with the subscriber's MIN, it interprets this message as a request for a special call-delivery service. The MSC then sends a message, over a network that has been established for this purpose, to the subscriber station's home MSC. This message requests that the home MSC forward all calls to the mobile station's home directory number to a special temporary directory number at the visited MSC. When a call arrives at the temporary directory number at the visited MSC, the MSC translates this number to the actual directory number of the roaming subscriber station, and issues a page request using the MIN derived from this directory number.

When this technique is used, the calling party does not need to know anything about the location of the subscriber to whom she is placing a call. However, the service is not completely automatic, because the subscriber must still take some action to invoke the service, which may or may not be desirable. Furthermore, it is not completely general, because it may be desirable for the subscriber to move between two or more service areas, have the cellular network keep track of her whereabouts, and be able to deliver calls to her regardless of location. These goals can be accomplished using the *home location register* (HLR) and *visitor location register* (VLR) functions shown in the TIA network reference model of Figure 10.5.

To show how this structure can provide enhanced mobility features, consider the act of registration by a roaming mobile subscriber. The MSC in a service area may become aware of the presence of a roaming subscriber station in a variety of ways: autonomous registration, a call origination, or some other means. When this happens, the MSC will send a registration notification to its associated VLR. The VLR may react to this message in a variety of ways.

If the VLR has no record of the subscriber station that is the object of the registration notification, the VLR will forward a registration notification to the HLR serving the subscriber station's home MSC. This notice informs the HLR that the subscriber station in question is now in a service area associated with the VLR that sent the message. The HLR records this information and returns an acknowledgment to the VLR. If the subscriber station was previously roaming in a service area associated with a different VLR, the HLR will send a registration cancellation to this previous serving VLR. The previous serving VLR then removes its records of the subscriber station.

After these actions are taken, the new serving VLR has a record of the location of the roaming subscriber station (which MSC is associated with the service area in which the subscriber station is currently located, if the VLR serves more than one MSC), and the subscriber station's HLR also has a record of its location (which VLR is associated with the service area in which it is roaming). Further actions may or may not take place. The VLR may send a message to the HLR seeking to establish a qualification procedure that will serve to verify the authenticity of the subscriber station. The VLR may also request a service profile from the HLR, so that it can determine the services that the subscriber station subscribes to in its home service area.

10.7 CONNECTIONLESS DATA SERVICE FOR CELLULAR SYSTEMS

The AMPS cellular technology has obviously succeeded in providing voice services to a large and growing customer base, and the CDMA and TDMA digital standards will extend the capacity and functionality to a larger user base. To date, data services over the cellular network in North America have not been widely available or well supported. Part of the reason for this deficiency is that the AMPS standard was not developed with the need to provide reliable data services in mind. Users would like to be able to take advantage of the large installed base of wireline data modems and fax machines. However, CCITT standard modems are not designed to deal with all the impairments encountered on a cellular connection. Some techniques have been developed to enhance standard modems to provide reliable operation over analog cellular connections, but these are not entirely satisfactory, for various reasons.

A major drawback in using connection-oriented wireline modem technology over cellular voice connections is cost. Cellular "air time" is significantly more expensive than landline local telephone service. There is a large class of applications for which the connection is idle for a large percentage of the time that the connection is up. For this class of applications, a connectionless data service would be preferable to the wireline modem approach due to its increased efficiency.

In this section we briefly describe a connectionless data service that has recently been defined for use as an overlay on existing AMPS cellular networks.

10.7.1 The CDPD Specification

The *cellular digital packet data* (CDPD) specification[20] was developed by a consortium of cellular service providers to define a technology that provides connectionless packet-data access in the cellular band, without significantly interfering with the provision of voice services. CDPD uses a 19.2-kbps data stream that occupies the same 30-kHz bandwidth used by AMPS and IS-54 systems. The physical layer was designed to have as much as possible in common with AMPS, so that readily available, off-the-shelf components could be used in implementing subscriber stations to the greatest extent possible.

The CDPD reverse link *medium access control* (MAC) layer uses a random-access technique called *digital sense multiple access* (DSMA) that is in many ways similar to the CSMA/CD access method used in Ethernet. But because CDPD mobile stations cannot reliably detect activity in other mobile stations, they must rely on feedback in the form of flags on the forward-channel data stream to determine when the reverse channel is busy.

The data-link layer in CDPD uses an adaptation of HDLC.[2] On the forward link, the data-link layer frames ride on a continuous data stream made up of Reed-Solomon code blocks that have MAC layer control flags and synchronization information interleaved into them. On the reverse link, the data-link layer frames are embedded in bursts that consist of one or more Reed-Solomon code blocks with some interleaved MAC layer control.

Above the data-link layer a subnetwork-dependent convergence sublayer serves as an interface to industry standard TCP/IP and OSI network and higher layers. This sublayer takes care of segmenting IP or CLNP datagrams, compressing IP[3] or CLNP[7] headers for efficient use of the radio channel, and providing an interface to encryption services.

10.7.2 Channel Hopping

CDPD is intended to operate as an invisible overlay on AMPS cellular systems, using channel resources that are idle due to the statistical nature of call arrivals in a trunked, circuit-switched voice system. These channels are available to CDPD only when they are not required by the voice system. The CDPD system is intended to be sufficiently intelligent to abandon an AMPS voice channel whenever the channel is required for voice service, without interfering with voice service. When this departure occurs, a CDPD radio in a *mobile data base station* (MDBS) providing service will tune to a new frequency that is available to it. This process is referred to as *channel hopping*.

If there is time, the CDPD MDBS will broadcast a message that informs M-ESs of the new channel to which the MDBS is about to tune. However, there will also be occasions on which the MDBS will be required to perform an emergency channel hop, without broadcasting a new channel. When this hop occurs, the M-ESs tuned to the original channel must be capable of acquiring the MDBS channel stream on the new channel.

10.7.3 Mobility and Routing in a CDPD Network

A block diagram of CDPD network elements and interfaces is shown in Figure 10.10. The elements are

*   *Mobile end system (M-ES)*   CDPD subscriber station

*   *Mobile data base station (MDBS)*   CDPD radio base station

*   *Mobile data intermediate system (MD-IS)*   Packet switch/router that serves a role analogous to that played by the MSC voice cellular system. This system provides conventional packet switching and routing functions, as well as mobility management functions.

*   *Fixed end system (F-ES)*   Fixed-network host, either internal to the CDPD network, where it may be providing a value-added service or a service associated with network functionality, or external to the CDPD network

10.7.3.1 *CDPD Mobility Management: Cell Transfer*

Because CDPD operation is connectionless, local mobility operates in a somewhat different manner than in the voice cellular systems described in preceding sections. Unlike a handover procedure that is controlled by the switch, when an M-ES moves out of the range of an MDBS with which it is associated, the M-ES initiates a cell-transfer procedure, by which it seeks to associate itself with another MDBS that will provide it with good service. This operation has much in common with the manner in which an AMPS subscriber station chooses a control channel, and therefore a radio base station, with which to communicate.

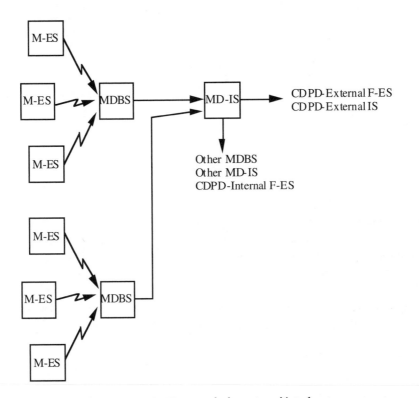

Figure 10.10   CDPD network elements and interfaces

An M-ES executes an initialization procedure on power up, during which it finds a CDPD forward channel that it can decode reliably. Once the M-ES has completed this procedure, it can attempt to register itself with the CDPD system providing service on the channel stream that it has acquired. Once registered, the M-ES can proceed to access the reverse channel and can receive packets on the forward channel.

When the M-ES begins to move out of range of the MDBS from which it is receiving service, the quality of its connection will begin to deteriorate. The M-ES observes the deterioration through decreased signal level, increased errors in decoding the Reed-Solomon code blocks, loss of synchronization, or a combination of these events. When this sequence happens, the M-ES will initiate reacquisition, during which it attempts to find a new channel that can provide it with high quality service. In most cases, the M-ES will have a short list of candidate channels on which neighbor MDBSs are operating CDPD channel streams, so that this reacquisition can take place rapidly.

When an acknowledged data-link layer connection has been established, and the M-ES and MDBS are exchanging link-layer information and acknowledgment frames, an M-ES determines that it is out of range of the MDBS with which it has

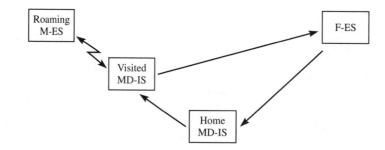

Figure 10.11   Packet routing for a roaming M-ES

established the connection when the MDBS fails to set MAC-layer Busy/Idle flags in response to its access attempts. When this sequence happens, the M-ES will initiate cell transfer. The objective is for the M-ES to complete the cell transfer before the link-layer frame counter wraps around and triggers a link-layer retransmit on the old MDBS. When the M-ES reregisters on the new MDBS, the link-layer connection will be switched to the new MDBS, and any unacknowledged link-layer frames will be retransmitted on the channel stream of the new MDBS.

10.7.3.2 CDPD Mobility Management: Roaming

The CDPD network will take advantage of the powerful routing and addressing capabilities of packet-switched data networks to route traffic to roaming M-ESs. Each CDPD system will have a mobile serving function and mobile home function, which are similar to the HLR and VLR functions described in preceding sections. The mobile serving function is responsible for tracking the location of M-ESs that are registered on the system, and routing traffic to them, whether this is their home system or they are visiting M-ESs roaming in the system.

When an M-ES registers on a CDPD system that is not its home system, the visited mobile serving function will inform the mobile home function in the M-ES's home system of that M-ES's presence in the visited system. Datagrams addressed to the M-ES will be routed initially to the M-ES's home system, where the mobile home function will encapsulate them and route them to the mobile serving function at the visited CDPD system. The visited mobile serving function is then responsible for decapsulating the forwarded datagrams and routing them to the MDBS that is serving the M-ES in question.

Traffic originated by a roaming M-ES is routed directly to its destination, without being forwarded first to the mobile home function in the M-ES's home system. Routing paths for traffic associated with a roaming M-ES are shown in Figure 10.11.

10.8 CONCLUSION

In cellular mobile radio networks, the nature of the radio channel and the mobility of subscribers are the dominant factors affecting routing. We discuss the implications of these factors, present the general cellular system architecture, and compare the cellular standards for voice communications. Next, we focus on the routing problems of locating and tracking subscribers and maintaining calls during subscriber movement. We conclude with a discussion of the cellular data service provided by CDPD.

REFERENCES

1 N. Abramson, "The ALOHA System," in N. Abramson and F. Kuo, eds., *Computer Communication Networks,* Englewood Cliffs: Prentice Hall, 1973.

2 U. Black, *X.25 and Related Protocols*, Los Alamitos, CA: IEEE Computer Society Press, 1991.

3 D. Comer, *Internetworking with TCP/IP, Volume I: Principles, Protocols, and Architecture,* 2nd ed., Englewood Cliffs: Prentice Hall, 1991.

4 K. S. Gilhousen, I. M. Jacobs, R. Padovani, A. J. Viterbi, L. A. Weaver, and C. E. Wheatley, "On the Capacity of a Cellular CDMA System," *IEEE Transactions on Vehicular Technology,* Vol. 40, May 1991.

5 D. J. Goodman, "Second Generation Wireless Information Networks," *IEEE Transactions on Vehicular Technology,* Vol. 40, May 1991.

6 W. C. Jakes, Jr., *Microwave Mobile Communications,* New York: Wiley, 1974. Reprint. Piscataway, NJ: IEEE Press, 1993.

7 D. Katz and P. S. Ford, "TUBA: Replacing IP with CLNP," *IEEE Network,* May 1993.

8 W. C. Y. Lee, *Mobile Communications Engineering*, New York: McGraw-Hill, 1982.

9 M. Mouly and M-B Pautet, *The GSM System for Mobile Communications,* Palaiseau, France: M. Mouly and Marie-B. Pautet, 49, rue Louise Bruneau, F-91120, 1992.

10 K. Raith and J. Uddenfeldt, "Capacity of Digital Cellular TDMA Systems," *IEEE Transactions on Vehicular Technology,* Vol. 40, May 1991.

11 W. R. Young, "Advanced Mobile Phone Service: Introduction, Background, and Objectives," *Bell Systems Technical Journal,* Vol. 58, No. 1, January 1979, pp. 1–41. This entire issue of the *Bell Systems Technical Journal* is devoted to papers on the introduction of AMPS.

12   "Mobile Station–Land Station Compatibility Specification," Electronic Industry Association, Document No. ANSI/EIA/TIA-553-1989, 1989.

13   "Recommended Minimum Standards for 800–MHz Cellular Subscriber Units," Electronic Industry Association, Document No. EIA/IS-19-B, 1988.

14   "Recommended Minimum Standards for 800–MHz Cellular Land Stations," Electronic Industry Association, Document No. EIA/IS-20-A, 1988.

15   "Cellular System Dual-Mode Mobile Station–Base Station Compatibility Standard," Telecommunications Industry Association, Document No. EIA/TIA/IS-54–B, April 1992.

16   "Recommended Minimum Performance Standards of 800 MHz Dual-Mode Mobile Stations," Telecommunications Industry Association, Document No. TIA/EIA/IS-55–A, September 1993.

17   "Recommended Minimum Performance Standards for 800 MHz Base Stations Supporting Dual-Mode Mobile Stations," Telecommunications Industry Association, Document No. TIA/EIA/IS-56–A, October 1993.

18   "Mobile Station–Base Station Compatibility Standard for Dual-Mode Wideband Spread Spectrum Cellular System," Telecommunications Industry Association, Document No. TIA/EIA/IS-95, July 1993.

19   "Cellular Radiotelecommunications Intersystem Operations," Rev. B, Electronic Industry Association, Document No. IS-41B, 1991.

20   "Cellular Digital Packet Data System Specification," Release 1.0, Ameritech Mobile Communications, Inc., Bell Atlantic Mobile Systems, Contel Cellular, Inc., GTE Mobile Communications, Inc., McCaw Cellular Communications, Inc., NYNEX Mobile Communications, Inc., PacTel Cellular, Southwestern Bell Mobile Systems, July 1993.

CHAPTER 11 ❖ ❖ ❖ ❖

_____

Packet-Radio Routing

GREGORY S. LAUER

CONTENTS

351

Multihop mobile packet-radio networks are the preferred technology for tactical networking because of their ability to self-organize and rapidly adapt to change. Such packet-radio networks pose routing constraints that are unique among those of packet-switched networks. First, the network topology may be highly dynamic, because each mobile radio unit also functions as a packet switch. Second, the network transmission capacity may be limited by the power of the portable radio units as well as by radio signal interference and obstruction. Thus, routing procedures for packet-radio networks must accommodate frequent and rapid changes in network topology while making efficient use of the limited network transmission capacity. This chapter presents a variety of routing strategies for packet-radio networks, concentrating on those developed as part of the ARPA SURAN packet-radio project. It also includes routing techniques applicable to very large packet-radio networks, specifically those techniques involving hierarchical network organization.

11.1 INTRODUCTION AND OVERVIEW

A packet-radio network consists of a number of nodes (fixed or mobile) that communicate with each other via radio. In many packet-radio networks the packet radios do *not* have direct radio links to all other packet radios in the network and thus store-and-forward routing of the packets is required. Using radio for communication between nodes has two major benefits: it speeds up deploying a network because links need not be installed, and radio links directly support mobile nodes. However, the use of radio introduces two complicating factors: the nodes share their communication medium and the network topology can be highly dynamic. (The links between radios may exist for as little as tens of seconds; links may come in and out of existence by the movement of the packet radios, by changes in the propagation environment, or by external interference.)

Packet-radio networks are used in a wide range of settings and use a wide spectrum of technologies. Examples include: the DARPA packet-radio project[8] (wide-band spread-spectrum mobile nodes for defense research), Amateur Packet Radio[65] (narrow-band, mainly fixed-site nodes for amateur use), Part 15 Radio LANs[72] (low-power spread-spectrum for local-area networking), military packet-radio overlays[1,3,4,5] (narrow-band HF packet overlays for military use), and Cellular Digital Packet Data[2] (which overlays a data network on cellular systems).

The routing algorithms used in these networks range from single-hop to multihop, from single frequency to multifrequency, from virtual-circuit to datagram, and from nearly static to highly adaptive.[6,12] It is beyond the scope of this chapter to

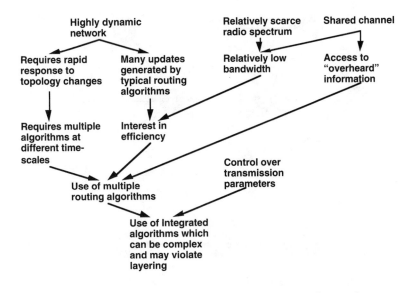

Figure 11.1   Why packet-radio routing algorithms can be complex

discuss the routing algorithms used in each of these networks. Instead in this chapter we will focus on routing in highly mobile, multihop, shared-channel datagram networks: a demanding environment raising issues that rarely occur in other networks.[7]

At first blush, packet-radio networks seem to raise no special routing issues other than having to deal with a very dynamic topology. In reality, packet-radio routing algorithms can be much more complex than those designed for wireline networks. The reason is efficiency.

Figure 11.1 illustrates the logic that drives the design of packet-radio routing algorithms. The packet-radio network can be highly dynamic, implying that (1) traditional routing algorithms will either not stabilize or will generate many routing updates, and (2) rapid response to topology change is needed (because dropping packets until the topology stabilizes is not a viable solution). The need for rapid response means that multiple algorithms working at different time scales are required (fast algorithms that work with local information and longer-term algorithms that use more global information).

Radio spectrum is a scarce resource, which means that packet-radio networks typically have limited bandwidth available. Because the radios must share access to the radio channel, the bandwidth available to any node is even more limited. Relatively low bandwidth combined with the potential for routing algorithms to generate large numbers of packets means that efficiency is paramount in designing packet-radio routing algorithms.

Efficiency and layered design (e.g., the OSI protocol stack) are generally in conflict. The goal of layering is to reduce complexity by hiding implementation details in

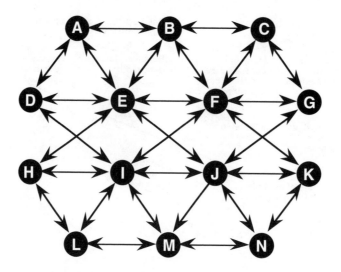

Figure 11.2   Graphical illustration of a packet-radio network

one layer (e.g., the link layer) from the layer (e.g., routing) that uses it. Efficiency is attained by taking advantage of all the information available. In packet-radio networks the availability of "overheard" information, the ability to control transmitter parameters, and the need for efficiency combine to generate interest in integrated algorithms that may violate layering principles (and thus may be more complex).

For example, consider the following algorithms used in the DARPA packet-radio program.[9] Figure 11.2 graphically illustrates a multihop packet-radio network with which we illustrate these algorithms. The lines between nodes indicate which radios can hear a transmission. For example, if node A transmits a packet, nodes D, E, and B can receive the transmission. Links need not be bidirectional, for sources of interference may be closer to one node than another (e.g., node M can hear node J transmit, but not vice versa).

- *Passive acknowledgments*   Consider node E, forwarding a packet to node F that was received from node D. The transmission to node F can be overheard by node D; that overheard transmission indicates that node E successfully received the packet and thus can act as a *passive acknowledgment* to node D. If node E can adjust the power used when transmitting a packet (power control) then passive acknowledgments will require that the power used to forward a packet be selected not just so that it can be heard by the destination (node F), but also so it can be heard by the previous node (node D).

- *Alternate routing on retransmission*   While packets are broadcast, their header normally indicates the node to which they are directed; other nodes that receive these packets do not attempt to forward them. If no acknowledgment is received after three attempts, the sending node will change the header to indicate that any node closer to the ultimate destination may forward the packet.

- *Filtering based on overheard traffic*   Alternate routing creates an undesirable "limited flood" where several nodes may be forwarding the same packet. To reduce the effect of this phenomenon, nodes filter their send-queue based on overheard traffic. For example, if node E overhears another radio closer to the destination transmit a packet that node E has queued to send, then node E will treat that overheard transmission as an acknowledgment and remove that packet from its send-queue, *even if node E has never sent the packet.*

Because the routing algorithms developed for a packet-radio network depend strongly on the technology used in the network it is difficult to discuss general algorithms in detail and to directly apply the algorithms used in one setting to another.[11] In this chapter we thus take a twin-track approach: in each of the following sections we briefly discuss some general issues that are relevant to dynamic multihop shared-channel datagram packet-radio networks and then discuss in more detail the algorithms developed for the DARPA packet-radio network.

The remainder of this chapter is organized as follows. In Section 11.2 we consider issues associated with packet-radio channel access, connectivity determination (and control), and discuss the overheard information that may be used in routing. In Section 11.3 we describe the DARPA packet-radio project and the *low-cost packet radio* (LPR), which was developed as part of that project. In Section 11.4 we consider broadcast routing algorithms that are appropriate for networks consisting of up to a few hundred nodes. One of the algorithms described here has been used in moderate-size field tests; most of the other algorithms have been simulated and analyzed extensively. These algorithms, called *flat routing algorithms,* do not scale as the network size increases to thousands of nodes. In Section 11.5 we consider routing algorithms for large packet-radio networks. Two types of algorithms are considered: *hierarchical algorithms* that attempt to scale to large networks by hiding the details of topology in distant places and *nonhierarchical algorithms* that are an attempt to reduce the information required to route in large networks. In Section 11.6 we briefly consider routing algorithms that have been developed for networks that use transmission control (either by using receiver-directed transmissions or by changing the link parameters).

11.2   PACKET-RADIO NETWORKS

11.2.1   Channel Access and Hidden Terminals

Packet-radio nodes that have a neighbor in common but that are not neighbors are called *hidden terminals* (e.g., nodes D and B in Figure 11.2). Because hidden terminals have no way of knowing when the other one is sending a packet, a hidden terminal may transmit a packet to a node that is currently receiving a packet. In many broadcast networks if two packets are transmitted so that their receptions at a node overlap in time, then neither is successfully received. Hidden terminals mean that even when CSMA channel-access mechanisms are used, the performance of a packet-radio channel can be as bad as that of ALOHA channels (e.g., a maximum throughput of 18 to 36 percent). (These two figures correspond to unslotted and slotted channel-access procedures. The DARPA packet radios used an unslotted channel-access procedure to minimize problems with mobile nodes.)

This problem can be reduced by having the packet radios use *spread-spectrum signaling*.[55] Spread spectrum operates by replacing each symbol in a packet with many independent chips. Each bit of the packet is indirectly transmitted by sending the waveform corresponding to the many chips that make it up. The chip sequences frequently have the property that transmissions starting at different times (even if they use the same spread-spectrum sequence) have low correlation due to their offset in time. This low correlation makes transmissions that start in the middle of a packet reception look like noise. Spread spectrum thus provides a *capture* mechanism, which allows a node to receive the first of a sequence of overlapping time-offset transmissions unless the undesired transmissions are much more powerful than the desired one.

Even if spread-spectrum signaling is used, the hidden terminal problem means that when multiple packets are sent simultaneously to a node at most one of the packets will be received. Without effective channel-access mechanisms, the performance of spread-spectrum packet-radio channels can be as bad as that of slotted ALOHA (e.g., a maximum throughput of 36 percent).

Channel-access schemes such as *busy-tone multiple access*[60] have been proposed to alleviate the hidden terminal problem, but they require hardware support and emit an easily detected signal, which makes them undesirable in tactical environments. Approaches that schedule transmissions are difficult to implement because they require significant amounts of information and computation. Other distributed channel-access approaches, such as MACA,[59] have been proposed but not yet implemented.

11.2.2 Throughput

The throughput of packet-radio networks is difficult to compute because it is a complex function of the channel-access protocols, topology, traffic matrix, radio capabilities (e.g., power control), environment, routing algorithm, and so on. A simple model of slotted, multihop packet-radio networks[71] that assumes no capture and no acknowledgment traffic, indicates that packet radios should transmit only $1/K$ of the time, where K is the average number of neighbors. For this model the probability of successful transmission is 36 percent. If all traffic went only one hop, the "end-user" bandwidth would be $(.36/K)$ times the channel bandwidth.

In a multihop network the amount of "new" traffic that can be sent is further reduced by the need for the packet radios to forward traffic that was generated elsewhere and is destined for other nodes. If the traffic pattern is uniform and the average number of hops between nodes is H, then each packet must be forwarded H times. Because only one out of H packets is new (the others are transit traffic), the amount of new end-user traffic is reduced by a factor of H to $(.36/KH)$.

In a network with $K = 5$ neighbors and $H = 5$ hops, this model would predict a maximum end-user bit rate of as little as 1.4 percent of the channel bit rate. The throughput is likely to be lower in systems with acknowledgments and an unslotted channel. In the DARPA packet-radio network (which is a high-bandwidth network) the channel bit rate ranges from 50 to 400 kilobits per second, which corresponds to a maximum end-user bit rate of approximately 720 to 5800 bits per second.

Because packet-radio links are limited in range, the number of hops that packets must travel in large networks will on average be higher than in wireline networks that can install long-distance backbone links. Thus large values of H that reduce the end-user traffic that can be carried may be typical.

If the traffic matrix is not uniform, then the bandwidth available to an end user can be much higher. Consider a situation in which the only traffic is one source sending packets to a destination. Each packet radio on the route between the source and destination must receive a packet, transmit that packet, and receive an acknowledgment for that transmission. Thus the maximum throughput is $1/3$ the channel bandwidth, which for the DARPA packet radio would be between 16 and 132 kilobits per second.

Packet-radio networks are thus best suited for applications which generate bursts of data and which access the network sporadically, because this arrangement minimizes the losses due to contention. Notice, however, that sophisticated channel-access and congestion-control algorithms are required to adapt to changes in traffic patterns. These problems make bandwidth a precious resource. Routing algorithms for packet-radio networks thus emphasize efficiency and reducing the number of control-traffic packets to a minimum.

11.2.3 Connectivity

Because links in a packet-radio network are affected by node mobility, propagation effects, and interference, packet-radio nodes must be able to dynamically determine their own connectivity. Because radio channels are unreliable, packet radios typically use a link-level acknowledgment strategy that requires bidirectional links. This tactic requires that the packet radios determine which nodes can hear them and which nodes they can hear.

The simplest approach is to have the radios periodically transmit a packet that is used to determine connectivity. Nodes keep track of how many of these packets have been received out of the number transmitted and use that ratio to determine the link quality. If the ratio is high enough in both directions, then the link is declared up or *good*; otherwise it is marked down or *bad*. Links can also be marked bad if too many retransmissions are required to send a packet to a neighbor. Enhancements to this procedure include measuring signal strength, signal-to-noise ratio, using overheard traffic, and so on.

Because packet-radio network connectivity may not be controllable, network partitions are a real possibility and links must be established as quickly as possible. Thus the connectivity packets need to be broadcast relatively often. Although network partitions are the most obvious problem of variable connectivity, another problem is that some packet radios may have too many neighbors. Establishing connectivity with a neighbor uses resources (bandwidth and storage) that may be excessive for large numbers of neighbors. References 66, 69, and 73 discuss algorithms for selecting the neighbors in situations where connectivity is too dense. In particular they discuss how to select neighbors without causing network partitions.

11.2.4 Broadcast Channels

The broadcast nature of radio channels means that packet radios have access to information that would be unavailable in other networks. Specifically, the nodes can overhear the forwarding of packets that they have sent to another node and can overhear packets being sent between other nodes. These overheard transmissions can be used as passive acknowledgments and, if packet headers include information about the distance traveled and the distance yet to go, as sources of routing information.

Packets broadcast by a radio can indicate that they are for a specific node, a group of nodes, or all nodes. The latter two types of transmission can be used to:

- Send network-control traffic to all neighbors (or to the whole network).

- Support algorithms for broadcasting user traffic.

- Request help in getting a packet to its destination when a link fails.

Some packet-radio nodes may be able to adjust various gain parameters (e.g., power, data rate, forward-error-correcting (FEC) code rate) either on a per-packet basis or on a longer time scale. The choice of gain parameters will affect which neighboring nodes can hear a packet transmission and can therefore affect the network capacity.

11.3 DARPA PACKET-RADIO NETWORK

In 1972 the Defense Advanced Research Projects Agency (DARPA) initiated a packet-radio program. It was based on the (then) recent development of inexpensive VLSI chips, surface acoustic-wave devices that could be used in spread-spectrum signaling, and packet switching. The goal of the program was to explore the use of packet radios as an easy-to-deploy tactical data-communications network.[8]

By 1983, the packet-radio network program had developed a number of spread-spectrum packet radios that could automatically configure themselves into a packet-switching network. Algorithms included channel-access protocols, link-layer protocols for monitoring link performance, adapting the link-data rate, and retransmitting packets on a hop-by-hop basis, and network routing and management strategies.[9,49] In 1983 DARPA established a successor to the packet-radio program which it called the Survivable Adaptive Networks (SURAN) program. The goals of the SURAN program were to extend the algorithms developed in the packet-radio network program, to support large (thousands of nodes) networks, and to develop adaptive network algorithms that could deal with the dynamics expected in a tactical environment.[14]

In parallel with the SURAN program, DARPA initiated a program to develop LPRs that could operate in noisy environments that might include jammers. The LPRs developed employ several techniques to diminish bit-error rates in these circumstances.[52,64] These techniques include using spread-spectrum signaling, multiple transmission rates (100 and 400 kbps), and *forward error correcting* (FEC) codes (with rates of 1/2, 3/4, 7/8). To reduce interference, each LPR can attenuate its transmissions in four steps of 8 dB. Full power is 5 watts for a nominal range of 10 kilometers.

The spread-spectrum chip sequences are generated with a pseudorandom algorithm that is initialized with a (masked) clock value and a seed value. A receiver must know the spreading sequence before it can decode a packet. A receiver uses the seed value and its current (masked) clock value when it listens to the channel; packets encoded in any other way will be indistinguishable from noise. The mask can be set so that the seed for the spreading sequence changes as frequently as every 5.12 milliseconds.*

The packet-radio hardware supports two modes of packet transmission: *broadcast* and *receiver-directed*. Each packet starts with a preamble, which indicates how the rest of the packet is to be decoded (i.e., data rate, FEC rate, and transmission mode). In broadcast transmissions a seed value known to all radios is used to generate the

---

* The radios maintain synchronization by time stamping packets with an accuracy of approximately 5 microseconds and a "double-ended" protocol that accounts for propagation delay. The radios then adjust their clocks to that of the neighbor that is closest to the packet radio with the lowest ID. These synchronization algorithms are similar to those discussed in references 13 and 63.

spread-spectrum sequence and thus these packets can be received by all neighboring nodes. Broadcast-channel access lets nodes learn about their neighbors by overhearing transmissions and facilitates rapid updating of routing tables.

The seed used in spreading a receiver-directed transmission is unique to the radio to which the packet is being sent. If the preamble indicates that the packet is receiver-directed then each radio receiving it uses its unique seed to generate the spread-spectrum sequence for decoding the packet. If the packet is not destined for that node then the radio will lose bit synchronization and be free to receive another packet. This phenomenon prevents nodes from wasting time receiving packets that they must later discard and gives them more time to receive packets they will keep, which in turn reduces the retransmission rate and increases effective channel capacity.

11.4 ROUTING ALGORITHMS FOR SMALL TO MEDIUM-SIZED NETWORKS

11.4.1 Routing Overview

The general goal of routing in datagram networks is to get packets reliably from the source to the destination while maximizing the capacity of the network to carry user traffic and minimizing the delay experienced by the packets. "Optimal" routing algorithms that maximize capacity or minimize delay typically need an estimate of the network flows (the amount of traffic to be carried from each source to each destination), fixed topology, information about the "incremental delay" or the "residual capacity" of links or paths, and need to assume that these metrics are only a function of the traffic carried on that link or path.[20] Applying these algorithms in packet-radio networks is difficult because:

- Information about network flows is typically *not* available in datagram networks.

- Network topology can vary rapidly.

- Incremental delay and residual capacity change more quickly than the physical topology, increasing routing overhead.

- Even if a radio generates timely routing information that reflects changes in delay and capacity, the delay incurred in getting that information throughout the network may be such that the information is stale by the time it reaches a distant node.

- The incremental delay and residual capacity of a link are affected by the traffic being carried on other links.

As an example of this last issue, consider a stream of traffic flowing from node D to node G along the route D–E–F–G in Figure 11.2. Assume that the route has a capacity of c bits per second. Now consider another stream of traffic flowing from node H to node K along the route H–I–J–K. Transmission by the nodes along these two routes will interfere with each other and reduce the capacity of each route to fewer than c bits per second.

For these reasons it is not currently feasible to implement packet-radio routing algorithms that attempt to directly minimize delay or to maximize capacity. Many packet-radio routing algorithms can be viewed as having the (slightly) simpler goals of efficiency and reliability. Routing algorithms can thus be differentiated by the metric they use to define "efficiency."

In most networks minimum-hop routing is efficient, for it computes routes that use the fewest network resources (because each route traverses the fewest nodes and links possible). This result does not necessarily apply in packet-radio networks. For example, consider two streams of traffic that must flow from D to G and from H to K. The minimum-hop routes are D–E–F–G (3 hops) and H–I–J–K (3 hops), but transmissions by the nodes along these two routes will interfere with each other and retransmissions will be required to forward packets between nodes. If the traffic were routed along the paths D–A–B–C–G (4 hops) and H–L–M–N–K (4 hops) then there would be no interference and no contention-based retransmission. These longer routes will use fewer network resources if the average number of transmissions required to forward a packet on the minimum-hop route is greater than $4/3$. Although minimum-hop routing is not necessarily efficient, it is well understood and has been used as the foundation for several packet-radio routing algorithms.

Alternative metrics have been proposed for routing:

- *Least-interference routing (LIR) algorithm*[47]   Computes minimum-cost routes where the cost of a link is the number of other packet radios that overhear the transmission (i.e., which could be subject to interference). This metric is independent of the traffic and only neighbor connectivity information (which is already available) is needed. The LIR route from D to G is via A–B–C.

- *Maximum–minimum residual capacity routing (MMRCR) algorithm*[1]   Selects minimum-cost routes where the cost of using a link is a traffic *dependent* metric that reflects the probability of successful transmission and of interference.

- *Least-resistance routing (LRR) algorithm*[39]   Computes minimum-cost routes where the link cost is a quantitative assessment of the interference environment at a radio that accounts for transmissions from other radios and partial-band jamming.

Attempts to improve the reliability of routing include:

- Using many algorithms working at different time scales (see Section 11.4.2).

- Precomputing multiple disjoint paths from a source to a destination, so that link or node failures will cause minimal disruption.[36]

- Ensuring that topology changes do not cause route loops.[21,42]

Once an objective has been selected, routing algorithms can be further subdivided based on how the routes are computed. Alternatives include (1) centralized (one node computes the routes and distributes them to the other nodes), (2) decentralized (each node computes routes for itself using information about the topology of the network), and (3) distributed (the nodes cooperate to compute routes without any node having information about the overall network topology). The main problems with centralized routing are the complexity required to provide a hot standby (in case the routing node fails) and the delay in adapting to changes in topology (each node must wait for an update from the central server when a route fails).

The decentralized algorithm (also known as link state and discussed in Chapter 5 of this volume) works by having each node determine its own connectivity and then flooding this link-state information to all other nodes in the network. These link-state updates provide the other nodes with the information needed to determine the packet-radio network topology and to compute routes to each destination.

The distributed algorithm (also known as distance vector and discussed in Chapter 3 of this volume) works by having each node broadcast information about the shortest distances it knows to destinations in the network. Radios receiving this broadcast can then determine the distance to each destination via each neighbor and select the shortest route (which is then broadcast to its neighbors).

The relative merits of decentralized and distributed algorithms are discussed in reference 16. Briefly, the differences are:

- The basic distance-vector algorithm needs several iterations to converge, can have problems with route loops when path lengths increase, and can take a long time to detect that destinations are unreachable. Modifications to the distance-vector algorithm to ameliorate or eliminate these problems have been developed[22,27,50] but have not yet been implemented in packet-radio networks.

- The link-state algorithm can be made robust against misbehaving nodes by digitally signing the link-state updates.[68] The distance-vector algorithm cannot, because the computations are distributed (though see reference 67 for algorithms to detect some problems).

- The link-state algorithm gives each node a topological map of the network, so that when a link fails, an alternative path can be generated rapidly. Efficient algorithms have been developed that allow distance-vector routing to compute one alternate path,[36,37] but not without major modifications to the basic algorithm.

- A pure link-state algorithm generates more traffic than a pure distance-vector routing algorithm, but the overhead of most real algorithms is protocol dependent and must be analyzed case by case.

11.4.2 Routing Overhead

Bandwidth is such a scarce resource that the overhead of the link-state and distance-vector routing algorithms are of interest. Versions of the algorithms that send updates periodically are of most interest in packet-radio networks for three reasons:

- They produce a known amount of traffic regardless of network dynamics (not true for algorithms that are event driven).

- The shared radio channel provides a foundation for relatively inexpensive (though unreliable) broadcast of routing updates. These broadcast algorithms are made reliable by periodic transmission of routing information.

- The need to determine connectivity means that radios must broadcast packets periodically. The routing algorithm can "piggyback" information into these packets or the connectivity algorithm can use the periodically broadcast routing updates to help determine link quality.

In the following analysis we consider two simple routing protocols that were considered for use in the DARPA packet-radio network and which have been used elsewhere. First, a few definitions:

- N is the number of nodes in the network.

- K is the average number of neighbors each packet radio has.

- L is the average link lifetime.

- T is the time between routing updates.

In the distance-vector algorithm, nodes broadcast a routing packet periodically; this packet includes information about the distances to all known destinations in the packet-radio network. The distance-vector routing update will thus have N entries. If the entries in the update are sorted by distance, then the distance to each entry will either be the same as the previous entry or one greater; a one-bit flag suffices to distinguish the cases.

In the periodic version of the link-state algorithm the latest link-state updates are "bundled" into a few packets* that are transmitted every T seconds. This approach

---

* The DARPA LPR uses an 8086 processor, which introduces significant per-packet processing delay. This slowness leads to an interest in algorithms which minimize the number of packets rather than those which minimize the number of bits.

slowly floods the updates across the network. Each link-state update includes the node ID of the original sender, a sequence number (so that the latest update can be identified), and a list of the neighbor packet radios.

A thousand-node packet-radio network is quite large, and so we'll assume that packet-radio IDs are only 10-bit IDs. The sequence number in the link-state updates needs to distinguish between current and old updates. A 16-bit sequence number is a conservative choice. The routing information is thus:

- *Distance vector* $(10 + 1)N = 11N$ bits

- *Link state* $[(10 + 16) + 10K] N = 26N + 10KN$ bits

Link-state routing thus takes $(26 + 10K)/11$ times more data per period per node than distance-vector routing. For low connectivity ($K = 3$), this is a factor of 5.09; for high connectivity ($K = 10$), this is a factor of 11.45. Thus a straightforward implementation of link state generates significantly more traffic than the distance-vector algorithm.

A modification that can significantly reduce the overhead of link-state routing is *incremental updating*, wherein nodes send only data that have changed. Sequence numbers are incremented only when connectivity changes; neighbors are listed in an update only if their connectivity has changed. Updates include the most recent sequence number of each node in the network and any changes in connectivity. Incremental updates require a protocol for updating nodes which are entering the network or which have missed updates. One approach is for nodes that notice they are out of date to request a full update from a neighboring node.

On average the number of link changes in a routing update will be $(KN/L)T$. The amount of data to be sent in a link-state routing packet is thus $26N + 10N(KT/L)$ bits. The ratio between incremental link-state routing and distance-vector routing is thus $(26 + KT/L)/11$. Table 11.1 tabulates this ratio for a wide range of connectivities and link lifetimes, with $T = 7.5$ seconds; it is typically less than 2.5.

Table 12.1   Incremental link-state versus distance-vector overhead

	L		
K	**30 seconds**	**2 minutes**	**10 minutes**
4	2.45	2.39	2.37
8	2.55	2.41	2.37
16	2.72	2.45	2.38

The link-state algorithm analyzed has more routing overhead than the distance-vector algorithm. Because the link-state algorithm can determine new routes more quickly than the distance-vector algorithm it is likely to require fewer end-to-end packet retransmissions (which occur when packets are dropped and a reliable end-to-end protocol is being used) and may therefore lead to a net reduction in network traffic. Recent studies of distance-vector algorithms that are loop free indicate that the amount of traffic generated by those algorithms is comparable to that of the link-state algorithm. Whether the advantages of the link-state algorithm (ease in computing alternate routes, robustness, responsiveness) outweigh the disadvantages (complexity, higher overhead) depends on the network and the design criteria.

11.4.3 DARPA Packet Radio

The DARPA packet-radio project initially used centralized routing,[8] but interest in robustness led to a decision to change to a different algorithm. The packet-radio project investigated using link-state and distance-vector routing and decided to use distance-vector routing for two reasons. First, distance-vector routing requires less bandwidth, and second, the ARPANET had recently switched from using distance-vector to using link-state, and DARPA was interested in seeing how well the distance-vector algorithm could be made to work.

The general approach in the packet-radio project in dealing with the issues of low bandwidth and rapid dynamics was: (1) take advantage of the broadcast nature of radio transmissions whenever possible to reduce the communications requirements, and (2) use multiple mechanisms that are complementary (e.g., a "slow" distance-vector routing algorithm, and "fast" alternate-path routing algorithms).

The packet-radio protocols circa 1985 are documented in references 28 and 30. Between 1985 and 1991, several significant extensions to these algorithms were incorporated. No general survey of these enhancements is available. A detailed specification of the algorithms is given in reference 70; reference 26 discusses one of the extensions known as "multiclass routing." In this section we review the basic algorithms and protocols that were implemented and tested in the LPRs, describe some of the enhancements to these algorithms, and describe some of the issues that were encountered in implementing these changes. These algorithms use only the broadcast mode of packet transmission and don't vary the FEC code rate or transmission power.

11.4.3.1 Basic Packet-Radio Routing

Tier Routing

Packet radios broadcast a PROP (*packet-radio organization packet*) every 7.5 seconds; they determine which radios can hear each other, identify the quality of the link between them, and exchange routing information. The packet radios use distance-vector routing to compute minimum-hop paths between themselves and all the other packet radios. Each node maintains the routing information in a tier table (hence the distance-vector algorithm is sometimes known as the *tier routing* algorithm), which includes this information for every other packet radio in the network:

- Destination packet radio.

- The next packet radio on the route to the destination.

- The number of hops to the destination (tier level).

- Whether the route is good (includes no poor-quality links) or bad (has some poor-quality links).

A PROP includes this routing information:

- A list of neighbors.

- A list of reachable destinations in the network for which a good route is known and the distances to them.

- A list of destinations in the network for which no good route is known.

A packet radio derives tier information in this way:

- It puts all its neighbors in the tier table at one hop away.

- The neighbors in a received PROP are considered two hops away unless they are also neighbors of this packet radio. The neighbor that transmitted the PROP is the next packet radio, also known as the *reporting packet radio*.

- Other destinations reported in a PROP are considered to be at one greater than the reported distance. The neighbor packet radio that transmitted the PROP is the next packet radio, or reporting packet radio.

If a PROP reports a good route to a destination, a packet radio will update its tier table to that destination if:

- No information is stored for the destination packet radio.

- The route to the destination is marked *bad* and that route has been reported in a PROP at least once.

- The new tier level is less than the stored tier level.

- The route to that destination is received from the reporting packet radio for that destination. The tier level will be updated even if it is greater than the current entry.

A route to a destination will be marked *bad* if:

- A PROP with a bad route to that destination is received from the reporting packet radio for that destination.

Figure 11.3 Tier-route loop formation

- The link goes down to the neighbor who is stored in the tier table as the reporting packet radio for that destination.

The requirement that a node report bad information in a PROP before accepting a new route is a form of holddown that is used in many distance-vector algorithms to reduce the chances of forming route loops.[15] Figure 11.3 illustrates how route loops can form. Node B has a route to destination node D, which is 2 hops long. Node A has a 3-hop path to node D via node B (i.e., node B is A's next packet radio to destination D). If the link between B and C fails and B accepts a route from A before reporting that its route has failed, then B will think it has a 4-hop route to node D. In turn, when A receives a PROP from node B, it will think it has a 5-hop route to node D via node B. This route loop will persist with the hop count incrementing upward until another route looks shorter. If no route to the destination exists, the hop count will continue incrementing until it reaches a maximum value, which is taken to indicate that the destination is unreachable.

A holddown reduces the chance of route loops by requiring that bad routes be reported before new routes are accepted. In Figure 11.3 if the failed route to D is reported by B to A, then A's PROP will not include a good route to D and B will not enter a route loop. However, PROPs are transmitted over an unreliable channel and neighbors may be receiving other packets when a PROP is transmitted. In this case the information about the failed route is not received and route loops will form.

Link-Layer Protocol

The DARPA packet radios use link-by-link acknowledgments because the channels are unreliable. When a packet radio transmits a packet to the next radio on the route to the destination, it waits for an acknowledgment that the packet was received. If the radio overhears the packet being forwarded, the radio is said to have received a passive acknowledgment. An active acknowledgment (consisting of only the packet routing header) is transmitted by the final destination packet radio.

A packet is retransmitted until an acknowledgment is received, or the packet has been retransmitted six times. The packet is discarded if an acknowledgment is still not received. If the passive acknowledgment is missed, the packet will be erroneously retransmitted. Then the receiving packet radio must generate an active acknowledgment because the packet will not be forwarded (and thus no passive acknowledgment will be generated).

Only one outstanding (unacknowledged) packet is allowed per neighbor. That is, the link-layer protocol has a per neighbor window size of one.

Alternate-Path Routing

The DARPA packet-radio network takes advantage of the fact that packets are broadcast and thus are typically heard by multiple radios. If the link-layer protocol fails to deliver a packet to a neighbor, the transmitting radio will set flags in the packet header that request any node closer to the destination to accept it. Because this mechanism causes the packet to take an "alternate" route to the destination, this procedure is called *alternate routing*.

The alternate-routing mechanism works as follows. If an acknowledgment is not received after three transmissions, the packet is retransmitted with the alternate-route request flag set in the packet header. A neighbor receiving a packet with the alternate-routing request flag set will forward the received packet as long as its distance to the destination is less than or equal to the packet's "hops-to-go" field. When it forwards the packet its transmission provides a passive acknowledgment to the packet radio requesting alternate routing help.

A radio accepts a packet as an acknowledgment if it meets two criteria:

- The packet must be a duplicate of one already transmitted (i.e., the source and sequence number match that of a packet previously transmitted).

- There must be an indication that the packet has been received by a node closer to the destination. This condition could be indicated by:
    - The packet was sent by the next packet radio on the route to the destination.
    - The packet came from this packet radio (i.e., the previous PR field in the packet is this packet radio).
    - The packet was sent by a radio that thinks it is closer to the destination (the "hops-to-go" field is smaller than this radio's tier entry).

Duplicate transmissions may occur if a packet radio retransmits a packet before the receiving packet radio has forwarded the packet, if the transmitting packet radio misses the acknowledgment from the receiving packet radio, or if alternate routing is being used. The routing header of a newly received packet is compared with the routing headers of packets to be transmitted and of packets that have been acknowledged. The newly received packet is discarded if any matches occur; an active acknowledgment is generated if needed.

The routing algorithm does not distinguish between packets with different type-of-service requirements. Two mechanisms, however, are used to help ensure that real-time traffic (e.g., voice traffic) is not delayed. Traffic that is marked as real-time is not delayed as long by the congestion-control algorithm[55] and alternate routing is invoked earlier (after one retransmission).[41] These mechanisms attempt to ensure that packets reach their destination quickly.

Updating from Traffic

PROPs are transmitted only once every 7.5 seconds and thus are a relatively slow mechanism for routing. The packet radios augment the PROP-based tier routing by updating their routing tables from traffic based on information in the routing headers put on user packets. Each header includes (among other things) the source and destination of the packet, the number of hops traveled, and the number of hops remaining to the destination.

When a node receives a packet (whether or not it is for that packet radio) it can use the information in the header to update its routing-table entries to the source of the packet and to the destination of the packet. The radio that transmitted the packet is treated as if it had sent a PROP and the source and destination (and associated hop counts) are treated as if they were PROP entries. Updating to the source is not done if:

- The packet was ever received over a bad link.

- The packet was received from a radio that is not a good neighbor.

- The packet was originally sent by this radio.

Updating to the destination is not done if:

- The packet was received from a radio that is not a good neighbor.

- The packet was originally sent by this radio.

- The packet is a retransmission (which might indicate that the packet is being forwarded over a poor-quality link).

11.4.3.2 Extensions

Propagating Information about Bad Routes

The tier routing algorithm uses a holddown approach to minimize the formation of route loops. Bad information (routes getting longer or going away) must be reported to neighbors before a good route can be accepted from a neighbor. Because it is desirable to find new routes quickly, the original version of the algorithm required that the bad information be reported in only one PROP before a new route could be accepted. This decision meant, however, that if the one PROP including the information about the bad route was not received by a neighbor, route loops would be formed. Increasing the number of times PROPs must be used to report the bad route would reduce the chance of route loops forming, but would also slow finding new routes.

Because reporting tier data in the routing header of a transmitted packet is the same as reporting that information in a PROP, the routing algorithm was modified to require packet radios to report bad information three times (rather than one) but to allow packet radios to count transmissions of packets with routing headers that include the bad information.

Multiclass Routing

The basic DARPA packet-radio routing algorithm does not use a route unless *all* links in the route have confirmed bidirectional connectivity. Becuase it can take tens of seconds to establish bidirectional connectivity (several PROPs must be exchanged), this approach slowed, and in some cases prevented, nodes in the network from being able to route traffic under dynamic conditions.

The multiclass routing algorithm generates *unconfirmed* routes, which include links that are coming up. These unconfirmed routes are used until a confirmed route is available. The multiclass routing algorithm has three classes of routes: first class (confirmed), second class (unconfirmed), and *marked for erasure*. Routes that are marked for erasure have one or more of the links along the route being deleted from the network.

This extension modifies the route-selection rules: a first-class route of any length is preferred to a shorter second-class route. If neighbors report routes of the same class to the same destination, then the route with the smaller hop count is selected. The tier holddown mechanism (bad routes must be reported three times before a new route can be accepted) is extended so that whenever a route changes to a less preferred class, the tier data must be reported three times before the route status is allowed to be changed again. When a route is marked for erasure, each packet radio must report that route's status three times before deleting it from the tier table or replacing it with another route.

Event-Driven Updates

When a link between two packet radios goes down, any delay in reporting this information will increase the chances of route loops and lost traffic. Although the modified routing algorithm that propagates information about bad routes speeds up notification, it depends on the rate at which user traffic is transmitted. Because user traffic is subject to congestion-control mechanisms, there may be substantial delay in propagating information about bad routes. The solution implemented involves modifying how active acknowledgments are generated.

In the basic packet-radio algorithms, when a radio loses its link to a neighbor (and thus to some destinations) and then receives a packet for one of the unreachable destinations, the packet radio transmits an active acknowledgment with a routing header indicating that the route to the destination has failed. Each packet radio that overhears the acknowledgment and has that radio as the reporting packet radio for that destination will mark the route to be erased.

This extension modifies active acknowledgment processing to allow rapid propagation of routing information. This extension has three components.

- If a packet radio receives an active acknowledgment from its reporting packet radio indicating that a route has failed, it is required to broadcast an active acknowledgment indicating the route has failed and then to mark the route "to be erased." (If the transmitting radio is not the reporting packet radio for that destination, then the active acknowledgment is ignored.)

- A packet radio that has reported a route as being bad three times (either in active acknowledgments or in PROPs) requests a new route to that destination from its neighbors by setting a flag in the routing header of any packet it transmits (forwards) toward that destination.

- Packet radios with a good route to a destination respond to requests for a new route by reporting their good route in an active acknowledgment.

Because active acknowledgments are not subject to congestion-control mechanisms, the information about the failed route will spread rapidly to all packet radios that are routing to that destination through the failed link. Packet radios use a failed route until it is deleted or replaced with a good route, and so a packet radio with a failed link will rapidly generate three waves of active acknowledgments (a wave will be launched when the packet radio receives new packets or retransmissions of old packets for the unreachable destination). Once the affected packet radios have reported the data about the failed route three times, they set a bit in the routing header of the next packet to be forwarded to that destination to request a new route. Any packet radio that overhears a request and has a good route to the destination generates an active acknowledgment including the information about the new route. The information about the good route floods back to the affected packet radios, repairing the failed route.

Figure 11.4 illustrates how this extension works. In diagram 11.4a the next hop to destination D for each packet radio is indicated by the solid arrow. When the link between A and B fails and A receives a packet for D, it broadcasts an active acknowledgment that causes other active acknowledgments marking the route *bad* to be generated (these flow along the dotted lines). Once the failed route has been reported three times, information about good routes flows along the dotted lines in diagram 11.4b, generating the routes indicated by the solid arrows.

Any packet radio that does not have the failed route in its tier table is unaffected by this "controlled flood" of tier data. Because a node generates an active acknowledgment only when its reporting packet radio for that destination sends an active acknowledgment, a link failure causes three active acknowledgments to be sent by each affected node.

The use of active acknowledgments rapidly spreads the tier data about the failed route, which reduces the chance for growing tier data and route loops to occur. By using active acknowledgments to spread the tier data (indicating a route failure) and to spread the new route (which replaces the failed route), the entire procedure can be

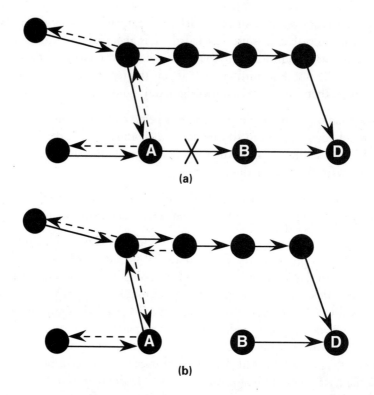

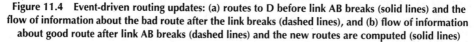

Figure 11.4   Event-driven routing updates: (a) routes to D before link AB breaks (solid lines) and the flow of information about the bad route after the link breaks (dashed lines), and (b) flow of information about good route after link AB breaks (dashed lines) and the new routes are computed (solid lines)

completed in less than a second rather than tens of seconds using the previous routing algorithms.

One danger of event-driven routing updates is the risk of congesting the network with these updates if connectivity changes rapidly. In the current SURAN protocol it takes several PROP periods or several failed packet transmissions to change a neighbor status, limiting the frequency of these updates. If the link-up/down protocol were modified to allow rapid changes in neighbor status (e.g., by measuring signal strength), then other ways of minimizing the effects of these event-driven route updates would need to be considered (e.g., collecting route updates for some minimal time before transmitting them).

A second danger of event-driven routing updates is that they may expose the network to denial-of-service attacks: if an enemy can cause a condition in which radios are forced to generate updates frequently (which in turn forces their neighbors to generate updates) the network could become so congested that it would affect user traffic. Further analysis is required to determine if defenses against this attack can be devised.

11.4.3.3 Interactions and Complexities

The multiple routing algorithms have the benefit of providing mechanisms which operate at different time scales and which take advantage of the different kinds of information available. These multiple algorithms mean, however, that many interactions can occur. The following examples indicate the kinds of issues that arise.

Interactions between Tier and Overheard Routing

When a packet radio that is receiving traffic becomes unreachable, packets to that destination will be alternate routed. These alternate-routed packets may have been received when the route to the destination was good. If the routing information to be included in the header is determined when the packet is received, then the packets will include out-of-date routing information when transmitted. Packet radios receiving these packets will mark routes good when they are really bad. Thus each packet radio must, just before transmitting any packet, update the routing data in that header to match the current routing data.

Routing vs. Duplicate Filtering

Nodes attempt to identify and filter out duplicate packets (which may have been generated by alternate routing or by unnecessary retransmissions). In the basic version of the tier algorithm, duplicates are defined as packets with the same source ID and sequence number. The extensions above mean that if a link fails and a route changes, packets may be routed back through nodes that have already transmitted them. It is thus necessary to ensure that duplicate filtering is not done solely on source ID and sequence number: the "next-hop" destination of the transmission is also used.

Partitioned Networks

If there are no good routes to a destination (e.g., the destination has failed or the network has partitioned) then packet radios will continue to send active acknowledgments indicating a failed route until the destination is erased from the tier data tables (a minimum of seven PROP periods). To stop these packets from congesting the network, packet radios are limited to advertising a failed route in only six active acknowledgments.

11.5 LARGE-NETWORK ROUTING ALGORITHMS

11.5.1 Large Networks

Large multihop shared-channel packet-radio networks have a problem: the bandwidth available to an end user *decreases* as the number of nodes in the network increases. If the number of nodes in the network (N) is increased, while the density of packet-radio nodes (nodes per square mile) is held constant, then the average number of hops between nodes will increase as $N^{1/2}$. Because the network bandwidth increases as N, the bandwidth available to each user (assuming a uniform traffic pattern) decreases as $N^{1/2}$.

In large wireline networks, *backbone* links, which carry traffic long distances in one hop, can be installed to ensure that route lengths grow slowly with network size. Shared-channel packet-radio networks cannot use this strategy, for their links are limited to the range of their radio transmission. Large packet-radio networks may interest military users for whom ease of deployment is paramount or users with mainly local traffic (in which case a large packet-radio network is almost a set of independent small networks).

The protocols discussed in Section 11.4 are not directly extensible to very large networks. Periodic transmission of updates means that routing information is forwarded one hop approximately every $T/2$ seconds, where T is the time between routing transmissions. The time for information to cross the network grows as $N^{1/2}$ and thus, if the delay in receiving information is to be constant as the network grows, T must decrease as $N^{1/2}$. This condition is not feasible because it would generate too many updates. Event-driven updates do not solve the problem, either. Consider link-state routing in a network with N nodes, connectivity K, and an average link lifetime of L. The routing information required to keep each node up to date is proportional to $N\lambda$, where λ is the rate at which the network topology changes (NK/L). Thus the routing information required is proportional to N^2. The network bandwidth grows linearly with network size, implying an upper bound to the size a network can reach before all the bandwidth is dedicated to distributing routing information.

These problems can be addressed in a variety of ways:

- Hide details of faraway parts of the network. This approach takes advantage of the observation that the next hop in a route is likely to depend only on the region of the network where the destination is located. Hierarchical algorithms are based on this observation.

- Send out information about faraway parts of the network less frequently.[29] This approach is similar to the previous approach and is based on the observation that the next hop in a route is unlikely to change dramatically because of topology changes in faraway parts of the network. Up-to-date information is used to forward the packet when it gets near the destination. The *prioritized tier connectivity information exchange algorithm* is based on this approach.

- Send information only to the nodes that need it. If a change in topology makes a route only a little suboptimal, then information about that change is not sent out. The *threshold distance vector routing algorithm* is based on this approach.

11.5.2 Hierarchic Algorithms

Hierarchic algorithms work by hiding details of the network's topology.[32,43,44] This concealing is done by aggregating nodes into clusters and clusters into superclusters, and so on.* The hierarchical address of a node is given by its membership in a cluster and supercluster, and can be written as supercluster.cluster.node. Routing decisions are based on the addresses of the destination and the node that is forwarding the packet. If they belong to different superclusters, then forwarding will be done with an intersupercluster route; if they belong to the same supercluster but to different clusters, forwarding will be done using intercluster routes; if they belong to the same cluster, forwarding will be done using intracluster routes. Routing to a packet radio in a hierarchic network thus requires that the source node be able to determine the hierarchic address of the destination.

Hierarchic algorithms thus require a description of how:

- Clusters and superclusters are generated.

- The address of the destination node is determined.

- Routes are computed.

- Packets are forwarded.

In wireline networks the hierarchy is defined administratively and is relatively static. This approach does not work in packet-radio networks, for nodes may be highly dynamic: nodes that are now neighbors (and in the same cluster) may later be very far apart (and need to be in different clusters). Thus in packet-radio networks the hierarchy must be dynamically defined. The easiest way to generate (super)clusters is to elect (super)clusterheads and have nodes join the nearest (super)clusterhead. Election algorithms will depend on the information available to the nodes: they are easier to devise if the link-state routing algorithm is used for intracluster routing and harder to devise if distance-vector routing is used.

In wireline networks the hierarchic address of a node is relatively static. This condition does not occur in packet-radio networks and thus determining the address of the destination node is more difficult in packet-radio networks than in wireline

---

* For simplicity, only clusters and superclusters are used in examples.

networks. The fundamental problem is that hierarchic routing attempts to reduce traffic by hiding information about the contents of (super)clusters but address determination requires that any node be able to determine which nodes are in a (super)cluster.

All approaches to determining addresses require that some nodes (address servers) keep track of the address of specific nodes and that any node be able to find the appropriate address server. Reference 35 considers a single-level hierarchy (clusters only) where there is one address server per cluster and address servers keep track of the membership of their cluster. Three schemes for determining an address are analyzed:

1   An address server sends a query to other address servers to determine if the destination is in that cluster.

2   Address servers send updates to other address servers when the membership of their cluster changes.

3   A modification of scheme 1 in which information about a cluster's membership is returned along with an answer to a query and cached for future use.

Reference 48 analyzes an address service that involves all the nodes in the network and works as follows. Node X takes its own ID (X) and applies a hashing algorithm to it to generate a hierarchical address (e.g., A(X).B(X).C(X)). X then sends a message to A.B.C that includes its own hierarchical address (e.g., V.W.X). Node A.B.C now acts as the address server for X. Any other node in the network can use the same hashing algorithm to determine that A.B.C knows X's address and send a query to A.B.C to determine X's address. Because there may be no node A.B.C, the routing algorithm in reference 48 is modified so that packets will be sent to the "nearest" address that does exist.

Hierarchical routing algorithms can be divided into quasi-hierarchic and strict hierarchic approaches.[17,18] The quasi-hierarchic approach routes the packet along the shortest path to the destination supercluster; once in the destination supercluster, on the shortest path to the cluster; once in the destination cluster, on the shortest path to the destination node. Strict hierarchic routing has the packet routed from the source supercluster through a sequence of intermediate superclusters (determined by the intersupercluster routing algorithm) to the destination supercluster; in each supercluster the packet is routed through a sequence of intermediate clusters (determined by the intercluster routing algorithm) to the next supercluster; in each cluster the packet is routed by the shortest path to the next cluster. When the packet arrives in the destination supercluster, the packet is routed to the destination cluster and then to the destination node. Figure 11.5 sketches the different routes generated by the two algorithms.

Reference 34 discusses the theoretical performance of various hierarchical algorithms (quasi-hierarchic and strict hierarchic, timer based and event driven) in more

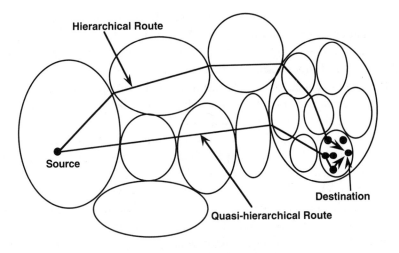

Figure 11.5 **Hierarchical and quasi-hierarchical routes**

detail. References 23 and 24 analyze the optimality of path lengths and the time it takes to attain consistent routes in all the nodes.

11.5.2.1 *Quasi-Hierarchic*

The *quasi-hierarchic algorithm* is an extension of the tier-routing algorithm. Each packet radio broadcasts a routing update (PROP) including its shortest path to other packet radios in its cluster, to other clusters in its supercluster, and to other superclusters in the network. Using this information, each packet-radio node calculates the minimum distance and required next packet-radio node for the optimal route to each cluster in its supercluster, and to each supercluster.

Different versions of this algorithm are possible depending on how the distance computation is initialized. The initialization occurs when a *border* packet radio receives a PROP from a neighbor in another cluster or supercluster. One algorithm results from having packet radios report neighboring (super)clusters as *one* hop away. In this case each PR's path to a (super)cluster is the shortest path to the border of that cluster. A different algorithm results from having border packet radios report neighboring clusters as S hops away, where S is the average distance from the border packet radio to the members of the (super)cluster. In this case each PR's path to a (super)cluster minimizes the sum of the distance to the cluster border plus the average distance from the border to the members of the cluster.

Although this algorithm does not give the exact minimum route to any particular packet-radio unit in the destination cluster or supercluster, reference 31 shows that, as the network size and number of hierarchical levels increase, this method produces routes that are very close in average length to those produced by flat routing.

This algorithm requires each node to periodically broadcast a routing update to its neighbors. The size of the routing update is approximately $N_1 + N_2 + N_3$, where N_1 is the number of nodes in a cluster, N_2 is the number of clusters in a supercluster, and N_3 is the number of superclusters in the network.

The primary advantage of this algorithm is its simplicity. Although protocols are needed for determining cluster and supercluster membership, no extra protocol is needed for calculating and disseminating intercluster and intersupercluster routes.

The biggest disadvantage with the quasi-hierarchical approach is its poor response to network dynamics. This poor response is a result of three specific problems: (1) a small change in network topology can result in changes to the routing calculations throughout the packet-radio network (i.e., changes overpropagate), (2) long-distance propagation of changes can take a long time, and (3) bad news (such as a link going down) can require several iterations before stable routes are computed.

These problems can result in the algorithm requiring a long time to reach stable, consistent routes, or, if the network is sufficiently dynamic, in never reaching stable, consistent routes. For example, consider a 1000-node network with a diameter of 20 hops where routing updates are transmitted every 7.5 seconds. In this network, it could take more than a minute for a change to be reflected throughout the network. If this network has an average connectivity of 10, and thus includes 5000 duplex links, and if each link goes up or down once an hour, then more than a hundred changes will be in progress at any one time.

Although we have focused on timer-driven implementations of quasi-hierarchic routing, an event-driven version can be developed.[40] Link-state versions of this algorithm do not appear attractive, for they generate significantly more traffic.

11.5.2.2   Strict Hierarchic

In *strict-hierarchic routing*, clusters have special nodes, known as *clusterheads*, which cooperate to compute hierarchic routing tables (HRTs).* HRTs specify the next cluster that a packet should traverse to reach a given destination cluster. Clusterheads distribute this information to the packet radios in their clusters. Packets are delivered to a destination by forwarding the packet toward the cluster specified in the HRT for that destination cluster; once the packet reaches the destination cluster it is forwarded to the destination packet radio using a nonhierarchic routing algorithm.

Routing within a cluster is done using either a link-state or distance-vector algorithm. The intracluster routing algorithm is used to determine routes to nodes in the cluster as well as to neighbor clusters. Clusterheads compute HRTs by using either a link-state or distance-vector routing algorithm where the clusters are treated as nodes

---

*   For simplicity, a two-level hierarchy consisting of packet radios and clusters is discussed in this section.

and the links are determined by which clusters are neighbors (i.e., have packet radios that are neighbors). Event-driven routing appears attractive for intercluster routing because intercluster connectivity is likely to change slowly (and thus little event-driven routing traffic will be generated), but the algorithm reacts quickly when the connectivity changes. The intercluster routing algorithm computes an HRT that lists the next cluster to which a packet should be sent to get to any destination cluster. The HRT is flooded to the packet radios in the cluster.

Strict hierarchic routing saves communications bandwidth by reducing the amount of information that a node needs to make a routing decision. In particular, changes to the topology of a cluster are reported only to the packet radios in that cluster; changes to the intercluster topology are reported to all the packet radios in the network whose HRTs are affected.

The biggest problem with strict hierarchic routing is the central role played by the clusterheads. Although the clusterheads are *not* central to traffic forwarding, they are central to route computation and distribution. Robustness requires that there be a "hot standby" for the clusterhead; protocols for handing off control to the standby clusterhead must be developed and care must be taken to avoid electing clusterheads that have poor connectivity.

11.5.2.3 Landmark

Landmark routing[48] is a variation on quasi-hierarchic routing. Distance-vector routing is used to compute routes to other nodes, with the modification that destinations are dropped from the tier table if they are too many hops away (the number of hops increases with a node's position in the hierarchy). If a node is at the highest level in the hierarchy, it is included in every update (it's a global landmark); nodes at the lowest level in the hierarchy are included only in updates sent by nearby nodes. Each node adopts a higher-level node as its "parent" (except the highest-level nodes). The address of a node is a sequence of landmarks, starting with a global landmark and ending with the node's parent. Routing is done by forwarding the packet to the lowest-level landmark that is visible to the forwarding node.

The advantages and disadvantages of this approach are similar to those of the quasi-hierarchic approach. Reference 48 proposes using a modified distance-vector routing algorithm to eliminate some of the problems with looping. This approach, however, seems to require using a reliable broadcast protocol that does not take advantage of the packet-radio channel.

Landmark routing does have a unique advantage. It intrinsically generates overlapping clusters: a node will generally have more than one choice for parent. If a parent node fails (or resigns as a landmark), affected nodes can quickly affiliate themselves with another landmark.

11.5.3   Nonhierarchic Algorithms

In the next two sections we discuss approaches to reducing the routing traffic associated with tier routing in large networks. The two alternatives are to send routing information less frequently or to send it to fewer nodes.

11.5.3.1   Prioritized Tier Connectivity Information Exchange

The *prioritized tier connectivity information exchange algorithm*[46] classifies routes to destinations into different priority levels based upon the type of change experienced by that route and the length of time since it was last reported. In each reporting period a single distance-vector routing update is transmitted. The highest-priority information is transmitted in each reporting period. Nonchanging (low-priority) information is reported over multiple reporting periods, thus supporting larger networks without an increase in routing traffic.

Because only one update is sent in each period, packet radios entering a network may have to wait multiple reporting periods to obtain full routing information. This wait, though, is better than the performance of distance-vector routing algorithms that simply drop information that does not fit in a routing update. Once all packet radios have obtained full routing information, then, as long as the priority types corresponding to information that has changed fit in a routing update, the performance of the prioritized tier connectivity information exchange algorithm will be the same as if all connectivity information were sent in each reporting period.

11.5.3.2   Threshold Distance-Vector Routing Algorithm

In shortest-path algorithms, a topological change can generate routing updates that propagate across the network, causing excessive overhead in large networks. *Threshold distance-vector routing* (TDVR)[1] reduces the overhead of tier routing by reducing the distance that updates propagate. In TDVR, a node updates its estimated distance d to a destination only if the following bounds are violated:

$$d_j + c_j \leq d \leq d_j + \alpha c_j$$

where j is the next node on the path to the destination and j is chosen to minimize the estimated distance to it, c_j is the cost of using the link to neighbor j, and α is a number greater than one. If d does not satisfy this equation then the node changes d by the smallest amount satisfying the bounds and informs its neighbors of the new value.

For the special case $\alpha = 1$, TDVR reduces to the Bellman-Ford algorithm. As α is increased, fewer update messages are transmitted and path lengths increase slightly. By increasing α when updates are frequent and decreasing α when updates are infrequent, surges in update traffic can be smoothed out.

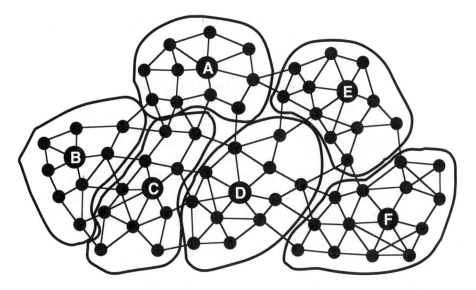

Figure 11.6 Hierarchically organized network

11.5.4 DARPA Packet Radio

11.5.4.1 Strict Hierarchic Routing

After considering alternative hierarchical routing algorithms, the DARPA packet-radio project selected a strict hierarchic algorithm. The reason was that the quasi-hierarchic algorithms might be unstable in highly dynamic networks. Although the hierarchic algorithm was never completely implemented, a detailed design was undertaken, packet-radio code was written, and extensive simulations were performed.* In this section we briefly review the hierarchical algorithm selected and then discuss issues that arose during the detailed design.

Though multilevel hierarchies were considered, a detailed analysis of the issues was undertaken only for two-level hierarchies. The first level of the hierarchy organizes packet radios into clusters; the second level organizes the clusters. Each cluster has a special node known as the clusterhead. Figure 11.6 illustrates a hierarchically organized network with six clusters (A, B, C, D, E, and F). The packet radios are indicated by small black dots, the clusterheads by the larger dots, and the intrapacket-radio links by lines.

---

* Because the LPR uses an 8086 processor, it was possible to implement the LPR operating system on a PC; using expanded memory it was possible to emulate hundreds of packet radios using an 80386.

The intracluster algorithm selected was the existing tier algorithm; the intercluster algorithm chosen was an event-driven link-state algorithm (selected to minimize the intercluster traffic while maximizing responsiveness).

11.5.4.2 *Packet-Radio Dynamics and Multiple-Cluster Membership*

As network connectivity changes, radios need to change clusters (the requirement that radios be able to route directly to all members of their cluster, and the use of tier routing means that clusters must be connected). When a destination packet radio changes clusters, source packet radios sending to it will send the packets to the wrong cluster (the *previous* destination cluster). A packet radio therefore is allowed to participate in the intracluster routing of its previous cluster until a timer expires. The timer value is selected so that most packet radios sending to it will have its new address before the timer expires (the new address will be included in any packets sent back from the destination packet radio to the source packet radio).

Tier routing takes a while to inform a cluster of new members: PROPs are broadcast only every 7.5 seconds, and so new member information can propagate as slowly as 7.5 times the diameter of the cluster. If an address server gives out the new address of a packet radio before all the members of that cluster learn of it, then packets sent to that address may be rejected as mislabeled. A packet radio is thus allowed to participate in the intracluster routing of its *next* cluster so that the nodes in a cluster will learn a route to the joining packet radio before that address is advertised. A packet radio is limited to participating in the routing of at most *two* clusters at a time (the current and either the previous or the next) because (1) a packet radio will generally stay in a cluster for a significant amount of time (and thus this restriction has little effect), (2) it simplifies the algorithm, and (3) it supports larger clusters. (Each PROP sent by a radio must include routes to all the packet radios in all the clusters that the packet radio has joined. Because the PROP size is fixed, clusters can be larger if a packet radio can join only two clusters.)

A cluster partition is undesirable. When a packet radio broadcasts a current cluster, it is claiming that it can deliver packets to any packet radio in that cluster; however, when a cluster partitions, the packet radio cannot fulfill that promise. In addition, it may not be possible to forward intercluster traffic through a partitioned cluster. Because of these problems, a packet radio will leave a cluster as quickly as possible once a partition has been detected (deduced by inability to route to the clusterhead).

A packet radio's cluster membership is represented using the notation **[P|C|N]**, where **P** stands for the previous cluster, **C** stands for the current cluster, and **N** stands for the next cluster. The interpretation of the packet-radio state is as follows:

- **[A|A|A]**   The typical state. The packet radio has been in cluster A for a while and is not planning to leave it.

- **[A|A|B]**   Cluster B is closer and the packet radio is going to join it.

- **[A|B|B]** The packet radio has changed its primary address to cluster B, but is maintaining routes in cluster A until all packet radios know the new address.

The transition rules are:

- **[A|A|A] → [A|A|B]** The route to clusterhead B is shorter than the route to clusterhead A, or the packet radio's route to clusterhead A is marked bad.

- **[A|A|B] → [A|A|A]** The route to A is good and clusterhead A is closer than clusterhead B, or clusterhead B resigns. This condition may occur if a packet radio elected itself as clusterhead B but too few packet radios selected it as their next cluster.

- **[A|A|B] → [A|B|B]** The packet radio has had B as its next cluster long enough for members of B to generate routes to it (indicated by a timer expiring), and the packet radio has received the HRT for cluster B.

- **[A|B|B] → [B|B|B]** All other packet radios know the new address (indicated by a timer expiring).

In nonoverlapping cluster architectures, it is possible for cluster births to disrupt intercluster links (Figure 11.7). For example, the birth of cluster C will take down the link between clusters A and B. This change causes a problem because the new links between A and C and between C and B (needed to forward traffic between clusters A and B) will not be formed until after the intercluster link between A and B has been broken. Thus the change in "logical" network structure could disrupt communication, an undesirable situation.

The cluster architecture discussed above provides a mechanism for avoiding this problem: when cluster C is being formed the packet radios joining it are in both cluster C and their original cluster. The cluster membership of the packet radios can be used to define three types of intercluster links:

- Neighboring packet radios with different previous clusters generate a *previous intercluster link*.

- Neighboring packet radios with different current clusters generate a *current intercluster link*.

- Neighboring packet radios with different next clusters generate a *next intercluster link*.

Thus it is possible to bring up a link between clusters A and C and between C and B before bringing down the link between A and B. The letters P, C, and N are used to denote the type of intercluster link (e.g., a PC link is previous and current). The desirable sequence of events corresponding to Figure 11.7 is:

1 The **A ↔ B** link is PCN.

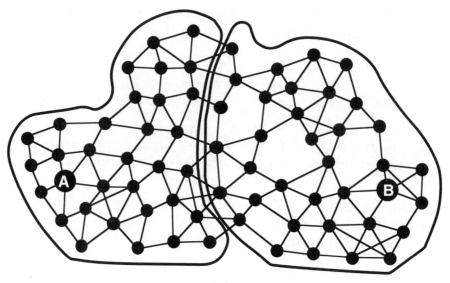

(a)

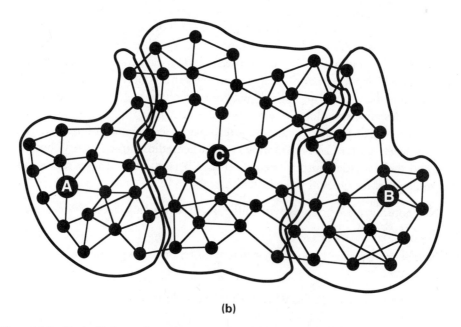

(b)

Figure 11.7   Cluster birth can disrupt intercluster connectivity: (a) clusters A and B are adjacent and there is a cluster link AB, and (b) the birth of cluster C breaks cluster link AB

2   The $A \leftrightarrow C$ and $B \leftrightarrow C$ links come up as N links (and are used to support the interchange of clusterhead information).

3   The $A \leftrightarrow B$ link becomes PC.

4   The **A** ↔ **C** and **B** ↔ **C** links become CN.

5   The **A** ↔ **B** link becomes P (and is only used when no C link exists).

6   The **A** ↔ **C** and **B** ↔ **C** links become PCN.

7   The **A** ↔ **B** link is erased.

This approach also handles the problems that arise when clusters die (i.e., the problem in nonoverlapping clusters of intercluster links failing before new ones can be formed).

The argument above implicitly assumes that the current links are preferred to previous links, but the situation is somewhat more complex: rules must be formulated for all possible combinations of possibilities.

This analysis indicates the difficulty in developing a reasonably simple design. Because the main issue is handling dynamics, one gets no insight from considering the static cases (each PR belongs to only one cluster) that are easy to analyze; instead one has to start with the much more complex dynamic cases.

11.6   ROUTING FOR NETWORKS WITH CONTROLLABLE TRANSMITTERS

11.6.1   Receiver-Directed Protocols

Receiver-directed spread-spectrum communication operates by having the packet radio use a spreading sequence that is a function of the radio to which the packet is addressed. Receiver-directed transmissions reduce the time a radio spends receiving unwanted transmission, thus increasing the probability that the radio will be available to receive desired transmissions. This tactic reduces the number of retransmissions in the network and increases network capacity. Reference 62 considers a network using receiver-directed transmissions and presents results indicating that receiver-directed transmissions can increase the throughput of a packet-radio network by a factor of five.

If the broadcast protocol is *replaced* with a receiver-directed protocol then these effects are felt:

1   Routing updates that would have been broadcast locally must be sent to each neighbor individually.

2   Alternate routing via broadcast cannot be used.

3   Passive acknowledgments are not available; active acknowledgments must be used.

4   Link-up/down protocols, which depend on overheard traffic, must be modified.

5   Updating routing tables from overheard traffic is not possible.

6   Overheard transmissions cannot be used to determine congestion.

If receiver-directed transmissions are available *in addition to* broadcast transmission, then issues 1 and 2 can be handled by broadcasting routing updates and by broadcasting alternate-routed packets; points 3, 4, 5, and 6 are unchanged.

Some radios can adjust the gain (e.g., power, data rate, choice of forward error-correcting code) used to transmit a packet. More gain implies that the packet can be received by nodes farther away, but high-gain transmissions also cause more interference. There have been numerous theoretical studies of power control and routing,[25,71,74] but many simplifying assumptions are needed to gain these results and it is unclear whether the results can be applied directly.

11.6.2   DARPA Packet Radio

The DARPA LPR is able to transmit using either broadcast or receiver-directed transmissions and can vary the link gain on a per packet basis. A new suite of protocols was developed for the SURAN program,[51,56,57,58] which took advantage of these features. The use of receiver-directed transmissions required no significant changes to the routing algorithm:

•   PROPs are broadcast.

•   Active acknowledgments including routing information are broadcast.

•   Distance-vector routing is used to determine the shortest path to each destination.

•   Updating routing tables based on overheard traffic is eliminated.

Using receiver-directed transmission did, however, greatly affect many other packet-radio algorithms:

•   Packets are sent using receiver-directed transmission unless they were being alternate routed, in which case they are broadcast.

•   Active acknowledgments are used for all packets.

•   A new channel-access protocol that gives priority to acknowledgments was developed.[61]

•   The link-up/down protocol had to be modified, for overheard traffic is not available to determine link quality.[10]

- The congestion-control algorithm had to be modified because of the absence of passive acknowledgments (which had been used to determine how long it was taking a node to forward packets).[54]

The use of gain control significantly affected the routing algorithms. Two algorithms (least-interference routing and subclass routing) were developed in an attempt to increase the network throughput by using gain control to decrease the interference caused by transmissions.

11.6.2.1 Least-Interference Routing

The *least-interference routing* (LIR) algorithm[47] computes a minimum-cost route where the link cost is a traffic-independent measure of the destructive interference caused by packet-radio transmissions.

The LIR algorithm consists of these three steps:

1   Nodes determine the potential destructive interference (interference metric) associated with sending a packet across each link.

2   The use of the interference metric as the routing metric to be minimized by a shortest-path routing algorithm.

3   The specification of the per packet transmission strategy at each packet radio.

The interference metric is selected as the number of neighbors that can receive a transmission (other than the target packet radio). In a network where the transmitter gain can be controlled, the interference metric associated with a neighbor is the one associated with the gain that is used to communicate with that neighbor. Because each packet radio must be able to determine the gain to be used in reaching a neighbor, computing this metric requires no extra communication. A shortest-path algorithm (either distance vector or link state) can be used to compute minimum-cost routes.

This algorithm increases the spatial reuse of the radio channel by giving preference to "short" links that minimize the link gain used. Reference 47 covers the results of multihop simulations that compare the end-to-end throughput and delay performance of LIR and minimum-hop routing both with and without dynamic power control. The ranking of the routing algorithms based upon the simulation performance results is (from best to worst) LIR with power control, minimum-hop routing with power control, LIR without power control, and minimum-hop routing without power control.

11.6.2.2 Subclass Routing

The subclass routing algorithm uses the link-gain information that is maintained by the transmission parameter-selection algorithm (TPSA)[57,58] to select routes. The TPSA selects (per neighbor) the minimum link gain that will allow successful forwarding of packets. The subclass routing algorithm uses these data to select routes that minimize the maximum gain required.

The subclass routing algorithm subdivides the "first class" used in the multiclass routing algorithm, based on the highest link gain used in the route. Like multiclass routing, a lower subclass (link gain) is preferred absolutely over a higher subclass (link gain). The seven subclasses used by the algorithm have a one-to-one correspondence to the gain indexes used by the TPSA.

Each candidate route is compared to the existing route using the multiclass, subclass, and hop-count metrics. The algorithm will first categorize a candidate route into a class, selecting a lower (better) class route. If both routes are first class, then the route is selected for its subclass. Again, a lower subclass is preferred over a higher subclass. If both routes have the same subclass or both routes are second class, then the route with the smaller hop count is selected.

The subclass routing algorithm minimizes the maximum link gain used along a route. While the subclass routing algorithm will tend to select longer routes, if interference is reduced the new routes may actually increase the network throughput.

11.7 CONCLUSION

In this chapter we try to highlight the issues that complicate the development of routing algorithms for highly mobile, multihop, shared-channel datagram packet-radio networks. Three types of routing algorithms are discussed: efficient algorithms for dealing with mobility, algorithms that can handle mobility and that scale as network size increases, and algorithms that can take advantage of radio-transmission gain control to reduce mutual interference.

The combination of limited bandwidth and highly dynamic topology stresses traditional routing algorithms: they either generate too many routing updates or fail to converge quickly enough to a feasible set of routes (in which case many packets may be dropped). An approach that avoids this problem uses multiple routing algorithms working at different time scales: fast algorithms which work with local information but which produce suboptimal routes and slower algorithms which use more global information to generate better routes. Using multiple routing algorithms, however, adds complexity and introduces the possibility of undesirable interactions between algorithms.

As packet-radio networks grow larger, a new problem is encountered. The total bandwidth in the network grows linearly with the number of nodes, but the average number of hops a packet must travel between source and destination also increases. Thus the bandwidth available to an end user *decreases* as the number of nodes in the network increases. In large networks, bandwidth is thus an even more precious resource, and routing algorithms that scale well as the network grows (e.g., hierarchic algorithms) are of interest.

Hierarchic routing is based on the idea that, far from the destination, the next hop in a route will not depend on the details of the network near the destination. Nodes are organized into clusters, clusters into superclusters, and so on, and each node keeps track of routes to nodes only in its cluster, to clusters in its supercluster, and so on. Implementing hierarchic routing in a highly dynamic network is complicated by these issues:

1 The hierarchy must be defined dynamically (because nodes that are now close together may later be far apart).

2 Routing algorithms must adapt to changes in hierarchic connectivity as well as to changes in radio connectivity.

3 Nodes must be able to determine the "hierarchical address" of a destination node. This step is quite difficult to do efficiently, for determining the hierarchical address of a node requires the very information about the network structure that hierarchic routing tries to hide.

Hierarchic routing algorithms based on overlapping clusters are one approach to addressing these issues, but the possibility of cluster "birth" and "death" and the type of intracluster routing algorithm used can cause complications.

Radio-transmission gain control allows for the possibility of reducing mutual interference, but several issues must be confronted. Is the goal to maximize network capacity (in which case routes are traffic dependent) or to develop a simple routing algorithm that takes the possibility of interference into consideration? In the latter case, options include minimizing the average power used in transmitting packets versus minimizing the maximum power used. Once the goals have been identified, a number of practical issues remain: integrating the routing algorithm and the link-gain selection algorithms, modifying packet-acknowledgment algorithms that depend on "overheard" traffic, and so on.

11.8 ACKNOWLEDGMENTS

In addition to the work cited in the references, this chapter draws upon email exchanges and unpublished work-group presentations that occurred with colleagues at BBN, Rockwell, and SRI as part of the DARPA-sponsored packet-radio programs. These email exchanges and presentations were an important resource used in writing this chapter, especially in the discussion of tier-routing issues.

REFERENCES

1   D. Beyer, M. Frankel, J. Hight, D. Lee, M. Lewis, P. McKenney, J. Naar, R. Ogier, N. Shacham, and W. Zaumen, "Packet Radio Network Research, Development and Application," *Proceedings of the SHAPE Packet Radio Symposium,* 1989.

2   *Cellular Digital Packet Data System Specification, Preliminary Release V. 0.9,* Kirkland, WA: CDPD Industry Input Coordinator, P.O. Box 97060, April 30, 1993.

3   B. Davies and T. Davies, "Packet Radio—A Survivable Data Communications System for the Forward Area," *Proceedings of the UK International Conference on Advances in Command, Control and Communication Systems: Theory and Applications,* Bournemouth, April 1985, pp. 129–137.

4   B. Davies and T. Davies, "The Application of Packet Switching Techniques to Combat Net Radio," *Proceedings of the IEEE,* Vol. 75, No. 1, January 1987, pp. 43–55.

5   M. Hazell and B. Davies, "A Fully Distributed Approach to the Design of a 16 Kbit/sec VHF Packet Radio Network," *Proceedings of the 1983 MILCOM,* Washington, DC, 1983, pp. 645–649.

6   J. Hahn and D. Stolle, "Packet Radio Network Routing Algorithms: A Survey," *IEEE Communications Magazine,* Vol. 22, No. 11, November 1984, pp. 41–47.

7   R. E. Kahn, "The Organization of Computer Resources into a Packet Radio Network," *IEEE Transactions on Communications,* Vol. COM-25, No. 1, January 1977, pp. 169–178.

8   R. E. Kahn, S. Gronemeyer, J. Burchfiel, and R. Kunzelman, "Advances in Packet Radio Technology," *Proceedings of the IEEE,* Vol. 66, No. 11, November 1978, pp. 1468–1496.

9   K. Klemba et al., "Packet Radio Executive Summary," Technical Report prepared for Defense Advanced Research Projects Agency by SRI International, July 1983.

10 G. Lauer, "Advanced Protocols for the SURAN Packet Radio Network," *Proceedings of the SHAPE Packet Radio Symposium,* 1989.

11 B. Leiner, D. Nielson, and F. Tobagi, "Issues in Packet Radio Network Design," *Proceedings of the IEEE,* Vol. 75, No. 1, January 1987, pp. 6–20.

12 C. Lynch, *Packet Radio Networks,* New York: Pergamon Press, 1987.

13 J. Rustad, R. Skaug, and A. Aasen, "New Radio Networks for Tactical Communication," *IEEE Journal on Selected Areas in Communications,* Vol. 8, No. 5, June 1990, pp. 713–727.

14 N. Shacham and J. Westcott, "Future Directions in Packet Radio Architectures and Protocols," *Proceedings of the IEEE,* Vol. 75, No. 1, January 1987, pp. 83–99.

15 D. Bertsekas and R. Gallager, *Data Networks,* Englewood Cliffs: Prentice Hall, 1987.

16 R. Callon, "A Comparison of 'Link State' and 'Distance Vector' Routing Algorithms," *Internet Engineering Task Force IDEA 002,* November 1987.

17 R. Callon and G. Lauer, "Hierarchical Routing for Packet Radio Networks," *SURAN Program Technical Note (SRNTN) 31,* Cambridge, MA: BBN Systems and Technologies Corporation, June 1985. Available from Defense Technical Information Center (DTIC).

18 R. Callon and G. Lauer, "More Issues in Hierarchical Routing for SURAP2," *SURAN Program Technical Note (SRNTN) 34,* Cambridge, MA: BBN Systems and Technologies Corporation, July 1985. Available from Defense Technical Information Center (DTIC).

19 J. S. Cline, "SURAP Version 1.3 Users Gguide," *SURAN Program Document (SRNDOC) 5,* Richardson, TX: Rockwell Inc., 1989. Available from Defense Technical Information Center (DTIC).

20 R. G. Gallager, "A Minimum Delay Routing Algorithm Using a Distributed Computation," *IEEE Transactions on Communications,* Vol. COM-25, No. 1, January 1977, pp. 73–85.

21 J. Garcia-Luna-Aceves, "On Loop Free Routing," *Proceedings of the ACM SIGCOMM '87*, 1987.

22 J. Garcia-Luna-Aceves, "Distributed Routing with Labeled Distances," *Proceedings of the INFOCOM '92,* June 1992, pp. 633–643.

23 J. Garcia-Luna and N. Shacham, "Analysis of Routing Strategies for Packet Radio Networks," *Proceedings of the IEEE INFOCOM '85,* Washington, DC, March 1985, pp. 292–302.

24 J. Garcia-Luna and N. Shacham, "Performance Analysis of Hierarchical Routing Schemes for Large Multihop Packet Radio Networks," *SURAN Program Technical Note (SRNTN) 30,* Menlo Park, CA: SRI International, October 1985. Available from Defense Technical Information Center (DTIC).

25 T. Hou and V. Li, "Performance Analysis of Routing Strategies in Multihop Packet Radio Networks," *Proceedings of the GLOBECOM '84 Conference Record,* Atlanta, November 1984, pp. 487–492.

26 J. Jubin and T. Barlow, "Multiclass Routing," *Proceedings of the MILCOM '90,* Monterey, CA, September 1990, pp. 622–626.

27 J. Jaffe and M. Moss, "A Responsive Distributed Routing Algorithm for Computer Networks," *IEEE Transactions on Communications,* Vol. COM-30, No. 7, July 1982, pp. 1758–1762.

28 J. Jubin and J. Tornow, "The DARPA Packet Radio Network Protocols," *Proceedings of the IEEE,* Vol. 75, No. 1, January 1987, pp. 21–32.

29 J. Jubin, "Uphill Tier Routing, Less Frequent Tier Data Updating, and Larger Networks," *SURAN Program Technical Note (SRNTN) 2,* Richardson, TX: Rockwell Inc., August 1983. Available from Defense Technical Information Center (DTIC).

30 J. Jubin, "Current Packet Radio Network Protocols," *Proceedings of the INFOCOM '85,* March 1985.

31 L. Kleinrock and F. Kamoun, "Hierarchical Routing for Large Networks," *Computer Networks,* No. 1, January 1977, pp. 155–174.

32 K. Klemba and N. Shacham, "An Architecture for Large Packet Radio Networks and Some Implementation Considerations," *SURAN Program Technical Note (SRNTN) 11,* Menlo Park, CA: SRI International, October 1983. Available from Defense Technical Information Center (DTIC).

33 P. Kung and N. Shacham, "An Algorithm for the Shortest Path under Multiple Constraints," *SURAN Program Technical Note (SRNTN) 7,* Menlo Park, CA: SRI International, November 1983. Available from Defense Technical Information Center (DTIC).

34 G. Lauer, "Hierarchical Routing Design for SURAN," *Proceedings of the International Conference on Communications,* June 1986.

35 G. Lauer, "Address Servers in Hierarchical Networks," in *Proceedings of the IEEE International Conference on Communications,* June 1988, pp. 443–451.

36 R. Ogier, V. Rutenburg, and N. Shacham, "Distributed Algorithms for Computing Shortest Pairs of Disjoint Paths," *IEEE Transactions on Information Theory,* March 1993, pp. 443–455.

37 R. Ogier and N. Shacham, "A Distributed Algorithm for Finding Shortest Pairs of Disjoint Paths," *Proceedings of the IEEE INFOCOM Conference,* Ottawa, April 1989.

38 M. Pursley and H. Russell, "Adaptive Forwarding and Routing in Frequency-Hop Spread-Spectrum Packet Radio Networks with Partial-Band Jamming," *Proceedings of the MILCOM '89 Conference,* Cambridge, MA, 1989, pp. 230–234.

39 M. Pursley, "Routing in Frequency-Hop Packet Radio Networks with Partial-Band Jamming," *Proceedings of the Tactical Communications Conference,* Fort Wayne, April 1990, pp. 117–126.

40 C. Ramamoorthy and W.-T. Tsai, "An Adaptive Hierarchical Routing Algorithm," in *Proceedings of the IEEE Computer Software and Applications Conference,* 1983, pp. 93–104.

41 N. Shacham and E. Craighill, "Dynamic Routing for Real-Time Data Transport in Packet Radio Networks," *Proceedings of the INFOCOM '82,* Las Vegas, April 1982, pp. 152–158.

42 A. Segall, "Advances in Verifiable Fail-Safe Routing Procedures," *IEEE Transactions on Communications,* Vol. COM-29, 1981, pp. 491–497.

43 N. Shacham, "Organization of Dynamic Radio Network by Overlapping Clusters: Architecture Considerations and Optimization," *Proceedings of the Tenth International Symposium on Computer Performance,* Paris, December 1984, pp. 435–447.

44 N. Shacham, "Hierarchical Routing in Large, Dynamic Ground Radio Networks," *Proceedings of the Eighteenth Hawaii International Conference on System Sciences,* 1985, pp. 292–301.

45 N. Shacham and P. King, "Architectures and Performance of Multi-channel, Multihop Packet Radio Networks," *SURAN Program Technical Note (SRNTN) 38,* Menlo Park, CA: SRI International, January 1986. Available from Defense Technical Information Center (DTIC).

46 J. Stevens, "Spreading Connectivity Information out over Multiple PROP Periods, and Timeliness of Information," *SURAN Program Technical Note (SRNTN) 21,* Richardson, TX: Rockwell Inc., May 1985. Available from Defense Technical Information Center (DTIC).

47 J. Stevens, "Spatial Reuse through Dynamic Power and Routing Control in Common-Channel Random-Access Packet Radio Networks," *SURAN Program Technical Note (SRNTN) 59,* Richardson, TX: Rockwell Inc., August 1988. Available from Defense Technical Information Center (DTIC).

48 P. F. Tsuchiya, "Landmark Routing: Architecture, Algorithms, and Issues," *Technical Report MTR-87W00174,* Cambridge, MA: MITRE Corporation, September 1987.

49 J. Westcott and J. Jubin, "A Distributed Routing Design for a Broadcast Environment," *Proceedings of the MILCOM '82,* 1982.

50 W. Zaumen and J. Garcia-Luan-Aceves, "Steady-State Response of Shortest-Path Routing Algorithms," *Proceedings of the IPCCC '92,* April 1992, pp. 323–332.

51 J. Zavgren and M. Leib, "High-Throughput, Survivable Protocols for CDMA Packet-Radio Networks," *SURAN Program Technical Note (SRNTN) 74,* Cambridge, MA: BBN Systems and Technologies Corporation, February 1990.

52 F. Bruno, W. Fifer, and D. Quinn, "Low Cost Packet Radio—Advanced Technology for Packet Radio Switching Applications," *Proceedings of the IEEE Military Communications Conference (MILCOM),* October 1987.

53 M. Pursley, "The Role of Spread Spectrum in Packet Radio Networks," *Proceedings of the IEEE,* Vol. 75, No. 1, January 1987, pp. 116–134.

54 J. Escobar, G. Lauer, and M. Steenstrup, "A Rate-Based Congestion Control Algorithm for the SURAP 4 Packet Radio Architecture," *SURAN Program Technical Note (SRNTN) 72,* Cambridge, MA: BBN Systems and Technologies Corporation, 1989.

55 N. Gower and J. Jubin, "Congestion Control Using Pacing in a Packet Radio Network," *Proceedings of the IEEE Military Communications Conference (MILCOM '82),* Vol. 1, October 1982, pp. 23.1-1–23.1-6.

56 P. Bausbacher, "Steady State Evaluation of Transmission Parameter Selection Algorithms Using Markov Techniques," *SURAN Program Technical Note (SRNTN) 87,* Richardson, TX: Rockwell Inc., January 1990.

57 P. Bausbacher and J. Kearns, "Link Quality Estimation and Transmission Parameter Selection in an Adaptive Packet-Radio Network," *Proceedings of the Tactical Communications Conference (TCC),* April 1990, pp. 51–68.

58 J. Escobar, "Radio-Parameter Selection Algorithm for Receiver-Directed Packet-Radio Networks," *SURAN Program Technical Note (SRNTN) 73,* Cambridge, MA: BBN Systems and Technologies Corporation, 1989.

59 P. Karn, "A New Channel Access Method for Packet Radio," *Proceedings of the Ninth American Radio Relay League Computer Networking Conference,* 1990.

60 M. Sidi and A. Segall, "Busy-Tone-Multiple-Access-Type Scheme for Packet-Radio Networks," *Proceedings of the Performance of Data Communication Systems and Their Applications Conference,* Paris, September 1981, pp. 1–10.

61 J. R. Zavgren, "The Moment of Silence Channel-Access Algorithm," *Proceedings of the MILCOM '89,* Cambridge, MA, October 1989.

62 J. Zavgren and G. Lauer, "The Performance Improvement from Receiver-Directed Transmissions in Packet-Radio Networks," *Proceedings of the IEEE Tactical Communications Conference,* Fort Wayne, May 1988, pp. 65–72.

63 A. Aasen, "Time Synchronization Strategy for a Packet Radio Network," *Proceedings of the SHAPE Packet Radio Symposium,* 1989.

64 W. Fifer and F. Bruno, "The Low Cost Packet Radio," *Proceedings of the IEEE,* Vol. 75, No. 1, January 1987.

65 P. Karn, H. Price, and R. Diersing, "Packet Radio in the Amateur Service," *IEEE Journal on Selected Areas in Communication,* Vol. SAC-3, No. 3, May 1985, pp. 431–439.

66 B. Miller, "Limiting Logical Neighborhood Size," *SURAN Program Technical Note (SRNTN) 43,* Richardson, TX: Rockwell Inc., September 1986. Available from Defense Technical Information Center (DTIC).

67 J. Ong, "Detecting Black Holes in Packet Radio Networks," *SURAN Program Technical Note (SRNTN) 56,* Cambridge, MA: BBN Systems and Technologies Corporation, 1986.

68 R. Perlman, "Network Layer Protocols with Byzantine Robustness," Ph.D. thesis, Massachusetts Institute of Technology, August 1988.

69 N. Shacham and D. Beyer, "A Distributed Protocol for Reducing Neighborhood Size in Radio Networks," *Proceedings of the International Conference on Communications ICC '88,* Philadelphia, June 1988.

70 J. Stevens, D. Young, et al., "SURAN Protocol (SURAP) Version 1.1 Working Specification," *SURAN Program Document (SRNDOC) 3,* Richardson, TX: Rockwell Inc., March 1986. Available from Defense Technical Information Center (DTIC).

71 H. Takagi and L. Kleinrock, "Optimal Transmission Ranges for Randomly Distributed Packet Radio Terminals," *IEEE Transactions on Communications,* Vol. COM-32, No. 3, March 1984, pp. 246–257.

72 B. Tuch, "An ISM Band Spread Spectrum Local Area Network: Wave-LAN," *Proceedings of the IEEE Workshop on Wireless Local Area Networks,* May 1991, pp. 103–116.

73 B. Willis, "Distributed Heuristics for Maintaining Connectivity in Mobile Networks," *SURAN Program Technical Note (SRNTN) 54,* Cambridge, MA: BBN Systems and Technologies Corporation, April 1989.

74 L. Klienrock and J. Silvester, "Optimum Transmission Radii for Packet Radio Networks, or Why Six Is a Magic Number," *Proceedings of the National Telecommunications Conference,* December 1978, pp. 4.3.1–4.3.5.

Index